Capitalism, Socialism and Democracy

Joseph A. Schumpeter

Capitalism,

Socialism

and

Democracy

*With a new introduction
by Tom Bottomore*

HARPER TORCHBOOKS
Harper & Row, Publishers
New York, Cambridge, Hagerstown, Philadelphia, San Francisco
London, Mexico City, São Paulo, Sydney

This book was originally published in 1942 by Harper & Brothers, with a second edition in 1947, and a third edition in 1950.

CAPITALISM, SOCIALISM, AND DEMOCRACY. Copyright, 1942, 1947 by Joseph R. Schumpeter. Copyright 1950 by Harper & Row, Publishers, Inc. Copyright © 1976 by George Allen & Unwin (Publishers) Ltd. Printed in the United States of America. All rights reserved. No part of this book may be used or reproduced in any manner whatsoever without written permission except in the case of brief quotations embodied in critical articles and reviews. For information address Harper & Row, Publishers, Inc., 10 East 53d Street, New York, N.Y. 10022.

First HARPER COLOPHON edition published 1975

ISBN: 0-06-133008-6

88 89 90   30 29 28 27

CONTENTS

Contents

COMMENTS ON FURTHER POSTWAR DEVELOPMENTS

INTRODUCTION

Schumpeter's book, as he remarked, was the fruit of almost forty years of reflection and research on the subject of socialism. Its message, as originally expressed in the preface, was that "a socialist form of society will inevitably emerge from an equally inevitable decomposition of capitalist society", but in a later paper entitled "The March into Socialism" which was added to the third edition of the book Schumpeter modified somewhat this forthright prophecy. He disclaimed any intention of predicting the future in such a definite way, and described his study as an analysis of "observable tendencies" which might have diverse outcomes depending upon the strength of various resistances and counter tendencies that it would be difficult or impossible to foresee. "The capitalist order," he now concluded, "tends to destroy itself and centralist socialism is . . . a likely heir apparent."

Almost another forty years on from the time when Schumpeter undertook his study, how plausible does his analysis of those "observable tendencies" appear? First, in what way does capitalism tend to destroy itself? Not, according to Schumpeter, because it generates insoluble economic problems. Writing towards the end of the economic depressions of the 1930s, he rejected outright the prevalent view that an economic breakdown of capitalism would occur. In particular, he argued vigorously against what he called the "theory of vanishing investment opportunity", according to which there is a long-run tendency in capitalism to economic stagnation as a result of the declining rate of profit and the lack of new opportunities for profitable investment and enterprise. Capitalism, in Schumpeter's view, would be killed by its economic successes, not by its failures, because these successes create an unfavourable social and political climate, or in his words, an "atmosphere of almost universal hostility to its own social order".

Three processes are important in generating this anti-capitalist outlook. First, the development of the capitalist economy itself undermines the entrepreneurial or innovative function, which Schumpeter regards as the essential feature of capitalism, because technological progress and the bureaucratic administration of large enterprises tend to make innovation itself a routine matter and to substitute the activities of committees and teams of experts for individual initiative. Second, capitalism erodes its own institutional framework by destroying the protective strata—the gentry, small businessmen, farmers and others—which had survived from an earlier form of society, and by weakening individual proprietorship in favour of a more diffuse kind of ownership in the modern corporation. Third, capitalism encourages a rational and critical attitude which is eventually turned against its own social system, and this process is greatly assisted by the creation of a large stratum of intellectuals who have, according to Schumpeter, "a vested interest in social unrest".

The events of the period since the end of the 1930s provide some support for Schumpeter's thesis. No doubt it was the war that made it possible for capitalism to recover initially from the depression, but in its postwar development there have been few signs of stagnation or of an imminent collapse. Even the recession of the mid-1970s now begins to appear as only a temporary setback, and over the postwar period as a whole economic growth has been exceptionally rapid. This was so evident in the 1950s and 1960s, when the doctrine of the "affluent society" became popular, that radical criticisms of capitalist society tended to move from economic analysis to cultural criticism, most dramatically expressed, perhaps, in the writings of Marcuse and in the ideas of the radical movements of the late 1960s. It was at this time that the doctrines of "cultural revolution" and the "counter-culture" acquired a considerable influence, and the large part played by intellectuals in recent radical movements may be thought to accord well with Schumpeter's account of one of the major elements in the process of capitalist decline.

But still there are some important differences. Much radical criticism in the past decade, rather than turning bourgeois rationalism against the capitalist social system, has been more inclined to challenge the ideological dominance of a rationalist outlook, embodied in scientific and technological thinking, in any form of highly organized industrial society, whether capitalist or socialist. And this movement, instead of becoming diffused as a general opposition to capitalism, has tended to create a division between a stratum of intellectuals engaged in cultural criticism, and large sections of the population who are mainly preoccupied with economic growth and hence with the further development and use of science and technology. From this aspect, therefore, it might be argued that the general hostility to capitalism has not increased and spread as Schumpeter expected, but has been held in check mainly by more rapid economic development, that is to say, by new economic "successes".

Yet the postwar trends, especially in recent years, suggest some other doubts about Schumpeter's analysis. The survival of the capitalist economic system depends upon innovation and expansion, and it may be argued that in conditions in which growth rates have to be restricted in order to conserve natural resources—involving limitations upon population growth, the use of energy, etc.—such expansion is likely to become increasingly difficult. And to these considerations may be added questions about the likelihood of technological innovation continuing at the pace that has been achieved in the past few decades, and about the possibility of new investment opportunities occurring on the scale that was provided by the development of the railways, and subsequently of the automobile. Schumpeter discussed some of these issues, but in a very different context from that which now exists, and his view of the economic prospects of capitalism, even over a medium-term future of about forty years with which he was concerned, may well appear too optimistic.

In any event, the decline of capitalism, however produced, does not entail the emergence of a socialist society, and Schumpeter's view of socialism as the "likely heir apparent" is based upon an argument to the effect that the economic process tends to socialize itself. The scheme of modern social development within which he conducts his analysis has three stages, which we might describe as entrepreneurial capitalism, organized or bureaucratic capitalism, and socialism. The transition from one stage to the next comes about as a consequence of economic changes, among which the most important are those which create the large business corporation based upon modern science and rational administration. It should be noted that Schumpeter defines socialism only as an economic system, as "an institutional pattern in which control over means of production and over production itself is vested with a central authority— or . . . in which, as a matter of principle, the economic affairs of society belong to the public and not to the private sphere". He puts aside any discussion of the cultural aims of socialism, referrring in a somewhat cavalier fashion to what he calls the "cultural indeterminateness of socialism". In consequence, there is no place in his analysis for a consideration of socialism as a class movement which seeks to abolish or attenuate class differences, and so achieve greater social equality and a liberation of the mass of the people from the constraints imposed by ruling classes. Schumpeter is concerned only with the economic reorganization of society, and when he asks whether socialism can work, what he means is whether it can be economically efficient and productive.

This is a very narrow view of the socialist movement, and one which exaggerates its cultural diversity. There is, unmistakably, in modern socialism, despite the variety of its forms, a central preoccupation with the related issues of social equality and individual autonomy and self-determination. On the other side, few socialists have equated socialism with centralized public ownership and planning of the economy, or to put the matter in broader terms, have conceived socialism only as a mode of production. If socialism had to be characterized in a single phrase it would be more appropriate to describe it as a movement of human liberation, in which the transformation of the economic system is only one element, and itself gives rise to diverse choices in the construction of a different type of system.

Schumpeter's discussion of democracy, in relation to capitalism and socialism, is also somewhat narrow. Alongside his definition of socialism in economic terms he formulates an economic definition of democracy, conceived as an institutional arrangement like the market, in which various groups and individuals—equivalent to enterprises and entrepreneurs— compete for the votes of electors, the political "consumers". Schumpeter emphasizes strongly this analogy between the economy and the polity, quoting by way of illustration the remark of a politician to the effect that

"What businessmen do not understand is that exactly as they are dealing in oil so I am dealing in votes". This theory of democracy as being only a *method* for selecting political leaders (an idea already expressed by Max Weber in his later political writings) is presented as an alternative to the "classical doctrine", which Schumpeter rejects, according to which democracy embodies specific political ideals concerning the participation of citizens in political life and the nature of the relationship between political leaders and the people.

It is true that Schumpeter does not always adhere quite strictly to his own conception, and that in discussing the historical association, and even a causal connection, between the emergence of capitalism and the rise of modern democracy, he introduces ideas of rational action, individual responsibility, self-discipline, tolerance, and so on, which seem to belong rather to the classical doctrine. Nevertheless, the view of democracy as competition for political leadership, as a form without any definite substance in the way of social or political ends, remains central; and this permits Schumpeter to exclude any consideration of democracy as a historical phenomenon in which there may be tendencies to development and extension, or to stagnation and decay. Schumpeter refers only to democracy being "workable" or "unworkable", better or worse in its functioning as a mechanism; within his scheme of ideas there seems to be no way of examining the question of whether a society is more or less democratic.

Yet it is just this issue, the extension of democracy, which has been a fundamental element in the intellectual and practical development of the socialist movement over the past century, and has found a new expression in recent years in the idea of "participatory democracy". All the class struggles and national liberation movements of this century have aimed in one way or another at creating a more democratic society in which larger numbers of people, and especially those hitherto excluded, would play a more direct and more effective part in making the decisions that affect their lives, whether in the workplace, the family, and the local community, or on a national and international scale. The difficulties of extending democracy in such ways are by now all too evident, not least in those socialist societies where economic backwardness, traditions of authoritarian rule, the absence of earlier liberal forms of democracy and the dominance of a single monolithic party have all worked against the establishment of institutions which would ensure genuine self-government by the people in the various spheres of social life.

It may also be the case, as Schumpeter suggested—and many later critics of socialism have followed him in this line of argument—that centralized economic planning is actually inimical to democratic participation and tends to produce a very great concentration of power in the hands of political leaders and planners, whatever the means by which they are selected. But here the contrast which Schumpeter draws between a market economy and centralist socialism (or in the language of more recent writers, between a market economy and a command economy) is too stark, and does not allow for all the possible alternatives. For an economy which is centrally planned in its broad outlines may still have a considerable degree of decentralization in decision making. One feature of such decentralization may be the emergence of a socialist market economy, so that in many spheres of economic life decisions would be made in numerous different centres of activity rather than being imposed uniformly from above. During the past decade there has been much discussion of such developments in the socialist countries, as well as some practical economic reforms which follow this direction.

Another aspect of decentralization, which Schumpeter simply dismisses in a brief comment on the Socialization Commission in Germany after the First World War, concerns the organization of production in individual enterprises in a socialist economy. Here again there are various choices, ranging from a more or less total authoritarian control from above to a system of self-management on the Yugoslav model. And despite all the problems that the Yugoslav system has encountered, it constitutes, in my view, a viable and promising form of publicly owned enterprise, and represents one of the most significant contributions that has yet been made in the twentieth century to the extension of democratic participation in social life. The idea of self-management has had a growing influence in recent years, in the socialist countries as well as in the labour movements in capitalist countries, and it seems probable that the debate about socialism and democracy, or socialist democracy, will come to be formulated more and more in these terms, and with reference to the historical experience of self-managed production that is now available.

Considering all its limitations is there anything of great value in Schumpeter's conception of democracy as a method of selecting political leaders? Probably its most important feature, though it is not one that Schumpeter emphasizes, is the idea of dissent and opposition that is embodied in it. Competition for political leadership makes it possible for those social groups which are dissatisfied with their position in society, or with the general direction of social policy, to express their criticism and to bring some influence to bear upon those who are the political leaders for the time being. But this is still not the only important means of ensuring that a society is open to criticism and change, and that decisions are not made in an arbitrary way or in the service of particular interests. For the effective working of a thoroughly democratic society at least two other things are essential: first, that as many citizens as possible should share in making decisions, that is to say, should have the opportunity and experience, in diverse spheres and for some part of their lives, of exercising political leadership; and second, that there should exist a considerable variety of relatively autonomous associations (including publicly owned business enterprises) in which such self-government can be practised, and which provide a basis for a permanent, unimpeded criticism and reform of social arrangements.

The success that Schumpeter's book enjoyed when it first appeared, and its continuing appeal to readers, can be explained, I think, by the fact that it undertakes a serious and thorough examination of the great social transition of the present age, from capitalism to socialism (and prefaces this with an illuminating critical appraisal of Marx's theory, as the only socialist analysis of the transition that merits attention) rather than by the kind of judgement that it makes about the consequences of this process of social transformation. Schumpeter was far from welcoming the advent of socialism, which he seems to have contemplated with the same gloomy apprehension as did Max Weber. But this attitude did not prevent him from analysing as carefully and dispassionately as he could those tendencies which made it likely, and it may have enhanced his awareness of the difficulties and dangers presented by certain forms of socialism, which socialist thinkers themselves, after so many deceptions, can now more readily appreciate.

TOM BOTTOMORE
Brighton, 1976

PART I

The Marxian Doctrine

PROLOGUE

Most of the creations of the intellect or fancy pass away for good after a time that varies between an after-dinner hour and a generation. Some, however, do not. They suffer eclipses but they come back again, and they come back not as unrecognizable elements of a cultural inheritance, but in their individual garb and with their personal scars which people may see and touch. These we may well call the great ones—it is no disadvantage of this definition that it links greatness to vitality. Taken in this sense, this is undoubtedly the word to apply to the message of Marx. But there is an additional advantage to defining greatness by revivals: it thereby becomes independent of our love or hate. We need not believe that a great achievement must necessarily be a source of light or faultless in either fundamental design or details. On the contrary, we may believe it to be a power of darkness; we may think it fundamentally wrong or disagree with it on any number of particular points. In the case of the Marxian system, such adverse judgment or even exact disproof, by its very failure to injure fatally, only serves to bring out the power of the structure.

The last twenty years have witnessed a most interesting Marxian revival. That the great teacher of the socialist creed should have come into his own in Soviet Russia is not surprising. And it is only characteristic of such processes of canonization that there is, between the true meaning of Marx's message and bolshevist practice and ideology, at least as great a gulf as there was between the religion of humble Galileans and the practice and ideology of the princes of the church or the warlords of the Middle Ages.

But another revival is less easy to explain—the Marxian revival in the United States. This phenomenon is so interesting because until the twenties there was no Marxian strain of importance in either the American labor movement or in the thought of the American intellectual. What Marxism there was always had been superficial, insignificant and without standing. Moreover, the bolshevist type of revival produced no similar spurt in those countries which had previously been most steeped in Marxology. In Germany notably, which of all countries had the strongest Marxian tradition, a small orthodox sect indeed kept alive during the post-war socialist boom as it had during the previous depression. But the leaders of socialist thought (not only those allied to the Social Democratic party but also those who went much beyond its cautious conservatism in practical questions) betrayed little taste for reverting to the old tenets and, while worshiping the deity, took good care to keep it at a distance and to reason in economic matters exactly like other economists. Outside of Russia, therefore, the American phenomenon stands alone. We are not concerned with its causes. But it is worth while to survey the contours and the meaning of the message so many Americans have made their own.[1]

[1] References to Marx's writings will be confined to a minimum, and no data about his life will be given. This seems unnecessary because any reader who wishes for a list of the former and a general outline of the latter finds all he needs for our purposes in any dictionary, but especially in the *Encyclopedia Britannica* or the *Encyclopaedia of the Social Sciences*. A study of Marx begins most conveniently with the first volume of *Das Kapital* (first English translation by S. Moore and E. Aveling, edited by F. Engels, 1886). In spite of a huge amount of more recent work, I still think that F. Mehring's biography is the best, at least from the standpoint of the general reader.

CHAPTER I

MARX THE PROPHET

IT WAS not by a slip that an analogy from the world of religion was permitted to intrude into the title of this chapter. There is more than analogy. In one important sense, Marxism *is* a religion. To the believer it presents, first, a system of ultimate ends that embody the meaning of life and are absolute standards by which to judge events and actions; and, secondly, a guide to those ends which implies a plan of salvation and the indication of the evil from which mankind, or a chosen section of mankind, is to be saved. We may specify still further: Marxist socialism also belongs to that subgroup which promises paradise on this side of the grave. I believe that a formulation of these characteristics by an hierologist would give opportunities for classification and comment which might possibly lead much deeper into the sociological essence of Marxism than anything a mere economist can say.

The least important point about this is that it explains the success of Marxism.[1] Purely scientific achievement, had it even been much more perfect than it was in the case of Marx, would never have won the immortality in the historical sense which is his. Nor would his arsenal of party slogans have done it. Part of his success, although a very minor part, is indeed attributable to the barrelful of white-hot phrases, of impassioned accusations and wrathful gesticulations, ready for use on any platform, that he put at the disposal of his flock. All that needs to be said about this aspect of the matter is that this ammunition has served and is serving its purpose very well, but that the production of it carried a disadvantage: in order to forge such weapons for the arena of social strife Marx had occasionally to bend, or to deviate from, the opinions that would logically follow from his system. However, if Marx had not been more than a purveyor of phraseology, he would be dead by now. Mankind is not grateful for that sort of service and forgets quickly the names of the people who write the librettos for its political operas.

But he was a prophet, and in order to understand the nature of this achievement we must visualize it in the setting of his own time. It was the zenith of bourgeois realization and the nadir of bourgeois civilization, the time of mechanistic materialism, of a cultural milieu which had

[1] The religious quality of Marxism also explains a characteristic attitude of the orthodox Marxist toward opponents. To him, as to any believer in a Faith, the opponent is not merely in error but in sin. Dissent is disapproved of not only intellectually but also morally. There cannot be any excuse for it once the Message has been revealed.

as yet betrayed no sign that a new art and a new mode of life were in its womb, and which rioted in most repulsive banality. Faith in any real sense was rapidly falling away from all classes of society, and with it the only ray of light (apart from what may have been derived from Rochdale attitudes and saving banks) died from the workman's world, while intellectuals professed themselves highly satisfied with Mill's *Logic* and the Poor Law.

Now, to millions of human hearts the Marxian message of the terrestrial paradise of socialism meant a new ray of light and a new meaning of life. Call Marxist religion a counterfeit if you like, or a caricature of faith—there is plenty to be said for this view—but do not overlook or fail to admire the greatness of the achievement. Never mind that nearly all of those millions were unable to understand and appreciate the message in its true significance. That is the fate of all messages. The important thing is that the message was framed and conveyed in such a way as to be acceptable to the positivistic mind of its time—which was essentially bourgeois no doubt, but there is no paradox in saying that Marxism is essentially a product of the bourgeois mind. This was done, on the one hand, by formulating with unsurpassed force that feeling of being thwarted and ill treated which is the auto-therapeutic attitude of the unsuccessful many, and, on the other hand, by proclaiming that socialistic deliverance from those ills was a certainty amenable to rational proof.

Observe how supreme art here succeeds in weaving together those extra-rational cravings which receding religion had left running about like masterless dogs, and the rationalistic and materialistic tendencies of the time, ineluctable for the moment, which would not tolerate any creed that had no scientific or pseudo-scientific connotation. Preaching the goal would have been ineffectual; analyzing a social process would have interested only a few hundred specialists. But preaching in the garb of analysis and analyzing with a view to heartfelt needs, this is what conquered passionate allegiance and gave to the Marxist that supreme boon which consists in the conviction that what one is and stands for can never be defeated but must conquer victoriously in the end. This, of course, does not exhaust the achievement. Personal force and the flash of prophecy work independently of the contents of the creed. No new life and no new meaning of life can be effectively revealed without. But this does not concern us here.

Something will have to be said about the cogency and correctness of Marx's attempt to prove the inevitability of the socialist goal. One remark, however, suffices as to what has been called above his formulation of the feelings of the unsuccessful many. It was, of course, not a true formulation of actual feelings, conscious or subconscious. Rather we could call it an attempt at replacing actual feelings by a true or false revelation of the logic of social evolution. By doing this and by attributing—quite unrealistically—to the masses his own shibboleth of "class consciousness," he undoubtedly falsified the true psychology of the workman (which centers in the wish to become a small bourgeois and to be helped to that status by political force), but in so far as his teaching took effect he also expanded and ennobled it. He did not weep any sentimental tears about the beauty of the socialist idea. This is one of his claims to superiority over what he called the Utopian Socialists. Nor did he glorify the workmen into heroes of daily toil as bourgeois love to do when trembling for their dividends. He was perfectly free from any tendency, so conspicuous in some of his weaker followers, toward licking the workman's boots. He had probably a clear perception of what the masses are and he looked far above their heads toward social goals altogether beyond what they thought or wanted. Also, he never taught any ideals as set by himself. Such vanity was quite foreign to him. As every true prophet styles himself the humble mouthpiece of his deity, so Marx pretended no more than to speak the logic of the dialectic process of history. There is dignity in all this which compensates for many pettinesses and vulgarities with which, in his work and in his life, this dignity formed so strange an alliance.

Another point, finally, should not go unmentioned. Marx was personally much too civilized to fall in with those vulgar professors of socialism who do not recognize a temple when they see it. He was perfectly able to understand a civilization and the "relatively absolute" value of its values, however far removed from it he may have felt himself to be. In this respect no better testimony to his broad-mindedness can be offered than the *Communist Manifesto* which is an account nothing short of glowing[2] of the achievements of capitalism; and even in pronouncing *pro futuro* death sentence on it, he never failed to recognize its historical necessity. This attitude, of course, implies quite a lot of things Marx himself would have been unwilling to accept. But he was undoubtedly strengthened in it, and it was made more easy for him to take, because of that perception of the organic logic of things to which

[2] This may seem to be an exaggeration. But let us quote from the authorized English translation: "The bourgeoisie . . . has been the first to show what man's activity can bring about. It has accomplished wonders far surpassing Egyptian pyramids, Roman aqueducts and Gothic cathedrals. . . . The bourgeoisie . . . draws all nations . . . into civilization. . . . It has created enormous cities . . . and thus rescued a considerable part of the population from the idiocy [sic!] of rural life. . . . The bourgeoisie, during its rule of scarce one hundred years, has created more massive and more colossal productive forces than have all preceding generations together." Observe that all the achievements referred to are attributed *to the bourgeoisie alone* which is more than many thoroughly bourgeois economists would claim. This is all I meant by the above passage—and strikingly different from the views of the vulgarized Marxism of today or from the Veblenite stuff of the modern non-Marxist radical. Let me say at once: not more than that is implied in anything I shall say in the second part about the performance of capitalism.

his theory of history gives one particular expression. Things social fell into order for him, and however much of a coffeehouse conspirator he may have been at some junctures of his life, his true self despised that sort of thing. Socialism for him was no obsession which blots out all other colors of life and creates an unhealthy and stupid hatred or contempt for other civilizations. And there is, in more senses than one, justification for the title claimed for his type of socialist thought and of socialist volition which are welded together by virtue of his fundamental position: Scientific Socialism.

CHAPTER II

MARX THE SOCIOLOGIST

WE HAVE now to do a thing which is very objectionable to the faithful. They naturally resent any application of cold analysis to what for them is the very fountain of truth. But one of the things they resent most is cutting Marx's work into pieces and discussing them one by one. They would say that the very act displays the incapacity of the bourgeois to grasp the resplendent whole, all parts of which complement and explain one another, so that the true meaning is missed as soon as any one part or aspect is considered by itself. We have no choice, however. By committing the offense and next taking up Marx the sociologist after Marx the prophet, I do not mean to deny either the presence of a unity of social vision which succeeds in giving some measure of analytic unity, and still more a semblance of unity, to the Marxian work, or the fact that every part of it, however independent intrinsically, has been correlated by the author with every other. Enough independence remains nevertheless in every province of the vast realm to make it possible for the student to accept the fruits of his labors in one of them while rejecting those in another. Much of the glamour of the faith is lost in the process but something is gained by salvaging important and stimulating truth which is much more valuable by itself than it would be if tied to hopeless wreckage.

This applies first of all to Marx's philosophy which we may as well get out of our way once and for all. German-trained and speculative-minded as he was, he had a thorough grounding and a passionate interest in philosophy. Pure philosophy of the German kind was his starting point and the love of his youth. For a time he thought of it as his true vocation. He was a Neo-Hegelian, which roughly means that while accepting the master's fundamental attitudes and methods he and his group eliminated, and replaced by pretty much their opposites, the conservative interpretations put upon Hegel's philosophy by many of its other adherents. This background shows in all his writings wherever the opportunity offers itself. It is no wonder that his German and Russian readers, by bent of mind and training similarly disposed, should seize primarily upon this element and make it the master key to the system.

I believe this to be a mistake and an injustice to Marx's scientific powers. He retained his early love during the whole of his lifetime. He enjoyed certain formal analogies which may be found between his and

9

Hegel's argument. He liked to testify to his Hegelianism and to use Hegelian phraseology. But this is all. Nowhere did he betray positive science to metaphysics. He says himself as much in the preface to the second edition of the first volume of *Das Kapital,* and that what he says there is true and no self-delusion can be proved by analyzing his argument, which everywhere rests upon social fact, and the true sources of his propositions none of which lies in the domain of philosophy. Of course, those commentators or critics who themselves started from the philosophic side were unable to do this because they did not know enough about the social sciences involved. The propensity of the philosophic system-builder, moreover, made them averse to any other interpretation but the one which proceeds from some philosophic principle. So they saw philosophy in the most matter-of-fact statements about economic experience, thereby shunting discussion on to the wrong track, misleading friends and foes alike.

Marx the sociologist brought to bear on his task an equipment which consisted primarily of an extensive command over historical and contemporaneous fact. His knowledge of the latter was always somewhat antiquated, for he was the most bookish of men and therefore fundamental materials, as distinguished from the material of the newspapers, always reached him with a lag. But hardly any historical work of his time that was of any general importance or scope escaped him, although much of the monographic literature did. While we cannot extol the completeness of his information in this field as much as we shall his erudition in the field of economic theory, he was yet able to illustrate his social visions not only by large historical frescoes but also by many details most of which were as regards reliability rather above than below the standards of other sociologists of his time. These facts he embraced with a glance that pierced through the random irregularities of the surface down to the grandiose logic of things historical. In this there was not merely passion. There was not merely analytic impulse. There were both. And the outcome of his attempt to formulate that logic, the so-called Economic Interpretation of History,[1] is doubtless one of the greatest individual achievements of sociology to this day. Before it, the question sinks into insignificance whether or not this achievement was entirely original and how far credit has in part to be given to predecessors, German and French.

The economic interpretation of history does *not* mean that men are, consciously or unconsciously, wholly or primarily, actuated by economic motives. On the contrary, the explanation of the role and mechanism of non-economic motives and the analysis of the way in which social reality mirrors itself in the individual psyches is an es-

---

[1] First published in that scathing attack on Proudhon's *Philosophie de la Misère,* entitled *Das Elend der Philosophie,* 1847. Another version was included in the *Communist Manifesto,* 1848.

sential element of the theory and one of its most significant contributions. Marx did not hold that religions, metaphysics, schools of art, ethical ideas and political volitions were either reducible to economic *motives* or of no importance. He only tried to unveil the economic *conditions* which shape them and which account for their rise and fall. The whole of Max Weber's[2] facts and arguments fits perfectly into Marx's system. Social groups and classes and the ways in which these groups or classes explain to themselves their own existence, location and behavior were of course what interested him most. He poured the vials of his most bilious wrath on the historians who took those attitudes and their verbalizations (the ideologies or, as Pareto would have said, *derivations*) at their face value and who tried to interpret social reality by means of them. But if ideas or values were not for him the prime movers of the social process, neither were they mere smoke. If I may use the analogy, they had in the social engine the role of transmission belts. We cannot touch upon that most interesting post-war development of these principles which would afford the best instance by which to explain this, the Sociology of Knowledge.[3] But it was necessary to say this much because Marx has been persistently misunderstood in this respect. Even his friend Engels, at the open grave of Marx, defined the theory in question as meaning precisely that individuals and groups are swayed primarily by economic motives, which in some important respects is wrong and for the rest piteously trivial.

While we are about it, we may as well defend Marx against another misunderstanding: the *economic* interpretation of history has often been called the *materialistic* interpretation. It has been called so by Marx himself. This phrase greatly increased its popularity with some, and its unpopularity with other people. But it is entirely meaningless. Marx's philosophy is no more materialistic than is Hegel's, and his theory of history is not more materialistic than is any other attempt to account for the historic process by the means at the command of empirical science. It should be clear that this is logically compatible with any metaphysical or religious belief—exactly as any physical picture of the world is. Medieval theology itself supplies methods by which it is possible to establish this compatibility.[4]

What the theory really says may be put into two propositions: (1)

[2] The above refers to Weber's investigations into the sociology of religions and particularly to his famous study, *Die protestantische Ethik und der Geist des Kapitalismus,* republished in his collected works.

[3] The German word is *Wissenssoziologie,* and the best names to mention are those of Max Scheler and Karl Mannheim. The latter's article on the subject in the German Dictionary of Sociology (*Handwörterbuch der Soziologie*) can serve as an introduction.

[4] I have met several Catholic radicals, a priest among them, all devout Catholics, who took this view and in fact declared themselves Marxists in everything except in matters relating to their faith.

The forms or conditions of production are the fundamental determinant of social structures which in turn breed attitudes, actions and civilizations. Marx illustrates his meaning by the famous statement that the "hand-mill" creates feudal, and the "steam-mill," capitalist societies. This stresses the technological element to a dangerous extent, but may be accepted on the understanding that mere technology is not all of it. Popularizing a little and recognizing that by doing so we lose much of the meaning, we may say that it is our daily work which forms our minds, and that it is our location within the productive process which determines our outlook on things—or the sides of things we see—and the social elbowroom at the command of each of us. (2) The forms of production themselves have a logic of their own; that is to say, they change according to necessities inherent in them so as to produce their successors merely by their own working. To illustrate by the same Marxian example: the system characterized by the "hand-mill" creates an economic and social situation in which the adoption of the mechanical method of milling becomes a practical necessity that individuals or groups are powerless to alter. The rise and working of the "steam-mill" in turn creates new social functions and locations, new groups and views, which develop and interact in such a way as to outgrow their own frame. Here, then, we have the propeller which is responsible first of all for economic and, in consequence of this, for any other social change, a propeller the action of which does not itself require any impetus external to it.

Both propositions undoubtedly contain a large amount of truth and are, as we shall find at several turns of our way, invaluable working hypotheses. Most of the current objections completely fail, all those for instance which in refutation point to the influence of ethical or religious factors, or the one already raised by Eduard Bernstein, which with delightful simplicity asserts that "men have heads" and can hence act as they choose. After what has been said above, it is hardly necessary to dwell on the weakness of such arguments: of course men "choose" their course of action which is not directly enforced by the objective data of the environment; but they choose from standpoints, views and propensities that do not form another set of independent data but are themselves molded by the objective set.

Nevertheless, the question arises whether the economic interpretation of history is more than a convenient approximation which must be expected to work less satisfactorily in some cases than it does in others. An obvious qualification occurs at the outset. Social structures, types and attitudes are coins that do not readily melt. Once they are formed they persist, possibly for centuries, and since different structures and types display different degrees of this ability to survive, we almost always find that actual group and national behavior more or less departs from what we should expect it to be if we tried to infer it from the dominant forms of the productive process. Though this applies quite generally, it is most clearly seen when a highly durable structure transfers itself bodily from one country to another. The social situation created in Sicily by the Norman conquest will illustrate my meaning. Such facts Marx did not overlook but he hardly realized all their implications.

A related case is of more ominous significance. Consider the emergence of the feudal type of landlordism in the kingdom of the Franks during the sixth and seventh centuries. This was certainly a most important event that shaped the structure of society for many ages and *also influenced conditions of production, wants and technology included*. But its simplest explanation is to be found in the function of military leadership previously filled by the families and individuals who (retaining that function however) became feudal landlords after the definitive conquest of the new territory. This does not fit the Marxian schema at all well and could easily be so construed as to point in a different direction. Facts of this nature can no doubt also be brought into the fold by means of auxiliary hypotheses but the necessity of inserting such hypotheses is usually the beginning of the end of a theory.

Many other difficulties that arise in the course of attempts at historical interpretation by means of the Marxian schema could be met by admitting some measure of interaction between the sphere of production and other spheres of social life.[5] But the glamour of fundamental truth that surrounds it depends precisely on the strictness and simplicity of the one-way relation which it asserts. If this be called in question, the economic interpretation of history will have to take its place among other propositions of a similar kind—as one of many partial truths— or else to give way to another that does tell more fundamental truth. However, neither its rank as an achievement nor its handiness as a working hypothesis is impaired thereby.

To the faithful, of course, it is simply the master key to all the secrets of human history. And if we sometimes feel inclined to smile at rather naïve applications of it, we should remember what sort of arguments it replaced. Even the crippled sister of the economic interpretation of history, the Marxian Theory of Social Classes, moves into a more favorable light as soon as we bear this in mind.

Again, it is in the first place an important contribution that we have to record. Economists have been strangely slow in recognizing the phenomenon of social classes. Of course they always classified the agents whose interplay produced the processes they dealt with. But these classes were simply sets of individuals that displayed some common character:

[5] In his later life, Engels admitted that freely. Plekhanov went still further in this direction.

thus, some people were classed as landlords or workmen because they owned land or sold the services of their labor. Social classes, however, are not the creatures of the classifying observer but live entities that exist as such. And their existence entails consequences that are entirely missed by a schema which looks upon society as if it were an amorphous assemblage of individuals or families. It is fairly open to question precisely how important the phenomenon of social classes is for research in the field of purely economic theory. That it is very important for many practical applications and for all the broader aspects of the social process in general is beyond doubt.

Roughly speaking, we may say that the social classes made their entrance in the famous statement contained in the *Communist Manifesto* that the history of society is the history of class struggles. Of course, this is to put the claim at its highest. But even if we tone it down to the proposition that historical events may often be interpreted in terms of class interests and class attitudes and that existing class structures are always an important factor in historical interpretation, enough remains to entitle us to speak of a conception nearly as valuable as was the economic interpretation of history itself.

Clearly, success on the line of advance opened up by the principle of class struggle depends upon the validity of the particular theory of classes we make our own. Our picture of history and all our interpretations of cultural patterns and the mechanism of social change will differ according to whether we choose, for instance, the racial theory of classes and like Gobineau reduce human history to the history of the struggle of races or, say, the division of labor theory of classes in the fashion of Schmoller or of Durkheim and resolve class antagonisms into antagonisms between the interests of vocational groups. Nor is the range of possible differences in analysis confined to the problem of the nature of classes. Whatever view we may hold about it, different interpretations will result from different definitions of class interest[6] and from different opinions about how class action manifests itself. The subject is a hotbed of prejudice to this day, and as yet hardly in its scientific stage.

Curiously enough, Marx has never, as far as we know, worked out systematically what it is plain was one of the pivots of his thought. It is possible that he deferred the task until it was too late, precisely because his thinking ran so much in terms of class concepts that he did not feel it necessary to bother about definitive statement at all. It is

[6] The reader will perceive that one's views about what classes are and about what calls them into existence do not uniquely determine what the *interests* of those classes are and how each class will act on what "it"—its leaders for instance or the rank and file—considers or feels, in the long run or in the short, erroneously or correctly, to be its interest or interests. The problem of group interest is full of thorns and pitfalls of its own, quite irrespective of the nature of the groups under study.

equally possible that some points about it remained unsettled in his own mind, and that his way toward a full-fledged theory of classes was barred by certain difficulties he had created for himself by insisting on a purely economic and over-simplified conception of the phenomenon. He himself and his disciples both offered applications of this under-developed theory to particular patterns of which his own *History of the Class Struggles in France* is the outstanding example.[7] Beyond that no real progress has been achieved. The theory of his chief associate, Engels, was of the division of labor type and essentially un-Marxian in its implications. Barring this we have only the sidelights and *aperçus*—some of them of striking force and brilliance—that are strewn all over the writings of the master, particularly in *Das Kapital* and the *Communist Manifesto*.

The task of piecing together such fragments is delicate and cannot be attempted here. The basic idea is clear enough, however. The stratifying principle consists in the ownership, or the exclusion from ownership, of means of production such as factory buildings, machinery, raw materials and the consumers' goods that enter into the workman's budget. We have thus, fundamentally, two and only two classes, those owners, the capitalists, and those have-nots who are compelled to sell their labor, the laboring class or proletariat. The existence of intermediate groups, such as are formed by farmers or artisans who employ labor but also do manual work, by clerks and by the professions is of course not denied; but they are treated as anomalies which tend to disappear in the course of the capitalist process. The two fundamental classes are, by virtue of the logic of their position and quite independently of any individual volition, essentially antagonistic to each other. Rifts within each class and collisions between subgroups occur and may even have historically decisive importance. But in the last analysis, such rifts or collisions are incidental. The one antagonism that is not incidental but inherent in the basic design of capitalist society is founded upon the private control over the means to produce: the very nature of the relation between the capitalist class and the proletariat is strife—class war.

As we shall see presently, Marx tries to show how in that class war capitalists destroy each other and eventually will destroy the capitalist system too. He also tries to show how the ownership of capital leads to further accumulation. But this way of arguing as well as the very definition that makes the ownership of something the constituent char-

[7] Another example is the socialist theory of imperialism which will be noticed later on. O. Bauer's interesting attempt to interpret the antagonisms between the various races that inhabited the Austro-Hungarian Empire in terms of the class struggle between capitalists and workers (*Die Nationalitätenfrage*, 1905) also deserves to be mentioned, although the skill of the analyst only serves to show up the inadequacy of the tool.

acteristic of a social class only serves to increase the importance of the question of "primitive accumulation," that is to say, of the question how capitalists came to be capitalists in the first instance or how they acquired that stock of goods which according to the Marxian doctrine was necessary in order to enable them to start exploiting. On this question Marx is much less explicit.[8] He contemptuously rejects the bourgeois nursery tale *(Kinderfibel)* that some people rather than others became, and are still becoming every day, capitalists by superior intelligence and energy in working and saving. Now he was well advised to sneer at that story about the good boys. For to call for a guffaw is no doubt an excellent method of disposing of an uncomfortable truth, as every politician knows to his profit. Nobody who looks at historical and contemporaneous fact with anything like an unbiased mind can fail to observe that this children's tale, while far from telling the whole truth, yet tells a good deal of it. Supernormal intelligence and energy account for industrial success and in particular for the *founding* of industrial positions in nine cases out of ten. And precisely in the initial stages of capitalism and of every individual industrial career, saving was and is an important element in the process though not quite as explained in classic economics. It is true that one does not ordinarily attain the status of capitalist (industrial employer) by saving from a wage or salary in order to equip one's factory by means of the fund thus assembled. The bulk of accumulation comes from profits and hence presupposes profits—this is in fact the *sound* reason for distinguishing saving from accumulating. The means required in order to start enterprise are typically provided by borrowing other people's savings, the presence of which in many small puddles is easy to explain or the deposits which banks create for the use of the would-be entrepreneur. Nevertheless, the latter does save as a rule: the function of his saving is to raise him above the necessity of submitting to daily drudgery for the sake of his daily bread and to give him breathing space in order to look around, to develop his plans and to secure cooperation. As a matter of economic theory, therefore, Marx had a real case—though he overstated it—when he denied to saving the role that the classical authors attributed to it. Only his inference does not follow. And the guffaw is hardly more justified than it would be if the classical theory were correct.[9]

[8] See *Das Kapital,* vol. i, ch. xxvi: "The Secret of Primitive Accumulation."

[9] I will not stay to stress, though I must mention, that even the classical theory is not as wrong as Marx pretended it was. "Saving up" in the most literal sense has been, especially in earlier stages of capitalism, a not unimportant method of "original accumulation." Moreover, there was another method that was akin to it though not identical with   Many a factory in the seventeenth and eighteenth centuries was just a shed that a man was able to put up by the work of his hands, and required only the simplest equipment to work it. In such cases the manual work of the prospective capitalist plus a quite small fund of savings was all that was needed—and brains, of course.

The guffaw did its work, however, and helped to clear the road for Marx's alternative theory of primitive accumulation. But this alternative theory is not as definite as we might wish. Force—robbery—subjugation of the masses facilitating their spoliation and the results of the pillage in turn facilitating subjugation—this was all right of course and admirably tallied with ideas common among intellectuals of all types, in our day still more than in the day of Marx. But evidently it does not solve the problem, which is to explain how some people acquired the power to subjugate and to rob. Popular literature does not worry about it. I should not think of addressing the question to the writings of John Reed. But we are dealing with Marx.

Now at least the semblance of a solution is afforded by the historical quality of all the major theories of Marx. For him, it is essential for the *logic* of capitalism, and not only a matter of *fact,* that it grew out of a feudal state of society. Of course the same question about the causes and the mechanism of social stratification arises also in this case, but Marx substantially accepted the bourgeois view that feudalism was a reign of force[10] in which subjugation and exploitation of the masses were already accomplished facts. The class theory devised primarily for the conditions of capitalist society was extended to its feudal predecessor—as was much of the conceptual apparatus of the economic theory of capitalism[11]—and some of the most thorny problems were stowed away in the feudal compound to reappear in a settled state, in the form of data, in the analysis of the capitalist pattern. The feudal exploiter was simply replaced by the capitalist exploiter. In those cases in which feudal lords actually turned into industrialists, this alone would solve what is thus left of the problem. Historical evidence lends a certain amount of support to this view: many feudal lords, particularly in Germany, in fact did erect and run factories, often providing the financial means from their feudal rents and the labor from the agricultural population (not necessarily but sometimes their serfs).[12] In all other cases the material available to stop the gap is distinctly inferior. The only frank way of expressing the situation is that from a Marxian standpoint there is no satisfactory

[10] Many socialist writers besides Marx have displayed that uncritical confidence in the explanatory value of the element of force and of the control over the physical means with which to exert force. Ferdinand Lassalle, for instance, has little beyond cannons and bayonets to offer by way of explanation of governmental authority. It is a source of wonder to me that so many people should be blind to the weakness of such a sociology and to the fact that it would obviously be much truer to say that power leads to control over cannons (and men willing to use them) than that control over cannons generates power.

[11] This constitutes one of the affinities of the teaching of Marx to that of K. Rodbertus.

[12] W. Sombart, in the first edition of his *Theorie des modernen Kapitalismus,* tried to make the most of those cases. But the attempt to base primitive accumulation entirely on the accumulation of ground rent showed its hopelessness as Sombart himself eventually recognized.

explanation, that is to say, no explanation without resorting to non-Marxian elements suggestive of non-Marxian conclusions.[13]

This, however, vitiates the theory at both its historical and its logical source. Since most of the methods of primitive accumulation also account for later accumulation—primitive accumulation, as it were, continues throughout the capitalist era—it is not possible to say that Marx's theory of social classes is all right *except* for the difficulties about processes in a distant past. But it is perhaps superfluous to insist on the shortcomings of a theory which not even in the most favorable instances goes anywhere near the heart of the phenomenon it undertakes to explain, and which never should have been taken seriously. These instances are to be found mainly in that epoch of capitalist evolution which derived its character from the prevalence of the medium-sized owner-managed firm. Beyond the range of that type, class positions, though in most cases reflected in more or less corresponding economic positions, are more often the cause than the consequence of the latter: business achievement is obviously not everywhere the only avenue to social eminence and only where it is can ownership of means of production causally determine a group's position in the social structure. Even then, however, it is as reasonable to make that ownership the defining element as it would be to define a soldier as a man who happens to have a gun. The water-tight division between people who (together with their descendants) are supposed to be capitalists once for all and others who (together with their descendants) are supposed to be proletarians once for all is not only, as has often been pointed out, utterly unrealistic but it misses the salient point about social classes—the incessant rise and fall of individual families into and out of the upper strata. The facts I am alluding to are all obvious and indisputable. If they do not show on the Marxian canvas, the reason can only be in their un-Marxian implications.

It is not superfluous, however, to consider the role which that theory plays within Marx's structure and to ask ourselves what analytic intention—as distinguished from its use as a piece of equipment for the agitator—he meant it to serve.

On the one hand, we must bear in mind that for Marx the theory of Social Classes and the Economic Interpretation of History were not what they are for us, viz., two independent doctrines. With Marx, the former implements the latter in a particular way and thus restricts—

---

[13] This holds true even if we admit robbery to the utmost extent to which it is possible to do so without trespassing upon the sphere of the intellectual's folklore. Robbery actually entered into the building up of commercial capital at many times and places. Phoenician as well as English wealth offers familiar examples. But even then the Marxian explanation is inadequate because in the last resort successful robbery must rest on the personal superiority of the robbers. And as soon as this is admitted, a very different theory of social stratification suggests itself.

makes more definite—the *modus operandi* of the conditions or forms of production. These determine the social structure and, through the social structure, all manifestations of civilization and the whole march of cultural and political history. But the social structure is, for all non-socialist epochs, defined in terms of classes—those two classes—which are the true dramatis personae and at the same time the only *immediate* creatures of the logic of the capitalist system of production which affects everything else through them. This explains why Marx was forced to make his classes purely economic phenomena, and even phenomena that were economic in a very narrow sense: he thereby cut himself off from a deeper view of them, but in the precise spot of his analytic schema in which he placed them he had no choice but to do so.

On the other hand, Marx wished to define capitalism by the same trait that also defines his class division. A little reflection will convince the reader that this is not a necessary or natural thing to do. In fact it was a bold stroke of analytic strategy which linked the fate of the class phenomenon with the fate of capitalism in such a way that socialism, which in reality has nothing to do with the presence or absence of social classes, became, by definition, the only possible kind of classless society, excepting primitive groups. This ingenious tautology could not equally well have been secured by any definitions of classes *and* of capitalism other than those chosen by Marx—the definition by private ownership of means of production. Hence there had to be just two classes, owners and non-owners, and hence all other principles of division, much more plausible ones among them, had to be severely neglected or discounted or else reduced to that one.

The exaggeration of the definiteness and importance of the dividing line between the capitalist class in that sense and the proletariat was surpassed only by the exaggeration of the antagonism between them. To any mind not warped by the habit of fingering the Marxian rosary it should be obvious that their relation is, in normal times, primarily one of cooperation and that any theory to the contrary must draw largely on pathological cases for verification. In social life, antagonism and synagogism are of course both ubiquitous and in fact inseparable except in the rarest of cases. But I am almost tempted to say that there was, if anything, less of absolute nonsense in the old harmonistic view—full of nonsense though that was too—than in the Marxian construction of the impassable gulf between tool owners and tool users. Again, however, he had no choice, not because he wanted to arrive at revolutionary results—these he could have derived just as well from dozens of other possible schemata—but because of the requirements of his own analysis. *If* class struggle was the subject matter of history and also the means of bringing about the socialist dawn, and *if* there had to be just those two classes, then their relation had to be antagonistic on principle or else the force in his system of social dynamics would have been lost.

Now, though Marx *defines* capitalism sociológically, i.e., by the institution of private control over means of production, the *mechanics* of capitalist society are provided by his economic theory. This economic theory is to show how the sociological data embodied in such conceptions as class, class interest, class behavior, exchange between classes, work out through the medium of economic values, profits, wages, investment, etc., and how they generate precisely the economic process that will eventually break its own institutional framework and at the same time create the conditions for the emergence of another social world. This particular theory of social classes is the analytic tool which, by linking the economic interpretation of history with the concepts of the profit economy, marshals all social facts, makes all phenomena confocal. It is therefore not simply a theory of an individual phenomenon which is to explain that phenomenon and nothing else. It has an organic function which is really much more important to the Marxian system than the measure of success with which it solves its immediate problem. This function must be seen if we are to understand how an analyst of the power of Marx could ever have borne with its shortcomings.

There are, and always have been, some enthusiasts who admired the Marxian theory of social classes as such. But far more understandable are the feelings of all those who admire the force and grandeur of that synthesis as a whole to the point of being ready to condone almost any number of shortcomings in the component parts. We shall try to appraise it for ourselves (Chapter IV). But first we must see how Marx's economic mechanics acquits itself of the task that his general plan imposes upon it.

CHAPTER III

MARX THE ECONOMIST

As an economic theorist Marx was first of all a very learned man. It may seem strange that I should think it necessary to give such prominence to this element in the case of an author whom I have called a genius and a prophet. Yet it is important to appreciate it. Geniuses and prophets do not usually excel in professional learning, and their originality, if any, is often due precisely to the fact that they do not. But nothing in Marx's economics can be accounted for by any want of scholarship or training in the technique of theoretical analysis. He was a voracious reader and an indefatigable worker. He missed very few contributions of significance. And whatever he read he digested, wrestling with every fact or argument with a passion for detail most unusual in one whose glance habitually encompassed entire civilizations and secular developments. Criticizing and rejecting or accepting and coordinating, he always went to the bottom of every matter. The outstanding proof of this is in his work, *Theories of Surplus Value,* which is a monument of theoretical ardor. This incessant endeavor to school himself and to master whatever there was to master went some way toward freeing him from prejudices and extra-scientific aims, though he certainly worked in order to verify a definite vision. To his powerful intellect, the interest in the problem as a problem was paramount in spite of himself; and however much he may have bent the import of his final *results,* while at work he was primarily concerned with sharpening the tools of analysis proffered by the science of his day, with straightening out logical difficulties and with building on the foundation thus acquired a theory that in nature and intent was truly scientific whatever its shortcomings may have been.

It is easy to see why both friends and foes should have misunderstood the nature of his performance in the purely economic field. For the friends, he was so much more than a mere professional theorist that it would have seemed almost blasphemy to them to give too much prominence to this aspect of his work. The foes, who resented his attitudes and the setting of his theoretic argument, found it almost impossible to admit that in some parts of his work he did precisely the kind of thing which they valued so highly when presented by other hands. Moreover, the cold metal of economic theory is in Marx's pages immersed in such a wealth of steaming phrases as to acquire a temperature not naturally its own. Whoever shrugs his shoulders at Marx's claim to be considered

21

an analyst in the scientific sense thinks of course of those phrases and not of the thought, of the impassioned language and of the glowing indictment of "exploitation" and "immiserization" (this is probably the best way to render the word *Verelendung,* which is no more good German than that English monster is good English. It is *immiserimento* in Italian). To be sure, all these things and many others, such as his spiteful innuendoes or his vulgar comment on Lady Orkney,[1] are important parts of the show, were important to Marx himself and are so both for the faithful and for the unbelievers. They explain in part why many people insist on seeing in Marx's theorems something more than, and even something fundamentally different from, the analogous propositions of his master. But they do not affect the nature of his analysis.

Marx had a master then? Yes. Real understanding of his economics begins with recognizing that, as a theorist, he was a pupil of Ricardo. He was his pupil not only in the sense that his own argument evidently starts from Ricardo's propositions but also in the much more significant sense that he had learned the art of theorizing from Ricardo. He always used Ricardo's tools, and every theoretical problem presented itself to him in the form of difficulties which occurred to him in his profound study of Ricardo and of suggestions for further work which he gleaned from it. Marx himself admitted much of this, although of course he would not have admitted that his attitude toward Ricardo was typically that of a pupil who goes to the professor, hears him speak several times in almost successive sentences of redundancy of population and of population that is redundant and again of machinery making population redundant, and then goes home and tries to work the thing out. That both parties to the Marxian controversy should have been averse to admitting this is perhaps understandable.

Ricardo's is not the only influence which acted on Marx's economics, but no other than that of Quesnay, from whom Marx derived his fundamental conception of the economic process as a whole, need be mentioned in a sketch like this. The group of English writers who between 1800 and 1840 tried to develop the labor theory of value may have furnished many suggestions and details, but this is covered for our purpose by the reference to the Ricardian current of thought. Several authors, to some of whom Marx was unkind in inverse proportion to their distance from him and whose work ran in many points parallel to his (Sismondi, Rodbertus, John Stuart Mill), must be left out of account, as must everything not directly pertaining to the main argument—so, for instance, Marx's distinctly weak performance in the field of money, in which he did not succeed in coming up to the Ricardian standard.

Now for a desperately abbreviated outline of the Marxian argument, unavoidably unjust on many counts to the structure of *Das Kapital*

[1] The friend of William III—the king who, so unpopular in his own day, had by that time become an idol of the English bourgeoisie.

which, partly unfinished, partly battered by successful attack, still stretches its mighty skyline before us!

1. Marx fell in with the ordinary run of the theorists of his own and also of a later epoch by making a theory of value the corner stone of his theoretical structure. His theory of value is the Ricardian one. I believe that such an outstanding authority as Professor Taussig disagreed with this and always stressed the differences. There is plenty of difference in wording, method of deduction and sociological implication, but there is none in the bare theorem, which alone matters to the theorist of today.[2] Both Ricardo and Marx say that the value of every commodity is (in perfect equilibrium and perfect competition) proportional to the quantity of labor contained in the commodity, provided this labor is in accordance with the existing standard of efficiency of production (the "socially necessary quantity of labor"). Both measure this quantity in hours of work and use the same method in order to reduce different qualities of work to a single standard. Both encounter the threshold difficulties incident to this approach similarly (that is to say, Marx encounters them as he had learned to do from Ricardo). Neither has anything useful to say about monopoly or what we now call imperfect competition. Both answer critics by the same arguments. Marx's arguments are merely less polite, more prolix and more "philosophical" in the worst sense of this word.

Everybody knows that this theory of value is unsatisfactory. In the voluminous discussion that has been carried on about it, the right is not indeed all on one side and many faulty arguments have been used by its opponents. The essential point is not whether labor is the true "source" or "cause" of economic value. This question may be of primary interest to social philosophers who want to deduce from it ethical claims to the product, and Marx himself was of course not indifferent to this aspect of the problem. For economics as a positive science, however, which has to describe or explain actual processes, it is much more

---

[2] It may, however, be open to question whether this is all that mattered to Marx himself. He was under the same delusion as Aristotle, viz., that value, though a factor in the determination of relative prices, is yet something that is different from, and exists independently of, relative prices or exchange relations. The proposition that the value of a commodity *is* the amount of labor embodied in it can hardly mean anything else. If so, then there *is* a difference between Ricardo and Marx, since Ricardo's values are simply exchange values or relative prices. It is worth while to mention this because, if we could accept this view of value, much of his theory that seems to us untenable or even meaningless would cease to be so. Of course we cannot. Nor would the situation be improved if, following some Marxologists, we took the view that whether a distinct "substance" or not, Marx's labor-quantity values are merely intended to serve as tools by which to display the division of total social income into labor income and capital income (the theory of individual relative prices being then a secondary matter). For, as we shall see presently, Marx's theory of value also fails at this task (granted that we can divorce that task from the problem of individual prices).

important to ask how the labor theory of value works as a tool of analysis, and the real trouble with it is that it does so very badly.

To begin with, it does not work at all outside of the case of perfect competition. Second, even with perfect competition it never works *smoothly* except if labor is the only factor of production and, moreover, if labor is all of one kind.[3] If either of these two conditions is not fulfilled, additional assumptions must be introduced and analytical difficulties increase to an extent that soon becomes unmanageable. Reasoning on the lines of the labor theory of value is hence reasoning on a very special case without practical importance, though something might be said for it if it be interpreted in the sense of a rough approximation to the historical tendencies of relative values. The theory which replaced it—in its earliest and now outmoded form, known as the theory of marginal utility—may claim superiority on many counts but the real argument for it is that it is much more general and applies equally well, on the one hand, to the cases of monopoly and imperfect competition and, on the other hand, to the presence of other factors and of labor of many different kinds and qualities. Moreover, if we introduce into this theory the restrictive assumptions mentioned, proportionality between value and quantity of labor applied follows from it.[4] It should be clear, therefore, not only that it was perfectly absurd for Marxists to question, as at first they tried to do, the validity of the marginal utility theory of value (which was what confronted them),

[3] The necessity for the second assumption is particularly damaging. The labor theory of value may be able to deal with differences in quality of labor that are due to training (acquired skill): appropriate quota of the work that goes into the process of training would then have to be added to every hour of skilled work so that we might, without leaving the range of the principle, put the hour of work done by a skilled workman equal to a determined multiple of an hour of unskilled work. But this method fails in the case of "natural" differences in quality of work due to differences in intelligence, will power, physical strength or agility. Then recourse must be had to the difference in value of the hours respectively worked by the naturally inferior and the naturally superior workmen—a value that is not itself explainable on the labor-quantity principle. In fact Ricardo does precisely this: he simply says that those different qualities will somehow be put into their right relation by the play of the market mechanism so that we may after all speak of an hour's work done by workman A being equivalent to a definite multiple of the work done by workman B. But he completely overlooks that in arguing in this way he appeals to another principle of valuation and really surrenders the labor-quantity principle which thus fails from the start, within its own precincts, and before it has the chance to fail because of the presence of factors other than labor.

[4] In fact, it follows from the marginal utility theory of value that for equilibrium to exist each factor must be so distributed over the productive uses open to it that the last unit allocated to any use produces the same value as the last unit allocated to each of the other uses. If there be no other factors except labor of one kind and quality, this obviously means that the relative values or prices of all commodities must be proportional to the numbers of man-hours contained in them, provided there is perfect competition and mobility.

but also that it is incorrect to call the labor theory of value "wrong." In any case it is dead and buried.

2. Though neither Ricardo nor Marx seems to have been fully aware of all the weaknesses of the position in which they had placed themselves by adopting this starting point, they perceived some of them quite clearly. In particular, they both grappled with the problem of eliminating the element of Services of Natural Agents which of course are deprived of their proper place in the process of production and distribution by a theory of value that rests upon quantity of labor alone. The familiar Ricardian theory of the rent of land is essentially an attempt to accomplish that elimination and the Marxian theory is another. As soon as we are in possession of an analytical apparatus which takes care of rent as naturally as it does of wages, the whole difficulty vanishes. Hence nothing more need be said about the intrinsic merits or demerits of Marx's doctrine of absolute as distinguished from differential rent, or about its relation to that of Rodbertus.

But even if we let that pass we are still left with the difficulty arising out of the presence of capital in the sense of a stock of means of production that are themselves produced. To Ricardo it presented itself very simply: in the famous Section IV of the first chapter of his *Principles* he introduces and accepts as a fact, without attempting to question it, that, where capital goods such as plant, machinery and raw materials are used in the production of a commodity, this commodity will sell at a price which will yield a net return to the owner of those capital goods. He realized that this fact has something to do with the period of time that elapses between the investment and the emergence of salable products and that it will enforce deviations of the actual values of these from proportionality to the man-hours "contained" in them—including the man-hours that went into the production of the capital goods themselves—whenever these periods are not the same in all industries. To this he points as coolly as if it followed from, instead of contradicting, his fundamental theorem about value, and beyond this he does not really go, confining himself to some secondary problems that arise in this connection and obviously believing that his theory still describes the basic determinant of value.

Marx also introduced, accepted and discussed that same fact and never questioned it as a fact. He also realized that it seems to give the lie to the labor theory of value. But he recognized the inadequacy of Ricardo's treatment of the problem and, while accepting the problem itself in the shape in which Ricardo presented it, set about to attack it in earnest, devoting to it about as many hundreds of pages as Ricardo devoted sentences.

3. In doing so he not only displayed much keener perception of the nature of the problem involved, but he also improved the conceptual apparatus he received. For instance, he replaced to good

purpose Ricardo's distinction between fixed and circulating capital by the distinction between constant and variable (wage) capital, and Ricardo's rudimentary notions about duration of the processes of production by the much more rigorous concept of "organic structure of capital" which turns on the relation between constant and variable capital. He also made many other contributions to the theory of capital. We will however confine ourselves now to his explanation of the net return to capital, his Theory of Exploitation.

The masses have not always felt themselves to be frustrated and exploited. But the intellectuals that formulated their views for them have always told them that they were, without necessarily meaning by it anything precise. Marx could not have done without the phrase even if he had wanted to. His merit and achievement were that he perceived the weakness of the various arguments by which the tutors of the mass mind before him had tried to show how exploitation came about and which even today supply the stock in trade of the ordinary radical. None of the usual slogans about bargaining power and cheating satisfied him. What he wanted to prove was that exploitation did not arise from individual situations occasionally and accidentally; but that it resulted from the very logic of the capitalist system, unavoidably and quite independently of any individual intention.

This is how he did it. The brain, muscles and nerves of a laborer constitute, as it were, a fund or stock of potential labor (*Arbeitskraft*, usually translated not very satisfactorily by labor power). This fund or stock Marx looks upon as a sort of substance that exists in a definite quantity and in capitalist society is a commodity like any other. We may clarify the thought for ourselves by thinking of the case of slavery: Marx's idea is that there is no essential difference, though there are many secondary ones, between the wage contract and the purchase of a slave—what the employer of "free" labor buys is not indeed, as in the case of slavery, the laborers themselves but a definite quota of the sum total of their potential labor.

Now since labor in that sense (not the labor *service* or the actual man-hour) is a commodity the law of value must apply to it. That is to say, it must in equilibrium and perfect competition fetch a wage proportional to the number of labor *hours* that entered into its "production." But what number of labor *hours* enters into the "production" of the stock of potential labor that is stored up within a workman's skin? Well, the number of labor *hours* it took and takes to rear, feed, clothe and house the laborer.[5] This constitutes the value of that stock, and if he sells parts of it—expressed in days or weeks

[5] That is, barring the distinction between "labor power" and labor, the solution which S. Bailey (*A Critical Discourse on the Nature, Measure and Causes of Value*, 1825) by anticipation voted absurd, as Marx himself did not fail to notice (*Das Kapital*, vol. i, ch. xix).

or years—he will receive wages that correspond to the labor value of these parts, just as a slave trader selling a slave would in equilibrium receive a price proportional to the total number of those labor *hours*. It should be observed once more that Marx thus keeps carefully clear of all those popular slogans which in one form or another hold that in the capitalist labor market the workman is robbed or cheated or that, in his lamentable weakness, he is simply compelled to accept any terms imposed. The thing is not as simple as this: he gets the full value of his labor potential.

But once the "capitalists" have acquired that stock of potential services they are in a position to make the laborer work more hours—render more actual services—than it takes to produce that stock or potential stock. They can exact, in this sense, more actual hours of labor than they have paid for. Since the resulting products also sell at a price proportional to the man-hours that enter into their production, there is a difference between the two values—arising from nothing but the *modus operandi* of the Marxian law of values—which necessarily and by virtue of the mechanism of capitalist markets goes to the capitalist. This is the Surplus Value (*Mehrwert*).[6] By appropriating it the capitalist "exploits" labor, though he pays to the laborers not less than the full value of their labor potential and receives from consumers not more than the full value of the products he sells. Again it should be observed that there is no appeal to such things as unfair pricing, restriction of production or cheating in the markets for the products. Marx did of course not mean to deny the existence of such practices. But he saw them in their true perspective and hence never based any fundamental conclusions upon them.

Let us admire, in passing, the pedagogics of it: however special and removed from its ordinary sense the meaning might be which the word Exploitation now acquires, however doubtful the support which it derives from the Natural Law and the philosophies of the schoolmen and the writers of the Enlightenment, it is received into the pale of scientific argument after all and thus serves the purpose of comforting the disciple marching on to fight his battles.

As regards the merits of this scientific argument we must carefully distinguish two aspects of it, one of which has been persistently neglected by critics. At the ordinary level of the theory of a stationary economic process it is easy to show that under Marx's own assumptions the doctrine of surplus value is untenable. The labor theory of value, even if we could grant it to be valid for every other commodity, can never be applied to the commodity labor, for this would imply that workmen, like machines, are being produced according to rational cost calculations. Since they are not, there is no warrant for assuming

---

[6] The rate of surplus value (degree of exploitation) is defined as the ratio between surplus value and the variable (wage) capital.

that the value of labor power will be proportional to the man-hours
that enter into its "production." Logically Marx would have improved
his position had he accepted Lassalle's Iron Law of Wages or simply
argued on Malthusian lines as Ricardo did. But since he very wisely
refused to do that, his theory of exploitation loses one of its essential
props from the start.[7]

Moreover, it can be shown that perfectly competitive equilibrium
cannot exist in a situation in which all capitalist-employers make exploitation gains. For in this case they would individually try to expand production, and the mass effect of this would unavoidably tend
to increase wage rates and to reduce gains of that kind to zero. It
would no doubt be possible to mend the case somewhat by appealing
to the theory of imperfect competition, by introducing friction and
institutional inhibitions of the working of competition, by stressing
all the possibilities of hitches in the sphere of money and credit and
so on. Only a moderate case could be made out in this manner, however, one that Marx would have heartily despised.

But there is another aspect of the matter. We need only look at
Marx's analytic aim in order to realize that he need not have accepted
battle on the ground on which it is so easy to beat him. This is so
easy only as long as we see in the theory of surplus value nothing but
a proposition about stationary economic processes in perfect equilibrium. Since what he aimed at analyzing was not a state of equilibrium
which according to him capitalist society can never attain, but on
the contrary a process of incessant change in the economic structure,
criticism along the above lines is not completely decisive. Surplus
values may be impossible in perfect equilibrium but can be ever
present because that equilibrium is never allowed to establish itself.
They may always *tend* to vanish and yet be always there because they
are constantly recreated. This defense will not rescue the labor theory
of value, particularly as applied to the commodity labor itself, or the
argument about exploitation as it stands. But it will enable us to
put a more favorable interpretation on the result, although a satisfactory theory of those surpluses will strip them of the specifically
Marxian connotation. This aspect proves to be of considerable importance. It throws a new light also on other parts of Marx's apparatus
of economic analysis and goes far toward explaining why that apparatus was not more fatally damaged by the successful criticisms
directed against its very fundaments.

4. If, however, we go on at the level on which discussion of Marxian
doctrines ordinarily moves, we get deeper and deeper into difficulties
or rather we perceive that the faithful do when they try to follow
the master on his way. To begin with, the doctrine of surplus value
does not make it any easier to solve the problems, alluded to above,

[7] We shall see later how Marx tried to replace that prop.

which are created by the discrepancy between the labor theory of value and the plain facts of economic reality. On the contrary it accentuates them because, according to it, constant capital—that is, non-wage capital—does not transmit to the product any more value than it loses in its production; only wage capital does that and the profits earned should in consequence vary, as between firms, according to the organic composition of their capitals. Marx relies on the competition between capitalists for bringing about a redistribution of the total "mass" of surplus value such that each firm should earn profits proportional to its total capital, or that individual rates of profits should be equalized. We readily see that the difficulty belongs to the class of spurious problems that always result from attempts to work an unsound theory,[8] and the solution to the class of counsels of despair. Marx, however, believed not only that the latter availed to establish the emergence of uniform rates of profits and to explain how, because of it, relative prices of commodities will deviate from their values in terms of labor,[9] but also that his theory offered an explanation of another "law" that held a great place in classical doctrine, namely, the statement that the rate of profit has an inherent tendency to fall. This follows in fact fairly plausibly from the increase in relative importance of the constant part of the total capital in the wage-good industries: if the relative importance of plant and equipment increases in those industries, as it does in the course of capitalist evolution, and if the

[8] There is, however, one element in it which is not unsound and the perception of which, however dim, should be recorded to Marx's credit. It is not, as almost all economists believe even today, an unquestionable fact that produced means of production would yield a net return in a perfectly stationary economy. If they in practice normally do seem to yield net returns, that may well be due to the fact that the economy never is stationary. Marx's argument about the net return to capital might be interpreted as a devious way of recognizing this.

[9] His solution of that problem he embodied in manuscripts from which his friend Engels compiled the posthumous third volume of *Das Kapital*. Therefore we have not before us what Marx himself might ultimately have wished to say. As it was, most critics felt no hesitation in convicting him of having by the third volume flatly contradicted the doctrine of the first. On the face of it that verdict is not justified. If we place ourselves on Marx's standpoint, as it is our duty in a question of this kind, it is not absurd to look upon surplus value as a "mass" produced by the social process of production considered as a unit and to make the rest a matter of the distribution of that mass. And if that is not absurd, it is still possible to hold that the relative prices of commodities, as deduced in the third volume, follow from the labor-quantity theory in the first volume. Hence it is not correct to assert, as some writers from Lexis to Cole have done, that Marx's theory of value is completely divorced from, and contributes nothing to, his theory of prices. But Marx stands to gain little by being cleared of contradiction. The remaining indictment is quite strong enough. The best contribution to the whole question of how values and prices are related to each other in the Marxian system, that also refers to some of the better performances in a controversy that was not exactly fascinating, is L. von Bortkiewicz, "Wertrechnung und Preisrechnung im Marxschen System," *Archiv für Sozialwissenschaft und Sozialpolitik*, 1907.

rate of surplus value or the degree of exploitation remains the same, then the rate of return to total capital will in general decrease. This argument has elicited much admiration, and was presumably looked upon by Marx himself with all the satisfaction we are in the habit of feeling if a theory of ours explains an observation that did not enter into its construction. It would be interesting to discuss it on its own merits and independently of the mistakes Marx committed in deriving it. We need not stay to do so, for it is sufficiently condemned by its premises. But a cognate though not identical proposition provides both one of the most important "forces" of Marxian dynamics and the link between the theory of exploitation and the next story of Marx's analytic structure, usually referred to as the Theory of Accumulation.

The main part of the loot wrung from exploited labor (according to some of the disciples, practically all of it) capitalists turn into capital—means of production. In itself and barring the connotations called up by Marx's phraseology, this is of course no more than a statement of a very familiar fact ordinarily described in terms of saving and investment. For Marx however this mere fact was not enough: if the capitalist process was to unfold in inexorable logic, that fact had to be part of this logic which means, practically, that it had to be necessary. Nor would it have been satisfactory to allow this necessity to grow out of the social psychology of the capitalist class, for instance in a way similar to Max Weber's who made Puritan attitudes—and abstaining from hedonist enjoyment of one's profits obviously fits well into their pattern—a causal determinant of capitalist behavior. Marx did not despise any support he felt able to derive from this method.[10] But there had to be something more substantial than this for a system designed as his was, something which compels capitalists to accumulate irrespective of what they feel about it, and which is powerful enough to account for that psychological pattern itself. And fortunately there is.

In setting forth the nature of that compulsion to save, I shall for the sake of convenience accept Marx's teaching on one point: that is to say, I shall assume as he does that saving by the capitalist class *ipso facto* implies a corresponding increase in real capital.[11] This

[10] For instance, in one place (*Das Kapital*, vol. i, p. 654, of the Everyman edition) he surpasses himself in picturesque rhetoric on the subject—going, I think, further than is proper for the author of the economic interpretation of history. Accumulating may or may not be "Moses and all the prophets"(!) for the capitalist class and such flights may or may not strike us as ridiculous—with Marx, arguments of that type and in that style are always suggestive of some weakness that must be screened.

[11] For Marx, saving or accumulating is identical with conversion of "surplus value into capital." With that I do not propose to take issue, though individual attempts at saving do not necessarily and automatically increase real capital. Marx's view

movement will in the first instance always occur in the variable part of total capital, the wage capital, even if the intention is to increase the constant part and in particular that part which Ricardo called fixed capital—mainly machinery.

When discussing Marx's theory of exploitation, I have pointed out that in a perfectly competitive economy exploitation gains would induce capitalists to expand production, or to attempt to expand it, because from the standpoint of every one of them that would mean more profit. In order to do so they would have to accumulate. Moreover the mass effect of this would tend to reduce surplus values through the ensuing rise in wage rates, if not also through an ensuing fall in the prices of products—a very nice instance of the contradictions inherent in capitalism that were so dear to Marx's heart. And that tendency itself would, also for the individual capitalist, constitute another reason why he should feel compelled to accumulate,[12] though again that would in the end make matters worse for the capitalist class as a whole. There would hence be a sort of compulsion to accumulate even in an otherwise stationary process which, as I mentioned before, could not reach stable equilibrium until accumulation had reduced surplus value to zero and thus destroyed capitalism itself.[13]

Much more important and much more drastically compelling is something else, however. As a matter of fact, capitalist economy is not and cannot be stationary. Nor is it merely expanding in a steady manner. It is incessantly being revolutionized *from within* by new enterprise, i.e., by the intrusion of new commodities or new methods of production or new commercial opportunities into the industrial structure as it exists at any moment. Any existing structures and all the conditions of doing business are always in a process of change.

---

seems to me to be so much nearer the truth than the opposite view sponsored by many of my contemporaries that I do not think it worth while to challenge it here.

[12] Less would of course in general be saved out of a smaller than out of a bigger income. But more will be saved out of any given income if it is not expected to last or if it is expected to decrease than would be saved out of the same income if it were known to be at least stable at its current figure.

[13] To some extent Marx recognizes this. But he thinks that if wages rise and thereby interfere with accumulation, the rate of the latter will decrease "because the stimulus of gain is blunted" so that "the mechanism of the process of capitalist production removes the very obstacles it temporarily creates." (*Das Kapital,* vol. i, ch. xxv, section 1.) Now *this* tendency of the capitalist mechanism to equilibrate itself is surely not above question and any assertion of it would require, to say the least, careful qualification. But the interesting point is that we should call that statement most un-Marxian if we happened to come across it in the work of another economist and that, as far as it is tenable, it greatly weakens the main drift of Marx's argument. In this point as in many others, Marx displays to an astonishing degree the shackles of the bourgeois economics of his time which he believed himself to have broken.

Every situation is being upset before it has had time to work itself out. Economic progress, in capitalist society, means turmoil. And, as we shall see in the next part, in this turmoil competition works in a manner completely different from the way it would work in a stationary process, however perfectly competitive. Possibilities of gains to be reaped by producing new things or by producing old things more cheaply are constantly materializing and calling for new investments. These new products and new methods compete with the old products and old methods not on equal terms but at a decisive advantage that may mean death to the latter. This is how "progress" comes about in capitalist society. In order to escape being undersold, *every* firm is in the end compelled to follow suit, to invest in its turn and, in order to be able to do so, to plow back part of its profits, i.e., to accumulate.[14] Thus, everyone else accumulates.

Now Marx saw this process of industrial change more clearly and he realized its pivotal importance more fully than any other economist of his time. This does not mean that he correctly understood its nature or correctly analyzed its mechanism. With him, that mechanism resolves itself into mere mechanics of masses of capital. He had no adequate theory of enterprise and his failure to distinguish the entrepreneur from the capitalist, together with a faulty theoretical technique, accounts for many cases of *non sequitur* and for many mistakes. But the mere vision of the process was in itself sufficient for many of the purposes that Marx had in mind. The *non sequitur* ceases to be a fatal objection if what does not follow from Marx's argument can be made to follow from another one; and even downright mistakes and misinterpretations are often redeemed by the substantial correctness of the general drift of the argument in the course of which they occur—in particular they may be rendered innocuous for the further steps of the analysis which, to the critic who fails to appreciate this paradoxical situation, seem condemned beyond appeal.

We had an example of this before. Taken as it stands, Marx's theory of surplus value is untenable. But since the capitalist process does produce recurrent waves of temporary surplus gains over cost which, though in a very un-Marxian way, other theories can account for all right, Marx's next step, inscribed to accumulation, is not completely vitiated by his previous slips. Similarly, Marx himself did not satisfactorily establish that compulsion to accumulate, which is so essential

[14] That is of course not the only method of financing technological improvement. But it is practically the only method that Marx considered. Since it actually is a very important one, we may here follow him in this, though other methods, particularly that of borrowing from banks, i.e., of creating deposits, produce consequences of their own, insertion of which would really be necessary in order to draw a correct picture of the capitalist process.

to his argument. But no great harm results from the shortcomings of his explanation because, in the way alluded to, we can readily supply a more satisfactory one ourselves, in which among other things the fall of profits drops into the right place by itself. The aggregate rate of profit on total industrial capital need not fall in the long run, either for the Marxian reason that the constant capital increases relatively to the variable capital[15] or for any other. It is sufficient that, as we have seen, the profit of every individual plant is incessantly being threatened by actual or potential competition from new commodities or methods of production which sooner or later will turn it into a loss. So we get the driving force required and even an analogon to Marx's proposition that constant capital does not produce surplus value—for no individual assemblage of capital goods remains a source of surplus gains forever—without having to rely on those parts of his argument which are of doubtful validity.

Another example is afforded by the next link in Marx's chain, his Theory of Concentration, that is, his treatment of the tendency of the capitalist process to increase the size both of industrial plants and of units of control. All he has to offer in explanation,[16] when stripped of his imagery, boils down to the unexciting statements that "the battle of competition is fought by cheapening commodities" which "depends, *caeteris paribus,* on the productiveness of labor"; that this again depends on the scale of production; and that "the larger capitals beat the smaller."[17] This is much like what the current textbook says on the matter, and not very deep or admirable in itself. In particular it is inadequate because of the exclusive emphasis placed on the size of the individual "capitals" while in his description of effects Marx is much hampered by his technique which is unable to deal effectively with either monopoly or oligopoly.

[15] According to Marx, profits can of course also fall for another reason, i.e., because of a fall in the rate of surplus value. That may be due either to increases in wage rates or to reductions, by legislation for instance, of the daily hours of work. It is possible to argue, even from the standpoint of Marxian theory, that this will induce "capitalists" to substitute labor-saving capital goods for labor, and hence also increase investment temporarily irrespective of the impact of new commodities and of technological progress. Into these questions we cannot enter however. But we may note a curious incident. In 1837, Nassau W. Senior published a pamphlet entitled *Letters on the Factory Act,* in which he tried to show that the proposed reduction of the duration of the working day would result in the annihilation of profits in the cotton industry. In *Das Kapital,* vol. i, ch. vii, section 3. Marx surpasses himself in fierce indictments against that performance. Senior's argument is in fact little short of foolish. But Marx should have been the last person to say so for it is quite in keeping with his own theory of exploitation.

[16] See *Das Kapital,* vol. i, ch. xxv, section 2.

[17] This conclusion, often referred to as the theory of expropriation, is with Marx the only purely economic basis of that struggle by which capitalists destroy one another.

Yet the admiration so many economists outside the fold profess to feel for this theory is not unjustified. For one thing, to predict the advent of big business was, considering the conditions of Marx's day, an achievement in itself. But he did more than that. He neatly hitched concentration to the process of accumulation or rather he visualized the former as part of the latter, and not only as part of its factual pattern but also of its logic. He perceived some of the consequences correctly—for instance that "the increasing bulk of individual masses of capital becomes the material basis of an uninterrupted revolution in the mode of production itself"—and others at least in a one-sided or distorted manner. He electrified the atmosphere surrounding the phenomenon by all the dynamos of class war and politics—that alone would have been enough to raise his exposition of it high above the dry economic theorems involved, particularly for people without any imagination of their own. And, most important of all, he was able to go on, almost entirely unhampered by the inadequate motivation of individual traits of his picture and by what to the professional appears to be lack of stringency in his argument, for after all the industrial giants actually were in the offing and so was the social situation which they were bound to create.

5. Two more items will complete this sketch: Marx's theory of *Verelendung* or, to use the English equivalent I have ventured to adopt, of immiserization, and his (and Engels') theory of the trade cycle. In the former, both analysis and vision fail beyond remedy; both show up to advantage in the latter.

Marx undoubtedly held that in the course of capitalist evolution real wage rates and the standard of life of the masses would fall in the better-paid, and fail to improve in the worst-paid, strata and that this would come about not through any accidental or environmental circumstances but by virtue of the very logic of the capitalist process.[18] As a prediction, this was of course singularly infelicitous and Marxists of all types have been hard put to it to make the best of the clearly adverse evidence that confronted them. At first, and in some isolated instances even to our day, they displayed a remarkable tenacity in trying to save that "law" as a statement of an actual tendency borne out by wage statistics. Then attempts were made to read into it a different meaning, that is to say, to make it refer not

[18] There is a first-line defense which Marxists, like most apologists, are wont to set against the critical intention lurking behind any such clear-cut statement. It is that Marx did not entirely fail to see the other side of the medal and that he very often "recognized" cases of rising wages and so on—as indeed nobody could possibly fail to do—the implication being that he fully anticipated whatever a critic might have to say. So prolix a writer who interlards his argument with such rich layers of historical analysis naturally gives more scope for such defense than any of the fathers of the church did. But what is the good of "recognizing" recalcitrant fact if it is not allowed to influence conclusions?

to rates of real wages or to the absolute share that goes to the working class but to the relative share of labor incomes in total national income. Though some passages in Marx will in fact bear interpretation in this sense, this clearly violates the meaning of most. Moreover, little would be gained by accepting this interpretation, because Marx's main conclusions presuppose that the *absolute* per capita share of labor should fall or, at the very least, not increase: if he really had been thinking of the relative share that would only add to Marxian troubles. Finally the proposition itself would still be wrong. For the relative share of wages and salaries in total income varies but little from year to year and is remarkably constant over time—it certainly does not reveal any tendency to fall.

There seems, however, to be another way out of the difficulty. A tendency may fail to show in our statistical time series—which may even show the opposite one as they do in this case—and yet it might be inherent in the system under investigation, for it might be suppressed by exceptional conditions. This is in fact the line that most modern Marxists take. The exceptional conditions are found in colonial expansion or, more generally, in the opening up of new countries during the nineteenth century, which is held to have brought about a "closed season" for the victims of exploitation.[19] In the next part we shall have occasion to touch upon this matter. Meanwhile, let us note that facts lend some *prima facie* support to this argument which is also unexceptionable in logic and therefore might resolve the difficulty if that tendency were otherwise well established.

But the real trouble is that Marx's theoretical structure is anything but trustworthy in that sector: along with the vision, the analytic groundwork is there at fault. The basis of the theory of immiserization is the theory of the "industrial reserve army," i.e., of the unemployment created by the mechanization of the process of production.[20] And the theory of the reserve army is in turn based upon the doctrine expounded in Ricardo's chapter on machinery. Nowhere else—excepting of course the theory of value—does Marx's argument so completely depend on that of Ricardo without adding anything essential.[21]

---

[19] This idea was suggested by Marx himself, though it has been developed by the Neo-Marxists.

[20] This kind of unemployment must of course be distinguished from others. In particular, Marx notices the kind which owes its existence to the cyclical variations in business activity. Since the two are not independent and since in his argument he often relies on the latter type rather than on the former, difficulties of interpretation arise of which not all critics seem to be fully aware.

[21] To any theorist this must be obvious, from a study not only of the *sedes materiae, Das Kapital,* vol. i, ch. xv, sections 3, 4, 5, and especially 6 (where Marx deals with the theory of compensation, to be noted above), but also of chs. xxiv and xxv where, in a partially different garb, the same things are repeated and elaborated.

I am speaking of course of the pure theory of the phenomenon only. Marx did add, as always, many minor touches such as the felicitous generalization by which the replacement of skilled by unskilled workers is made to enter into the concept of unemployment; also he added an infinite wealth of illustration and phraseology; and, most important of all, he added the impressive setting, the wide backgrounds of his social process.

Ricardo had at first been inclined to share the view, very common at all times, that the introduction of machines into the productive process could hardly fail to benefit the masses. When he came to doubt that opinion or, at all events, its general validity, he with characteristic frankness revised his position. No less characteristically, he leaned backwards in doing so and, using his customary method of "imagining strong cases," produced a numerical example, well known to all economists, to show that things could also turn out the other way. He did not mean to deny, on the one hand, that he was proving no more than a possibility—a not unlikely one though—or, on the other hand, that in the end net benefit to labor would result from mechanization through its ulterior effects on total output, prices and so on.

The example is correct as far as it goes.[22] The somewhat more refined methods of today support its result to the extent that they admit the possibility it aimed at establishing as well as the opposite one; they go beyond it by stating the formal conditions which determine whether the one or the other consequence will ensue. That is of course all that pure theory can do. Further data are necessary in order to predict the actual effect. But for our purpose, Ricardo's example presents another interesting feature. He considers a firm owning a given amount of capital and employing a given number of workmen that decides to take a step in mechanization. Accordingly, it assigns a group of those workmen to the task of constructing a machine which when installed will enable the firm to dispense with part of that group. Profits may eventually remain the same (after the competitive adjustments which will do away with any temporary gain) but gross revenue will be destroyed to the exact amount of the wages previously paid to the workmen that have now been "set free." Marx's idea of the replacement of variable (wage) capital by constant capital is almost the exact replica of this way of putting it. Ricardo's emphasis upon the ensuing *redundancy* of population is likewise exactly paralleled by Marx's emphasis upon *surplus* population which term he uses as an alternative to the term "industrial re-

---

[22] Or it can be made correct without losing its significance. There are a few doubtful points about the argument that are probably due to its lamentable technique—which so many economists would love to perpetuate.

serve army." Ricardo's teaching is indeed being swallowed hook, line and sinker.

But what may pass muster as long as we move within the restricted purpose Ricardo had in view becomes utterly inadequate—in fact the source of another *non sequitur*, not redeemed this time by a correct vision of ultimate results—as soon as we consider the superstructure Marx erected on that slender foundation. Some such feeling he seems to have had himself. For with an energy that has something desperate about it he clutched the conditionally pessimistic result of his teacher as if the latter's strong case were the only possible one, and with energy even more desperate he fought those authors who had developed the implications of Ricardo's hint at compensations that the machine age might hold out to labor even where the immediate effect of the introduction of machinery spelled injury (theory of compensation, the pet aversion of all Marxists).

He had every reason for taking this course. For he badly needed a firm foundation for his theory of the reserve army which was to serve two fundamentally important purposes, besides some minor ones. First, we have seen that he deprived his doctrine of exploitation of what I have called an essential prop by his aversion, quite understandable in itself, to making use of the Malthusian theory of population. That prop was replaced by the ever-present, because ever-recreated[23] reserve army. Second, the particularly narrow view of the process of mechanization he adopted was essential in order to motivate the resounding phrases in Chapter XXXII of the first volume of *Das Kapital* which in a sense are the crowning finale not only of that volume but of Marx's whole work. I will quote them in full—more fully than the point under discussion requires—in order to give my readers a glimpse of Marx in the attitude which accounts equally well for the enthusiasm of some and for the contempt of others. Whether a compound of things that are not so or the very heart of prophetic truth, here they are:

"Hand in hand with this centralization, or this expropriation of many capitalists by few, develops . . . the entanglement of all nations in the net of the world market, and with this, the international character of the capitalist régime. Along with the constantly diminishing number of the magnates of capital, who usurp and monopolize all advantages of this process of transformation, grows the mass of misery, oppression, slavery, degradation, exploitation; but with this too grows

[23] It is of course necessary to stress the incessant creation. It would be quite unfair to Marx's words as well as meaning to imagine, as some critics have done, that he assumed that the introduction of machinery threw people out of work who then would remain individually unemployed ever after. He did not deny absorption, and criticism that is based on the proof that any unemployment created will each time be absorbed entirely misses the target.

the revolt of the working class, a class always increasing in numbers, and disciplined, united, organized by the very mechanism of the process of capitalist production itself. The monopoly of capital becomes a fetter upon the mode of production, which has sprung up and flourished along with it, and under it. Centralization of the means of production and socialization of labor at last reach a point where they become incompatible with their capitalist integument. This integument bursts. The knell of capitalist private property sounds. The expropriators are expropriated."

6. Marx's performance in the field of business cycles is exceedingly difficult to appraise. The really valuable part of it consists of dozens of observations and comments, most of them of a casual nature, which are scattered over almost all his writings, many of his letters included. Attempts at reconstruction from such *membra disjecta* of a body that nowhere appears in the flesh and perhaps did not even exist in Marx's own mind except in an embryonic form, may easily yield different results in different hands and be vitiated by the understandable tendency of the admirer to credit Marx, by means of suitable interpretation, with practically all those results of later research of which the admirer himself approves.

The common run of friends and foes never realized and does not realize now the kind of task which confronts the commentator because of the nature of Marx's kaleidoscopic contribution to that subject. Seeing that Marx so frequently pronounced upon it and that it was obviously very relevant to his fundamental theme, they took it for granted that there must be some simple and clear-cut Marxian cycle theory which it should be possible to make grow out of the rest of his logic of the capitalist process much as, for instance, the theory of exploitation grows out of the labor theory. Accordingly they set about finding such a theory, and it is easy to guess what it was that occurred to them.

On the one hand, Marx no doubt extols—though he does not quite adequately motivate—the tremendous power of capitalism to develop society's capacity to produce. On the other hand, he incessantly places emphasis on the growing misery of the masses. Is it not the most natural thing in the world to conclude that crises or depressions are due to the fact that the exploited masses cannot buy what that ever-expanding apparatus of production turns out or stands ready to turn out, and that for this and also other reasons which we need not repeat the rate of profits drops to bankruptcy level? Thus we seem indeed to land, according to which element we want to stress, at the shores of either an under-consumption or an over-production theory of the most contemptible type.

The Marxian explanation has in fact been classed with the underconsumption theories of crises.[24] There are two circumstances that may be invoked in support. First, in the theory of surplus value and also in other matters, the affinity of Marx's teachings with that of Sismondi and Rodbertus is obvious. And these men did espouse the underconsumption view. It was not unnatural to infer that Marx might have done the same. Second, some passages in Marx's works particularly the brief statement about crises contained in the *Communist Manifesto* undoubtedly lend themselves to this interpretation, though Engels' utterances do so much more.[25] But this is of no account since Marx, showing excellent sense, expressly repudiated it.[26]

The fact is that he had no simple theory of business cycles. And none can be made to follow logically from his "laws" of the capitalist process. Even if we accept his explanation of the emergence of surplus value and agree to allow that accumulation, mechanization (relative increase of constant capital) and surplus population, the latter inexorably deepening mass misery, do link up into a logical chain that ends in the catastrophe of the capitalist system—even then we are left without a factor that would necessarily impart of cyclical fluctuation to the process and account for an *immanent* alternation of prosperities and depressions.[27] No doubt plenty of accidents and incidents

[24] Though this interpretation has become a fashion, I will mention two authors only, one of whom is responsible for a modified version of it, while the other may testify to its persistence: Tugan-Baranowsky, *Theoretische Grundlagen des Marxismus*, 1905, who condemned Marx's theory of crises on that ground; and M. Dobb, *Political Economy and Capitalism*, 1937, who is more sympathetic toward it.

[25] Engels' somewhat commonplace view of the matter is best expressed in his polemical book entitled *Herrn Eugen Dührings Umwälzung der Wissenschaft*, 1878, in what has become one of the most frequently quoted passages in socialist literature. He presents there a very graphic account of the morphology of crises that is good enough no doubt for the purposes of popular lectures, but also the opinion, standing in the place in which one would look for an explanation, that "the expansion of the market cannot keep pace with the expansion of production." Also he approvingly refers to Fourier's opinion, conveyed by the self-explanatory phrase, *crises pléthoriques*. It cannot be denied however that Marx wrote part of ch. x and shares responsibility for the whole book.

I observe that the few comments on Engels that are contained in this sketch are of a derogatory nature. This is unfortunate and not due to any intention to belittle the merits of that eminent man. I do think however that it should be frankly admitted that intellectually and especially as a theorist he stood far below Marx. We cannot even be sure that he always got the latter's meaning. His interpretations must therefore be used with care.

[26] *Das Kapital*, vol. ii, p. 476, of the English translation of 1907. See, however, also *Theorien über den Mehrwert*, vol. ii, ch. iii.

[27] To the layman, the opposite seems so obvious that it would not be easy to establish this statement, even if we had all the space in the world. The best way for the reader to convince himself of its truth is to study Ricardo's argument on machinery. The process there described might cause any amount of unemployment and yet go on indefinitely without causing a breakdown other than the final one of the system itself. Marx would have agreed with this.

are always at hand for us to draw upon in order to make up for the missing fundamental explanation. There are miscalculations, mistaken expectations and other errors, waves of optimism and pessimism, speculative excesses and reactions to speculative excesses, and there is the inexhaustible source of "external factors." All the same, Marx's mechanical process of accumulation going on at an even rate—and there is nothing to show why, on principle, it should not—the process he describes *might* also go on at even rates; as far as its logic is concerned, it is essentially prosperityless and depressionless.

Of course this is not necessarily a misfortune. Many other theorists have held and do hold simply that crises happen whenever something of sufficient importance goes wrong. Nor was it altogether a handicap because it released Marx, for once, from the thralldom of his system and set him free to look at facts without having to do violence to them. Accordingly, he considers a wide variety of more or less relevant elements. For instance, he uses somewhat superficially the intervention of money in commodity transactions—and nothing else—in order to invalidate Say's proposition about the impossibility of a general glut; or easy money markets in order to explain disproportionate developments in the lines characterized by heavy investment in durable capital goods; or special stimuli such as the opening of markets or the emergence of new social wants in order to motivate sudden spurts in "accumulation." He tries, not very successfully, to turn the growth of population into a factor making for fluctuations.[28] He observes, though he does not really explain, that the scale of production expands "by fits and starts" that are "the preliminary to its equally sudden contraction." He aptly says that "the superficiality of Political Economy shows itself in the fact that it looks upon expansion and contraction of credit, which is a mere symptom of the periodic changes of the industrial cycle, as their cause."[29] And the chapter of incidents and accidents he of course lays under heavy contribution.

All that is common sense and substantially sound. We find practically all the elements that ever entered into any serious analysis of business cycles, and on the whole very little error. Moreover, it must not be forgotten that the mere perception of the existence of cyclical movements was a great achievement at the time. Many economists who went before him had an inkling of it. In the main, however, they focused their attention on the spectacular breakdowns that came

[28] In this also he does not stand alone. However it is but fair to him to expect that he would eventually have seen the weaknesses of this approach, and it is relevant to note that his remarks on the subject occur in the third volume and cannot be trusted to render what might have been his final view.

[29] *Das Kapital*, vol. i, ch. xxv, section 3. Immediately after this passage he takes a step in a direction that is also very familiar to the student of modern business cycle theories: "Effects, in their turn become causes, and the varying accidents of the whole process, *which always reproduces its own conditions* [my italics], take on the form of periodicity."

to be referred to as "crises." And those crises they failed to see in their true light, that is to say, in the light of the cyclical process of which they are mere incidents. They considered them, without looking beyond or below, as isolated misfortunes that will happen in consequence of errors, excesses, misconduct or of the faulty working of the credit mechanism. Marx was, I believe, the first economist to rise above that tradition and to anticipate—barring the statistical complement—the work of Clément Juglar. Though, as we have seen, he did not offer an adequate explanation of the business cycle, the phenomenon stood clearly before his eyes and he understood much of its mechanism. Also like Juglar, he unhesitatingly spoke of a decennial cycle "interrupted by minor fluctuations."[30] He was intrigued by the question of what the cause of that period might be and considered the idea that it might have something to do with the life of machinery in the cotton industry. And there are many other signs of preoccupation with the problem of business cycles as distinguished from that of crises. This is enough to assure him high rank among the fathers of modern cycle research.

Another aspect must be mentioned. In most cases Marx used the term crisis in its ordinary sense, speaking of the crisis of 1825 or that of 1847 as other people do. But he also used it in a different sense. Believing that capitalist evolution would some day disrupt the institutional framework of capitalist society, he thought that before the actual breakdown occurred, capitalism would begin to work with increasing friction and display the symptoms of fatal illness. To this stage, to be visualized of course as a more or less prolonged historical period, he applied the same term. And he displays a tendency to link those recurrent crises with this unique crisis of the capitalist order. He even suggests that the former may in a sense be looked upon as previews of the ultimate breakdown. Since to many readers this might look like a clue to Marx's theory of crises in the ordinary sense, it is necessary to point out that the factors which according to Marx will be responsible for the ultimate breakdown cannot, without a good dose of additional hypotheses, be made responsible for the recurrent depressions,[31] and that the clue does not get us beyond the trivial

[30] Engels went further than this. Some of his notes to Marx's third volume reveal that he suspected also the existence of a longer swing. Though he was inclined to interpret the comparative weakness of prosperities and the comparative intensity of depressions in the seventies and eighties as a structural change rather than as the effect of the depression phase of a wave of longer span (exactly as many modern economists do with respect to the post-war developments and especially to those of the last decade) some anticipation of Kondratieff's work on Long Cycles might be seen in this.

[31] In order to convince himself of this, the reader need only glance again at the quotation on p. 37. In fact, though Marx so often plays with the idea, he avoids committing himself to it, which is significant because it was not his way to miss the opportunity for a generalization.

proposition that the "expropriation of the expropriators" may be an easier matter in a depression than it would be in a boom.

7. Finally, the idea that capitalist evolution will burst—or outgrow—the institutions of capitalist society (*Zusammenbruchstheorie,* the theory of the inevitable catastrophe) affords a last example of the combination of a *non sequitur* with profound vision which helps to rescue the result.

Based as Marx's "dialectic deduction" is on the growth of misery and oppression that will goad the masses into revolt, it is invalidated by the *non sequitur* that vitiates the argument which was to establish that inevitable growth of misery. Moreover, otherwise orthodox Marxists have long ago begun to doubt the validity of the proposition that concentration of industrial control is necessarily incompatible with the "capitalist integument." The first of them to voice this doubt by means of a well-organized argument was Rudolf Hilferding,[32] one of the leaders of the important group of Neo-Marxists, who actually inclined toward the opposite inference, viz., that through concentration capitalism might gain in stability.[33] Deferring to the next part what I have to say upon the matter, I will state that Hilferding seems to me to go too far although there is, as we shall see, no foundation for the belief, at present current in this country, that big business "becomes a fetter upon the mode of production," and although Marx's conclusion does in fact not follow from his premises.

However, even though Marx's facts and reasoning were still more at fault than they are, his result might nevertheless be true so far as it simply avers that capitalist evolution will destroy the foundations of capitalist society. I believe it is. And I do not think I am exaggerating if I call profound a vision in which that truth stood revealed beyond doubt in 1847. It is a commonplace now. The first to make it that was Gustav Schmoller. His Excellency, Professor Von Schmoller, Prussian Privy Councellor and Member of the Prussian House of Lords, was not much of a revolutionary or much given to agi-

---

[32] *Das Finanzkapital,* 1910. Doubts based on a number of secondary circumstances that were held to show that Marx made too much of the tendencies he thought he had established and that social evolution was a much more complex and a much less consistent process than he made out, had of course often arisen before. It is sufficient to mention E. Bernstein; see ch. xxvi. But Hilferding's analysis does not plead extenuating circumstances, but fights that conclusion on principle and on Marx's own ground.

[33] This proposition has often (even by its author) been confused with the proposition that business fluctuations tend to become milder as time goes on. That may or may not be so (1929-32 would not disprove it) but greater stability of the capitalist *system,* i.e., a somewhat less temperamental behavior of our time series of prices and quantities, does not necessarily imply, nor is it necessarily implied by, greater stability, i.e., a greater ability of the capitalist *order* to withstand attack. Both things are related, of course, but they are not the same.

tatorial gesticulations. But he quietly stated the same truth. The Why and How of it he likewise left unsaid.

It is hardly necessary to sum up elaborately. However imperfect, our sketch should suffice to establish: first, that nobody who cares at all for purely economic analysis can speak of unqualified success; second, that nobody who cares at all for bold construction can speak of unqualified failure.

In the court that sits on theoretical technique, the verdict must be adverse. Adherence to an analytic apparatus that always had been inadequate and was in Marx's own day rapidly becoming obsolete; a long list of conclusions that do not follow or are downright wrong; mistakes which if corrected change essential inferences, sometimes into their opposites—all this can be rightfully charged against Marx, the theoretical technician.

Even in that court, however, qualification of the verdict will be necessary on two grounds.

First, though Marx was often—sometimes hopelessly—wrong, his critics were far from being always right. Since there were excellent economists among them, the fact should be recorded to his credit, particularly because most of them he was not able to meet himself.

Second, so should Marx's contributions, both critical and positive, to a great many individual problems. In a sketch like this, it is not possible to enumerate them, let alone to do them justice. But we have had a view of some of them in our discussion of his treatment of the business cycle. I have also mentioned some that improved our theory of the structure of physical capital. The schemata which he devised in that field, though not irreproachable, have again proved serviceable in recent work that looks quite Marxian in places.

But a court of appeal—even though still confined to theoretical matters—might feel inclined to reverse this verdict altogether. For there is one truly great achievement to be set against Marx's theoretical misdemeanors. Through all that is faulty or even unscientific in his analysis runs a fundamental idea that is neither—the idea of a theory, not merely of an indefinite number of disjointed individual patterns or of the logic of economic quantities in general, but of the actual sequence of those patterns or of the economic process as it goes on, under its own steam, in historic time, producing at every instant that state which will of itself determine the next one. Thus, the author of so many misconceptions was also the first to visualize what even at the present time is still the economic theory of the future for which we are slowly and laboriously accumulating stone and mortar, statistical facts and functional equations.

And he not only conceived that idea, but he tried to carry it out All the shortcomings that disfigure his work must, because of the great purpose his argument attempted to serve, be judged differently even where they are not, as they are in some cases, fully redeemed thereby. There is however one thing of fundamental importance for the methodology of economics which he actually achieved. Economists always have either themselves done work in economic history or else used the historical work of others. But the facts of economic history were assigned to a separate compartment. They entered theory, if at all, merely in the role of illustrations, or possibly of verifications of results. They mixed with it only mechanically. Now Marx's mixture is a chemical one; that is to say, he introduced them into the very argument that produces the results. He was the first economist of top rank to see and to teach systematically how economic theory may be turned into historical analysis and how the historical narrative may be turned into *histoire raisonnée.*[34] the analogous problem with respect to statistics he did not attempt to solve. But in a sense it is implied in the other. This also answers the question how far, in the way explained at the end of the preceding chapter, Marx's economic theory succeeds in implementing his sociological setup. It does not succeed; but in failing, it establishes both a goal and a method.

[34] If devoted disciples should therefore claim that he set the goal for the historical school of economics, that claim could not be lightly dismissed, though the work of the Schmoller school was certainly quite independent of Marx's suggestion. But if they went on to claim that Marx, and Marx only, knew how to rationalize history, whereas the men of the historical school only knew how to describe facts without getting at their meaning, they would be spoiling their case. For those men as a matter of fact knew how to analyze. If their generalizations were less sweeping and their narratives less selective, that is all to their credit.

CHAPTER IV

MARX THE TEACHER

THE main components of the Marxian structure are now before us. What about the imposing synthesis as a whole? The question is not otiose. If ever it is true, it is in this case that the whole is more than the sum of the parts. Moreover, the synthesis may have so spoiled the wheat or so utilized the chaff, both of which are present in almost every spot, that the whole might be more true or more false than any part of it is, taken by itself. Finally, there is the Message that proceeds only from the whole. Of the latter however no more will be said. Each of us must settle for himself what it means to him.

Our time revolts against the inexorable necessity of specialization and therefore cries out for synthesis, nowhere so loudly as in the social sciences in which the non-professional element counts for so much.[1] But Marx's system illustrates well that, though synthesis may mean new light, it also means new fetters.

We have seen how in the Marxian argument sociology and economics pervade each other. In intent, and to some degree also in actual practice, they are one. All the major concepts and propositions are hence both economic and sociological and carry the same meaning on both planes—if, from our standpoint, we may still speak of two planes of argument. Thus, the economic *category* "labor" and the social *class* "proletariat" are, on principle at least, made congruent, in fact identical. Or the economists' functional distribution—that is to say, the explanation of the way in which incomes emerge as returns to productive services irrespective of what social class any recipient of such a return may belong to—enters the Marxian system only in the form of distribution between social classes and thus acquires a different connotation. Or capital in the Marxian system is capital only if in the hands of a distinct capitalist class. The same things, if in the hands of the workmen, are not capital.

There cannot be any doubt about the access of vitality which comes to analysis thereby. The ghostly concepts of economic theory begin

[1] The non-professional element is particularly strongly represented among those admirers of Marx who, going beyond the attitude of the typical Marxian *economist*, still take at face value everything he wrote. This is very significant. In every national group of Marxists there are at least three laymen to every trained economist and even this economist is as a rule a Marxist only in that qualified sense defined in the introduction to this part: he worships at the shrine, but he turns his back upon it when he does his research.

to breathe. The bloodless theorem descends into *agmen, pulverem et clamorem*; without losing its logical quality, it is no longer a mere proposition about the logical properties of a system of abstractions; it is the stroke of a brush that is painting the wild jumble of social life. Such analysis conveys not only richer meaning of what all economic analysis describes but it embraces a much broader field—it draws every kind of class action into its picture, whether or not this class action conforms to the ordinary rules of business procedure. Wars, revolutions, legislation of all types, changes in the structure of governments, in short all the things that non-Marxian economics treats simply as external disturbances do find their places side by side with, say, investment in machinery or bargains with labor—everything is covered by a single explanatory schema.

At the same time, such procedure has its shortcomings. Conceptual arrangements that are subject to a yoke of this kind may easily lose in efficiency as much as they gain in vividness. The pair, worker-proletarian, may serve as a telling if somewhat trite example. In non-Marxian economics all returns to services of persons partake of the nature of wages, whether those persons are tophole lawyers, movie stars, company executives or street sweepers. Since all these returns have, from the standpoint of the economic phenomenon involved, much in common, this generalization is not futile or sterile. On the contrary, it may be enlightening, even for the sociological aspect of things. But by equating labor and proletariat we obscure it; in fact, we entirely banish it from our picture. Similarly, a valuable economic theorem may by its sociological metamorphosis pick up error instead of richer meaning and vice versa. Thus, synthesis in general and synthesis on Marxian lines in particular might easily issue in both worse economics and worse sociology.

Synthesis in general, i.e., coordination of the methods and results of different lines of advance, is a difficult thing which few are competent to tackle. In consequence it is ordinarily not tackled at all and from the students who are taught to see only individual trees we hear discontented clamor for the forest. They fail to realize however that the trouble is in part an *embarras de richesse* and that the synthetic forest may look uncommonly like an intellectual concentration camp.

Synthesis on Marxian lines, i.e., coordination of economic and sociological analysis with a view to bending everything to a single purpose, is of course particularly apt to look like that. The purpose—that *histoire raisonnée* of capitalist society—is wide enough but the analytic setup is not. There is indeed a grand wedding of political facts and of economic theorems; but they are wedded by force and neither of them can breathe. Marxists claim that their system solves all the great problems that baffle non-Marxian economics; so it does but only by emasculating them. This point calls for some elaboration.

I said a moment ago that Marx's synthesis embraces all those historical events—such as wars, revolutions, legislative changes—and all those social institutions—such as property, contractual relations, forms of government—that non-Marxian economists are wont to treat as disturbing factors or as data, which means that they do not propose to explain them but only to analyze their *modi operandi* and consequences. Such factors or data are of course necessary in order to delimit the object and range of any research program whatsoever. If they are not always expressly specified, that is only because everyone is expected to know what they are. The trait peculiar to the Marxian system is that it subjects those historical events and social institutions themselves to the explanatory process of economic analysis or, to use the technical lingo, that it treats them not as data but as variables.

Thus the Napoleonic Wars, the Crimean War, the American Civil War, the World War of 1914, the French Frondes, the great French Revolution, the revolutions of 1830 and 1848, English free trade, the labor movement as a whole as well as any of its particular manifestations, colonial expansion, institutional changes, the national and party politics of every time and country—all this enters the domain of Marxian economics which claims to find theoretical explanations in terms of class warfare, of attempts at and revolt against exploitation, of accumulation and of qualitative change in the capital structure, of changes in the rate of surplus value and in the rate of profit. No longer has the economist to be content with giving technical answers to technical questions; instead, he teaches humanity the hidden meaning of its struggles. No longer is "politics" an independent factor that may and must be abstracted from in an investigation of fundamentals and, when it does intrude, plays according to one's preferences either the role of a naughty boy who viciously tampers with a machine when the engineer's back is turned, or else the role of a *deus ex machina* by virtue of the mysterious wisdom of a doubtful species of mammals deferentially referred to as "statesmen." No—politics itself is being determined by the structure and state of the economic process and becomes a conductor of effects as completely within the range of economic theory as any purchase or sale.

Once more, nothing is easier to understand than the fascination exerted by a synthesis which does for us just this. It is particularly understandable in the young and in those intellectual denizens of our newspaper world to whom the gods seem to have granted the gift of eternal youth. Panting with impatience to have their innings, longing to save the world from something or other, disgusted with textbooks of undescribable tedium, dissatisfied emotionally and intellectually, unable to achieve synthesis by their own effort, they find what they crave for in Marx. There it is, the key to all the most intimate secrets, the magic wand that marshals both great events and small. They are beholding an explanatory schema that at the same time is—if I may for a moment lapse into Hegelianism—most general and most concrete. They need no longer feel out of it in the great affairs of life—all at once they see through the pompous marionettes of politics and business who never know what it is all about. And who can blame them, considering available alternatives?

Yes, of course—but apart from that, what does this service of the Marxian synthesis amount to? I wonder. The humble economist who describes England's transition to free trade or the early achievements of English factory legislation is not, and never was, likely to forget to mention the structural conditions of the English economy that produced those policies. If he does not do so in a course or book on pure theory that merely makes for neater and and more efficient analysis. What the Marxist has to add is only the insistence on the principle, and a particularly narrow and warped theory by which to implement it. This theory yields results no doubt, and very simple and definite ones to boot. But we need only apply it systematically to individual cases in order to grow thoroughly weary of the unending jingle about the class war between owners and non-owners and to become aware of a painful sense of inadequacy or, worse still, of triviality—of the former, if we do not swear by the underlying schema; of the latter, if we do.

Marxists are in the habit of pointing triumphantly to the success of the Marxian diagnosis of the economic and social tendencies that are supposed to be inherent in capitalist evolution. As we have seen, there is some justification for this: more clearly than any other writer of his day Marx discerned the trend toward big business and not only that but also some of the features of the consequent situations. We have also seen that in this case vision lent its aid to analysis so as to remedy some of the shortcomings of the latter and to make the import of the synthesis truer than the contributing elements of the analysis were themselves. But this is all. And against the achievement must be set the failure of the prediction of increasing misery, the joint result of wrong vision and faulty analysis, on which a great many Marxian speculations about the future course of social events had been based. He who places his trust in the Marxian synthesis as a whole in order to understand present situations and problems is apt to be woefully wrong.[2] This seems in fact to be felt by many a Marxist just now.

[2] Some Marxists would reply that non-Marxian economists have simply nothing to contribute to our understanding of our time so that the disciple of Marx is nevertheless better off in that respect. Waiving the question of whether it is better to say nothing or to say something that is wrong, we should bear in mind that this is not true, for both economists and sociologists of non-Marxian persuasions have as a matter of fact contributed substantially though mostly on individual questions. Least of all can this Marxist claim be based on a comparison of Marx's teachings with that of the Austrians or of the Walras or Marshall schools. The mem-

In particular there is no reason for taking pride in the manner in which the Marxian synthesis accounts for the experience of the last decade. Any prolonged period of depression or of unsatisfactory recovery will verify any pessimistic forecast exactly as well as it verifies the Marxian one. In this case an impression to the contrary is created by the talk of disheartened bourgeois and elated intellectuals which naturally acquired a Marxian hue from their fears and hopes. But no actual fact warrants any specifically Marxian diagnosis, still less an inference to the effect that what we have been witnessing was not simply a depression, but the symptoms of a structural change in the capitalist process such as Marx expected to occur. For, as will be noted in the next part, all the phenomena observed such as supernormal unemployment, lack of investment opportunity, shrinkage of money values, losses and so on, come within the well-known pattern of periods of predominating depression such as the seventies and eighties on which Engels commented with a restraint that should set an example to ardent followers of today.

Two outstanding examples will illustrate both the merits and the demerits of the Marxian synthesis considered as a problem-solving engine.

First we will consider the Marxist theory of Imperialism. Its roots are all to be found in Marx's chief work, but it has been developed by the Neo-Marxist school which flourished in the first two decades of this century and, without renouncing communion with the old defenders of the faith, such as Karl Kautsky, did much to overhaul the system. Vienna was its center; Otto Bauer, Rudolf Hilferding, Max Adler were its leaders. In the field of imperialism their work was continued, with but secondary shifts of emphasis, by many others, prominent among whom were Rosa Luxemburg and Fritz Sternberg. The argument runs as follows.

Since, on the one hand, capitalist society cannot exist and its economic system cannot function without profits and since, on the other hand, profits are constantly being eliminated by the very working of that system, incessant effort to keep them alive becomes the central aim of the capitalist class. Accumulation accompanied by qualitative change in the composition of capital is, as we have seen, a remedy which though alleviating for the moment the situation of the individual capitalist makes matters worse in the end. So capital, yielding to the pressure of a falling rate of profits—it falls, we recall, both because constant capital increases relative to variable capital and because, if wages tend to rise and hours are being shortened, the rate of surplus

---

bers of these groups were in most cases wholly, in all cases mainly, interested in economic theory. This performance is hence incommensurable with Marx's synthesis. It could only be compared with Marx's theoretical apparatus and in that field comparison is all to their advantage.

value falls—seeks for outlets in countries in which there is still labor that can be exploited at will and in which the process of mechanization has not as yet gone far. Thus we get an export of capital into undeveloped countries which is essentially an export of capital equipment or of consumers' goods to be used in order to buy labor or to acquire things with which to buy labor.[3] But it is also export of capital in the ordinary sense of the term because the exported commodities will not be paid for—at least not immediately—by goods, services or money from the importing country. And it turns into colonization if, in order to safeguard the investment both against hostile reaction of the native environment—or if you please, against its resistance to exploitation—and against competition from other capitalist countries, the undeveloped country is brought into political subjection. This is in general accomplished by military force supplied either by the colonizing capitalists themselves or by their home government which thus lives up to the definition given in the *Communist Manifesto*: "the executive of the modern State [is] . . . a committee for managing the common affairs of the whole bourgeoisie." Of course, that force will not be used for defensive purposes only. There will be conquest, friction between the capitalist countries and internecine war between rival bourgeoisies.

Another element completes this theory of imperialism as it is now usually presented. So far as colonial expansion is prompted by a falling rate of profit in the capitalist countries, it should occur in the later stages of capitalist evolution—Marxists in fact speak of imperialism as a stage, preferably the last stage, of capitalism. Hence it would coincide with a high degree of concentration of capitalist control over industry and with a decline of the type of competition that characterized the times of the small or medium-sized firm. Marx himself did not lay much stress on the resulting tendency toward monopolistic restriction of output and on the consequent tendency toward protecting the domestic game preserve against the intrusion of poachers from other capitalist countries. Perhaps he was too competent an economist to trust this line of argument too far. But the Neo-Marxists were glad to avail themselves of it. Thus we get not only another stimulus for imperialist policy and another source of imperialist imbroglios but

[3] Think of luxuries to be traded to chieftains against slaves or to be traded against wage goods with which to hire native labor. For the sake of brevity, I do not take account of the fact that capital export in the sense envisaged will in general arise as a part of the total trade of the two countries which also includes commodity transactions unconnected with the particular process we have in mind. These transactions of course greatly facilitate that capital export, but do not affect its principle. I shall also neglect other types of capital exports. The theory under discussion is not, and is not intended to be, a general theory of international trade and finance.

also, as a by-product, a theory of a phenomenon that is not necessarily imperialist in itself, modern protectionism.

Note one more hitch in that process that will stand the Marxist in good stead in the task of explaining further difficulties. When the undeveloped countries have been developed, capital export of the kind we have been considering will decline. There may then be a period during which the mother country and the colony will exchange, say, manufactured products for raw materials. But in the end the exports of manufacturers will also have to decline while colonial competition will assert itself in the mother country. Attempts to retard the advent of that state of things will provide further sources of friction, this time between each old capitalist country and its colonies, of wars of independence and so on. But in any case colonial doors will eventually be closed to domestic capital which will no longer be able to flee from vanishing profits at home into richer pastures abroad. Lack of outlets, excess capacity, complete deadlock, in the end regular recurrence of national bankruptcies and other disasters—perhaps world wars from sheer capitalist despair—may confidently be anticipated. History is as simple as that.

This theory is a fair—perhaps it is the best—example of the way in which the Marxian synthesis attempts to solve problems and acquires authority by doing so. The whole thing seems to follow beautifully from two fundamental premises that are both firmly embedded in the groundwork of the system: the theory of classes and the theory of accumulation. A series of vital facts of our time seems to be perfectly accounted for. The whole maze of international politics seems to be cleared up by a single powerful stroke of analysis. And we see in the process why and how class action, always remaining intrinsically the same, assumes the form of political or of business action according to circumstances that determine nothing but tactical methods and phraseology. If, the means and opportunities at the command of a group of capitalists being what they are, it is more profitable to negotiate a loan, a loan will be negotiated. If, the means and opportunities being what they are, it is more profitable to make war, war will be made. The latter alternative is no less entitled to enter economic theory than the former. Even mere protectionism now grows nicely out of the very logic of capitalist evolution.

Moreover, this theory displays to full advantage a virtue that it has in common with most of the Marxian concepts in the field of what is usually referred to as applied economics. This is its close alliance with historical and contemporaneous fact. Probably not one reader has perused my résumé without being struck by the ease with which supporting historical instances crowded in upon him at every single step of the argument. Has he not heard of the oppression by Europeans of native labor in many parts of the world, of what South and Central

American Indians suffered at the hands of the Spaniards for instance, or of slave-hunting and slave-trading and coolieism? Is capital export not actually ever-present in capitalist countries? Has it not almost invariably been accompanied by military conquest that served to subdue the natives and to fight other European powers? Has not colonization always had a rather conspicuous military side, even when managed entirely by business corporations such as the East India Company or the British South Africa Company? What better illustration could Marx himself have desired than Cecil Rhodes and the Boer War? Is it not pretty obvious that colonial ambitions were, to say the least, an important factor in European troubles, at all events since about 1700? As for the present time, who has not heard, on the one hand, about the "strategy of raw materials" and, on the other hand, of the repercussions on Europe of the growth of native capitalism in the tropics? And so on. As to protectionism—well, that is as plain as anything can be.

But we had better be careful. An apparent verification by prima facie favorable cases which are not analyzed in detail may be very deceptive. Moreover, as every lawyer and every politician knows, energetic appeal to familiar facts will go a long way toward inducing a jury or a parliament to accept also the construction he desires to put upon them. Marxists have exploited this technique to the full. In this instance it is particularly successful, because the facts in question combine the virtues of being superficially known to everyone and of being thoroughly understood by very few. In fact, though we cannot enter into detailed discussion here, even hasty reflection suffices to suggest a suspicion that "it is not so."

A few remarks will be made in the next part on the relation in which the bourgeoisie stands to imperialism. We shall now consider the question whether, if the Marxian interpretation of capital export, colonization and protectionism were correct, it would also be adequate as a theory of all the phenomena we think of when using that loose and misused term. Of course we can always define imperialism in such a way as to mean just what the Marxian interpretation implies; and we can always profess ourselves convinced that all those phenomena *must* be explainable in the Marxian manner. But then the problem of imperialism—always granting that the theory is in itself correct —would be "solved" only tautologically.[4] Whether the Marxian ap-

[4] The danger of empty tautologies being put over on us is best illustrated by individual cases. Thus, France conquered Algeria, Tunisia and Morocco, and Italy conquered Abyssinia, by military force without there being any significant capitalist interests to press for it. As a matter of fact, presence of such interests was a pretense that was very difficult to establish, and the subsequent development of such interests was a slow process that went on, unsatisfactorily enough, under government pressure. If that should not look very Marxist, it will be replied that action was taken under pressure of potential or anticipated capitalist interests or that in

proach or, for that matter, any purely economic approach yields a solution that is not tautological would still have to be considered. This, however, need not concern us here, because the ground gives way before we get that far.

At first sight, the theory seems to fit some cases tolerably well. The most important instances are afforded by the English and Dutch conquests in the tropics. But other cases, such as the colonization of New England, it does not fit at all. And even the former type of case is not satisfactorily described by the Marxian theory of imperialism. It would obviously not suffice to recognize that the lure of gain played a role in motivating colonial expansion.[5] The Neo-Marxists did not mean to aver such a horrible platitude. If these cases are to count for them, it is also necessary that colonial expansion came about, in the way indicated, under pressure of accumulation on the rate of profit, hence as a feature of decaying, or at all events of fully matured, capitalism. But the heroic time of colonial adventure was precisely the time of early and immature capitalism when accumulation was in its beginnings and any such pressure—also, in particular, any barrier to exploitation of domestic labor—was conspicuous by its absence. The element of monopoly was not absent. On the contrary it was far more evident than it is today. But that only adds to the absurdity of the construction which makes both monopoly and conquest specific properties of latter-day capitalism.

Moreover, the other leg of the theory, class struggle, is in no better condition. One must wear blinkers to concentrate on that aspect of colonial expansion which hardly ever played more than a secondary role, and to construe in terms of class struggle a phenomenon which affords some of the most striking instances of class cooperation. It was as much a movement toward higher wages as it was a movement toward higher profits, and in the long run it certainly benefited (in part because of the exploitation of *native* labor) the proletariat more than it benefited the capitalist interest. But I do not wish to stress its

the last analysis some capitalist interest or objective necessity "must" have been at the bottom of it. And we can then hunt for corroboratory evidence that will never be entirely lacking, since capitalist interests, like any others, will in fact be affected by, and take advantage of, any situation whatsoever, and since the particular conditions of the capitalist organism will always present some features which may without absurdity be linked up with those policies of national expansion. Evidently it is preconceived conviction and nothing else that keeps us going in a task as desperate as this; without such a conviction it would never occur to us to embark upon it. And we really need not take the trouble; we might just as well say that "it must be so" and leave it at that. This is what I meant by tautological explanation.

[5] Nor is it sufficient to stress the fact that each country actually did "exploit" its colonies. For that was exploitation of a country as a whole by a country as a whole (of all classes by all classes) and has nothing to do with the specifically Marxian kind of exploitation.

effects. The essential point is that its *causation* has not much to do with class warfare, and not more to do with class structure than is implied in the leadership of groups and individuals that belonged to, or by colonial enterprise rose into, the capitalist class. If however we shake off the blinkers and cease to look upon colonization or imperialism as a mere incident in class warfare, little remains that is specifically Marxist about the matter. What Adam Smith has to say on it does just as well—better in fact.

The by-product, the Neo-Marxian theory of modern protectionism, still remains. Classical literature is full of invectives against the "sinister interests"—at that time mainly, but never wholly, the agrarian interests—which in clamoring for protection committed the unforgivable crime against public welfare. Thus the classics had a causal theory of protection all right—not only a theory of its effects—and if now we add the protectionist interests of modern big business we have gone as far as it is reasonable to go. Modern economists with Marxist sympathies really should know better than to say that even now their bourgeois colleagues do not see the relation between the trend toward protectionism and the trend toward big units of control, though these colleagues may not always think it necessary to stress so obvious a fact. Not that the classics and their successors to this day were right about protection: their interpretation of it was, and is, as one-sided as was the Marxian one, besides being often wrong in the appraisal of consequences and of the interests involved. But for at least fifty years they have known about the monopoly component in protectionism all that Marxists ever knew, which was not difficult considering the commonplace character of the discovery.

And they were superior to the Marxist theory in one very important respect. Whatever the value of their economics—perhaps it was not great—they mostly[6] stuck to it. In this instance, that was an advantage. The proposition that many protective duties owe their existence to the pressure of large concerns that desire to use them for the purpose of keeping their prices at home above what they otherwise would be, possibly in order to be able to sell more cheaply abroad, is a platitude but correct, although no tariff was ever wholly or even mainly due to this particular cause. It is the Marxian synthesis that makes it inadequate or wrong. If our ambition is simply to understand all the causes and implications of modern protectionism, political, social and economic, then it is inadequate. For instance, the consistent support given by the American people to protectionist policy, whenever

---

[6] They did not always confine themselves to their economics. When they did not, results were anything but encouraging. Thus, James Mill's purely economic writings, while not particularly valuable, cannot be simply dismissed as hopelessly substandard. The real nonsense—and platitudinous nonsense at that—is in his articles on government and cognate subjects.

they had the opportunity to speak their minds, is accounted for not by any love for or domination by big business, but by a fervent wish to build and keep a world of their own and to be rid of all the vicissitudes of the rest of the world. Synthesis that overlooks such elements of the case is not an asset but a liability. But if our ambition is to reduce all the causes and implications of modern protectionism, whatever they may be, to the monopolistic element in modern industry as the sole *causa causans* and if we formulate that proposition accordingly, then it becomes wrong. Big business has been able to take advantage of the popular sentiment and it has fostered it; but it is absurd to say that it has created it. Synthesis that yields—we ought rather to say, postulates—such a result is inferior to no synthesis at all.

Matters become infinitely worse if, flying in the face of fact plus common sense, we exalt that theory of capital export and colonization into the fundamental explanation of international politics which thereupon resolves into a struggle, on the one hand, of monopolistic capitalist groups with each other and, on the other hand, of each of them with their own proletariat. This sort of thing may make useful party literature but otherwise it merely shows that nursery tales are no monopoly of bourgeois economics. As a matter of fact, very little influence on foreign policy has been exerted by big business—or by the *haute finance* from the Fuggers to the Morgans—and in most of the cases in which large-scale industry as such, or banking interests as such, have been able to assert themselves, their naïve dilettantism has resulted in discomfiture. The attitudes of capitalist groups toward the policy of their nations are predominantly adaptive rather than causative, today more than ever. Also, they hinge to an astonishing degree on short-run considerations equally remote from any deeply laid plans and from any definite "objective" class interests. At this point Marxism degenerates into the formulation of popular superstitions.[7]

There are other instances of a similar state of things in all parts of the Marxian structure. To mention one, the definition of the nature of governments that was quoted from the *Communist Mani-*

---

[7] This superstition is exactly on a par with another that is harbored by many worthy and simple-minded people who explain modern history to themselves on the hypothesis that there is somewhere a committee of supremely wise and malevolent Jews who behind the scenes control international or perhaps all politics. Marxists are not victims of this particular superstition but theirs is on no higher plane. It is amusing to record that, when faced with either doctrine, I have always experienced great difficulty in replying in anything like a fashion satisfactory to myself. This was not only due to the circumstance that it is always difficult to establish denial of factual assertions. The main difficulty came from the fact that people, lacking any first-hand knowledge of international affairs and their personnel, also lack any organ for the perception of absurdity.

festo a little while ago has certainly an element of truth in it. And in many cases that truth will account for governmental attitudes toward the more obvious manifestations of class antagonisms. But so far as true, the theory embodied in that definition is trivial. All that is worth while troubling about is the Why and How of that vast majority of cases in which the theory either fails to conform to fact or, even if conforming, fails to describe correctly the actual behavior of those "committees for managing the common affairs of the bourgeoisie." Again, in practically all cases the theory can be made tautologically true. For there is no policy short of exterminating the bourgeoisie that could not be held to serve some economic or extra-economic, short-run or long-run, bourgeois interest, at least in the sense that it wards off still worse things. This, however, does not make that theory any more valuable. But let us turn to our second example of the problem-solving power of the Marxian synthesis.

The badge of Scientific Socialism which according to Marx is to distinguish it from Utopian Socialism consists in the proof that socialism is inevitable irrespective of human volition or of desirability. As has been stated before, all this means is that by virtue of its very logic capitalist evolution tends to destroy the capitalist and to produce the socialist order of things.[8] How far has Marx succeeded in establishing the existence of these tendencies?

As regards the tendency toward self-destruction, the question has already been answered.[9] The doctrine that the capitalist economy will inevitably break down for purely economic reasons has not been established by Marx, as Hilferding's objections would suffice to show. On the one hand, some of his propositions about future facts that are essential to the orthodox argument, especially the one about the inevitable increase of misery and oppression, are untenable; on the other hand, the breakdown of the capitalist order would not necessarily follow from these propositions, even if they were all true. But other factors in the situation that the capitalist process tends to develop were correctly seen by Marx, as was, so I hope to show, the ultimate outcome itself. Concerning the latter, it may be necessary to replace the Marxian nexus by another, and the term "breakdown" may then turn out to be a misnomer, particularly if it be understood in the sense of a breakdown caused by the failure of the capitalist engine of production; but this does not affect the essence of the doctrine, however much it may affect its formulation and some of its implications.

As regards the tendency toward socialism, we must first realize that this is a distinct problem. The capitalist or any other order of things may evidently break down—or economic and social evolution may

[8] See also Part II, Prologue.
[9] See *supra*, ch. iii, § 7.

outgrow it—and yet the socialist phoenix may fail to rise from the ashes. There may be chaos and, unless we define as socialism any non-chaotic alternative to capitalism, there are other possibilities. The particular type of social organization that the average orthodox Marxist—before the advent of bolshevism at any rate—seemed to anticipate is certainly only one of many possible cases.

Marx himself, while very wisely refraining from describing socialist society in detail, emphasized conditions of its emergence: on the one hand, the presence of giant units of industrial control—which, of course, would greatly facilitate socialization—and, on the other hand, the presence of an oppressed, enslaved, exploited, but also very numerous, *disciplined,* united and organized proletariat. This suggests much about the final battle that is to be the acute stage of the secular warfare between the two classes which will then be arrayed against each other for the last time. It also suggests something about what is to follow; it suggests the idea that the proletariat as such will "take over" and, through its dictatorship, put a stop to the "exploitation of man by man" and bring about classless society. If our purpose were to prove that Marxism is a member of the family of chiliastic creeds this would indeed be quite enough. Since we are concerned not with that aspect but with a scientific forecast, it clearly is not. Schmoller was on much safer ground. For though he also refused to commit himself to details, he obviously visualized the process as one of progressive bureaucratization, nationalization and so on, ending in state socialism which, whether we like it or not, at least makes definite sense. Thus Marx fails to turn the socialist possibility into a certainty even if we grant him the breakdown theory in its entirety; if we do not, then failure follows *a fortiori.*

In no case, however—whether we accept Marx's reasoning or any other—will the socialist order be realized automatically; even if capitalist evolution provided all conditions for it in the most Marxian manner conceivable, distinct action would still be necessary to bring it about.[10] This of course is in accordance with Marx's teaching. His revolution is but the particular garb in which his imagination liked to clothe that action. The emphasis on violence is perhaps understandable in one who in his formative years had experienced all the excitement of 1848 and who was, though quite able to despise revolutionary ideology, yet never able to shake off its trammels. Moreover, the greater part of his audience would hardly have been willing to listen to a message that lacked the hallowed clarion call. Finally, though he saw the possibility of peaceful transition, at least for England, he may not have seen its likelihood. In his day it was not so easy to see, and his pet idea of the two classes in battle array made it still more difficult to see it. His friend Engels actually went to the

10 See Part III, ch. v.

trouble of studying tactics. But though the revolution can be relegated to the compound of non-essentials, the necessity for distinct action still remains.

This should also solve the problem that has divided the disciples: revolution or evolution? If I have caught Marx's meaning, the answer is not hard to give. Evolution was for him the parent of socialism. He was much too strongly imbued with a sense of the inherent logic of things social to believe that revolution can replace any part of the work of evolution. The revolution comes in nevertheless. But it only comes in order to write the conclusion under a complete set of premises. The Marxian revolution therefore differs entirely, in nature and in function, from the revolutions both of the bourgeois radical and of the socialist conspirator. It is essentially revolution in the fullness of time.[11] It is true that disciples who dislike this conclusion, and especially its application to the Russian case,[12] can point to many passages in the sacred books that seem to contradict it. But in those passages Marx himself contradicts his deepest and most mature thought which speaks out unmistakably from the analytic structure of *Das Kapital* and—as any thought must that is inspired by a sense of the inherent logic of things—carries, beneath the fantastic glitter of dubious gems, a distinctly conservative implication. And, after all, why not? No serious argument ever supports any "ism" unconditionally.[13] To say that Marx, stripped of phrases, admits of interpretation in a conservative sense is only saying that he can be taken seriously.

[11] This should be noticed for later reference. We shall repeatedly return to the subject and, among other things, discuss the criteria of that "fullness of time."

[12] Karl Kautsky, in his preface to *Theorien über den Mehrwert*, even claimed the revolution of 1905 for Marxian socialism, although it is patent that the Marxian phraseology of a few intellectuals was all that was socialist about it.

[13] This argument could be carried much further. In particular, there is nothing specifically socialist in the labor theory of value; this of course everyone would admit who is familiar with the historical development of that doctrine. But the same is true (excepting of course the phrase) of the theory of exploitation. We need only recognize that existence of the surpluses so dubbed by Marx is—or at least was—a necessary condition for the emergence of all that we comprise in the term civilization (which in fact it would be difficult to deny), and there we are. In order to be a socialist, it is of course not necessary to be a Marxist; but neither is it sufficient to be a Marxist in order to be a socialist. Socialist or revolutionary conclusions can be impressed on any scientific theory; no scientific theory necessarily implies them. And none will keep us in what Bernard Shaw somewhere describes as sociological rage, unless its author goes out of his way in order to work us up.

PART II

Can Capitalism Survive?

PROLOGUE

CAN capitalism survive? No. I do not think it can. But this opinion of mine, like that of every other economist who has pronounced upon the subject, is in itself completely uninteresting. What counts in any attempt at social prognosis is not the Yes or No that sums up the facts and arguments which lead up to it but those facts and arguments themselves. They contain all that is scientific in the final result. Everything else is not science but prophecy. Analysis, whether economic or other, never yields more than a statement about the tendencies present in an observable pattern. And these never tell us what *will* happen to the pattern but only what *would* happen if they continued to act as they have been acting in the time interval covered by our observation and if no other factors intruded. "Inevitability" or "necessity" can never mean more than this.

What follows must be read with that proviso. But there are other limitations to our results and their reliability. The process of social life is a function of so many variables many of which are not amenable to anything like measurement that even mere diagnosis of a given state of things becomes a doubtful matter quite apart from the formidable sources of error that open up as soon as we attempt prognosis. These difficulties should not be exaggerated, however. We shall see that the dominant traits of the picture clearly support certain inferences which, whatever the qualifications that may have to be added, are too strong to be neglected on the ground that they cannot be proved in the sense in which a proposition of Euclid's can.

One more point before we start. The thesis I shall endeavor to establish is that the actual and prospective performance of the capitalist system is such as to negative the idea of its breaking down under the weight of economic failure, but that its very success undermines the social institutions which protect it, and "inevitably" creates conditions in which it will not be able to live and which strongly point to socialism as the heir apparent. My final conclusion therefore does not differ, however much my argument may, from that of most socialist writers and in particular from that of all Marxists. But in order to accept it one does not need to be a socialist. Prognosis does not imply anything about the desirability of the course of events that one predicts. If a doctor predicts that his patient will die presently, this does not mean that he desires it. One may hate socialism or at least look upon it with cool criticism, and yet foresee its advent. Many conservatives did and do.

Nor need one accept this conclusion in order to qualify as a social-ist. One may love socialism and ardently believe in its economic, cultural and ethical superiority but nevertheless believe at the same time that capitalist society does not harbor any tendency toward self-destruction. There are in fact socialists who believe that the capitalist order is gathering strength and is entrenching itself as time goes on, so that it is chimerical to hope for its breakdown.

CHAPTER V

THE RATE OF INCREASE OF TOTAL OUTPUT

THE atmosphere of hostility to capitalism which we shall have to explain presently makes it much more difficult than it otherwise would be to form a rational opinion about its economic and cultural performance. The public mind has by now so thoroughly grown out of humor with it as to make condemnation of capitalism and all its works a foregone conclusion—almost a requirement of the etiquette of discussion. Whatever his political preference, every writer or speaker hastens to conform to this code and to emphasize his critical attitude, his freedom from "complacency," his belief in the inadequacies of capitalist achievement, his aversion to capitalist and his sympathy with anti-capitalist interests. Any other attitude is voted not only foolish but anti-social and is looked upon as an indication of immoral servitude. This is of course perfectly natural. New social religions will always have that effect. Only it does not make it easier to fulfill the analyst's task: in 300 A.D. it would not have been easy to expound the achievements of ancient civilization to a fervent believer in Christianity. On the one hand, the most obvious truths are simply put out of court *a limine*;[1] on the other hand, the most obvious misstatements are borne with or applauded.

A first test of economic performance is total output, the total of all the commodities and services produced in a unit of time—a year or a quarter of a year or a month. Economists try to measure variations in this quantity by means of indices derived from a number of series representing the output of individual commodities. "Strict logic is a stern master, and if one respected it, one would never construct or use any production index,"[2] for not only the material and the technique of constructing such an index, but the very concept of a total output of different commodities produced in ever-changing proportions, is a highly doubtful matter.[3] Nevertheless, I believe that this device is sufficiently reliable to give us a general idea.

[1] There is however another method of dealing with obvious though uncomfortable truth, viz., the method of sneering at its triviality. Such a sneer will serve as well as a refutation would, for the average audience is as a rule perfectly unaware of the fact that it often covers the impossibility of denial—a pretty specimen of social psychology.

[2] A. F. Burns, *Production Trends in the United States Since 1870*, p. 262.

[3] We cannot enter into this problem here. A little will, however, be said about it when we meet it again in the next chapter. For a fuller treatment see my book on *Business Cycles*, ch. ix.

For the United States, individual series good and numerous enough to warrant construction of such an index of output are available since the Civil War. Choosing what is known as the Day-Persons index of total production[4] we find that, from 1870 to 1930, the average annual rate of growth was 3.7 per cent and, in the division of manufactures alone, 4.3 per cent. Let us concentrate on the former figure and try to visualize what it means. In order to do this we must first apply a correction: since the durable equipment of industry was always increasing in relative importance, output available for consumption cannot have increased at the same rate as total production. We must allow for that. But I believe that an allowance of 1.7 per cent is ample;[5] thus we arrive at a rate of increase in "available output" of 2 per cent (compound interest) per year.

Now suppose that the capitalist engine keeps on producing at that rate of increase for another half century starting from 1928. To this assumption there are various objections which will have to be noticed later on, but it cannot be objected to on the ground that in the decade from 1929 to 1939 capitalism had already failed to live up to that standard. For the depression that ran its course from the last quarter of 1929 to the third quarter of 1932 does not prove that a secular break has occurred in the propelling mechanism of capitalist production because depressions of such severity have repeatedly occurred—roughly once in fifty-five years—and because the effects of one of them—the one from 1873 to 1877—are taken account of in the annual average of 2 per cent. The subnormal recovery to 1935, the subnormal prosperity to 1937 and the slump after that are easily accounted for by the difficulties incident to the adaptation to a new fiscal policy, new labor legislation and a general change in the attitude of government to private enterprise all of which can, in a sense to be defined later, be distinguished from the working of the productive apparatus as such.

Since misunderstandings at this point would be especially undesirable, I wish to emphasize that the last sentence does not in itself imply either an adverse criticism of the New Deal policies or the proposition—which I do believe to be true but which I do not need just now—that policies of that type are in the long run incompatible with the effective working of the system of private enterprise. All I now mean to imply is that so extensive and rapid a change of the social scene naturally affects productive performance for a time, and so much the most ardent New Dealer must *and also can* admit. I for one do not see how it would otherwise be possible to account for the

[4] See W. M. Persons, *Forecasting Business Cycles*, ch. xi.

[5] That allowance is in fact absurdly large. See also Professor F. C. Mill's estimate of 3.1 per cent for the period 1901-1913, and of 3.8 per cent for the period 1922-1929 (construction excluded; *Economic Tendencies in the United States*, 1932).

fact that this country which had the best chance of recovering quickly was precisely the one to experience the most unsatisfactory recovery. The only somewhat similar case, that of France, supports the same inference. It follows that the course of events during the decade from 1929 to 1939 does not *per se* constitute a valid reason for refusing to listen to the argument in hand which, moreover, may in any case serve to illustrate the meaning of past performance.

Well, if from 1928 on available production under the conditions of the capitalist order continued to develop as it did before, i.e., at a long-run average rate of increase of 2 per cent per year, it would after fifty years, in 1978, reach an amount of roughly 2.7 (2.6916) times the 1928 figure. In order to translate this into terms of average real income *per head of population*, we first observe that our rate of increase in total output may be roughly equated to the rate of increase in the sum total of private money incomes available for consumption,[6] corrected for changes in the purchasing power of the consumers' dollars. Second, we must form an idea about the increase in population we are to expect; we will choose Mr. Sloane's estimate, which gives 160 millions for 1978. Average income per head during those fifty years would therefore increase to a little more than double its 1928 amount, which was about $650, or to about $1300 *of 1928 purchasing power*.[7]

Perhaps some readers feel that a proviso should be added about the distribution of the total monetary income. Until about forty years ago, many economists besides Marx believed that the capitalist process tended to change relative shares in the national total so that the obvious inference from our average might be invalidated by the rich growing richer and the poor growing poorer, at least relatively. But there is no such tendency. Whatever may be thought of the statistical measures devised for the purpose, this much is certain: that the structure of the pyramid of incomes, expressed in terms of money, has not greatly changed during the period covered by our material

---

[6] "Consumption" includes the acquisition of durable consumers' goods such as motor cars, refrigerators and homes. We do not distinguish between transient consumers' goods and what is sometimes referred to as "consumers' capital."

[7] That is to say, average real income per head would increase at a compound interest rate of 1⅜ per cent. It so happens that in England, during the century preceding the First World War, real income per head of population increased at almost exactly that rate (see Lord Stamp in *Wealth and Taxable Capacity*). No great confidence can be placed in this coincidence. But I think it serves to show that our little calculation is not wildly absurd. In Number 241 of the *National Industrial Conference Board Studies*, Table I, pp. 6 and 7, we find that "per capita realized national income" adjusted by the Federal Reserve Bank of New York and the National Industrial Conference Board cost of living index, was in 1929 a little over four times the 1829 figure—a similar result, though open to still more serious doubts as to reliability.

—which for England includes the whole of the nineteenth century[8]
—and that the relative share of wages plus salaries has also been
substantially constant over time. There is, so long as we are discussing what the capitalist engine might do if left to itself, no reason to
believe that the distribution of incomes or the dispersion about our
average would in 1978 be significantly different from what it was
in 1928.

One way of expressing our result is that, if capitalism repeated its
past performance for another half century starting with 1928, this
would do away with anything that according to present standards
could be called poverty, even in the lowest strata of the population,
pathological cases alone excepted.

Nor is this all. Whatever else our index may do or may not do, it
certainly does not overstate the actual rate of increase. It does not
take account of the commodity, Voluntary Leisure. New commodities
escape or are inadequately represented by an index which must rest
largely on basic commodities and intermediate products. For the
same reason improvements in quality almost completely fail to assert
themselves although they constitute, in many lines, the core of the
progress achieved—there is no way of expressing adequately the
difference between a motorcar of 1940 and a motorcar of 1900 or
the extent to which the price of motorcars per unit of utility has
fallen. It would be more nearly possible to estimate the rate at which
given quantities of raw materials or semi-finished products are made
to go further than they used to—a steel ingot or a ton of coal, though
they may be unchanged in physical quality, represent a multiple of
their economic efficiency sixty years ago. But little has been done
along this line. I have no idea about what would happen to our
index if there were a method for correcting it for these and similar
factors. It is certain, however, that its percentage rate of change would
be increased and that we have here a reserve that should make the
estimate adopted proof against the effects of any conceivable downward revision. Moreover, even if we had the means of measuring the
change in the technological efficiency of industrial products, this
measure would still fail to convey an adequate idea of what it means
for the dignity or intensity or pleasantness of human life—for all that
the economists of an earlier generation subsumed under the heading
of Satisfaction of Wants. And this, after all, is for us the relevant
consideration, the true "output" of capitalist production, the reason

[8] See Stamp, op. cit. The same phenomenon can be observed in all countries for
which there is sufficient statistical information, if we clear the latter of the disturbing effect of the cycles of various span that are covered by the available material.
The measure of income distribution (or of inequality of incomes) devised by
Vilfredo Pareto is open to objection. But the fact itself is independent of its shortcomings.

why we are interested in the index of production and the pounds and gallons that enter into it and would hardly be worth while in themselves.

But let us keep to our 2 per cent. There is one more point that is important for a correct appraisal of that figure. I have stated above that, broadly speaking, relative shares in national income have remained substantially constant over the last hundred years. This, however, is true only if we measure them in money. Measured in real terms, relative shares have substantially changed in favor of the lower income groups. This follows from the fact that the capitalist engine is first and last an engine of mass production which unavoidably means also production for the masses, whereas, climbing upward in the scale of individual incomes, we find that an increasing proportion is being spent on personal services and on handmade commodities, the prices of which are largely a function of wage rates.

Verification is easy. There are no doubt some things available to the modern workman that Louis XIV himself would have been delighted to have yet was unable to have—modern dentistry for instance. On the whole, however, a budget on that level had little that really mattered to gain from capitalist achievement. Even speed of traveling may be assumed to have been a minor consideration for so very dignified a gentleman. Electric lighting is no great boon to anyone who has money enough to buy a sufficient number of candles and to pay servants to attend to them. It is the cheap cloth, the cheap cotton and rayon fabric, boots, motorcars and so on that are the typical achievements of capitalist production, and not as a rule improvements that would mean much to the rich man. Queen Elizabeth owned silk stockings. The capitalist achievement does not typically consist in providing more silk stockings for queens but in bringing them within the reach of factory girls in return for steadily decreasing amounts of effort.

The same fact stands out still better if we glance at those long waves in economic activity, analysis of which reveals the nature and mechanism of the capitalist process better than anything else. Each of them consists of an "industrial revolution" and the absorption of its effects. For instance, we are able to observe statistically and historically—the phenomenon is so clear that even our scanty information suffices to establish it—the rise of such a long wave toward the end of the 1780's, its culmination around 1800, its downward sweep and then a sort of recovery ending at the beginning of the 1840's. This was the Industrial Revolution dear to the heart of textbook writers. Upon its heels, however, came another such revolution producing another long wave that rose in the forties, culminated just before 1857 and ebbed away to 1897, to be followed in turn by the one that reached its peak about 1911 and is now in the act of ebbing away.[9]

These revolutions periodically reshape the existing structure of industry by introducing new methods of production—the mechanized factory, the electrified factory, chemical synthesis and the like; new commodities, such as railroad service, motorcars, electrical appliances; new forms of organization—the merger movement; new sources of supply—La Plata wool, American cotton, Katanga copper; new trade routes and markets to sell in and so on. This process of industrial change provides the ground swell that gives the general tone to business: while these things are being initiated we have brisk expenditure and predominating "prosperity"—interrupted, no doubt, by the negative phases of the shorter cycles that are superimposed on that ground swell—and while those things are being completed and their results pour forth we have elimination of antiquated elements of the industrial structure and predominating "depression." Thus there are prolonged periods of rising and of falling prices, interest rates, employment and so on, which phenomena constitute parts of the mechanism of this process of recurrent rejuvenation of the productive apparatus.

Now these results each time consist in an avalanche of consumers' goods that permanently deepens and widens the stream of real income although in the first instance they spell disturbance, losses and unemployment. And if we look at those avalanches of consumers' goods we again find that each of them consists in articles of mass consumption and increases the purchasing power of the wage dollar more than that of any other dollar—in other words, that the capitalist process, not by coincidence but by virtue of its mechanism, progressively raises the standard of life of the masses. It does so through a sequence of vicissitudes, the severity of which is proportional to the speed of the advance. But it does so effectively. One problem after another of the supply of commodities to the masses has been successfully solved[10] by being brought within the reach of the methods of capitalist production. The most important one of those that remain, housing, is approaching solution by means of the pre-fabricated house.

And still this is not all. Appraisal of an economic order would be incomplete—and incidentally un-Marxian—if it stopped at the output which the corresponding economic conveyor hands to the various groups of society and left out of account all those things that the conveyor does not serve directly but for which it provides the means

[9] These are the "long waves" which, in business cycle literature, are primarily associated with the name of N. D. Kondratieff.

[10] This of course also applies to agricultural commodities, the cheap mass production of which was entirely the work of large-scale capitalist enterprise (railroads, shipping, agricultural machinery, fertilizers).

as well as the political volition, and all those cultural achievements that are induced by the mentality it generates. Deferring consideration of the latter (Chapter XI), we shall now turn to some aspects of the former.

The technique and atmosphere of the struggle for social legislation obscures the otherwise obvious facts that, on the one hand, part of this legislation presupposes previous capitalist success (in other words, wealth which had previously to be created by capitalist enterprise) and that, on the other hand, much of what social legislation develops and generalizes had been previously initiated by the action of the capitalist stratum itself. Both facts must of course be added to the sum total of capitalist performance. Now if the system had another run such as it had in the sixty years preceding 1928 and really reached the $1300 *per head of population,* it is easy to see that all the desiderata that have so far been espoused by any social reformers—practically without exception, including even the greater part of the cranks—either would be fulfilled automatically or could be fulfilled *without significant interference with the capitalist process.* Ample provision for the unemployed in particular would then be not only a tolerable but a light burden. Irresponsibility in creating unemployment and in financing the support of the unemployed might of course at any time create insoluble problems. But managed with ordinary prudence, an *average* annual expenditure of 16 billions on an *average* number of 16 million unemployed including dependents (10 per cent of the population) would not in itself be a serious matter with an available national income of the order of magnitude of 200 billion dollars (purchasing power of 1928).

May I call the reader's attention to the reason why unemployment which everyone agrees must be one of the most important issues in any discussion of capitalism—with some critics so much so that they base their indictment exclusively on this element of the case—will play a comparatively small role in my argument? I do not think that unemployment is among those evils which, like poverty, capitalist evolution could ever eliminate of itself. I also do not think that there is any tendency for the unemployment percentage to increase in the long run. The only series covering a respectable time interval—roughly the sixty years preceding the First World War—gives the English trade-union percentage of unemployed members. It is a typically cyclical series and displays no trend (or a horizontal one).[11] Since this is theoretically understandable—there is no theoretical reason to call the evidence in question—those two propositions seem established for

[11] That series has often been charted and analyzed. See for instance, A. C. Pigou, *Industrial Fluctuations* or my *Business Cycles.* For every country there seems to be an irreducible minimum and, superimposed on that, a cyclical movement, the strongest component of which has a period of about nine to ten years.

the prewar time to 1913 inclusive. In the postwar time and in most countries unemployment was mostly at an abnormally high level even before 1930. But this and still more the unemployment during the thirties can be accounted for on grounds that have nothing to do with a long-run tendency of unemployment percentages to increase *from causes inherent in the capitalist mechanism itself*. I have mentioned above those industrial revolutions which are so characteristic of the capitalist process. Supernormal unemployment is one of the features of the periods of adaptation that follow upon the "prosperity phase" of each of them. We observe it in the 1820's and 1870's, and the period after 1920 is simply another of those periods. So far the phenomenon is essentially temporary in the sense that nothing can be inferred about it for the future. But there were a number of other factors which tended to intensify it—war effects, dislocations of foreign trade, wage policies, certain institutional changes that swelled the statistical figure, in England and Germany fiscal policies (also important in the United States since 1935) and so on. Some of these are no doubt symptoms of an "atmosphere" in which capitalism will work with decreasing efficiency. That however is another matter which will engage our attention later on.

But whether lasting or temporary, getting worse or not, unemployment undoubtedly is and always has been a scourge. In the next part of this book we shall have to list its possible elimination among the claims of the socialist order to superiority. Nevertheless, I hold that the real tragedy is not unemployment *per se*, but unemployment plus the impossibility of providing adequately for the unemployed *without impairing the conditions of further economic development*: for obviously the suffering and degradation—the destruction of human values—which we associate with unemployment, though not the waste of productive resources, would be largely eliminated and unemployment would lose practically all its terror if the private life of the unemployed were not seriously affected by their unemployment. The indictment stands that in the past—say, roughly, to the end of the nineteenth century—the capitalist order was not only unwilling but also quite incapable of guaranteeing this. But since it will be able to do so if it keeps up its past performance for another half century this indictment would in that case enter the limbo filled by the sorry specters of child labor and sixteen-hour working days and five persons living in one room which it is quite proper to emphasize when we are talking about the past social costs of capitalist achievement but which are not necessarily relevant to the balance of alternatives for the future. Our own time is somewhere between the disabilities of earlier stages in capitalist evolution and the abilities of the system in full maturity. In this country at least, the better part of the task could even now be accomplished without undue strain on the system. The difficulties do not seem to consist so much in the lack of a surplus sufficient to blot out the darkest hues in the picture: they consist, on the one hand, in the fact that the unemployment figure has been increased by anti-capitalist policies beyond what it need have been in the thirties and, on the other hand, in the fact that public opinion as soon as it becomes at all alive to the duty in question, immediately insists on economically irrational methods of financing relief and on lax and wasteful methods of administering it.

Much the same argument applies to the future—and to a great extent the present—possibilities held out by capitalist evolution for the care of the aged and sick, for education and hygiene and so on. Also, an increasing number of commodities might reasonably be expected, from the standpoint of the individual household, to pass out of the class of economic goods and to be available practically up to the satiety point. This could be brought about either by arrangements between public agencies and producing concerns or by nationalization or municipalization, gradual progress with which would of course be a feature of the future development even of an otherwise unfettered capitalism.

CHAPTER VI

PLAUSIBLE CAPITALISM

THE argument of the preceding chapter seems to be exposed to a reply that is as damaging as it is obvious. The average rate of increase in total available production that obtained during the sixty years preceding 1928 has been projected into the future. So far as this was merely a device in order to illustrate the significance of past development, there was nothing in this procedure that could have shocked the statistical conscience. But as soon as I implied that the following fifty years might actually display a similar average rate of increase, I apparently did commit a statistical crime; it is, of course, clear that a historical record of production over any given period does not in itself justify any extrapolation at all,[1] let alone an extrapolation over half a century. It is therefore necessary to emphasize again that my extrapolation is not intended to forecast the actual behavior of output in the future. Beyond illustrating the meaning of past performance, it is merely intended to give us a quantitative idea of what the capitalist engine might conceivably accomplish if, for another half century, it repeated its past performance—which is a very different matter. The question whether it can be expected to do so will be answered quite independently of the extrapolation itself. For this purpose we have now to embark upon a long and difficult investigation.

Before we can discuss the chance of capitalism repeating its past performance we must evidently try to find out in what sense the observed rate of increase in output really measures that past performance. No doubt, the period that furnished our data was one of comparatively unfettered capitalism. But this fact does not in itself provide a sufficient link between the performance and the capitalist engine. In order to believe that this was more than coincidence we must satisfy ourselves first, that there is an understandable relation between the capitalist order and the observed rate of increase in output; second, that, given such a relation, the rate of increase was actually due to it and not to

[1] This proposition holds, on general principles, for any *historical* time series, since the very concept of historical sequence implies the occurrence of irreversible changes in the economic structure which must be expected to affect the law of any given economic quantity. Theoretical justification and, as a rule, statistical treatment are therefore necessary for even the most modest extrapolations. It may however be urged that our case is somewhat favored by the fact that within the comprehensive compound represented by the output series, idiosyncrasies of individual items will to some extent cancel each other.

particularly favorable conditions which had nothing to do with capitalism.

These two problems must be solved before the problem of a "repetition of performance" can arise at all. The third point then reduces to the question whether there is any reason why the capitalist engine should, during the next forty years, fail to go on working as it did in the past.

We shall deal with these three points in turn.

Our first problem may be reformulated as follows. On the one hand, we have a considerable body of statistical data descriptive of a rate of "progress" that has been admired even by very critical minds. On the other hand, we have a body of facts about the structure of the economic system of that period and about the way it functioned; from these facts, analysis has distilled what is technically called a "model" of capitalist reality, i.e., a generalized picture of its essential features. We wish to know whether that type of economy was favorable, irrelevant, or unfavorable to the performance we observe and, if favorable, whether those features may be reasonably held to yield adequate explanation of this performance. Waiving technicalities as much as possible, we shall approach the question in a common-sense spirit.

1. Unlike the class of feudal lords, the commercial and industrial bourgeoisie rose by business success. Bourgeois society has been cast in a purely economic mold: its foundations, beams and beacons are all made of economic material. The building faces toward the economic side of life. Prizes and penalties are measured in pecuniary terms. Going up and going down means making and losing money. This, of course, nobody can deny. But I wish to add that, within its own frame, that social arrangement is, or at all events was, singularly effective. In part it appeals to, and in part it creates, a schema of motives that is unsurpassed in simplicity and force. The promises of wealth and the threats of destitution that it holds out, it redeems with ruthless promptitude. Wherever the bourgeois way of life asserts itself sufficiently to dim the beacons of other social worlds, these promises are strong enough to attract the large majority of supernormal brains and to identify success with business success. They are not proffered at random; yet there is a sufficiently enticing admixture of chance: the game is not like roulette, it is more like poker. They are addressed to ability, energy and supernormal capacity for work; but if there were a way of measuring either that ability in general or the personal achievement that goes into any particular success, the premiums actually paid out would probably not be found proportional to either. Spectacular prizes much greater than would have been necessary to call forth the particular effort are thrown to a small minority of winners, thus propelling much more efficaciously than a

more equal and more "just" distribution would, the activity of that large majority of businessmen who receive in return very modest compensation or nothing or less than nothing, and yet do their utmost because they have the big prizes before their eyes and overrate their chances of doing equally well. Similarly, the threats are addressed to incompetence. But though the incompetent men and the obsolete methods are in fact eliminated, sometimes very promptly, sometimes with a lag, failure also threatens or actually overtakes many an able man, thus whipping up *everyone*, again much more efficaciously than a more equal and more "just" system of penalties would. Finally, both business success and business failure are ideally precise. Neither can be talked away.

One aspect of this should be particularly noticed, for future reference as well as because of its importance for the argument in hand. In the way indicated and also in other ways which will be discussed later on, the capitalist arrangement, as embodied in the institution of private enterprise, effectively chains the bourgeois stratum to its tasks. But it does more than that. The same apparatus which conditions for performance the individuals and families that at any given time form the bourgeois class, *ipso facto* also selects the individuals and families that are to rise into that class or to drop out of it. This combination of the conditioning and the selective function is not a matter of course. On the contrary, most methods of social selection, unlike the "methods" of biological selection, do not guarantee performance of the selected individual; and their failure to do so constitutes one of the crucial problems of socialist organization that will come up for discussion at another stage of our inquiry. For the time being, it should merely be observed how well the capitalist system solves that problem: in most cases the man who rises first *into* the business class and then *within* it is also an able businessman and he is likely to rise exactly as far as his ability goes—simply because in that schema rising to a position and doing well in it generally is or was one and the same thing. This fact, so often obscured by the auto-therapeutic effort of the unsuccessful to deny it, is much more important for an appraisal of capitalist society and its civilization than anything that can be gleaned from the pure theory of the capitalist machine.

2. But is not all that we might be tempted to infer from "maximum performance of an optimally selected group" invalidated by the further fact that that performance is not geared to social service—production, so we might say, for consumption—but to money-making, that it aims at maximizing profits instead of welfare? Outside of the bourgeois stratum, this has of course always been the popular opinion. Economists have sometimes fought and sometimes espoused it. In doing so they have contributed something that was much more valuable than were the final judgments themselves at which they arrived

individually and which in most cases reflect little more than their social location, interests and sympathies or antipathies. They slowly increased our factual knowledge and analytic powers so that the answers to many questions we are able to give today are no doubt much more correct although less simple and sweeping than were those of our predecessors.

To go no further back, the so-called classical economists[2] were practically of one mind. Most of them disliked many things about the social institutions of their epoch and about the way those institutions worked. They fought the landed interest and approved of social reforms—factory legislation in particular—that were not all on the lines of *laissez faire*. But they were quite convinced that within the institutional framework of capitalism, the manufacturer's and the trader's self-interest made for maximum performance in the interest of all. Confronted with the problem we are discussing, they would have had little hesitation in attributing the observed rate of increase in total output to relatively unfettered enterprise and the profit motive —perhaps they would have mentioned "beneficial legislation" as a condition but by this they would have meant the removal of fetters, especially the removal or reduction of protective duties during the nineteenth century.

It is exceedingly difficult, at this hour of the day, to do justice to these views. They were of course the typical views of the English bourgeois class, and bourgeois blinkers are in evidence on almost every page the classical authors wrote. No less in evidence are blinkers of another kind: the classics reasoned in terms of a particular historical situation which they uncritically idealized and from which they uncritically generalized. Most of them, moreover, seem to have argued exclusively in terms of the English interests and problems of their time. This is the reason why, in other lands and at other times, people disliked their economics, frequently to the point of not even caring to understand it. But it will not do to dismiss their teaching on these grounds. A prejudiced man may yet be speaking the truth. Propositions developed from special cases may yet be generally valid. And the enemies and successors of the classics had and have only different but not fewer blinkers and preconceptions; they envisaged and envisage different but not less special cases.

From the standpoint of the economic analyst, the chief merit of the classics consists in their dispelling, along with many other gross errors, the naïve idea that economic activity in capitalist society, because it

[2] The term Classical Economists will in this book be used to designate the leading English economists whose works appeared between 1776 and 1848. Adam Smith, Ricardo, Malthus, Senior and John Stuart Mill are the outstanding names. It is important to keep this in mind because a much broader use of the term has come into fashion of late.

turns on the profit motive, must by virtue of that fact alone necessarily run counter to the interests of consumers; or, to put it differently, that moneymaking necessarily deflects producing from its social goal; or, finally, that private profits, both in themselves and through the distortion of the economic process they induce, are always a net loss to all excepting those who receive them and would therefore constitute a net gain to be reaped by socialization. If we look at the logic of these and similar propositions which no trained economist ever thought of defending, the classical refutation may well seem trivial. But as soon as we look at all the theories and slogans which, consciously or subconsciously, imply them and which are once more served up today, we shall feel more respect for that achievement. Let me add at once that the classical writers also clearly perceived, though they may have exaggerated, the role of saving and accumulation and that they linked saving to the rate of "progress" they observed in a manner that was fundamentally, if only approximately, correct. Above all, there was practical wisdom about their doctrine, a responsible long-run view and a manly tone that contrast favorably with modern hysterics.

But between realizing that hunting for a maximum of profit and striving for maximum productive performance are not necessarily incompatible, to proving that the former will necessarily—or in the immense majority of cases—imply the latter, there is a gulf much wider than the classics thought. And they never succeeded in bridging it. The modern student of their doctrines never ceases to wonder how it was possible for them to be satisfied with their arguments or to mistake these arguments for proofs; in the light of later analysis their *theory* was seen to be a house of cards whatever measure of truth there may have been in their *vision*.[3]

3. This later analysis we will take in two strides—as much of it, that is, as we need in order to clarify our problem. Historically, the first will carry us into the first decade of this century, the second will cover some of the postwar developments of scientific economics. Frankly I do not know how much good this will do the non-professional reader; like every other branch of our knowledge, economics, as its analytic engine improves, moves fatally away from that happy stage in which all problems, methods and results could be made accessible to every educated person without special training. I will, however, do my best.

The first stride may be associated with two great names revered to

[3] The reader will recall my emphasis on the distinction between one's theory and one's vision in the case of Marx. It is however always important to remember that the ability to see things in their correct perspective may be, and often is, divorced from the ability to reason correctly and vice versa. That is why a man may be a very good theorist and yet talk absolute nonsense whenever confronted with the task of diagnosing a concrete historical pattern as a whole.

this day by numberless disciples—so far at least as the latter do not think it bad form to express reverence for anything or anybody, which many of them obviously do—Alfred Marshall and Knut Wicksell.[4] Their theoretical structure has little in common with that of the classics—though Marshall did his best to hide the fact—but it conserves the classic proposition that in the case of perfect competition the profit interest of the producer tends to maximize production. It even supplied almost satisfactory proof. Only, in the process of being more correctly stated and proved, the proposition lost much of its content—it does emerge from the operation, to be sure, but it emerges emaciated, barely alive.[5] Still it can be shown, within the general assumptions of the Marshall-Wicksell analysis, that firms which cannot by their own individual action exert any influence upon the price of their products or of the factors of production they employ—so that there would be no point in their weeping over the fact that any increase in production tends to decrease the former and to increase the latter—will expand their output until they reach the point at which the additional cost that must be incurred in order to produce another small increment of product (marginal cost) just equals the price they

[4] Marshall's *Principles* (first edition 1890) and Wicksell's *Lectures* (first Swedish edition 1901, English translation 1934) are entitled to the prominence I am here giving to them, because of the influence they exerted on many minds in their formative stages and because they dealt with theory in a thoroughly practical spirit. On purely scientific grounds, precedence should be given to the work of Léon Walras. In America, the names to mention are J. B. Clark, Irving Fisher and F. W. Taussig.

[5] Anticipating later argument (see below, ch. viii, § 6) I shall in this note briefly clarify the above passage. Analysis of the mechanism of the profit economy led not only to the discovery of exceptions to the principle that competitive industry tends to maximize output, but also to the discovery that proof of the principle itself requires assumptions which reduce it to little more than a truism. Its practical value is however particularly impaired by the two following considerations:

1. The principle, as far as it can be proved at all, applies to a state of static equilibrium. Capitalist reality is first and last a process of change. In appraising the performance of competitive enterprise, the question whether it would or would not tend to maximize production in a perfectly equilibrated stationary condition of the economic process is hence almost, though not quite, irrelevant.

2. The principle, as stated by Wicksell, is what was left of a more ambitious proposition that, though in a rarefied form, can still be found in Marshall—the theorem that competitive industry tends to produce a state of maximum satisfaction of wants. But this theorem, even if we waive the serious objections to speaking of non-observable psychic magnitudes, is readily seen to boil down to the triviality that, whatever the data and in particular the institutional arrangements of a society may be, human action, as far as it is rational, will always try to make the best of any given situation. In fact it boils down to a definition of rational action and can hence be paralleled by analogous theorems for, say, a socialist society. But so can the principle of maximum production. Neither formulates any specific virtue of private competitive enterprise. This does not mean that such virtues do not exist. It does mean however that they are not simply inherent in the *logic* of competition.

can get for that increment, i.e., that they will produce as much as they can without running into loss. And this can be shown to be as much as it is in general "socially desirable" to produce. In more technical language, in that case prices are, from the standpoint of the individual firm, not variables but parameters; and where this is so, there exists a state of equilibrium in which all outputs are at their maximum and all factors fully employed. This case is usually referred to as perfect competition. Remembering what has been said about the selective process which operates on all firms and their managers, we might in fact conceive a very optimistic idea of the results to be expected from a highly selected group of people forced, within that pattern, by their profit motive to strain every nerve in order to maximize output and to minimize costs. In particular, it might seem at first sight that a system conforming to this pattern would display remarkable absence of some of the major sources of social waste. As a little reflection should show, this is really but another way of stating the content of the preceding sentence.

4. Let us take the second stride. The Marshall-Wicksell analysis of course did not overlook the many cases that fail to conform to that model. Nor, for that matter, had the classics overlooked them. They recognized cases of "monopoly," and Adam Smith himself carefully noticed the prevalence of devices to restrict competition[6] and all the differences in flexibility of prices resulting therefrom. But they looked upon those cases as exceptions and, moreover, as exceptions that could and would be done away with in time. Something of that sort is true also of Marshall. Although he developed the Cournot theory of monopoly[7] and although he anticipated later analysis by calling attention to the fact that most firms have special markets of their own in which they set prices instead of merely accepting them,[8] he as well as Wicksell framed his general conclusions on the pattern of perfect competition so as to suggest, much as the classics did, that perfect competition was the rule. Neither Marshall and Wicksell nor the classics saw that perfect competition is the exception and that even if it were the rule there would be much less reason for congratulation than one might think.

If we look more closely at the conditions—not all of them explicitly stated or even clearly seen by Marshall and Wicksell—that must be fulfilled in order to produce perfect competition, we realize imme-

---

[6] In a manner strikingly suggestive of present-day attitudes he even emphasized the discrepancy between the interests of every trade and those of the public and talked about conspiracies against the latter which, so he thought, might originate at any businessmen's dinner party.

[7] Augustin Cournot, 1938.

[8] This is why the later theory of imperfect competition may fairly be traced to him. Though he did not elaborate it, he saw the phenomenon more correctly than most of those who did. In particular he did not exaggerate its importance.

diately that outside of agricultural mass production there cannot be many instances of it. A farmer supplies his cotton or wheat in fact under those conditions: from his standpoint the ruling prices of cotton or wheat are data, though very variable ones, and not being able to influence them by his individual action he simply adapts his output; since all farmers do the same, prices and quantities will in the end be adjusted as the theory of perfect competition requires. But this is not so even with many agricultural products—with ducks, sausages, vegetables and many dairy products for instance. And as regards practically all the finished products and services of industry and trade, it is clear that every grocer, every filling station, every manufacturer of gloves or shaving cream or handsaws has a small and precarious market of his own which he tries—must try—to build up and to keep by price strategy, quality strategy—"product differentiation"—and advertising. Thus we get a completely different pattern which there seems to be no reason to expect to yield the results of perfect competition and which fits much better into the monopolistic schema. In these cases we speak of Monopolistic Competition. Their theory has been one of the major contributions to postwar economics.[9]

There remains a wide field of substantially homogeneous products —mainly industrial raw materials and semi-finished products such as steel ingots, cement, cotton gray goods and the like—in which the conditions for the emergence of monopolistic competition do not seem to prevail. This is· so. But in general, similar results follow for that field inasmuch as the greater part of it is covered by largest-scale firms which, either individually or in concert, are able to manipulate prices even without differentiating products—the case of Oligopoly. Again the monopoly schema, suitably adapted, seems to fit this type of behavior much better than does the schema of perfect competition.

As soon as the prevalence of monopolistic competition or of oligopoly or of combinations of the two is recognized, many of the propositions which the Marshall-Wicksell generation of economists used to teach with the utmost confidence become either inapplicable or much more difficult to prove. This holds true, in the first place, of the propositions turning on the fundamental concept of equilibrium, i.e., a determinate state of the economic organism, toward which any given state of it is always gravitating and which displays certain simple properties. In the general case of oligopoly there is in fact no determinate equilibrium at all and the possibility presents itself that there may be an endless sequence of moves and countermoves, an indefinite state of warfare between firms. It is true that there are many special cases in which a state of equilibrium theoretically exists. In the second place, even in these cases not only is it much harder to attain than

9 See, in particular, E. S. Chamberlin, *Theory of Monopolistic Competition,* and Joan Robinson, *The Economics of Imperfect Competition.*

the equilibrium in perfect competition, and still harder to preserve, but the "beneficial" competition of the classic type seems likely to be replaced by "predatory" or "cutthroat" competition or simply by struggles for control in the financial sphere. These things are so many sources of social waste, and there are many others such as the costs of advertising campaigns, the suppression of new methods of production (buying up of patents in order not to use them) and so on. And most important of all: under the conditions envisaged, equilibrium, even if eventually attained by an extremely costly method, no longer guarantees either full employment or maximum output in the sense of the theory of perfect competition. It *may* exist without full employment; it is *bound* to exist, so it seems, at a level of output below that maximum mark, because profit-conserving strategy, impossible in conditions of perfect competition, now not only becomes possible but imposes itself.

Well, does not this bear out what the man in the street (unless a businessman himself) always thought on the subject of private business? Has not modern analysis completely refuted the classical doctrine and justified the popular view? Is it not quite true after all, that there is little parallelism between producing for profit and producing for the consumer and that private enterprise is little more than a device to curtail production in order to extort profits which then are correctly described as tolls and ransoms?

CHAPTER VII

THE PROCESS OF CREATIVE DESTRUCTION

THE theories of monopolistic and oligopolistic competition and their popular variants may in two ways be made to serve the view that capitalist reality is unfavorable to maximum performance in production. One may hold that it always has been so and that all along output has been expanding in spite of the secular sabotage perpetrated by the managing bourgeoisie. Advocates of this proposition would have to produce evidence to the effect that the observed rate of increase can be accounted for by a sequence of favorable circumstances unconnected with the mechanism of private enterprise and strong enough to overcome the latter's resistance. This is precisely the question which we shall discuss in Chapter IX. However, those who espouse this variant at least avoid the trouble about historical fact that the advocates of the alternative proposition have to face. This avers that capitalist reality once tended to favor maximum productive performance, or at all events productive performance so considerable as to constitute a major element in any serious appraisal of the system; but that the later spread of monopolist structures, killing competition, has by now reversed that tendency.

First, this involves the creation of an entirely imaginary golden age of perfect competition that at some time somehow metamorphosed itself into the monopolistic age, whereas it is quite clear that perfect competition has at no time been more of a reality than it is at present. Secondly, it is necessary to point out that the rate of increase in output did not decrease from the nineties from which, I suppose, the prevalence of the largest-size concerns, at least in manufacturing industry, would have to be dated; that there is nothing in the behavior of the time series of total output to suggest a "break in trend"; and, most important of all, that the modern standard of life of the masses evolved during the period of relatively unfettered "big business." If we list the items that enter the modern workman's budget and from 1899 on observe the course of their prices not in terms of money but in terms of the hours of labor that will buy them—i.e., each year's money prices divided by each year's hourly wage rates—we cannot fail to be struck by the rate of the advance which, considering the spectacular improvement in qualities, seems to have been greater and not smaller than it ever was before. If we economists were given less to wishful thinking and more to the observation of facts, doubts would immediately arise as to the realistic virtues of a theory that would have led us to expect a very different result. Nor is this all. As soon as we go into details and inquire into the individual items in which progress was most conspicuous, the trail leads not to the doors of those firms that work under conditions of comparatively free competition but precisely to the doors of the large concerns—which, as in the case of agricultural machinery, also account for much of the progress in the competitive sector—and a shocking suspicion dawns upon us that big business may have had more to do with creating that standard of life than with keeping it down.

The conclusions alluded to at the end of the preceding chapter are in fact almost completely false. Yet they follow from observations and theorems that are almost completely[1] true. Both economists and popular writers have once more run away with some fragments of reality they happened to grasp. These fragments themselves were mostly seen correctly. Their formal properties were mostly developed correctly. But no conclusions about capitalist reality as a whole follow from such fragmentary analyses. If we draw them nevertheless, we can be right only by accident. That has been done. And the lucky accident did not happen.

The essential point to grasp is that in dealing with capitalism we are dealing with an evolutionary process. It may seem strange that anyone can fail to see so obvious a fact which moreover was long ago emphasized by Karl Marx. Yet that fragmentary analysis which yields the bulk of our propositions about the functioning of modern capitalism persistently neglects it. Let us restate the point and see how it bears upon our problem.

Capitalism, then, is by nature a form or method of economic change and not only never is but never can be stationary. And this evolutionary character of the capitalist process is not merely due to the fact that economic life goes on in a social and natural environment which changes and by its change alters the data of economic action; this fact is important and these changes (wars, revolutions and so on) often condition industrial change, but they are not its prime movers. Nor is this evolutionary character due to a quasi-automatic increase in population and capital or to the vagaries of monetary systems of

---

[1] As a matter of fact, those observations and theorems are not completely satisfactory. The usual expositions of the doctrine of imperfect competition fail in particular to give due attention to the many and important cases in which, even as a matter of static theory, imperfect competition approximates the results of perfect competition. There are other cases in which it does not do this, but offers compensations which, while not entering any output index, yet contribute to what the output index is in the last resort intended to measure—the cases in which a firm defends its market by establishing a name for quality and service for instance. However, in order to simplify matters, we will not take issue with that doctrine on its own ground.

which exactly the same thing holds true. The fundamental impulse that sets and keeps the capitalist engine in motion comes from the new consumers' goods, the new methods of production or transportation, the new markets, the new forms of industrial organization that capitalist enterprise creates.

As we have seen in the preceding chapter, the contents of the laborer's budget, say from 1760 to 1940, did not simply grow on unchanging lines but they underwent a process of qualitative change. Similarly, the history of the productive apparatus of a typical farm, from the beginnings of the rationalization of crop rotation, plowing and fattening to the mechanized thing of today—linking up with elevators and railroads—is a history of revolutions. So is the history of the productive apparatus of the iron and steel industry from the charcoal furnace to our own type of furnace, or the history of the apparatus of power production from the overshot water wheel to the modern power plant, or the history of transportation from the mail-coach to the airplane. The opening up of new markets, foreign or domestic, and the organizational development from the craft shop and factory to such concerns as U. S. Steel illustrate the same process of industrial mutation—if I may use that biological term—that incessantly revolutionizes[2] the economic structure *from within*, incessantly destroying the old one, incessantly creating a new one. This process of Creative Destruction is the essential fact about capitalism. It is what capitalism consists in and what every capitalist concern has got to live in. This fact bears upon our problem in two ways.

First, since we are dealing with a process whose every element takes considerable time in revealing its true features and ultimate effects, there is no point in appraising the performance of that process *ex visu* of a given point of time; we must judge its performance over time, as it unfolds through decades or centuries. A system—any system, economic or other—that at *every* given point of time fully utilizes its possibilities to the best advantage may yet in the long run be inferior to a system that does so at *no* given point of time, because the latter's failure to do so may be a condition for the level or speed of ·long-run performance.

Second, since we are dealing with an organic process, analysis of what happens in any particular part of it—say, in an individual concern or industry—may indeed clarify details of mechanism but is inconclusive beyond that. Every piece of business strategy acquires its true significance only against the background of that process ànd

---

[2] Those revolutions are not strictly incessant; they occur in discrete rushes which are separated from each other by spans of comparative quiet. The process as a whole works incessantly however, in the sense that there always is either revolution or absorption of the results of revolution, both together forming what are known as business cycles.

within the situation created by it. It must be seen in its role in the
perennial gale of creative destruction; it cannot be understood irrespective of it or, in fact, on the hypothesis that there is a perennial lull.

But economists who, *ex visu* of a point of time, look for example
at the behavior of an oligopolist industry—an industry which consists of a few big firms—and observe the well-known moves and
countermoves within it that seem to aim at nothing but high prices
and restrictions of output are making precisely that hypothesis. They
accept the data of the momentary situation as if there were no past or
future to it and think that they have understood what there is to
understand if they interpret the behavior of those firms by means of
the principle of maximizing profits with reference to those data. The
usual theorist's paper and the usual government commission's report
practically never try to see that behavior, on the one hand, as a result
of a piece of past history and, on the other hand, as an attempt to
deal with a situation that is sure to change presently—as an attempt
by those firms to keep on their feet, on ground that is slipping away
from under them. In other words, the problem that is usually being
visualized is how capitalism administers existing structures, whereas
the relevant problem is how it creates and destroys them. As long as
this is not recognized, the investigator does a meaningless job. As
soon as it is recognized, his outlook on capitalist practice and its
social results changes considerably.[3]

The first thing to go is the traditional conception of the *modus
operandi* of competition. Economists are at long last emerging from
the stage in which price competition was all they saw. As soon as
quality competition and sales effort are admitted into the sacred
precincts of theory, the price variable is ousted from its dominant
position. However, it is still competition within a rigid pattern of
invariant conditions, methods of production and forms of industrial
organization in particular, that practically monopolizes attention.
But in capitalist reality as distinguished from its textbook picture, it
is not that kind of competition which counts but the competition
from the new commodity, the new technology, the new source of
supply, the new type of organization (the largest-scale unit of control
for instance)—competition which commands a decisive cost or quality
advantage and which strikes not at the margins of the profits and the
outputs of the existing firms but at their foundations and their very
lives. This kind of competition is as much more effective than the
other as a bombardment is in comparison with forcing a door, and

---

[3] It should be understood that it is only our appraisal of economic performance
and not our moral judgment that can be so changed. Owing to its autonomy, moral
approval or disapproval is entirely independent of our appraisal of social (or any
other) results, unless we happen to adopt a moral system such as utilitarianism

which makes moral approval and disapproval turn on them *ex definitione*.

so much more important that it becomes a matter of comparative indifference whether competition in the ordinary sense functions more or less promptly; the powerful lever that in the long run expands output and brings down prices is in any case made of other stuff.

It is hardly necessary to point out that competition of the kind we now have in mind acts not only when in being but also when it is merely an ever-present threat. It disciplines before it attacks. The businessman feels himself to be in a competitive situation even if he is alone in his field or if, though not alone, he holds a position such that investigating government experts fail to see any effective competition between him and any other firms in the same or a neighboring field and in consequence conclude that his talk, under examination, about his competitive sorrows is all make-believe. In many cases, though not in all, this will in the long run enforce behavior very similar to the perfectly competitive pattern.

Many theorists take the opposite view which is best conveyed by an example. Let us assume that there is a certain number of retailers in a neighborhood who try to improve their relative position by service and "atmosphere" but avoid price competition and stick as to methods to the local tradition—a picture of stagnating routine. As others drift into the trade that quasi-equilibrium is indeed upset, but in a manner that does not benefit their customers. The economic space around each of the shops having been narrowed, their owners will no longer be able to make a living and they will try to mend the case by raising prices in tacit agreement. This will further reduce their sales and so, by successive pyramiding, a situation will evolve in which increasing potential supply will be attended by increasing instead of decreasing prices and by decreasing instead of increasing sales.

Such cases do occur, and it is right and proper to work them out. But as the practical instances usually given show, they are fringe-end cases to be found mainly in the sectors furthest removed from all that is most characteristic of capitalist activity.[4] Moreover, they are transient by nature. In the case of retail trade the competition that matters arises not from additional shops of the same type, but from the department store, the chain store, the mail-order house and the supermarket which are bound to destroy those pyramids sooner or later.[5]

---

[4] This is also shown by a theorem we frequently meet with in expositions of the theory of imperfect competition, viz., the theorem that, under conditions of imperfect competition, producing or trading businesses tend to be irrationally small. Since imperfect competition is at the same time held to be an outstanding characteristic of modern industry we are set to wondering what world these theorists live in, unless, as stated above, fringe-end cases are all they have in mind.

[5] The mere threat of their attack cannot, in the particular conditions, environmental and personal, of small-scale retail trade, have its usual disciplining influence, for the small man is too much hampered by his cost structure and, however

Now a theoretical construction which neglects this essential element of the case neglects all that is most typically capitalist about it; even if correct in logic as well as in fact, it is like *Hamlet* without the Danish prince.

---

well he may manage within his inescapable limitations, he can never adapt himself to the methods of competitors who can afford to sell at the price at which he buys.

CHAPTER VIII

MONOPOLISTIC PRACTICES

WHAT has been said so far is really sufficient to enable the reader to deal with the large majority of the practical cases he is likely to meet and to realize the inadequacy of most of those criticisms of the profit economy which, directly or indirectly, rely on the absence of perfect competition. Since, however, the bearing of our argument on some of those criticisms may not be obvious at a glance, it will be worth our while to elaborate a little in order to make a few points more explicit.

1. We have just seen that, both as a fact and as a threat, the impact of new things—new technologies for instance—on the existing structure of an industry considerably reduces the long-run scope and importance of practices that aim, through restricting output, at conserving established positions and at maximizing the profits accruing from them. We must now recognize the further fact that restrictive practices of this kind, as far as they are effective, acquire a new significance in the perennial gale of creative destruction, a significance which they would not have in a stationary state or in a state of slow and balanced growth. In either of these cases restrictive strategy would produce no result other than an increase in profits at the expense of buyers except that, in the case of balanced advance, it might still prove to be the easiest and most effective way of collecting the means by which to finance additional investment.[1] But in the process of creative destruction, restrictive practices may do much to steady the ship and to alleviate temporary difficulties. This is in fact a very familiar argument which always turns up in times of depression and, as everyone knows, has become very popular with governments and their economic advisers—witness the NRA. While it has been so much misused and so faultily acted upon that most economists heartily despise it, those

[1] Theorists are apt to look upon anyone who admits this possibility as guilty of gross error, and to prove immediately that financing by borrowing from banks or from private savers or, in the case of public enterprise, financing from the proceeds of an income tax is much more rational than is financing from surplus profits collected through a restrictive policy. For some patterns of behavior they are quite right. For others they are quite wrong. I believe that both capitalism and communism of the Russian type belong in the latter category. But the point is that theoretical considerations, especially theoretical considerations of the short-run kind, cannot solve, although they contribute to the solution of, the problem which we shall meet again in the next part.

same advisers who are responsible for this[2] invariably fail to see its much more general rationale.

Practically any investment entails, as a necessary complement of entrepreneurial action, certain safeguarding activities such as insuring or hedging. Long-range investing under rapidly changing conditions, especially under conditions that change or may change at any moment under the impact of new commodities and technologies, is like shooting at a target that is not only indistinct but moving—and moving jerkily at that. Hence it becomes necessary to resort to such protecting devices as patents or temporary secrecy of processes or, in some cases, long-period contracts secured in advance. But these protecting devices which most economists accept as normal elements of rational management[3] are only special cases of a larger class comprising many others which most economists condemn although they do not differ fundamentally from the recognized ones.

If for instance a war risk is insurable, nobody objects to a firm's collecting the cost of this insurance from the buyers of its products. But that risk is no less an element in long-run costs, if there are no facilities for insuring against it, in which case a price strategy aiming at the same end will seem to involve unnecessary restriction and to be productive of excess profits. Similarly, if a patent cannot be secured or would not, if secured, effectively protect, other means may have to be used in order to justify the investment. Among them are a price policy that will make it possible to write off more quickly than would otherwise be rational, or additional investment in order to provide excess capacity to be used only for aggression or defense. Again, if long-period contracts cannot be entered into in advance, other means may have to be devised in order to tie prospective customers to the investing firm.

In analyzing such business strategy *ex visu* of a given point of time, the investigating economist or government agent sees price policies that seem to him predatory and restrictions of output that seem to him synonymous with loss of opportunities to produce. He does not see that restrictions of this type are, in the conditions of the perennial gale, incidents, often unavoidable incidents, of a long-run process of expansion which they protect rather than impede. There is no more of paradox in this than there is in saying that motorcars are traveling faster than they otherwise would *because* they are provided with brakes.

[2] In particular, it is easy to show that there is no sense, and plenty of harm, in a policy that aims at preserving "price parities."

[3] Some economists, however, consider that even those devices are obstructions to progress which, though perhaps necessary in capitalist society, would be absent in a socialist one. There is some truth in this. But that does not affect the proposition that the protection afforded by patents and so on is, in the conditions of a profit economy, on balance a propelling and not an inhibiting factor.

2. This stands out most clearly in the case of those sectors of the economy which at any time happen to embody the impact of new things and methods on the existing industrial structure. The best way of getting a vivid and realistic idea of industrial strategy is indeed to visualize the behavior of new concerns or industries that introduce new commodities or processes (such as the aluminum industry) or else reorganize a part or the whole of an industry (such as, for instance, the old Standard Oil Company).

As we have seen, such concerns are aggressors by nature and wield the really effective weapon of competition. Their intrusion can only in the rarest of cases fail to improve total output in quantity or quality, both through the new method itself—even if at no time used to full advantage—and through the pressure it exerts on the preexisting firms. But these aggressors are so circumstanced as to require, for purposes of attack and defense, also pieces of armor other than price and quality of their product which, moreover, must be strategically manipulated all along so that at any point of time they seem to be doing nothing but restricting their output and keeping prices high.

On the one hand, largest-scale plans could in many cases not materialize at all if it were not known from the outset that competition will be discouraged by heavy capital requirements or lack of experience, or that means are available to discourage or checkmate it so as to gain the time and space for further developments. Even the conquest of financial control over competing concerns in otherwise unassailable positions or the securing of advantages that run counter to the public's sense of fair play—railroad rebates—move, as far as long-run effects on total output alone are envisaged, into a different light;[4] they *may* be methods for removing obstacles that the institution of private property puts in the path of progress. In a socialist society that time and space would be no less necessary. They would have to be secured by order of the central authority.

On the other hand, enterprise would in most cases be impossible if

[4] The qualification added removes, I think, any just cause for offense that the above proposition might conceivably cause. In case that qualification is not explicit enough, I beg leave to repeat that the moral aspect is in this case, as it must be in every case, entirely unaffected by an economic argument. For the rest, let the reader reflect that even in dealing with indubitably criminal actions every civilized judge and every civilized jury take account of the ulterior purpose in pursuit of which a crime has occurred and of the difference it makes whether an action that is a crime has or has not also effects they consider socially desirable.

Another objection would be more to the point. If an enterprise can succeed only by such means, does not that prove in itself that it cannot spell social gain? A very simple argument can be framed in support of this view. But it is subject to a severe *ceteris paribus* proviso. That is to say, it holds for conditions which are just about equivalent to excluding the process of creative destruction—capitalist reality. On reflection, it will be seen that the analogy of the practices under discussion with patents is sufficient to show this.

it were not known from the outset that exceptionally favorable situations are likely to arise which if exploited by price, quality and quantity manipulation will produce profits adequate to tide over exceptionally unfavorable situations provided these are similarly managed Again this requires strategy that in the short run is often restrictive. In the majority of successful cases this strategy just manages to serve its purpose. In some cases, however, it is so successful as to yield profits far above what is necessary in order to induce the corresponding investment. These cases then provide the baits that lure capital on to untried trails. Their presence explains in part how it is possible for so large a section of the capitalist world to work for nothing: in the midst of the prosperous twenties just about half of the business corporations in the United States were run at a loss, at zero profits, or at profits which, if they had been foreseen, would have been inadequate to call forth the effort and expenditure involved.

Our argument however extends beyond the cases of new concerns, methods and industries. Old concerns and established industries, whether or not directly attacked, still live in the perennial gale. Situations emerge in the process of creative destruction in which many firms may have to perish that nevertheless would be able to live on vigorously and usefully if they could weather a particular storm. Short of such general crises or depressions, sectional situations arise in which the rapid change of data that is characteristic of that process so disorganizes an industry for the time being as to inflict functionless losses and to create avoidable unemployment. Finally, there is certainly no point in trying to conserve obsolescent industries indefinitely; but there is point in trying to avoid their coming down with a crash and in attempting to turn a rout, which may become a center of cumulative depressive effects, into orderly retreat. Correspondingly there is, in the case of industries that have sown their wild oats but are still gaining and not losing ground, such a thing as orderly advance.[5]

[5] A good example illustrative of this point—in fact of much of our general argument—is the postwar history of the automobile and the rayon industry. The first illustrates very well the nature and value of what we might call "edited" competition. The bonanza time was over by about 1916. A host of firms nevertheless crowded into the industry afterwards, most of which were eliminated by 1925. From a fierce life and death struggle three concerns emerged that by now account for over 80 per cent of total sales. They are under competitive pressure inasmuch as, in spite of the advantages of an established position, an elaborate sales and service organization and so on, any failure to keep up and improve the quality of their products or any attempt at monopolistic combination would call in new competitors. Among themselves, the three concerns behave in a way which should be called corespective rather than competitive: they refrain from certain aggressive devices (which, by the way, would also be absent in perfect competition); they keep up with each other and in doing so play for points at the frontiers. This has now gone on for upwards of fifteen years and it is not obvious that if conditions of theoretically perfect competition had prevailed during that period, better

All this is of course nothing but the tritest common sense. But it is being overlooked with a persistence so stubborn as sometimes to raise the question of sincerity. And it follows that, within the process of creative destruction, all the realities of which theorists are in the habit of relegating to books and courses on business cycles, there is another side to industrial self-organization than that which these theorists are contemplating. "Restraints of trade" of the cartel type as well as those which merely consist in tacit understandings about price competition may be effective remedies under conditions of depression. As far as they are, they may in the end produce not only steadier but also greater expansion of total output than could be secured by an entirely uncontrolled onward rush that cannot fail to be studded with catastrophes. Nor can it be argued that these catastrophes occur in any case. We know what has happened in each historical case. We have a very imperfect idea of what might have happened, considering the tremendous pace of the process, if such pegs had been entirely absent.

Even as now extended however, our argument does not cover all cases of restrictive or regulating strategy, many of which no doubt have that injurious effect on the long-run development of output which is uncritically attributed to all of them. And even in the cases our argument does cover, the net effect is a question of the circumstances and of the way in which and the degree to which industry regulates itself in each individual case. It is certainly as conceivable that an all-pervading cartel system might sabotage all progress as it is that it might realize, with smaller social and private costs, all that perfect competition is supposed to realize. This is why our argument does not amount to a case against state regulation. It does show that there is no general case for indiscriminate "trust-busting" or for the prosecution of everything that qualifies as a restraint of trade. Rational as distinguished from vindictive regulation by public authority turns out to be an extremely delicate problem which not every government agency, particularly when in full cry against big business, can be trusted to solve.[6] But our argument, framed to refute a preva-

---

or cheaper cars would now be offered to the public, or higher wages and more or steadier employment to the workmen. The rayon industry had its bonanza time in the twenties. It presents the features incident to introducing a commodity into fields fully occupied before and the policies that impose themselves in such conditions still more clearly than does the automobile industry. And there are a number of other differences. But fundamentally the case is similar. The expansion in quantity and quality of rayon output is common knowledge. Yet restrictive policy presided over this expansion at each individual point of time.

[6] Unfortunately, this statement is almost as effective a bar to agreement on policy as the most thoroughgoing denial of any case for government regulation could be. In fact it may embitter discussion. Politicians, public officers and economists can stand what I may politely term the whole-hog opposition of "economic royalists." Doubts about their competence, such as crowd upon us particularly when we see the legal mind at work, are much more difficult for them to stand.

lent *theory* and the inferences drawn therefrom about the relation between modern capitalism and the development of total output, only yields another *theory*, i.e., another outlook on facts and another principle by which to interpret them. For our purpose that is enough. For the rest, the facts themselves have the floor.

3. Next, a few words on the subject of Rigid Prices which has been receiving so much attention of late. It really is but a particular aspect of the problem we have been discussing. We shall define rigidity as follows: a price is rigid if it is less sensitive to changes in the conditions of demand and supply than it would be if perfect competition prevailed.[7]

Quantitatively, the extent to which prices are rigid in that sense depends on the material and the method of measurement we select and is hence a doubtful matter. But whatever the material or method, it is certain that prices are not nearly as rigid as they seem to be. There are many reasons why what in effect is a change in price should not show in the statistical picture; in other words, why there should be much spurious rigidity. I shall mention only one class of them which is closely connected with the facts stressed by our analysis.

I have adverted to the importance, for the capitalist process in general and for its competitive mechanism in particular, of the intrusion of new commodities. Now a new commodity may effectively bring down the preexisting structure and satisfy a given want at much lower prices per unit of service (transportation service for instance), and yet not a single recorded price need change in the process; flexibility in the relevant sense may be accompanied by rigidity in a formal sense. There are other cases, not of this type, in which price reduction is the sole motive for bringing out a new brand while the old one is left at the previous quotation—again a price reduction that does not show. Moreover, the great majority of new consumers' goods—particularly all the gadgets of modern life—are at first introduced in an experimental and unsatisfactory form in which they could never conquer their potential markets. Improvement in the quality of products is hence a practically universal feature of the development of individual concerns and of industries. Whether or not this improvement involves additional costs, a constant price per unit of an improving commodity should not be called rigid without further investigation.

Of course, plenty of cases of genuine price rigidity remain—of

[7] This definition suffices for our purposes but would not be satisfactory for others. See D. D. Humphrey's article in the *Journal of Political Economy*, October 1937, and E. S. Mason's article in the *Review of Economic Statistics*, May 1938. Professor Mason has shown, among other things, that contrary to a widespread belief price rigidity is not increasing or, at all events, that it is no greater than it was forty years ago, a result which in itself suffices to invalidate some of the implications of the current doctrine of rigidity.

prices which are being kept constant as a matter of business policy or which remain unchanged because it is difficult to change, say, a price set by a cartel after laborious negotiations. In order to appraise the influence of this fact on the long-run development of output, it is first of all necessary to realize that this rigidity is essentially a short-run phenomenon. There are no major instances of long-run rigidity of prices. Whichever manufacturing industry or group of manufactured articles of any importance we choose to investigate over a period of time, we practically always find that in the long run prices do not fail to adapt themselves to technological progress—frequently they fall spectacularly in response to it[8]—unless prevented from doing so by monetary events and policies or, in some cases, by autonomous changes in wage rates which of course should be taken into account by appropriate corrections exactly as should changes in quality of products.[9] And our previous analysis shows sufficiently why in the process of capitalist evolution this must be so.

What the business strategy in question really aims at—all, in any case, that it can achieve—is to avoid seasonal, random and cyclical fluctuations in prices and to move only in response to the more fundamental changes in the conditions that underlie those fluctuations. Since these more fundamental changes take time in declaring themselves, this involves moving slowly by discrete steps—keeping to a price until new relatively durable contours have emerged into view. In technical language, this strategy aims at moving along a step function that will approximate trends. And that is what genuine and voluntary price rigidity in most cases amounts to. In fact, most economists do admit this, at least by implication. For though some of their arguments about rigidity would hold true only if the phenomenon were a long-run one—for instance most of the arguments averring that price rigidity keeps the fruits of technological progress from consumers—in practice they measure and discuss primarily cyclical rigidity and especially the fact that many prices do not, or do not promptly, fall in recessions and depressions. The real question is there-

[8] They do not as a rule fall as they would under conditions of perfect competition. But this is true only *ceteris paribus*, and this proviso robs the proposition of all practical importance. I have adverted to this point before and shall return to it below (§ 5).

[9] From a welfare standpoint, it is proper to adopt a definition different from ours, and to measure price changes in terms of the hours of labor that are currently necessary to earn the dollars which will buy given quantities of manufactured consumers' goods, taking account of changes of quality. We have already done this in the course of a previous argument. A long-run downward flexibility is then revealed that is truly impressive. Changes in price level raise another problem. So far as they reflect monetary influences they should be eliminated for most of the purposes of an investigation into rigidity. But so far as they reflect the combined effect of increasing efficiencies in all lines of production they should not.

fore how this short-run rigidity[10] may affect the long-run development of total output. Within this question, the only really important issue is this: prices that stay up in recession or depression no doubt influence the business situation in those phases of the cycles; if that influence is strongly injurious—making matters much worse than they would be with perfect flexibility all round—the destruction wrought each time might also affect output in the subsequent recoveries and prosperities and thus permanently reduce the rate of increase in total output below what it would be in the absence of those rigidities. Two arguments have been put forth in favor of this view.

In order to put the first into the strongest possible light, let us assume that an industry which refuses to reduce prices in recession goes on selling exactly the same quantity of product which it would sell if it had reduced them. Buyers are therefore out of pocket by the amount to which the industry profits from the rigidity. If these buyers are the kind of people who spend all they can and if the industry or those to whom its net returns go does not spend the increment it gets but either keeps it idle or repays bank loans, then total expenditure in the economy may be reduced thereby. If this happens, other industries or firms may suffer and if thereupon they restrict in turn, we may get a cumulation of depressive effects. In other words, rigidity may so influence the amount and distribution of national income as to decrease balances or to increase idle balances or, if we adopt a popular misnomer, savings. Such a case is conceivable. But the reader should have little difficulty in satisfying himself[11] that its practical importance, if any, is very small.

The second argument turns on the dislocating effects price rigidity may exert if, in the individual industry itself or elsewhere, it leads to an additional restriction of output, i.e., to a restriction greater than that which must in any case occur during depression. Since the most important conductor of those effects is the incident increase in unemployment—unstabilization of employment is in fact the indict-

[10] It should, however, be observed that this short run may last longer than the term "short run" usually implies—sometimes ten years and even longer. There is not one cycle, but there are many simultaneous ones of varying duration. One of the most important ones lasts on the average about nine years and a half. Structural changes requiring price adjustments do in important cases occur in periods of about that length. The full extent of the spectacular changes reveals itself only in periods much longer than this. To do justice to aluminum, rayon, or motorcar prices one must survey a period of about forty-five years.

[11] The best method of doing this is to work out carefully *all* the assumptions involved, not only in the strong case imagined but also in the weaker cases that are less unlikely to occur in practice. Moreover, it should not be forgotten that the profit due to keeping prices up may be the means of avoiding bankruptcy or at least the necessity of discontinuing operations, both of which might be much more effective in starting a downward "vicious spiral" than is a possible reduction in total expenditure. See the comments on the second argument.

ment most commonly directed against price rigidity—and the consequent decrease in total expenditure, this argument then follows in the tracks of the first one. Its practical weight is considerably reduced, although economists greatly differ as to the extent, by the consideration that in the most conspicuous cases price rigidity is motivated precisely by the low sensitiveness of demand to short-run price changes within the practicable range. People who in depression worry about their future are not likely to buy a new car even if the price were reduced by 25 per cent, especially if the purchase is easily postponable and if the reduction induces expectations of further reductions.

Quite irrespective of this however, the argument is inconclusive because it is again vitiated by a *ceteris paribus* clause that is inadmissible in dealing with our process of creative destruction. From the fact, so far as it is a fact, that at more flexible prices greater quantities could *ceteris paribus* be sold, it does not follow that either the output of the commodities in question, or total output and hence employment, would actually be greater. For inasmuch as we may assume that the refusal to lower prices strengthens the position of the industries which adopt that policy either by increasing their revenue or simply by avoiding chaos in their markets—that is to say, so far as this policy is something more than a mistake on their part—it may make fortresses out of what otherwise might be centers of devastation. As we have seen before, from a more general standpoint, total output and employment may well keep on a higher level with the restrictions incident to that policy than they would if depression were allowed to play havoc with the price structure.[12] In other words, under the conditions created by capitalist evolution, perfect and universal flexibility of prices might in depression further unstabilize the system, instead of stabilizing it as it no doubt would under the conditions envisaged by general theory. Again this is to a large extent recognized in those cases in which the economist is in sympathy with the interests immediately concerned, for instance in the case of labor and of agriculture; in those cases he admits readily enough that what looks like rigidity may be no more than regulated adaptation.

Perhaps the reader feels some surprise that so little remains of a doctrine of which so much has been made in the last few years. The rigidity of prices has become, with some people, the outstanding defect of the capitalist engine and—almost—the fundamental factor in the explanation of depressions. But there is nothing to wonder at in this. Individuals and groups snatch at anything that will qualify as a discovery lending support to the political tendencies of the hour. The

[12] The theorist's way to put the point is that in depression demand curves might shift downwards much more violently if all pegs were withdrawn from under all prices.

doctrine of price rigidity, with a modicum of truth to its credit, is not the worst case of this kind by a long way.

4. Another doctrine has crystallized into a slogan, viz., that in the era of big business the maintenance of the value of existing investment—conservation of capital—becomes the chief aim of entrepreneurial activity and bids fair to put a stop to all cost-reducing improvement. Hence the capitalist order becomes incompatible with progress.

Progress entails, as we have seen, destruction of capital values in the strata with which the new commodity or method of production competes. In perfect competition the old investments must be adapted at a sacrifice or abandoned; but when there is no perfect competition and when each industrial field is controlled by a few big concerns, these can in various ways fight the threatening attack on their capital structure and try to avoid losses on their capital accounts; that is to say, they can and will fight progress itself.

So far as this doctrine merely formulates a particular aspect of restrictive business strategy, there is no need to add anything to the argument already sketched in this chapter. Both as to the limits of that strategy and as to its functions in the process of creative destruction, we should only be repeating what has been said before. This becomes still more obvious if we observe that conserving capital values is the same thing as conserving profits. Modern theory tends in fact to use the concept Present Net Value of Assets (= capital values) in place of the concept of Profits. Both asset values and profits are of course not being simply conserved but maximized.

But the point about the sabotage of cost-reducing improvement still calls for comment in passing. As a little reflection will show, it is sufficient to consider the case of a concern that controls a technological device—some patent, say—the use of which would involve scrapping some or all of its plant and equipment. Will it, in order to conserve its capital values, refrain from using this device when a management not fettered by capitalist interests such as a socialist management could and would use it to the advantage of all?

Again it is tempting to raise the question of fact. The first thing a modern concern does as soon as it feels that it can afford it is to establish a research department every member of which knows that his bread and butter depends on his success in devising improvements. This practice does not obviously suggest aversion to technological progress. Nor can we in reply be referred to the cases in which patents acquired by business concerns have not been used promptly or not been used at all. For there may be perfectly good reasons for this; for example, the patented process may turn out to be no good or at least not to be in shape to warrant application on a commercial basis. Neither the inventors themselves nor the investigating economists or government officials are unbiased judges of this, and from their remonstrances or reports we may easily get a very distorted picture.[13]

But we are concerned with a question of theory. Everyone agrees that private and socialist managements will introduce improvements if, with the new method of production, the total cost per unit of product is expected to be smaller than the prime cost per unit of product with the method actually in use. If this condition is not fulfilled, then it is held that private management will not adopt a cost-reducing method until the existing plant and equipment is entirely written off, whereas socialist management would, to the social advantage, replace the old by any new cost-reducing method as soon as such a method becomes available, i.e., without regard to capital values. This however is not so.[14]

Private management, if actuated by the profit motive, cannot be interested in maintaining the values of any given building or machine any more than a socialist management would be. All that private management tries to do is to maximize the present net value of total assets which is equal to the discounted value of expected net returns. This amounts to saying that it will always adopt a new method of production which it believes will yield a larger stream of future income per unit of the corresponding stream of future outlay, both discounted to the present, than does the method actually in use. The value of past investment, whether or not paralleled by a bonded debt that has to be amortized, does not enter at all except in the sense and to the extent that it would also have to enter into the calculation underlying the decisions of a socialist management. So far as the use of the old machines saves future costs as compared with the immediate introduction of the new methods, the remainder of their service value is of course an element of the decision for both the capitalist and the socialist manager; otherwise bygones are bygones for both of them and any attempt to conserve the value of past investment would conflict as much with the rules following from the profit motive as it would conflict with the rules set for the behavior of the socialist manager.

---

[13] Incidentally, it should be noticed that the kind of restrictive practice under discussion, granted that it exists to a significant extent, would not be without compensatory effects on social welfare. In fact, the same critics who talk about sabotage of progress at the same time emphasize the *social* losses incident to the pace of capitalist progress, particularly the unemployment which that pace entails and which slower advance might mitigate to some extent. Well, is technological progress too quick or too slow for them? They had better make up their minds.

[14] It should be observed that even if the argument were correct, it would still be inadequate to support the thesis that capitalism is, under the conditions envisaged, "incompatible with technological progress." All that it would prove is, for some cases, the presence of a lag of ordinarily moderate length in the introduction of new methods.

It is however not true that private firms owning equipment the value of which is endangered by a new method which they also control—if they do not control it, there is no problem and no indictment—will adopt the new method only if total unit cost with it is smaller than prime unit cost with the old one, or if the old investment has been completely written off *according to the schedule decided on before the new method presented itself.* For if the new machines when installed are expected to outlive the rest of the period previously set for the use of the old machines, their discounted remainder value as of that date is another asset to be taken account of. Nor is it true, for analogous reasons, that a socialist management, if acting rationally, would always and immediately adopt any new method which promises to produce at smaller total unit costs or that this would be to the social advantage.

There is however another element[15] which profoundly affects behavior in this matter and which is being invariably overlooked. This is what might be called *ex ante* conservation of capital in expectation of further improvement. Frequently, if not in most cases, a going concern does not simply face the question whether or not to adopt a definite new method of production that is the best thing out and, in the form immediately available, can be expected to retain that position for some length of time. A new type of machine is in general but a link in a chain of improvements and may presently become obsolete. In a case like this it would obviously not be rational to follow the chain link by link regardless of the capital loss to be suffered each time. The real question then is at which link the concern should take action. The answer must be in the nature of a compromise between considerations that rest largely on guesses. But it will as a rule involve some waiting in order to see how the chain behaves. And to the outsider this may well look like trying to stifle improvement in order to conserve *existing* capital values. Yet even the most patient of comrades would revolt if a socialist management were so foolish as to follow the advice of the theorist and to keep on scrapping plant and equipment every year.

5. I have entitled this chapter as I did because most of it deals with the facts and problems that common parlance associates with monopoly or monopolistic practice. So far I have as much as possible refrained from using those terms in order to reserve for a separate section some comments on a few topics specifically connected with them. Nothing will be said however that we have not already met in one form or another.

(a) To begin with, there is the term itself. Monopolist means Single

---

[15] There are of course many other elements. The reader will please understand that in dealing with a few questions of principles it is impossible to do full justice to any of the topics touched upon.

Seller. Literally therefore anyone is a monopolist who sells anything that is not in every respect, wrapping and location and service included, exactly like what other people sell: every grocer, or every haberdasher, or every seller of "Good Humors" on a road that is not simply lined with sellers of the same brand of ice cream. This however is not what we mean when talking about monopolists. We mean only those single sellers whose markets are not open to the intrusion of would-be producers of the same commodity and of actual producers of similar ones or, speaking slightly more technically, only those single sellers who face a given demand schedule that is severely independent of their own action as well as of any reactions to their action by other concerns. The traditional Cournot-Marshall theory of monopoly as extended and amended by later authors holds only if we define it in this way and there is, so it seems, no point in calling anything a monopoly to which that theory does not apply.

But if accordingly we do define it like this, then it becomes evident immediately that pure cases of long-run monopoly must be of the rarest occurrence and that even tolerable approximations to the requirements of the concept must be still rarer than are cases of perfect competition. The power to exploit at pleasure a given pattern of demand—or one that changes independently of the monopolist's action and of the reactions it provokes—can under the conditions of intact capitalism hardly persist for a period long enough to matter for the analysis of total output, unless buttressed by public authority, for instance, in the case of fiscal monopolies. A modern business concern not *so* protected—i.e., even if protected by import duties or import prohibitions—and yet wielding that power (except temporarily) is not easy to find or even to imagine. Even railroads and power and light concerns had first to create the demand for their services and, when they had done so, to defend their market against competition. Outside the field of public utilities, the position of a single seller can in general be conquered—and retained for decades—only on the condition that he does not behave like a monopolist. Short-run monopoly will be touched upon presently.

Why then all this talk about monopoly? The answer is not without interest for the student of the psychology of political discussion. Of course, the concept of monopoly is being loosely used just like any other. People speak of a country's having a monopoly of something or other[16] even if the industry in question is highly competitive and so

[16] These so-called monopolies have of late come to the fore in connection with the proposal to withhold certain materials from aggressor nations. The lessons of this discussion have some bearing upon our problem by way of analogy. At first, much was thought of the possibilities of that weapon. Then, on looking more closely at it, people found their lists of such materials to be shrinking, because it became increasingly clear that there are very few things that cannot be either produced or substituted for in the areas in question. And finally a suspicion began

on. But this is not all. Economists, government agents, journalists and politicians in this country obviously love the word because it has come to be a term of opprobrium which is sure to rouse the public's hostility against any interest so labeled. In the Anglo-American world monopoly has been cursed and associated with functionless exploitation ever since, in the sixteenth and seventeenth centuries, it was English administrative practice to create monopoly positions in large numbers which, on the one hand, answered fairly well to the theoretical pattern of monopolist behavior and, on the other hand, fully justified the wave of indignation that impressed even the great Elizabeth.

Nothing is so retentive as a nation's memory. Our time offers other and more important instances of a nation's reaction to what happened centuries ago. That practice made the English-speaking public so monopoly-conscious that it acquired a habit of attributing to that sinister power practically everything it disliked about business. To the typical liberal bourgeois in particular, monopoly became the father of almost all abuses—in fact, it became his pet bogey. Adam Smith,[17] thinking primarily of monopolies of the Tudor and Stuart type, frowned on them in awful dignity. Sir Robert Peel—who like most conservatives occasionally knew how to borrow from the arsenal of the demagogue—in his famous epilogue to his last period of office that gave so much offense to his associates, spoke of a monopoly of bread or wheat, though English grain production was of course perfectly competitive in spite of protection.[18] And in this country monopoly is being made practically synonymous with any large-scale business.

(b) The theory of simple and discriminating monopoly teaches that, excepting a limiting case, monopoly price is higher and monopoly output smaller than competitive price and competitive output. This is true provided that the method and organization of production—and everything else—are exactly the same in both cases. Actually how-

to dawn to the effect that even though some pressure can be exerted on them in the short run, long-run developments might eventually destroy practically all that was left on the lists.

[17] There was more excuse for that uncritical attitude in the case of Adam Smith and the classics in general than there is in the case of their successors because big business in our sense had not then emerged. But even so they went too far. In part this was due to the fact that they had no satisfactory theory of monopoly which induced them not only to apply the term rather promiscuously (Adam Smith and even Senior interpreted for instance the rent of land as a monopoly gain) but also to look upon the monopolists' power of exploitation as practically unlimited which is of course wrong even for the most extreme cases.

[18] This instance illustrates the way in which the term keeps on creeping into illegitimate uses. Protection of agriculture and a monopoly of agrarian products are entirely different things. The struggle was over protection and not over a nonexistent cartel of either landowners or farmers. But in fighting protection it was just as well to beat up for applause. And there was evidently no simpler means of doing so than by calling protectionists monopolists.

ever there are superior methods available to the monopolist which either are not available at all to a crowd of competitors or are not available to them so readily: for there are advantages which, though not strictly unattainable on the competitive level of enterprise, are as a matter of fact secured only on the monopoly level, for instance, because monopolization may increase the sphere of influence of the better, and decrease the sphere of influence of the inferior, brains,[19] or because the monopoly enjoys a disproportionately higher financial standing. Whenever this is so, then that proposition is no longer true. In other words, this element of the case for competition may fail completely because monopoly prices are not necessarily higher or monopoly outputs smaller than competitive prices and outputs would be at the levels of productive and organizational efficiency that are within the reach of the type of firm compatible with the competitive hypothesis.

There cannot be any reasonable doubt that under the conditions of our epoch such superiority is as a matter of fact the outstanding feature of the typical large-scale unit of control, though mere size is neither necessary nor sufficient for it. These units not only arise in the process of creative destruction and function in a way entirely different from the static schema, but in many cases of decisive importance they provide the necessary form for the achievement. They largely create what they exploit. Hence the usual conclusion about their influence on long-run output would be invalid even if they were genuine monopolies in the technical sense of the term.

Motivation is quite immaterial. Even if the opportunity to set monopolist prices were the sole object, the pressure of the improved methods or of a huge apparatus would in general tend to shift the point of the monopolist's optimum toward or beyond the competitive cost price in the above sense, thus doing the work—partly, wholly, or more than wholly—of the competitive mechanism,[20] *even if re-*

[19] The reader should observe that while, as a broad rule, that particular type of superiority is simply indisputable, the inferior brains, especially if their owners are entirely eliminated, are not likely to admit it and that the public's and the recording economists' hearts go out to them and not to the others. This may have something to do with a tendency to discount the cost or quality advantages of quasi-monopolist combination that is at present as pronounced as was the exaggeration of them in the typical prospectus or announcement of sponsors of such combinations.

[20] The Aluminum Company of America is not a monopoly in the technical sense as defined above, among other reasons because it had to build up its demand schedule, which fact suffices to exclude a behavior conforming to the Cournot-Marshall schema. But most economists call it so and in the dearth of genuine cases we will for the purposes of this note do the same. From 1890 to 1929 the price of the basic product of this single seller fell to about 12 per cent or, correcting for the change in price level (B.L.S. index of wholesale prices), to about 8.8 per cent. Output rose from 30 metric tons to 103,400. Protection by patent ceased in 1909. Argument from costs and profits in criticism of this "monopoly" must

striction is practiced and excess capacity is in evidence all along. Of course if the methods of production, organization and so on are not improved by or in connection with monopolization as is the case with an ordinary cartel, the classical theorem about monopoly price and output comes into its own again.[21] So does another popular idea, viz., that monopolization has a soporific effect. For this, too, it is not difficult to find examples. But no general theory should be built upon it. For, especially in manufacturing industry, a monopoly position is in general no cushion to sleep on. As it can be gained, so it can be retained only by alertness and energy. What soporific influence there is in modern business is due to another cause that will be mentioned later.

(c) In the short run, genuine monopoly positions or positions approximating monopoly are much more frequent. The grocer in a village on the Ohio may be a true monopolist for hours or even days during an inundation. Every successful corner may spell monopoly for the moment. A firm specializing in paper labels for beer bottles may be so circumstanced—potential competitors realizing that what seem to be good profits would be immediately destroyed by their entering the field—that it can move at pleasure on a moderate but still finite stretch of the demand curve, at least until the metal label smashes that demand curve to pieces.

New methods of production or new commodities, especially the latter, do not *per se* confer monopoly, even if used or produced by a single firm. The product of the new method has to compete with the products of the old ones and the new commodity has to be introduced, i.e., its demand schedule has to be built up. As a rule neither patents nor monopolistic practices avail against that. But they may in cases of spectacular superiority of the new device, particularly if it can be leased like shoe machinery; or in cases of new commodities, the permanent demand schedule for which has been established before the patent has expired.

Thus it is true that there is or may be an element of genuine monopoly gain in those entrepreneurial profits which are the prizes offered by capitalist society to the successful innovator. But the quantitative importance of that element, its volatile nature and its function in the process in which it emerges put it in a class by itself. The main value to a concern of a single seller position that is secured by patent or monopolistic strategy does not consist so much in the opportunity

---

take it for granted that a multitude of competing firms would have been about equally successful in cost-reducing research, in the economical development of the productive apparatus, in teaching new uses for the product and in avoiding wasteful breakdowns. This is, in fact, being assumed by criticism of this kind; i.e., the propelling factor of modern capitalism is being assumed away.

[21] See however *supra*, § 1.

to behave temporarily according to the monopolist schema, as in the protection it affords against temporary disorganization of the market and the space it secures for long-range planning. Here however the argument merges into the analysis submitted before.

6. Glancing back we realize that most of the facts and arguments touched upon in this chapter tend to dim the halo that once surrounded perfect competition as much as they suggest a more favorable view of its alternative. I will now briefly restate our argument from this angle.

Traditional theory itself, even within its chosen precincts of a stationary or steadily growing economy, has since the time of Marshall and Edgeworth been discovering an increasing number of exceptions to the old propositions about perfect competition and, incidentally, free trade, that have shaken that unqualified belief in its virtues cherished by the generation which flourished between Ricardo and Marshall—roughly, J. S. Mill's generation in England and Francesco Ferrara's on the Continent. Especially the propositions that a perfectly competitive system is ideally economical of resources and allocates them in a way that is optimal with respect to a given distribution of income—propositions very relevant to the question of the behavior of output—cannot now be held with the old confidence.[22]

Much more serious is the breach made by more recent work in the field of dynamic theory (Frisch, Tinbergen, Roos, Hicks and others). Dynamic analysis is the analysis of sequences in time. In explaining why a certain economic quantity, for instance a price, is what we find it to be at a given moment, it takes into consideration not only the state of other economic quantities at the same moment, as static theory does, but also their state at preceding points of time, and the expectations about their future values. Now the first thing we discover in working out the propositions that thus relate quantities belonging to different points of time[23] is the fact that, once equilibrium has been destroyed by some disturbance, the process of establishing a new one is not so sure and prompt and economical as the old theory of perfect competition made it out to be; and the possibility that the very struggle for adjustment might lead such a system farther away from instead of nearer to a new equilibrium. This will happen in most cases unless the disturbance is small. In many cases, lagged adjustment is sufficient to produce this result.

All I can do here is to illustrate by the oldest, simplest and most familiar example. Suppose that demand and *intended* supply are in

[22] Since we cannot enter into the subject, I will refer the reader to Mr. R. F. Kahn's paper entitled "Some Notes on Ideal Output" (*Economic Journal* for March 1935), which covers much of this ground.

[23] The term dynamics is loosely used and carries many different meanings. The above definition was formulated by Ragnar Frisch.

equilibrium in a perfectly competitive market for wheat, but that bad weather reduces the crop below what farmers intended to supply. If price rises accordingly and the farmers thereupon produce that quantity of wheat which it would pay them to produce if that new price were the equilibrium price, then a slump in the wheat market will ensue in the following year. If now the farmers correspondingly restrict production, a price still higher than in the first year may result to induce a still greater expansion of production than occurred in the second year. And so on (as far as the pure logic of the process is concerned) indefinitely. The reader will readily perceive, from a survey of the assumptions involved, that no great fear need be entertained of ever higher prices' and ever greater outputs' alternating till doomsday. But even if reduced to its proper proportions, the phenomenon suffices to show up glaring weaknesses in the mechanism of perfect competition. As soon as this is realized much of the optimism that used to grace the practical implications of the theory of this mechanism passes out through the ivory gate.

But from our standpoint we must go further than that.[24] If we try to visualize how perfect competition works or would work in the process of creative destruction, we arrive at a still more discouraging result. This will not surprise us, considering that all the essential facts of that process are absent from the general schema of economic life that yields the traditional propositions about perfect competition. At the risk of repetition I will illustrate the point once more.

Perfect competition implies free entry into every industry. It is quite true, within that general theory, that free entry into all industries is a condition for optimal allocation of resources and hence for maximizing output. If our economic world consisted of a number of established industries producing familiar commodities by established and substantially invariant methods and if nothing happened except that additional men and additional savings combine in order to set up new firms of the existing type, then impediments to their entry into any industry they wish to enter would spell loss to the community. But perfectly free entry into a *new* field may make it impos-

[24] It should be observed that the defining feature of dynamic theory has nothing to do with the nature of the economic reality to which it is applied. It is a general method of analysis rather than a study of a particular process. We can use it in order to analyze a stationary economy, just as an evolving one can be analyzed by means of the methods of statics ("comparative statics"). Hence dynamic theory need not take, and as a matter of fact has not taken, any special cognizance of the process of creative destruction which we have taken to be the essence of capitalism. It is no doubt better equipped than is static theory to deal with many questions of mechanism that arise in the analysis of that process. But it is not an analysis of that process itself, and it treats the resulting individual disturbances of given states and structures just as it treats other disturbances. To judge the functioning of perfect competition from the standpoint of capitalist evolution is therefore not the same thing as judging it from the standpoint of dynamic theory.

sible to enter it at all. The introduction of new methods of production and new commodities is hardly conceivable with perfect—and perfectly prompt—competition from the start. And this means that the bulk of what we call economic progress is incompatible with it. As a matter of fact, perfect competition is and always has been temporarily suspended whenever anything new is being introduced—automatically or by measures devised for the purpose—even in otherwise perfectly competitive conditions.

Similarly, within the traditional system the usual indictment of rigid prices stands all right. Rigidity is a type of resistance to adaptation that perfect and prompt competition excludes. And for the kind of adaptation and for those conditions which have been treated by traditional theory, it is again quite true that such resistance spells loss and reduced output. But we have seen that in the spurts and vicissitudes of the process of creative destruction the opposite may be true: perfect and instantaneous flexibility may even produce functionless catastrophes. This of course can also be established by the general dynamic theory which, as mentioned above, shows that there are attempts at adaptation that intensify disequilibrium.

Again, under its own assumptions, traditional theory is correct in holding that profits above what is necessary in each individual case to call forth the equilibrium amount of means of production, entrepreneurial ability included, both indicate and in themselves imply net social loss and that business strategy that aims at keeping them alive is inimical to the growth of total output. Perfect competition would prevent or immediately eliminate such surplus profits and leave no room for that strategy. But since in the process of capitalist evolution these profits acquire new organic functions—I do not want to repeat what they are—that fact cannot any longer be unconditionally credited to the account of the perfectly competitive model, so far as the secular rate of increase in total output is concerned.

Finally, it can indeed be shown that, under the same assumptions which amount to excluding the most characteristic features of capitalist reality, a perfectly competitive economy is comparatively free from waste and in particular from those kinds of waste which we most readily associate with its counterpart. But this does not tell us anything about how its account looks under the conditions set by the process of creative destruction.

On the one hand, much of what without reference to those conditions would appear to be unrelieved waste ceases to qualify as such when duly related to them. The type of excess capacity for example that owes its existence to the practice of "building ahead of demand" or to the practice of providing capacity for the cyclical peaks of demand would in a regime of perfect competition be much reduced. But when *all* the facts of the case are taken into consideration, it is no longer correct to say that perfect competition wins out on that score. For though a concern that has to accept and cannot set prices would, in fact, use all of its capacity that can produce at marginal costs covered by the ruling prices, it does not follow that it would ever have the quantity and quality of capacity that big business has created and was able to create precisely because it is in a position to use it "strategically." Excess capacity of this type may—it does in some and does not in other cases—constitute a reason for claiming superiority for a socialist economy. But it should not without qualification be listed as a claim to superiority of the perfectly competitive species of capitalist economy as compared with the "monopoloid" species.

On the other hand, working in the conditions of capitalist evolution, the perfectly competitive arrangement displays wastes of its own. The firm of the type that is compatible with perfect competition is in many cases inferior in internal, especially technological, efficiency. If it is, then it wastes opportunities. It may also in its endeavors to improve its methods of production waste capital because it is in a less favorable position to evolve and to judge new possibilities. And, as we have seen before, a perfectly competitive industry is much more apt to be routed—and to scatter the bacilli of depression—under the impact of progress or of external disturbance than is big business. In the last resort, American agriculture, English coal mining, the English textile industry are costing consumers much more and are affecting *total* output much more injuriously than they would if controlled, each of them, by a dozen good brains.

Thus it is not sufficient to argue that because perfect competition is impossible under modern industrial conditions—or because it always has been impossible—the large-scale establishment or unit of control must be accepted as a necessary evil inseparable from the economic progress which it is prevented from sabotaging by the forces inherent in its productive apparatus. What we have got to accept is that it has come to be the most powerful engine of that progress and in particular of the long-run expansion of total output not only in spite of, but to a considerable extent through, this strategy which looks so restrictive when viewed in the individual case and from the individual point of time. In this respect, perfect competition is not only impossible but inferior, and has no title to being set up as a model of ideal efficiency. It is hence a mistake to base the theory of government regulation of industry on the principle that big business should be made to work as the respective industry would work in perfect competition. And socialists should rely for their criticisms on the virtues of a socialist economy rather than on those of the competitive model.

CHAPTER IX

CLOSED SEASON

I<small>T</small> is for the reader to decide how far the preceding analysis has attained its object. Economics is only an observational and interpretative science which implies that in questions like ours the room for difference of opinion can be narrowed but not reduced to zero. For the same reason the solution of our first problem only leads to the door of another which in an experimental science would not arise at all.

The first problem was to find out whether there is, as I have put it (p. 72), "an understandable relation" between the structural features of capitalism as depicted by various analytic "models" and the economic performance as depicted, for the epoch of intact or relatively unfettered capitalism, by the index of total output. My affirmative answer to this question was based upon an analysis that ran on lines approved by most economists up to the point at which what is usually referred to as the modern tendency toward monopolistic control entered the scene. After that my analysis deviated from the usual lines in an attempt to show that what practically everyone concedes to the capitalism of perfect competition (whether a theoretical construction, or, at some time or other, a historical reality) must also to even a greater degree be conceded to big-business capitalism. Since however we cannot put the driving power and the engine into an experiment station in order to let them perform under carefully controlled conditions, there is no way of proving, beyond the possibility of doubt, their adequacy to produce just that result, viz., the observed development of output. All we can say is that there was a rather striking performance and that the capitalist arrangement was favorable to producing it. And this is precisely why we cannot stop at our conclusion but have to face another problem.

A priori it might still be possible to account for the observed performance by exceptional circumstances which would have asserted themselves in any institutional pattern. The only way to deal with this possibility is to examine the economic and political history of the period in question and to discuss such exceptional circumstances as we may be able to find. We will attack the problem by considering those candidates for the role of exceptional circumstances not inherent in the business processes of capitalism which have been put up by economists or historians. There are five of them.

The first is government action which, though I quite agree with

Marx in holding that politics and policies are not independent factors but elements of the social process we are analyzing, may be considered as a factor external to the world of business for the purposes of this argument. The period from about 1870 to 1914 presents an almost ideal case. It would be difficult to find another equally free from either the stimuli or the depressants that may proceed from the political sector of the social process. The removal of the fetters from entrepreneurial activity and from industry and trade in general had largely been accomplished before. New and different fetters and burdens—social legislation and so on—were being imposed, but nobody will hold that they were major factors in the economic situation before 1914. There were wars. But none of them was economically important enough to exert vital effects one way or another. The Franco-German war that issued in the foundation of the German Empire might suggest a doubt. But the economically relevant event was after all the foundation of the Zollverein. There was armament expenditure. But in the circumstances of the decade ending in 1914 in which it assumed really important dimensions, it was a handicap rather than a stimulus.

The second candidate is gold. It is very fortunate that we need not enter into the thicket of questions that surrounds the *modus operandi* of the new plethora of gold which burst forth from about 1890 on. For since in the first twenty years of the period gold actually was scarce and since the rate of increase in total output was then no smaller than it was later on, gold production cannot have been a major factor in the productive performance of capitalism whatever it might have had to do with prosperities and depressions. The same holds true as regards monetary management which at that time was not of an aggressive but rather of an adaptive type.

Third, there was the increase in population which, whether a cause or a consequence of economic advance, certainly was one of the dominating factors in the economic situation. Unless we are prepared to aver that it was *wholly* consequential and to assume that any variation in output will always entail a corresponding variation in population while refusing to admit the converse nexus, all of which is of course absurd, that factor must be listed as an eligible candidate. For the moment, a brief remark will suffice to clarify the situation.

A greater number of gainfully employed people will in general produce more than a smaller number would whatever the social organization. Hence, if any part of the actual rate of increase in population during that epoch can be assumed—as of course it can—to have occurred independently of the results produced by the capitalist system in the sense that it would have occurred under any system, population must to that extent be listed as an external factor. To the same extent, the observed increase in total output does not measure, but exaggerates, capitalist performance.

Other things being equal, however, a greater number of gainfully employed people will in general produce less per head of employed or of population than a somewhat smaller number would whatever the social organization. This follows from the fact that the greater the number of workers, the smaller will be the amount of other factors with which the individual worker cooperates.[1] Hence, if output per head of population is chosen for measuring capitalist performance, then the observed increased is apt to understate the actual achievement, because part of this achievement has all along been absorbed in compensating for the fall in per capita output that would have occurred in its absence. Other aspects of the problem will be considered later on.

The fourth and fifth candidates command more support among economists but can easily be dismissed as long as we are dealing with past performance. The one is new land. The wide expanse of land that, economically speaking, entered the Americo-European sphere during that period; the huge mass of foodstuffs and raw materials, agricultural and other, that poured forth from it; all the cities and industries that everywhere grew up on the basis proffered by them—was this not a quite exceptional factor in the development of output, in fact a unique one? And was not this a boon that would have produced a vast access of wealth whatever the economic system it happened to impinge upon? There is a school of socialist thought that takes this view and in fact explains in this way the failure of Marx's predictions about ever-increasing misery to come true. The results of the exploitation of virgin environments they hold responsible for the fact that we did not see more of exploitation of labor; owing to that factor, the proletariat was permitted to enjoy a closed season.

There is no question about the importance of the opportunities afforded by the existence of new countries. And of course they were unique. But "objective opportunities"—that is to say, opportunities that exist independently of any social arrangement—are always prerequisites of progress, and each of them is historically unique. The presence of coal and iron ore in England or of petroleum in this and other countries is no less important and constitutes an opportunity that is no less unique. The whole capitalist process, like any other economic process that is evolutionary, consists in nothing else but exploiting such opportunities as they enter the businessman's horizon and there is no point in trying to single out the one under discussion in order to construe it as an external factor. There is less reason for doing so because the opening up of these new countries was achieved step by step through business enterprise and because business enter-

---

[1] This statement is far from satisfactory, but it seems to suffice for our purpose. The capitalist part of the world taken as a whole had by then certainly developed beyond the limits within which the opposite tendency is operative.

prise provided all the conditions for it (railroad and power plant construction, shipping, agricultural machinery and so on). Thus that process was part and parcel of capitalist achievement and on a par with the rest. Therefore the results rightfully enter our two per cent. Again we might invoke the *Communist Manifesto* in support.

The last candidate is technological progress. Was not the observed performance due to that stream of inventions that revolutionized the technique of production rather than to the businessman's hunt for profits? The answer is in the negative. The carrying into effect of those technological novelties was of the essence of that hunt. And even the inventing itself, as will be more fully explained in a moment, was a function of the capitalist process which is responsible for the mental habits that will produce invention. It is therefore quite wrong—and also quite un-Marxian—to say, as so many economists do, that capitalist enterprise was one, and technological progress a second, distinct factor in the observed development of output; they were essentially one and the same thing or, as we may also put it, the former was the propelling force of the latter.

Both the new land and the technological progress may become troublesome as soon as we proceed to extrapolation. Though achievements of capitalism, they may conceivably be achievements that cannot be repeated. And though we now have established a reasonable case to the effect that the observed behavior of output per head of population during the period of full-fledged capitalism was not an accident but may be held to measure roughly capitalist performance, we are faced by still another question, viz., the question to what extent it is legitimate to assume that the capitalist engine will—or would if allowed to do so—work on in the near future, say for another forty years, about as successfully as it did in the past.

CHAPTER X

THE VANISHING OF INVESTMENT OPPORTUNITY

T HE nature of this problem can be most tellingly displayed against the background of contemporaneous discussion. The present generation of economists has witnessed not only a world-wide depression of unusual severity and duration but also a subsequent period of halting and unsatisfactory recovery. I have already submitted my own interpretation[1] of these phenomena and stated the reasons why I do not think that they necessarily indicate a break in the trend of capitalist evolution. But it is natural that many if not most of my fellow economists should take a different view. As a matter of fact they feel, exactly as some of their predecessors felt between 1873 and 1896— though then this opinion was mainly confined to Europe—that a fundamental change is upon the capitalist process. According to this view, we have been witnessing not merely a depression and a bad recovery, accentuated perhaps by anti-capitalist policies, but the symptoms of a permanent loss of vitality which must be expected to go on and to supply the dominating theme for the remaining movements of the capitalist symphony; hence no inference as to the future can be drawn from the functioning of the capitalist engine and of its performance in the past.

This view is being held by many with whom the wish is not father to the thought. But we shall understand why socialists with whom it is, should have with particular alacrity availed themselves of the windfall—some of them to the point of shifting the base of their anti-capitalist argument completely to this ground. In doing so, they reaped the additional advantage of being able to fall back once more upon Marxian tradition which, as I have pointed out before, the trained economists among them had felt compelled to discard more and more. For, in the sense explained in the first chapter, Marx had predicted such a state of things: according to him capitalism, before actually breaking down, would enter into a stage of permanent crisis, temporarily interrupted by feeble upswings or by favorable chance occurrences. Nor is this all. One way of putting the matter from a Marxian standpoint is to stress the effects of capital accumulation and capital agglomeration on the rate of profits and, through the rate of profits, on the opportunity to invest. Since the capitalist process always

[1] See ch. V, p. 64.

has been geared to a large amount of current investment, even partial elimination of it would suffice to make plausible the forecast that the process is going to flop. This particular line in the Marxist argument no doubt seems to agree well not only with some outstanding facts of the past decade—unemployment, excess reserves, gluts in money markets, unsatisfactory margins of profits, stagnation of private investment—but also with several non-Marxist interpretations. There is surely no such gulf between Marx and Keynes as there was between Marx and Marshall or Wicksell. Both the Marxist doctrine and its non-Marxist counterpart are well expressed by the self-explanatory phrase that we shall use: the theory of vanishing investment opportunity.[2]

It should be observed that this theory really raises three distinct problems. The first is akin to the question that heads this part. Since nothing in the social world can ever be *aere perennius* and since the capitalist order is essentially the framework of a process not only of economic but also of social change, there is not much room for difference about the answer. The second question is whether the forces and mechanisms offered by the theory of vanishing investment opportunity are the ones to stress. In the following chapters I am going to submit another theory of what will eventually kill capitalism, but a number of parallelisms will remain. There is however a third problem. Even if the forces and mechanisms stressed by the theory of vanishing investment opportunity were in themselves adequate to establish the presence in the capitalist process of a long-run tendency toward ultimate deadlock, it does not necessarily follow that the vicissitudes of the past decade have been due to them and—which it is important to add for our purpose—that similar vicissitudes should therefore have to be expected to persist for the next forty years.

For the moment we are mainly concerned with the third problem. But much of what I am going to say also bears on the second. The factors that are held to justify a pessimistic forecast concerning the performance of capitalism in the near future and to negative the idea that past performance may be repeated may be divided into three groups.

There are, first, the environmental factors. It has been stated and will have to be established that the capitalist process produces a distribution of political power and a socio-psychological attitude—expressing itself in corresponding policies—that are hostile to it and may be expected to gather force so that they will eventually prevent the capitalist engine from functioning. This phenomenon I will set aside for later consideration. What follows now must be read with the appropriate proviso. But it should be noted that that attitude and cognate factors also affect the motive power of the bourgeois profit

[2] See my *Business Cycles*, ch. xv.

economy itself, and that hence the proviso covers more than one might think at first sight—more, at any rate, than mere "politics."

Then there is the capitalist engine itself. The theory of vanishing investment opportunity does not necessarily include, but as a matter of fact is apt to be in alliance with, the other theory that modern largest-scale business represents a petrified form of capitalism in which restrictive practices, price rigidities, exclusive attention to the conservation of existing capital values and so on are naturally inherent. This has been dealt with already.

Finally, there is what may be described as the "material" the capitalist engine feeds on, i.e., the opportunities open to new enterprise and investment. The theory under discussion puts so much emphasis on this element as to justify the label we have affixed to it. The main reasons for holding that opportunities for private enterprise and investment are vanishing are these: saturation, population, new lands, technological possibilities, and the circumstance that many existing investment opportunities belong to the sphere of public rather than of private investment.

1. For every given state of human wants and of technology (in the widest possible sense of the term) there is of course for every rate of real wages a definite amount of fixed and circulating capital that will spell saturation. If wants and methods of production had been frozen for good at their state in 1800, such a point would have been reached long ago. But is it not conceivable that wants may some day be so completely satisfied as to become frozen forever after? Some implications of this case will presently be developed, but so long as we deal with what may happen during the next forty years we evidently need not trouble ourselves about this possibility.

If ever it should materialize, then the current decline in birth rate, still more an actual fall in population, would indeed become an important factor in reducing opportunities for investment other than replacement. For if everyone's wants were satisfied or nearly satisfied, increase in the number of consumers would *ex hypothesi* be the only major source of additional demand. But independently of that possibility, decrease in the rate of increase in population does not *per se* endanger investment opportunity or the rate of increase in total output per head.[3] Of this we can easily satisfy ourselves by a brief examination of the usual argument to the contrary.

[3] This also holds true for a small decline in absolute numbers of people such as may occur in Great Britain before very long (see E. Charles, *London and Cambridge Economic Service*, Memo. No. 40). A considerable absolute decline would raise additional problems. These we shall neglect however because this cannot be expected to occur during the space of time under consideration. Still other problems, economic as well as political and socio-psychological, are presented by the aging of a population. Though they are beginning to assert themselves already—there is practically such a thing as a "lobby of the old"—we cannot enter into

On the one hand it is being held that a declining rate of increase in total population *ipso facto* spells a declining rate of increase in output and hence of investment because it restricts the expansion of demand. This does not follow. Want and effective demand are not the same thing. If they were, the poorest nations would be the ones to display the most vigorous demand. As it is, the income elements set free by the falling birth rate may be diverted to other channels and they are particularly apt to be so diverted in all those cases in which the desire to expand alternative demands is the very motive of childlessness. A modest argument can indeed be made out by stressing the fact that the lines of demand characteristic of an increasing population are particularly calculable and thus afford particularly reliable investment opportunities. But the desires that provide alternative opportunities are, in the given state of satisfaction of wants, not much less so. Of course the prognosis for certain individual branches of production, especially for agriculture, is in fact not a bright one. But this must not be confused with the prognosis for total output.[4]

On the other hand, we might argue that the declining rate of increase in population will tend to restrict output from the supply side. Rapid increase was in the past frequently one of the conditions of the observed development of output, and we might conclude *a contrario* that increasing scarcity of the labor factor might be expected to be a limiting factor. However, we do not hear much of this argument and for very good reasons. The observation that at the beginning of 1940 output of manufacturing industry in the United States was about 120 per cent of the average for 1923-1925 whereas factory employment was at about 100 per cent supplies an answer that is adequate for the calculable future. The extent of current unemployment; the fact that with a falling birth rate women are increasingly set free for productive work and that the falling death rate means prolongation of the useful period of life; the unexhausted stream of labor-saving devices; the possibility, increasing relatively to what it would be in the case of rapid increase of population, of avoiding complementary factors of production of inferior quality (warding off in part the operation of the law of diminishing-returns)—all this gives

---

them either. But it should be observed that, as long as retiring ages remain the same, the percentage share of those who have to be provided for without contributing need not be affected by a decreasing percentage of persons under fifteen.

[4] There seems to be an impression, prevalent with many economists, to the effect that an increase in population *per se* provides another source of demand for investment. Why—must not all these new workmen be equipped with tools and their complement of raw material? This however is by no means obvious. Unless the increase is allowed to depress wages, the implication as to investment opportunity lacks motivation, and even in that case reduction of investment per head employed would have to be expected.

ample support to Mr. Colin Clark's expectation that product per man-hour is going to rise during the next generation.[5]

Of course, the labor factor may be made artificially scarce through high-wage and short-hour policies and through political interference with the discipline of the labor force. Comparison of the economic performance in the United States and France from 1933 to 1940 with the economic performance of Japan and Germany during the same years suggests in fact that something of this kind has already occurred. But this belongs to the group of environmental factors.

As my argument will abundantly show before long, I am very far indeed from making light of the phenomenon under discussion. The falling birth rate seems to me to be one of the most significant features of our time. We shall see that even from a purely economic standpoint it is of cardinal importance, both as a symptom and as a cause of changing motivation. This however is a more complicated matter. Here we are concerned only with the mechanical effects of a decreasing rate of increase in population and these certainly do not support any pessimistic forecast as to the development of output per head during the next forty years. As far as that goes, those economists who predict a "flop" on this ground simply do what unfortunately economists have always been prone to do: as once they worried the public, on quite inadequate grounds, with the economic dangers of excessive numbers of mouths to feed,[6] so they worry it now, on no better grounds, with the economic dangers of deficiencies.

2. Next as to the opening up of new lands—that unique opportunity for investment which cannot ever recur. Even if, for the sake of argument, we grant that humanity's geographical frontier is closed for good—which is not in itself very obvious in view of the fact that at present there are deserts where once there were fields and populous cities—and even if we further grant that nothing will ever contribute to human *welfare* as much as did the foodstuffs and raw materials from those new lands—which is more plausible—it does not follow that total output per head must therefore decline, or increase at a smaller rate, during the next half-century. This would indeed have to be expected if the lands that in the nineteenth century entered the capitalist sphere had been exploited in the sense that diminishing

[5] *National Income and Outlay*, p. 21.

[6] Forecasts of future populations, from those of the seventeenth century on, were practically always wrong. For this, however, there is some excuse. There may be even for Malthus's doctrine. But I cannot see any excuse for its survival. In the second half of the nineteenth century it should have been clear to anyone that the only valuable things about Malthus's law of population are its qualifications. The first decade of this century definitely showed that it was a bogey. But no less an authority than Mr. Keynes attempted to revitalise it in the post-war period! And as late as 1925, Mr. H. Wright in his book on Population spoke of "wasting the gains of civilization on a mere increase in numbers." Will economics never come of age?

returns would now be due to assert themselves. This however is not the case and, as was just pointed out, the decreasing rate of increase in population removes from the range of practical considerations the idea that nature's response to human effort either already is or must soon become less generous than it has been. Technological progress effectively turned the tables on any such tendency, and it is one of the safest predictions that in the calculable future we shall live in an *embarras de richesse* of both foodstuffs and raw materials, giving all the rein to expansion of total output that we shall know what to do with. This applies to mineral resources as well.

There remains another possibility. Though the current output per head of foodstuffs and raw materials need not suffer and may even increase, the vast opportunities for enterprise and hence for investment that were afforded by the task of developing the new countries seem to have vanished with its completion and all sorts of difficulties are being predicted from the resulting reduction of outlets for savings. We will assume again for the sake of argument that those countries actually are developed for good and that savings, failing to adapt themselves to a reduction of outlets, might cause troubles and wastes unless other outlets open up instead. Both assumptions are indeed most unrealistic. But there is no necessity for us to question them because the conclusion as to the future development of output is contingent upon a third one that is completely gratuitous, viz., the absence of other outlets.

This third assumption is simply due to lack of imagination and exemplifies a mistake that very frequently distorts historical interpretation. The particular features of a historic process that impress the analyst tend in his mind to slip into the position of fundamental causes whether they have a claim to that role or not. For instance, what is usually referred to as the Rise of Capitalism roughly coincides with the influx of silver from the Potosí mines and with a political situation in which the expenditure of princes habitually outran their revenue so that they had to borrow incessantly. Both facts are obviously relevant in a variety of ways to the economic developments of those times—even peasants' revolts and religious upheavals may without absurdity be linked up with them. The analyst thereupon is apt to jump to the conclusion that the rise of the capitalist order of things is causally connected with them in the sense that without them (and a few other factors of the same type) the feudal world would have failed to transform itself into the capitalist one. But this is really another proposition and one for which there is, on the face of it, no warrant whatsoever. All that can be averred is that this was the road by which events traveled. It does not follow that there was no other. In this case, by the way, it cannot even be held that those factors favored capitalist development for though they certainly did do so in some respects they obviously retarded it in others.

Similarly, as we have seen in the preceding chapter, the opportunities for enterprise afforded by the new areas to be exploited were certainly unique, but only in the sense in which all opportunities are. It is gratuitous to assume not only that the "closing of the frontier" will cause a vacuum but also that whatever steps into the vacant place must necessarily be less important in any of the senses we may choose to give to that word. The conquest of the air may well be more important than the conquest of India was—we must not confuse geographical frontiers with economic ones.

It is true that the relative positions of countries or regions may significantly change as one type of investment opportunity is replaced by another. The smaller a country or region is and the more closely its fortunes are wedded to one particular element in the productive process, the less confidence we shall feel as to the future in store for it when that element is played out. Thus agricultural countries or regions *may* lose permanently by the competitive synthetic products (rayon, dyes, synthetic rubber for instance), and it may be no comfort to them that, if the process be taken as a whole, there may be net gain in total output. It is also true that the possible consequences of this may be much intensified by the division of the economic world into hostile national spheres. And it is finally true that all we can assert is that the vanishing of the investment opportunities incident to the development of new countries—if they are already vanishing—*need* not cause a void that would necessarily affect the rate of increase in total output. We cannot assert that they actually will be replaced by at least equivalent ones. We may point to the fact that from that development further developments naturally arise in those same countries or in others; we may put some trust in the ability of the capitalist engine to find or create ever new opportunities since it is geared to this very purpose; but such considerations do not carry us beyond our negative result. And recalling our reasons for embarking upon the subject, this is quite enough.

3. An analogous argument applies to the widely accepted view that the great stride in technological advance has been made and that but minor achievements remain. So far as this view does not merely render the impressions conceived from the state of things during and after the world crisis—when an apparent absence of novel propositions of the first magnitude was part of the familiar pattern of any great depression—it exemplifies still better than did the "closing of humanity's frontier" that error in interpretation economists are so prone to commit. We are just now in the downgrade of a wave of enterprise that created the electrical power plant, the electrical industry, the electrified farm and home and the motorcar. We find all that

very marvelous, and we cannot for our lives see where opportunities of comparable importance are to come from. As a matter of fact however, the promise held out by the chemical industry alone is much greater than what it was possible to anticipate in, say, 1880, not to mention the fact that the mere utilization of the achievement of the age of electricity and the production of modern homes for the masses would suffice to provide investment opportunities for quite a time to come.

Technological possibilities are an uncharted sea. We may survey a geographical region and appraise, though only with reference to a given technique of agricultural production, the relative fertility of individual plots. Given that technique and disregarding its possible future developments, we may then imagine (though this would be wrong historically) that the best plots are first taken into cultivation, after them the next best ones and so on. At any given time during this process it is only relatively inferior plots that remain to be exploited in the future. But we cannot reason in this fashion about the future possibilities of technological advance. From the fact that some of them have been exploited before others, it cannot be inferred that the former were more productive than the latter. And those that are still in the lap of the gods may be more or less productive than any that have thus far come within our range of observation. Again this yields only a negative result which even the fact that technological "progress" tends, through systemization and rationalization of research and of management, to become more effective and sure-footed, is powerless to turn into a positive one. But for us the negative result suffices: there is no reason to expect slackening of the rate of output through exhaustion of technological possibilities.

4. Two variants of this branch of the theory of vanishing investment opportunity remain to be noticed. Some economists have held that the labor force of every country had to be fitted out at some time or other with the necessary equipment. This, so they argue, has been accomplished roughly in the course of the nineteenth century. While it was being accomplished, it incessantly created new demand for capital goods, whereas, barring additions, only replacement demand remains forever after. The period of capitalist armament thus would turn out to be a unique intermezzo after all, characterized by the capitalist economy's straining every nerve in order to create for itself the necessary complement of tools and machines, and thus becoming equipped for the purpose of producing for further production at a rate which it is now impossible to keep up. This is a truly astounding picture of the economic process. Was there no equipment in the eighteenth century or, in fact, at the time our ancestors dwelled in caves? And if there was, why should the additions that occurred in the nineteenth century have been more saturating than any that went before? Moreover, additions to the armor of capitalism are as a rule competitive

with the preexisting pieces of it. They destroy the economic usefulness of the latter. Hence the task of providing equipment can never be solved once for all. The cases in which replacement reserves are adequate to solve it—as they normally would be in the absence of technological change—are exceptions. This is particularly clear where the new methods of production are embodied in new industries; obviously the automobile plants were not financed from the depreciation accounts of railroads.

The reader will no doubt observe that even if we were able to accept the premises of this argument, no pessimistic forecast about the rate of expansion of total output would necessarily follow. On the contrary he might draw the opposite inference, viz., that the possession of an extensive stock of capital goods that acquires economic immortality through continuous renewal should if anything facilitate further increase in total output. If so, he is quite right. The argument rests entirely on the disturbance to be expected if an economy geared to capital production faces a reduced rate of increase in the corresponding demand. But this disturbance which is not of sudden occurrence can easily be exaggerated. The steel industry for instance has not experienced great difficulties in transforming itself from an industry that produced capital goods almost exclusively into one that produces primarily durable consumers' goods or semi-finished products for the production of durable consumers' goods. And though compensation may not be possible within each existing capital goods industry, the principle involved is the same in all cases.

The other variant is this. The great bursts of economic activity that used to spread the symptoms of prosperity all over the economic organism have of course always been associated with expansions of producers' expenditure that were in turn associated with the construction of additional plant and equipment. Now some economists have discovered, or think they have discovered, that at the present time new technological processes tend to require less fixed capital in this sense than they used to in the past, particularly in the epoch of railroad building. The inference is that spending for capital construction will henceforth decrease in relative importance. Since this will adversely affect those intermittent bursts of economic activity that evidently have much to do with the observed rate of increase in total output, it further follows that this rate is bound to decline, especially if saving goes on at the old rate.

This tendency of new technological methods to become increasingly capital-saving has not so far been adequately established. Statistical evidence up to 1929—later data do not qualify for the purpose—point the other way. All that the sponsors of the theory in question have offered is a number of isolated instances to which it is possible to oppose others. But let us grant that such a tendency exists. We have then the same formal problem before us which exercised so many economists of the past in the case of labor-saving devices. These may affect the interests of labor favorably or adversely, but nobody doubts that on the whole they are favorable to an expansion of output. And this is—barring possible disturbances in the saving-investment process which it is the fashion to exaggerate—no different in the case of devices that economize outlay on capital goods *per unit of the final product*. In fact, it is not far from the truth to say that almost any new process that is economically workable economizes both labor and capital. Railroads were presumably capital-saving as compared with the outlay that transportation, by mailcoach or cart, of the same numbers of passengers and of the same quantities of goods that actually are being transported by railroads now would have involved. Similarly silk production by mulberry trees and silkworms may be more capital-consuming—I don't know—than the production of an equivalent amount of rayon fabric would be. That may be very sad for the owners of capital already sunk in the former. But it need not even mean decrease of investment opportunity. It certainly does not necessarily mean decrease in the expansion of output. Those who hope to see capitalism break down solely by virtue of the fact that the unit of capital goes further in productive effect than it used to, may have to wait long indeed.

5. Finally, since the subject is usually dealt with by economists who aim at impressing upon the public the necessity of governmental deficit spending, another point never fails to turn up, viz., that such opportunities for investment as remain are more suited for public than they are for private enterprise. This is true to some extent. First, with increasing wealth certain lines of expenditure are likely to gain ground which do not naturally enter into any cost-profit calculation, such as expenditure on the beautification of cities, on public health and so on. Second, an ever-widening sector of industrial activity tends to enter the sphere of public management, such as means of communication, docks, power production, insurance and so on, simply because these industries become increasingly amenable to the methods of public administration. National and municipal investment could thus be expected to expand, absolutely and relatively, even in a thoroughly capitalist society, just as other forms of public planning would.

But that is all. In order to recognize it we need not make any hypothesis about the course of things in the private sector of industrial activity. Moreover, for the purpose in hand it is immaterial whether in the future investment and the incident expansion of output will to a greater or a lesser extent be financed and managed by public rather than by private agencies unless it be held in addition that public financing will impose itself because private business would not be able to face the deficits to be expected in the future from *any* investment. This however has been dealt with before.

CHAPTER XI

THE CIVILIZATION OF CAPITALISM

Leaving the precincts of purely economic considerations, we now turn to the cultural complement of the capitalist economy—to its socio-psychological *superstructure*, if we wish to speak the Marxian language—and to the mentality that is characteristic of capitalist society and in particular of the bourgeois class. In desperate brevity, the salient facts may be conveyed as follows.

Fifty thousand years ago man confronted the dangers and opportunities of his environment in a way which some "prehistorians," sociologists and ethnologists agree was roughly equivalent to the attitude of modern primitives.[1] Two elements of this attitude are particularly important for us: the "collective" and "affective" nature of the primitive mental process and, partly overlapping, the role of what, not quite correctly, I shall here call magic. By the first I designate the fact that in small and undifferentiated or not much differentiated social groups collective ideas impose themselves much more stringently on the individual mind than they do in big and complex groups; and that conclusions and decisions are arrived at by methods which for our purpose may be characterized by a negative criterion: the disregard of what we call logic and, in particular, of the rule that excludes contradiction. By the second I designate the use of a set of beliefs which are not indeed completely divorced from experience—no magic device can survive an unbroken sequence of failures—but which insert, into the sequence of observed phenomena, entities or influences derived from non-empirical sources.[2] The similarity of this type of mental

[1] Research of this type goes far back. But I believe that a new stage of it ought to be dated from the works of Lucien Lévy-Bruhl. See in particular his *Fonctions mentales dans les sociétés inférieures* (1909) and *Le surnaturel et la nature dans la mentalité primitive* (1931). There is a long way between the position held in the first and the position held in the second work, the milestones of which are discernible in *Mentalité primitive* (1921) and *L'ame primitive* (1927). For us, Lévy-Bruhl is a particularly useful authority because he fully shares our thesis—in fact his work starts from it—that the "executive" functions of thinking and the mental structure of man are determined, partly at least, by the structure of the society within which they develop. It is immaterial that, with Lévy-Bruhl, this principle hails not from Marx but from Comte.

[2] A friendly critic of the above passage expostulated with me on the ground that I could not possibly mean what it says because in that case I should have to call the physicist's "force" a magic device. That is precisely what I do mean, unless it is agreed that the term Force is merely a name for a constant times the second time derivative of displacement. See the next but one sentence in the text.

process with the mental processes of neurotics has been pointed out by G. Dromard (1911; his term, *délire d'interpretation,* is particularly suggestive) and S. Freud (*Totem und Tabu,* 1913). But it does not follow that it is foreign to the mind of normal man of our own time. On the contrary, any discussion of political issues may convince the reader that a large and—for action—most important body of our own processes is of exactly the same nature.

Rational thought or behavior and a rationalistic civilization therefore do not imply absence of the criteria mentioned but only a slow though incessant widening of the sector of social life within which individuals or groups go about dealing with a given situation, first, by trying to make the best of it more or less—never wholly—according to their own lights; second, by doing so according to those rules of consistency which we call logic; and third, by doing so on assumptions which satisfy two conditions: that their number be a minimum and that every one of them be amenable to expression in terms of potential experience.[3]

All this is very inadequate of course but it suffices for our purpose. There is however one more point about the concept of rationalist civilizations that I will mention here for future reference. When the habit of rational analysis of, and rational behavior in, the daily tasks of life has gone far enough, it turns back upon the mass of collective ideas and criticizes and to some extent "rationalizes" them by way of such questions as why there should be kings and popes or subordination or tithes or property. Incidentally, it is important to notice that, while most of us would accept such an attitude as the symptom of a "higher stage" of mental development, this value judgment is not necessarily and in every sense borne out by the results. The rationalist attitude may go to work with information and technique so inadequate that actions—and especially a general surgical propensity—induced by it may, to an observer of a later period, appear to be, even from a purely intellectual standpoint, inferior to the actions and anti-surgical propensities associated with attitudes that at the time most people felt inclined to attribute to a low I.Q. A large part of the political thought of the seventeenth and eighteenth centuries illustrates this ever-forgotten truth. Not only in depth of social vision but also in logical analysis later "conservative" countercriticism was clearly superior although it would have been a mere matter of laughter for the writers of the enlightenment.

Now the rational attitude presumably forced itself on the human mind primarily from economic necessity; it is the everyday economic task to which we as a race owe our elementary training in rational thought and behavior—I have no hesitation in saying that all logic is

[3] This Kantian phrase has been chosen in order to guard against an obvious objection.

derived from the pattern of the economic decision or, to use a pet phrase of mine, that the economic pattern is the matrix of logic. This seems plausible for the following reason. Suppose that some "primitive" man uses that most elementary of all machines, already appreciated by our gorilla cousins, a stick, and that this stick breaks in his hand. If he tries to remedy the damage by reciting a magic formula— he might for instance murmur Supply and Demand or Planning and Control in the expectation that if he repeats this exactly nine times the two fragments will unite again—then he is within the precincts of pre-rational thought. If he gropes for the best way to join the fragments or to procure another stick, he is being rational in our sense. Both attitudes are possible of course. But it stands to reason that in this and most other economic actions the failure of a magic formula to work will be much more obvious than could be any failure of a formula that was to make our man victorious in combat or lucky in love or to lift a load of guilt from his conscience. This is due to the inexorable definiteness and, in most cases, the quantitative character that distinguish the economic from other spheres of human action, perhaps also to the unemotional drabness of the unending rhythm of economic wants and satisfactions. Once hammered in, the rational habit spreads under the pedagogic influence of favorable experiences to the other spheres and there also opens eyes for that amazing thing, the Fact.

This process is independent of any particular garb, hence also of the capitalistic garb, of economic activity. So is the profit motive and self-interest. Pre-capitalist man is in fact no less "grabbing" than capitalist man. Peasant serfs for instance or warrior lords assert their self-interest with a brutal energy all their own. But capitalism develops rationality and adds a new edge to it in two interconnected ways.

First it exalts the monetary unit—not itself a creation of capitalism —into a unit of account. That is to say, capitalist practice turns the unit of money into a tool of rational cost-profit calculations, of which the towering monument is double-entry bookkeeping.[4] Without going into this, we will notice that, primarily a product of the evolution of economic rationality, the cost-profit calculus in turn reacts upon that rationality; by crystallizing and defining numerically, it powerfully propels the logic of enterprise. And thus defined and quantified

[4] This element has been stressed, and *more suo* overstressed, by Sombart. Double-entry bookkeeping is the last step on a long and tortuous road. Its immediate predecessor was the practice of making up from time to time an inventory and figuring out profit or loss; see A. Sapori in *Biblioteca Storica Toscana*, VII, 1932. Luca Pacioli's treatise on bookkeeping, 1494, supplies by its date an important milestone. For the history and sociology of the state it is a vital fact to notice that rational bookkeeping did not intrude into the management of public funds until the eighteenth century and that even then it did so imperfectly and in the primitive form of "cameralist" bookkeeping.

for the economic sector, this type of logic or attitude or method then starts upon its conqueror's career subjugating—rationalizing—man's tools and philosophies, his medical practice, his picture of the cosmos, his outlook on life, everything in fact including his concepts of beauty and justice and his spiritual ambitions.

In this respect it is highly significant that modern mathematico-experimental science developed, in the fifteenth, sixteenth and seventeenth centuries, not only along with the social process usually referred to as the Rise of Capitalism, but also outside of the fortress of scholastic thought and in the face of its contemptuous hostility. In the fifteenth century mathematics was mainly concerned with questions of commercial arithmetic and the problems of the architect. The utilitarian mechanical device, invented by men of the craftsman type, stood at the source of modern physics. The rugged individualism of Galileo was the individualism of the rising capitalist class. The surgeon began to rise above the midwife and the barber. The artist who at the same time was an engineer and an entrepreneur—the type immortalized by such men as Vinci, Alberti, Cellini; even Dürer busied himself with plans for fortifications—illustrates best of all what I mean. By cursing it all, scholastic professors in the Italian universities showed more sense than we give them credit for. The trouble was not with individual unorthodox propositions. Any decent schoolman could be trusted to twist his texts so as to fit the Copernican system. But those professors quite rightly sensed the spirit behind such exploits—the spirit of rationalist individualism, the spirit generated by rising capitalism.

Second, rising capitalism produced not only the mental attitude of modern science, the attitude that consists in asking certain questions and in going about answering them in a certain way, but also the men and the means. By breaking up the feudal environment and disturbing the intellectual peace of manor and village (though there always was, of course, plenty to discuss and to fall out about in a convent), but especially by creating the social space for a new class that stood upon individual achievement in the economic field, it in turn attracted to that field the strong wills and the strong intellects. Precapitalist economic life left no scope for achievement that would carry over class boundaries or, to put it differently, be adequate to create social positions comparable to those of the members of the then ruling classes. Not that it precluded ascent in general.[5] But business activity was, broadly speaking, essentially subordinate, even at the peak of success within the craft guild, and it hardly ever led out of it. The

[5] We are too prone to look upon the medieval social structure as static or rigid. As a matter of fact, there was an incessant—to use Pareto's term—*circulation des aristocracies*. The elements that composed the uppermost stratum around 900 had practically disappeared by 1500.

main avenues to advancement and large gain were the church—nearly as accessible throughout the Middle Ages as it is now—to which we may add the chanceries of the great territorial magnates, and the hierarchy of warrior lords—quite accessible to every man who was physically and psychically fit until about the middle of the twelfth century, and not quite inaccessible thereafter. It was only when capitalist enterprise—first commercial and financial, then mining, finally industrial—unfolded its possibilities that supernormal ability and ambition began to turn to business as a third avenue. Success was quick and conspicuous, but it has been much exaggerated as regards the social weight it carried at first. If we look closely at the career of Jacob Fugger, for instance, or of Agostino Chigi, we easily satisfy ourselves that they had very little to do with steering the policies of Charles V or of Pope Leo X and that they paid heavily for such privileges as they enjoyed.[6] Yet entrepreneurial success was fascinating enough for everyone excepting the highest strata of feudal society to draw most of the best brains and thus to generate further success— to generate additional steam for the rationalist engine. So, in this sense, capitalism—and not merely economic activity in general—has after all been the propelling force of the rationalization of human behavior.

And now we are at long last face to face with the immediate goal[7] to which that complex yet inadequate argument was to lead. Not only the modern mechanized plant and the volume of the output that pours forth from it, not only modern technology and economic organization, but all the features and achievements of modern civilization are, directly or indirectly, the products of the capitalist process. They must be included in any balance sheet of it and in any verdict about its deeds or misdeeds.

There is the growth of rational science and the long list of its applications. Airplanes, refrigerators, television and that sort of thing are immediately recognizable as results of the profit economy. But although the modern hospital is not as a rule operated for profit, it is nonetheless the product of capitalism not only, to repeat, because the capitalist process supplies the means and the will, but much more fundamentally because capitalist rationality supplied the habits of

[6] The Medici are not really an exception. For though their wealth helped them to acquire control of the Florentine commonwealth, it was this control and not the wealth *per se* which accounts for the role played by the family. In any case they are the only merchants that ever rose to a footing of equality with the uppermost stratum of the feudal world. Real exceptions we find only where capitalist evolution *created* an environment or completely broke up the feudal stratum— in Venice and in the Netherlands for instance.

[7] The *immediate* goal, because the analysis contained in the last pages will stand us in good stead also for other purposes. It is in fact fundamental for any serious discussion of the great theme of Capitalism and Socialism.

mind that evolved the methods used in these hospitals. And the victories, not yet completely won but in the offing, over cancer, syphilis and tuberculosis will be as much capitalist achievements as motorcars or pipe lines or Bessemer steel have been. In the case of medicine, there is a capitalist profession behind the methods, capitalist both because to a large extent it works in a business spirit and because it is an emulsion of the industrial and commercial bourgeoisie. But even if that were not so, modern medicine and hygiene would still be by-products of the capitalist process just as is modern education.

There is the capitalist art and the capitalist style of life. If we limit ourselves to painting as an example, both for brevity's sake and because in that field my ignorance is slightly less complete than it is in others, and if (wrongly, as I think) we agree to start an epoch with Giotto's Arena frescoes and then follow the line (nothing short of damnable though such "linear" arguments are) Giotto—Masaccio—Vinci—Michelangelo—Greco, no amount of emphasis on mystical ardors in the case of Greco can obliterate my point for anyone who has eyes that see. And Vinci's experiments are offered to doubters who wish, as it were, to touch the capitalist rationality with their fingertips. This line if projected (yes, I know) could be made to land us (though perhaps gasping) in the contrast between Delacroix and Ingres. Well, and there we are; Cézanne, Van Gogh, Picasso or Matisse will do the rest. Expressionist liquidation of the object forms an admirably logical conclusion. The story of the capitalist novel (culminating in the Goncourt novel: "documents written up") would illustrate still better. But that is obvious. The evolution of the capitalist style of life could be easily—and perhaps most tellingly—described in terms of the genesis of the modern lounge suit.

There is finally all that may be grouped around the symbolic centerpiece of Gladstonian liberalism. The term Individualist Democracy would do just as well—better in fact because we want to cover some things that Gladstone would not have approved and a moral and spiritual attitude which, dwelling in the citadel of faith, he actually hated. At that I could leave this point if radical liturgy did not consist largely in picturesque denials of what I mean to convey. Radicals may insist that the masses are crying for salvation from intolerable sufferings and rattling their chains in darkness and despair, but of course there never was so much personal freedom of mind and body *for all*, never so much readiness to bear with and even to finance the mortal enemies of the leading class, never so much active sympathy with real and faked sufferings, never so much readiness to accept burdens, as there is in modern capitalist society; and whatever democracy there was, outside of peasant communities, developed historically in the wake of both modern and ancient capitalism. Again plenty of facts can be adduced from the past to make up a counterargument that will be effective but is irrelevant in a discussion of present conditions and future alternatives.[8] If we do decide to embark upon historical disquisition at all, then even many of those facts which to radical critics may seem to be the most eligible ones for their purpose will often look differently if viewed in the light of a comparison with the corresponding facts of pre-capitalist experience. And it cannot be replied that "those were different times." For it is precisely the capitalist process that made the difference.

Two points in particular must be mentioned. I have pointed out before that social legislation or, more generally, institutional change for the benefit of the masses is not simply something which has been forced upon capitalist society by an ineluctable necessity to alleviate the ever-deepening misery of the poor but that, besides raising the standard of living of the masses by virtue of its automatic effects, the capitalist process also provided for that legislation the means "and the will." The words in quotes require further explanation that is to be found in the principle of spreading rationality. The capitalist process rationalizes behavior and ideas and by so doing chases from our minds, along with metaphysical belief, mystic and romantic ideas of all sorts. Thus it reshapes not only our methods of attaining our ends but also these ultimate ends themselves. "Free thinking" in the sense of materialistic monism, laicism and pragmatic acceptance of the world this side of the grave follow from this not indeed by logical necessity but nevertheless very naturally. On the one hand, our inherited sense of duty, deprived of its traditional basis, becomes focused in utilitarian ideas about the betterment of mankind which, quite illogically to be sure, seem to withstand rationalist criticism better than, say, the fear of God does. On the other hand, the same rationalization of the soul rubs off all the glamour of super-empirical sanction from every species of classwise rights. This then, together with the typically capitalist enthusiasm for Efficiency and Service—so completely different from the body of ideas which would have been associated with those terms by the typical knight of old—breeds that "will" within the bourgeoisie itself. Feminism, an essentially capitalist phenomenon, illustrates the point still more clearly. The reader will realize that these tendencies must be understood "objectively" and that therefore no amount of anti-feminist or anti-reformist *talk* or even of temporary opposition to any particular measure proves anything against this analysis. These things are the very symptoms of the tendencies they pretend to fight. Of this, more in the subsequent chapters.

Also, capitalist civilization is rationalistic "and anti-heroic." The

[8] Even Marx, in whose time indictments of this kind were not anything like as absurd as they are today, evidently thought it desirable to strengthen his case by dwelling on conditions that even then were either past or visibly passing.

two go together of course. Success in industry and commerce requires
a lot of stamina, yet industrial and commercial activity is essentially
unheroic in the knight's sense—no flourishing of swords about it, not
much physical prowess, no chance to gallop the armored horse into
the enemy, preferably a heretic or heathen—and the ideology that
glorifies the idea of fighting for fighting's sake and of victory for victory's sake understandably withers in the office among all the columns
of figures. Therefore, owning assets that are apt to attract the robber
or the tax gatherer and not sharing or even disliking warrior ideology
that conflicts with its "rational" utilitarianism, the industrial and
commercial bourgeoisie is fundamentally pacifist and inclined to
insist on the application of the moral precepts of private life to international relations. It is true that, unlike most but like some other
features of capitalist civilization, pacifism and international morality
have also been espoused in non-capitalist environments and by pre-
capitalist agencies, in the Middle Ages by the Roman Church for
instance. Modern pacifism and modern international morality are
nonetheless products of capitalism.

In view of the fact that Marxian doctrine—especially Neo-Marxian
doctrine and even a considerable body of non-socialist opinion—is,
as we have seen in the first part of this book, strongly opposed to this
proposition[9] it is necessary to point out that the latter is not meant to
deny that many a bourgeoisie has put up a splendid fight for hearth
and home, or that almost purely bourgeois commonwealths were often
aggressive when it seemed to pay—like the Athenian or the Venetian
commonwealths—or that no bourgeoisie ever disliked war profits and
advantages to trade accruing from conquest or refused to be trained
in warlike nationalism by its feudal masters or leaders or by the
propaganda of some specially interested group. All I hold is, first, that
such instances of capitalist combativeness are not, as Marxism has it,
to be explained—exclusively or primarily—in terms of class interests
or class situations that systematically engender capitalist wars of conquest; second, that there is a difference between doing that which you
consider your normal business in life, for which you prepare yourself
in season and out of season and in terms of which you define your
success or failure, and doing what is not in your line, for which your
normal work and your mentality do not fit you and success in which
will increase the prestige of the most unbourgeois of professions; and
third, that this difference steadily tells—in international as well as in
domestic affairs—against the use of military force and for peaceful
arrangements, even where the balance of pecuniary advantage is clearly
on the side of war which, under modern circumstances, is not in
general very likely. As a matter of fact, the more completely capitalist
the structure and attitude of a nation, the more pacifist—and the

[9] See our discussion of the Marxian theory of imperialism, Part I, ch. iv.

more prone to count the costs of war—we observe it to be. Owing to the complex nature of every individual pattern, this could be fully brought out only by detailed historical analysis. But the bourgeois attitude to the military (standing armies), the spirit in which and the methods by which bourgeois societies wage war, and the readiness with which, in any serious case of prolonged warfare, they submit to non-bourgeois rule are conclusive in themselves. The Marxist theory that imperialism is the last stage of capitalist evolution therefore fails quite irrespective of purely economic objections.

But I am not going to sum up as the reader presumably expects me to. That is to say, I am not going to invite him, before he decides to put his trust in an untried alternative advocated by untried men, to look once more at the impressive economic and the still more impressive cultural achievement of the capitalist order and at the immense promise held out by both. I am not going to argue that that achievement and that promise are in themselves sufficient to support an argument for allowing the capitalist process to work on and, as it might easily be put, to lift poverty from the shoulders of mankind.

There would be no sense in this. Even if mankind were as free to choose as a businessman is free to choose between two competing pieces of machinery, no determined value judgment necessarily follows from the facts and relations between facts that I have tried to convey. As regards the economic performance, it does not follow that men are "happier" or even "better off" in the industrial society of today than they were in a medieval manor or village. As regards the cultural performance, one may accept every word I have written and yet hate it— its utilitarianism and the wholesale destruction of Meanings incident to it—from the bottom of one's heart. Moreover, as I shall have to emphasize again in our discussion of the socialist alternative, one may care less for the efficiency of the capitalist process in producing economic and cultural values than for the kind of human beings that it turns out and then leaves to their own devices, free to make a mess of their lives. There is a type of radical whose adverse verdict about capitalist civilization rests on nothing except stupidity, ignorance or irresponsibility, who is unable or unwilling to grasp the most obvious facts, let alone their wider implications. But a completely adverse verdict may also be arrived at on a higher plane.

However, whether favorable or unfavorable, value judgments about capitalist performance are of little interest. For mankind is not free to choose. This is not only because the mass of people are not in a position to compare alternatives rationally and always accept what they are being told. There is a much deeper reason for it. Things economic and social move by their own momentum and the ensuing situations compel individuals and groups to behave in certain ways whatever they may wish to do—not indeed by destroying their freedom of choice but by shaping the choosing mentalities and by narrowing the list of possibilities from which to choose. If this is the quintessence of Marxism then we all of us have got to be Marxists. In consequence, capitalist performance is not even relevant for prognosis. Most civilizations have disappeared before they had time to fill to the full the measure of their promise. Hence I am not going to argue, on the strength of that performance, that the capitalist intermezzo is likely to be prolonged. In fact, I am now going to draw the exactly opposite inference.

CHAPTER XII

CRUMBLING WALLS

I. THE OBSOLESCENCE OF THE ENTREPRENEURIAL FUNCTION

IN OUR discussion of the theory of vanishing investment opportunity, a reservation was made in favor of the possibility that the economic wants of humanity might some day be so completely satisfied that little motive would be left to push productive effort still further ahead. Such a state of satiety is no doubt very far off even if we keep within the present scheme of wants; and if we take account of the fact that, as higher standards of life are attained, these wants automatically expand and new wants emerge or are created,[1] satiety becomes a flying goal, particularly if we include leisure among consumers' goods. However, let us glance at that possibility, assuming, still more unrealistically, that methods of production have reached a state of perfection which does not admit of further improvement.

A more or less stationary state would ensue. Capitalism, being essentially an evolutionary process, would become atrophic. There would be nothing left for entrepreneurs to do. They would find themselves in much the same situation as generals would in a society perfectly sure of permanent peace. Profits and along with profits the rate of interest would converge toward zero. The bourgeois strata that live on profits and interest would tend to disappear. The management of industry and trade would become a matter of current administration, and the personnel would unavoidably acquire the characteristics of a bureaucracy. Socialism of a very sober type would almost automatically come into being. Human energy would turn away from business. Other than economic pursuits would attract the brains and provide the adventure.

For the calculable future this vision is of no importance. But all the greater importance attaches to the fact that many of the effects on the structure of society and on the organization of the productive process that we might expect from an approximately complete satisfaction of wants or from absolute technological perfection can also be expected from a development that is clearly observable already. Progress itself may be mechanized as well as the management of a stationary economy, and this mechanization of progress may affect entrepreneurship and capitalist society nearly as much as the cessation of economic progress would. In order to see this it is only necessary to restate,

[1] Wilhelm Wundt called this the Heterogony of Aims (*Heterogonie der Zwecke*).

first, what the entrepreneurial function consists in and, secondly, what it means for bourgeois society and the survival of the capitalist order.

We have seen that the function of entrepreneurs is to reform or revolutionize the pattern of production by exploiting an invention or, more generally, an untried technological possibility for producing a new commodity or producing an old one in a new way, by opening up a new source of supply of materials or a new outlet for products, by reorganizing an industry and so on. Railroad construction in its earlier stages, electrical power production before the First World War, steam and steel, the motorcar, colonial ventures afford spectacular instances of a large genus which comprises innumerable humbler ones —down to such things as making a success of a particular kind of sausage or toothbrush. This kind of activity is primarily responsible for the recurrent "prosperities" that revolutionize the economic organism and the recurrent "recessions" that are due to the disequilibrating impact of the new products or methods. To undertake such new things is difficult and constitutes a distinct economic function, first, because they lie outside of the routine tasks which everybody understands and, secondly, because the environment resists in many ways that vary, according to social conditions, from simple refusal either to finance or to buy a new thing, to physical attack on the man who tries to produce it. To act with confidence beyond the range of familiar beacons and to overcome that resistance requires aptitudes that are present in only a small fraction of the population and that define the entrepreneurial type as well as the entrepreneurial function. This function does not essentially consist in either inventing anything or otherwise creating the conditions which the enterprise exploits. It consists in getting things done.

This social function is already losing importance and is bound to lose it at an accelerating rate in the future even if the economic process itself of which entrepreneurship was the prime mover went on unabated. For, on the one hand, it is much easier now than it has been in the past to do things that lie outside familiar routine—innovation itself is being reduced to routine. Technological progress is increasingly becoming the business of teams of trained specialists who turn out what is required and make it work in predictable ways. The romance of earlier commercial adventure is rapidly wearing away, because so many more things can be strictly calculated that had of old to be visualized in a flash of genius.

On the other hand, personality and will power must count for less in environments which have become accustomed to economic change— best instanced by an incessant stream of new consumers' and producers' goods—and which, instead of resisting, accept it as a matter of course. The resistance which comes from interests threatened by an innovation in the productive process is not likely to die out as long as the capitalist order persists. It is, for instance, the great obstacle on the road toward mass production of cheap housing which presupposes radical mechanization and wholesale elimination of inefficient methods of work on the plot. But every other kind of resistance—the resistance, in particular, of consumers and producers to a new kind of thing because it is new—has well-nigh vanished already.

Thus, economic progress tends to become depersonalized and automatized. Bureau and committee work tends to replace individual action. Once more, reference to the military analogy will help to bring out the essential point.

Of old, roughly up to and including the Napoleonic Wars, generalship meant leadership and success meant the personal success of the man in command who earned corresponding "profits" in terms of social prestige. The technique of warfare and the structure of armies being what they were, the individual decision and driving power of the leading man—even his actual presence on a showy horse—were essential elements in the strategical and tactical situations. Napoleon's presence was, and had to be, actually felt on his battlefields. This is no longer so. Rationalized and specialized office work will eventually blot out personality, the calculable result, the "vision." The leading man no longer has the opportunity to fling himself into the fray. He is becoming just another office worker—and one who is not always difficult to replace.

Or take another military analogy. Warfare in the Middle Ages was a very personal affair. The armored knights practiced an art that required lifelong training and every one of them counted individually by virtue of personal skill and prowess. It is easy to understand why this craft should have become the basis of a social class in the fullest and richest sense of that term. But social and technological change undermined and eventually destroyed both the function and the position of that class. Warfare itself did not cease on that account. It simply became more and more mechanized—eventually so much so that success in what now is a mere profession no longer carries that connotation of individual achievement which would raise not only the man but also his group into a durable position of social leadership.

Now a similar social process—in the last analysis the same social process—undermines the role and, along with the role, the social position of the capitalist entrepreneur. His role, though less glamorous than that of medieval warlords, great or small, also is or was just another form of individual leadership acting by virtue of personal force and personal responsibility for success. His position, like that of warrior classes, is threatened as soon as this function in the social process loses its importance, and no less if this is due to the cessation of the social needs it served than if those needs are being served by other, more impersonal, methods.

But this affects the position of the entire bourgeois stratum. Although entrepreneurs are not necessarily or even typically elements of that stratum from the outset, they nevertheless enter it in case of success. Thus, though entrepreneurs do not *per se* form a social class, the bourgeois class absorbs them and their families and connections, thereby recruiting and revitalizing itself currently while at the same time the families that sever their active relation to "business" drop out of it after a generation or two. Between, there is the bulk of what we refer to as industrialists, merchants, financiers and bankers; they are in the intermediate stage between entrepreneurial venture and mere current administration of an inherited domain. The returns on which the class lives are produced by, and the social position of the class rests on, the success of this more or less active sector—which of course may, as it does in this country, form over 90 per cent of the bourgeois stratum—and of the individuals who are in the act of rising into that class. Economically and sociologically, directly and indirectly, the bourgeoisie therefore depends on the entrepreneur and, as a class, lives and will die with him, though a more or less prolonged transitional stage—eventually a stage in which it may feel equally unable to die and to live—is quite likely to occur, as in fact it did occur in the case of the feudal civilization.

To sum up this part of our argument: if capitalist evolution—"progress"—either ceases or becomes completely automatic, the economic basis of the industrial bourgeoisie will be reduced eventually to wages such as are paid for current administrative work excepting remnants of quasi-rents and monopoloid gains that may be expected to linger on for some time. Since capitalist enterprise, by its very achievements, tends to automatize progress, we conclude that it tends to make itself superfluous—to break to pieces under the pressure of its own success. The perfectly bureaucratized giant industrial unit not only ousts the small or medium-sized firm and "expropriates" its owners, but in the end it also ousts the entrepreneur and expropriates the bourgeoisie as a class which in the process stands to lose not only its income but also what is infinitely more important, its function. The true pacemakers of socialism were not the intellectuals or agitators who preached it but the Vanderbilts, Carnegies and Rockefellers. This result may not in every respect be to the taste of Marxian socialists, still less to the taste of socialists of a more popular (Marx would have said, vulgar) description. But so far as prognosis goes, it does not differ from theirs.

II. The Destruction of the Protecting Strata

So far we have been considering the effects of the capitalist process upon the economic bases of the upper strata of capitalist society and upon their social position and prestige. But effects further extend to the institutional framework that protected them. In showing this we shall take the term in its widest acceptance so as to include not only legal institutions but also attitudes of the public mind and policies.

1. Capitalist evolution first of all destroyed, or went far toward destroying, the institutional arrangements of the feudal world—the manor, the village, the craft guild. The facts and mechanisms of this process are too familiar to detain us. Destruction was wrought in three ways. The world of the artisan was destroyed primarily by the automatic effects of the competition that came from the capitalist entrepreneur; political action in removing atrophic organizations and regulations only registered results. The world of the lord and the peasant was destroyed primarily by political—in some cases revolutionary—action and capitalism merely presided over adaptive transformations say, of the German manorial organizations into large-scale agricultural units of production. But along with these industrial and agrarian revolutions went a no less revolutionary change in the general attitude of legislative authority and public opinion. Together with the old economic organization vanished the economic and political privileges of the classes or groups that used to play the leading role in it, particularly the tax exemptions and the political prerogatives of the landed nobility and gentry and of the clergy.

Economically all this meant for the bourgeoisie the breaking of so many fetters and the removal of so many barriers. Politically it meant the replacement of an order in which the bourgeois was a humble subject by another that was more congenial to his rationalist mind and to his immediate interests. But, surveying that process from the standpoint of today, the observer might well wonder whether in the end such complete emancipation was good for the bourgeois and his world. For those fetters not only hampered, they also sheltered. Before proceeding further we must carefully clarify and appraise this point.

2. The related processes of the rise of the capitalist bourgeoisie and of the rise of national states produced, in the sixteenth, seventeenth and eighteenth centuries, a social structure that may seem to us amphibial though it was no more amphibial or transitional than any other. Consider the outstanding instance that is afforded by the monarchy of Louis XIV. The royal power had subjugated the landed aristocracy and at the same time conciliated it by proffering employment and pensions and by conditionally accepting its claim to a ruling or leading class position. The same royal power had subjugated and allied itself with the clergy.[2] It had finally strengthened its sway over the bourgeoisie, its old ally in the struggle with the territorial magnates, protecting and propelling its enterprise in order to exploit it the more effectively in turn. Peasants and the (small) industrial proletariat were

[2] Gallicanism was nothing else but the ideological reflex of this.

likewise managed, exploited and protected by public authority—though the protection was in the case of the French *ancien régime* very much less in evidence than for instance in the Austria of Maria Theresa or of Joseph II—and, vicariously, by landlords or industrialists. This was not simply a government in the sense of nineteenth-century liberalism, i.e., a social agency existing for the performance of a few limited functions to be financed by a minimum of revenue. On principle, the monarchy managed everything, from consciences to the patterns of the silk fabrics of Lyons, and financially it aimed at a maximum of revenue. Though the king was never really absolute, public authority was all-comprehensive.

Correct diagnosis of this pattern is of the utmost importance for our subject. The king, the court, the army, the church and the bureaucracy lived to an increasing extent on revenue created by the capitalist process, even purely feudal sources of income being swelled in consequence of contemporaneous capitalist developments. To an increasing extent also, domestic and foreign policies and institutional changes were shaped to suit and propel that development. *As far as that goes,* the feudal elements in the structure of the so-called absolute monarchy come in only under the heading of atavisms which in fact is the diagnosis one would naturally adopt at first sight.

Looking more closely, however, we realize that those elements meant more than that. The steel frame of that structure still consisted of the human material of feudal society and this material still behaved according to precapitalist patterns. It filled the offices of state, officered the army, devised policies—it functioned as a *classe dirigente* and, though taking account of bourgeois interests, it took care to distance itself from the bourgeoisie. The centerpiece, the king, was king by the grace of God, and the root of his position was feudal, not only in the historical but also in the sociological sense, however much he availed himself of the economic possibilities offered by capitalism. All this was more than atavism. It was an active symbiosis of two social strata, one of which no doubt supported the other economically but was in turn supported by the other politically. Whatever we may think of the achievements or shortcomings of this arrangement, whatever the bourgeois himself may have thought of it at the time or later—and of the aristocratic scapegrace or idler—it was of the essence of that society.

3. Of *that* society only? The subsequent course of things, best exemplified by the English case, suggests the answer. The aristocratic element continued to rule the roost *right to the end of the period of intact and vital capitalism*. No doubt that element—though nowhere so effectively as in England—currently absorbed the brains from other strata that drifted into politics; it made itself the representative of bourgeois interests and fought the battles of the bourgeoisie; it

had to surrender its last legal privileges; but with these qualifications, and for ends no longer its own, it continued to man the political engine, to manage the state, to govern.

The economically operative part of the bourgeois strata did not offer much opposition to this. On the whole, that kind of division of labor suited them and they liked it. Where they did revolt against it or where they got into the political saddle without having to revolt, they did not make a conspicuous success of ruling and did not prove able to hold their own. The question arises whether it is really safe to assume that these failures were merely due to lack of opportunity to acquire experience and, with experience, the attitudes of a politically ruling class.

It is not. There is a more fundamental reason for those failures such as are instanced by the French or German experiences with bourgeois attempts at ruling—a reason which again will best be visualized by contrasting the figure of the industrialist or merchant with that of the medieval lord. The latter's "profession" not only qualified him admirably for the defense of his own class interest— he was not only able to fight for it physically—but it also cast a halo around him and made of him a ruler of men. The first was important, but more so were the mystic glamour and the lordly attitude— that ability and habit to command and to be obeyed that carried prestige with all classes of society and in every walk of life. That prestige was so great and that attitude so useful that the class position outlived the social and technological conditions which had given rise to it and proved adaptable, by means of a transformation of the class function, to quite different social and economic conditions. With the utmost ease and grace the lords and knights metamorphosed themselves into courtiers, administrators, diplomats, politicians and into military officers of a type that had nothing whatever to do with that of the medieval knight. And—most astonishing phenomenon when we come to think of it—a remnant of that old prestige survives even to this day, and not only with our ladies.

Of the industrialist and merchant the opposite is true. There is surely no trace of any mystic glamour about him which is what counts in the ruling of men. The stock exchange is a poor substitute for the Holy Grail. We have seen that the industrialist and merchant, as far as they are entrepreneurs, also fill a function of leadership. But economic leadership of this type does not readily expand, like the medieval lord's military leadership, into the leadership of nations. On the contrary, the ledger and the cost calculation absorb and confine.

I have called the bourgeois rationalist and unheroic. He can only use rationalist and unheroic means to defend his position or to bend a nation to his will. He can impress by what people may expect from his economic performance, he can argue his case, he can promise to pay out money or threaten to withhold it, he can hire the treacherous services of a *condottiere* or politician or journalist. But that is all and all of it is greatly overrated as to its political value. Nor are his experiences and habits of life of the kind that develop personal fascination. A genius in the business office may be, and often is, utterly unable outside of it to say boo to a goose—both in the drawing room and on the platform. Knowing this he wants to be left alone and to leave politics alone.

Again exceptions will occur to the reader. But again they do not amount to much. Aptitude for, and interest and success in, city management is the only important exception in Europe, and this will be found to strengthen our case instead of weakening it. Before the advent of the modern metropolis, which is no longer a bourgeois affair, city management was akin to business management. Grasp of its problems and authority within its precincts came naturally to the manufacturer and trader, and the local interests of manufacturing and trading supplied most of the subject matter of its politics which therefore lent itself to treatment by the methods and in the spirit of the business office. Under exceptionally favorable conditions, exceptional developments sprouted from those roots, such as the developments of the Venetian or Genoese republics. The case of the Low Countries enters into the same pattern, but it is particularly instructive by virtue of the fact that the merchants' republic invariably failed in the great game of international politics and that in practically every emergency it had to hand over the reins to a warlord of feudal complexion. As regards the United States, it would be easy to list the uniquely favorable circumstances—rapidly waning —that explain its case.[3]

4. The inference is obvious: barring such exceptional conditions, the bourgeois class is ill equipped to face the problems, both domestic and international, that have normally to be faced by a country of any importance. The bourgeois themselves feel this in spite of all the phraseology that seems to deny it, and so do the masses. Within a protecting framework not made of bourgeois material, the bourgeoisie may be successful, not only in the political defensive but also in the offensive, especially as an opposition. For a time it felt so safe as to be able to afford the luxury of attacking the protective frame itself; such bourgeois opposition as there was in imperial Germany illustrates this to perfection. But without protection by some non-bourgeois group, the bourgeoisie is politically helpless and unable not only to lead its nation but even to take care of its particular class interest. Which amounts to saying that it needs a master.

But the capitalist process, both by its economic mechanics and by

[3] This line of reasoning will be taken up again in Part IV.

its psycho-sociological effects, did away with this protecting master or, as in this country, never gave him, or a substitute for him, a chance to develop. The implications of this are strengthened by another consequence of the same process. Capitalist evolution eliminates not only the king *Dei Gratia* but also the political entrenchments that, had they proved tenable, would have been formed by the village and the craft guild. Of course, neither organization was tenable in the precise shape in which capitalism found it. But capitalist policies wrought destruction much beyond what was unavoidable. They attacked the artisan in reservations in which he could have survived for an indefinite time. They forced upon the peasant all the blessings of early liberalism—the free and unsheltered holding and all the individualist rope he needed in order to hang himself.

In breaking down the pre-capitalist framework of society, capitalism thus broke not only barriers that impeded its progress but also flying buttresses that prevented its collapse. That process, impressive in its relentless necessity, was not merely a matter of removing institutional deadwood, but of removing partners of the capitalist stratum, symbiosis with whom was an essential element of the capitalist schema. Having discovered this fact which so many slogans obscure, we might well wonder whether it is quite correct to look upon capitalism as a social form *sui generis* or, in fact, as anything else but the last stage of the decomposition of what we have called feudalism. On the whole, I am inclined to believe that its peculiarities suffice to make a type and to accept that symbiosis of classes which owe their existence to different epochs and processes as the rule rather than as an exception —at least it has been the rule these 6000 years, i.e., ever since primitive tillers of the soil became the subjects of mounted nomads. But there is no great objection that I can see against the opposite view alluded to.

III. The Destruction of the Institutional Framework of Capitalist Society

We return from our digression with a load of ominous facts. They are almost, though not quite, sufficient to establish our next point, viz., that the capitalist process in much the same way in which it destroyed the institutional framework of feudal society also undermines its own.

It has been pointed out above that the very success of capitalist enterprise paradoxically tends to impair the prestige or social weight of the class primarily associated with it and that the giant unit of control tends to oust the bourgeoisie from the function to which it owed that social weight. The corresponding change in the meaning, and the incidental loss in vitality, of the institutions of the bourgeois world and of its typical attitudes are easy to trace.

On the one hand, the capitalist process unavoidably attacks the economic standing ground of the small producer and trader. What it did to the pre-capitalist strata it also does—and by the same competitive mechanism—to the lower strata of capitalist industry. Here of course Marx scores. It is true that the facts of industrial concentration do not quite live up to the ideas the public is being taught to entertain about it (see Chapter XIX). The process has gone less far and is less free from setbacks and compensatory tendencies than one would gather from many a popular exposition. In particular, large-scale enterprise not only annihilates but also, to some extent, creates space for the small producing, and especially trading, firm. Also, in the case of the peasants and farmers, the capitalist world has at last proved both willing and able to pursue an expensive but on the whole effective policy of conservation. In the long run, however, there can be little doubt about the fact we are envisaging, or about its consequences. Outside of the agrarian field, moreover, the bourgeoisie has shown but little awareness of the problem[4] or its importance for the survival of the capitalist order. The profits to be made by rationalizing the organization of production and especially by cheapening the tortuous way of commodities from the factory to the ultimate consumer are more than the mind of the typical businessman can resist.

Now it is important to realize precisely what these consequences consist in. A very common type of social criticism which we have already met laments the "decline of competition" and equates it to the decline of capitalism because of the virtues it attributes to competition and the vices it attributes to modern industrial "monopolies." In this schema of interpretation, monopolization plays the role of arteriosclerosis and reacts upon the fortunes of the capitalist order through increasingly unsatisfactory economic performance. We have seen the reasons for rejecting this view. Economically neither the case for competition nor the case against concentration of economic control is anything like as strong as this argument implies. And, whether weak or strong, it misses the salient point. Even if the giant concerns were all managed so perfectly as to call forth applause from the angels in heaven, the political consequences of concentration would still be what they are. The political structure of a nation is profoundly affected by the elimination of a host of small and medium-sized firms the owner-managers of which, together with their dependents, henchmen and connections, count quantitatively at the polls and have a hold on what we may term the foreman class that no management of a large unit can ever have; the very foundation of private property and free contracting wears away in a nation in

---

[4] Although some governments did; the government of imperial Germany did much to fight this particular kind of rationalization, and there is now a strong tendency to do the same in this country.

which its most vital, most concrete, most meaningful types disappear
from the moral horizon of the people.

On the other hand, the capitalist process also attacks its own institutional framework—let us continue to visualize "property" and
"free contracting" as *partes pro toto*—within the precincts of the
big units. Excepting the cases that are still of considerable importance
in which a corporation is practically owned by a single individual or
family, the figure of the proprietor and with it the specifically propri-
etary interest have vanished from the picture. There are the salaried
executives and all the salaried managers and submanagers. There are
the big stockholders. And then there are the small stockholders. The
first group tends to acquire the employee attitude and rarely if ever
identifies itself with the stockholding interest even in the most favorable cases, i.e., in the cases in which it identifies itself with the interest of the concern as such. The second group, even if it considers
its connection with the concern as permanent and even if it actually
behaves as financial theory would have stockholders behave, is at
one remove from both the functions and the attitudes of an owner.
As to the third group, small stockholders often do not care much
about what for most of them is but a minor source of income and,
whether they care or not, they hardly ever bother, unless they or
some representatives of theirs are out to exploit their nuisance value;
being often very ill used and still more often thinking themselves ill
used, they almost regularly drift into an attitude hostile to "their"
corporations, to big business in general and, particularly when things
look bad, to the capitalist order as such. No element of any of those
three groups into which I schematized the typical situation unconditionally takes the attitude characteristic of that curious phenomenon,
so full of meaning and so rapidly passing, that is covered by the term
Property.

Freedom of contracting is in the same boat. In its full vitality it
meant individual contracting regulated by individual choice between
an indefinite number of possibilities. The stereotyped, unindividual,
impersonal and bureaucratized contract of today—this applies much
more generally, but *a potiori* we may fasten upon the labor contract
—which presents but restricted freedom of choice and mostly turns
on a *c'est à prendre ou à laisser*, has none of the old features the most
important of which become impossible with giant concerns dealing
with other giant concerns or impersonal masses of workmen or consumers. The void is being filled by a tropical growth of new legal
structures—and a little reflection shows that this could hardly be
otherwise.

Thus the capitalist process pushes into the background all those
institutions, the institutions of property and free contracting in particular, that expressed the needs and ways of the truly "private"

economic activity. Where it does not abolish them, as it already has
abolished free contracting in the labor market, it attains the same end
by shifting the relative importance of existing legal forms—the legal
forms pertaining to corporate business for instance as against those
pertaining to the partnership or individual firm—or by changing
their contents or meanings. The capitalist process, by substituting a
mere parcel of shares for the walls of and the machines in a factory,
takes the life out of the idea of property. It loosens the grip that
once was so strong—the grip in the sense of the legal right and the
actual ability to do as one pleases with one's own; the grip also in
the sense that the holder of the title loses the will to fight, economically, physically, politically, for "his" factory and his control over it,
to die if necessary on its steps. And this evaporation of what we may
term the material substance of property—its visible and touchable
reality—affects not only the attitude of holders but also that of the
workmen and of the public in general. Dematerialized, defunctional-
ized and absentee ownership does not impress and call forth moral
allegiance as the vital form of property did. Eventually there will be
nobody left who really cares to stand for it—nobody within and nobody without the precincts of the big concerns.

CHAPTER XIII

GROWING HOSTILITY

I. The Social Atmosphere of Capitalism

FROM the analysis of the two preceding chapters, it should not be difficult to understand how the capitalist process produced that atmosphere of almost universal hostility to its own social order to which I have referred at the threshold of this part. The phenomenon is so striking and both the Marxian and the popular explanations are so inadequate that it is desirable to develop the theory of it a little further.

1. The capitalist process, so we have seen, eventually decreases the importance of the function by which the capitalist class lives. We have also seen that it tends to wear away protective strata, to break down its own defenses, to disperse the garrisons of its entrenchments. And we have finally seen that capitalism creates a critical frame of mind which, after having destroyed the moral authority of so many other institutions, in the end turns against its own; the bourgeois finds to his amazement that the rationalist attitude does not stop at the credentials of kings and popes but goes on to attack private property and the whole scheme of bourgeois values.

The bourgeois fortress thus becomes politically defenseless. Defenseless fortresses invite aggression especially if there is rich booty in them. Aggressors will work themselves up into a state of rationalizing hostility[1]—aggressors always do. No doubt it is possible, for a time, to buy them off. But this last resource fails as soon as they discover that they can have all. In part, this explains what we are out to explain. So far as it goes—it does not go the whole way of course—this element of our theory is verified by the high correlation that exists historically between bourgeois defenselessness and hostility to the capitalist order: there was very little hostility on principle as long as the bourgeois position was safe, although there was then much more reason for it; it spread *pari passu* with the crumbling of the protecting walls.

2. But, so it might well be asked—in fact, so it is being asked in naïve bewilderment by many an industrialist who honestly feels he

[1] It is hoped that no confusion will arise from my using the verb "to rationalize" in two different meanings. An industrial plant is being "rationalized" when its productive efficiency per unit of expenditure is being increased. We "rationalize" an action of ours when we supply ourselves and others with reasons for it that satisfy our standard of values regardless of what our true impulses may be.

is doing his duty by all classes of society—why should the capitalist order need any protection by extra-capitalist powers or extra-rational loyalties? Can it not come out of the trial with flying colors? Does not our own previous argument sufficiently show that it has plenty of utilitarian credentials to present? Cannot a perfectly good case be made out for it? And those industrialists will assuredly not fail to point out that a sensible workman, in weighing the pro's and con's of his contract with, say, one of the big steel or automobile concerns, might well come to the conclusion that, everything considered, he is not doing so badly and that the advantages of this bargain are not all on one side. Yes—certainly, only all that is quite irrelevant.

For, first, it is an error to believe that political attack arises primarily from grievance and that it can be turned by justification. Political criticism cannot be met effectively by rational argument. From the fact that the criticism of the capitalist order proceeds from a critical attitude of mind, i.e., from an attitude which spurns allegiance to extra-rational values, it does not follow that rational refutation will be accepted. Such refutation may tear the rational garb of attack but can never reach the extra-rational driving power that always lurks behind it. Capitalist rationality does not do away with sub- or super-rational impulses. It merely makes them get out of hand by removing the restraint of sacred or semi-sacred tradition. In a civilization that lacks the means and even the will to discipline and to guide them, they will revolt. And once they revolt it matters little that, in a rationalist culture, their manifestations will in general be rationalized somehow. Just as the call for utilitarian credentials has never been addressed to kings, lords and popes in a judicial frame of mind that would accept the possibility of a satisfactory answer, so capitalism stands its trial before judges who have the sentence of death in their pockets. They are going to pass it, whatever the defense they may hear; the only success victorious defense can possibly produce is a change in the indictment. Utilitarian reason is in any case weak as a prime mover of group action. In no case is it a match for the extra-rational determinants of conduct.

Second, the success of the indictment becomes quite understandable as soon as we realize what acceptance of the case for capitalism would imply. That case, were it even much stronger than it actually is, could never be made simple. People at large would have to be possessed of an insight and a power of analysis which are altogether beyond them. Why, practically every nonsense that has ever been said about capitalism has been championed by some professed economist. But even if this is disregarded, rational recognition of the economic performance of capitalism and of the hopes it holds out for the future would require an almost impossible moral feat by the have-not. That performance stands out only if we take a long-run view; any pro-capitalist argument must rest on long-run considerations. In the short run, it is profits and inefficiencies that dominate the picture. In order to accept his lot, the leveler or the chartist of old would have had to comfort himself with hopes for his great-grandchildren. In order to identify himself with the capitalist system, the unemployed of today would have completely to forget his personal fate and the politician of today his personal ambition. The long-run interests of society are so entirely lodged with the upper strata of bourgeois society that it is perfectly natural for people to look upon them as the interests of that class only. For the masses, it is the short-run view that counts. Like Louis XV, they feel *après nous le déluge*, and from the standpoint of individualist utilitarianism they are of course being perfectly rational if they feel likè that.

Third, there are the daily troubles and expectations of trouble everyone has to struggle with in any social system—the frictions and disappointments, the greater and smaller unpleasant events that hurt, annoy and thwart. I suppose that every one of us is more or less in the habit of attributing them wholly to that part of reality which lies without his skin, and *emotional* attachment to the social order—i.e., the very thing capitalism is constitutionally unable to produce—is necessary in order to overcome the hostile impulse by which we react to them. If there is no emotional attachment, then that impulse has its way and grows into a permanent constituent of our psychic setup.

Fourth, the ever-rising standards of life and particularly the leisure that modern capitalism provides for the fully employed workman . . . well, there is no need for me to finish the sentence or to elaborate one of the tritest, oldest and most stodgy of all arguments which unfortunately is but too true. Secular improvement that is taken for granted and coupled with individual insecurity that is acutely resented is of course the best recipe for breeding social unrest.

II. The Sociology of the Intellectual

Nevertheless, neither the opportunity of attack nor real or fancied grievances are in themselves sufficient to produce, however strongly they may favor, the emergence of active hostility against a social order. For such an atmosphere to develop it is necessary that there be groups to whose interest it is to work up and organize resentment, to nurse it, to voice it and to lead it. As will be shown in Part IV, the mass of people never develops definite opinions on its own initiative. Still less is it able to articulate them and to turn them into consistent attitudes and actions. All it can do is to follow or refuse to follow such group leadership as may offer itself. Until we have discovered social groups that will qualify for that role our theory of the atmosphere of hostility to capitalism is incomplete. Broadly speaking, conditions favorable to general hostility to a social system or specific attack upon it will in any case tend to call forth groups that will exploit them. But in the case of capitalist society there is a further fact to be noted: unlike any other type of society, capitalism inevitably and by virtue of the very logic of its civilization creates, educates and subsidizes a vested interest in social unrest.[2] Explanation of this phenomenon, which is as curious as it is important, follows from our argument in Chapter XI, but may be made more telling by an excursion into the Sociology of the Intellectual.

1. This type is not easy to define. The difficulty is in fact symptomatic of the character of the species. Intellectuals are not a social class in the sense in which peasants or industrial laborers constitute social classes; they hail from all the corners of the social world, and a great part of their activities consist in fighting each other and in forming the spearheads of class interests not their own. Yet they develop group attitudes and group interests sufficiently strong to make large numbers of them behave in the way that is usually associated with the concept of social classes. Again, they cannot be simply defined as the sum total of all the people who have had a higher education; that would obliterate the most important features of the type. Yet anyone who had—and, save exceptional cases, nobody who had not—is a potential intellectual; and the fact that their minds are all similarly furnished facilitates understanding between them and constitutes a bond. Nor would it serve our purpose to make the concept coextensive with the membership of the liberal professions; physicians or lawyers for instance are not intellectuals in the relevant sense unless they talk or write about subjects outside of their professional competence which no doubt they often do—particularly the lawyers. Yet there is a close connection between the intellectuals and the professions. For *some* professions—especially if we count in journalism—actually do belong almost wholly to the domain of the intellectual type; the members of *all* professions have the opportunity of becoming intellectuals; and many intellectuals take to some profession for a living. Finally, a definition by means of the contrast to manual labor would be much too wide.[3] Yet the Duke of Wellington's "scribbling set" seems to be too narrow.[4] So is the meaning of *hommes de lettres*.

[2] Every social system is sensitive to revolt and in every social system stirring up revolt is a business that pays in case of success and hence always attracts both brain and brawn. It did in feudal times—very much so. But warrior nobles who revolted against their superiors attacked individual persons or positions. They did not attack the feudal system as such. And feudal society as a whole displayed no tendencies to encourage—intentionally or unintentionally—attacks upon its own social system as a whole.

[3] To my sorrow, I have found that the Oxford English Dictionary does not list the meaning I wish to attach to the term. It does give the turn of phrase "a dinner of intellectuals," but in connection with "superior powers of intellect" which points in a very different direction. I have been duly disconcerted, yet have not been able to discover another term that would serve my purpose equally well.

[4] The Duke's phrase occurs in *The Croker Papers* (ed. L. J. Jennings, 1884).

But we might do worse than take our lead from the Iron Duke. Intellectuals are in fact people who wield the power of the spoken and the written word, and one of the touches that distinguish them from other people who do the same is the absence of direct responsibility for practical affairs. This touch in general accounts for another—the absence of that first-hand knowledge of them which only actual experience can give. The critical attitude, arising no less from the intellectual's situation as an onlooker—in most cases also as an outsider—than from the fact that his main chance of asserting himself lies in his actual or potential nuisance value, should add a third touch. The profession of the unprofessional? Professional dilettantism? The people who talk about everything because they understand nothing? Bernard Shaw's journalist in *The Doctor's Dilemma*? No, no. I have not said that and I do not mean that. That sort of thing would be still more untrue than it would be offensive. Let us give up trying to define by words and instead define "epideiktically": in the Greek museum we can see the object, nicely labeled. The sophists, philosophers and rhetors—however strongly they objected to being thrown together, they were all of the same genus—of the fifth and fourth centuries B.C. illustrate ideally what I mean. That practically all of them were teachers does not destroy the value of the illustration.

2. When analyzing the rationalist nature of capitalist civilization (Chapter XI) I pointed out that the development of rational thought of course precedes the rise of the capitalist order by thousands of years; all that capitalism did was to give a new impulse and a particular bend to the process. Similarly—leaving aside the Graeco-Roman world—we find intellectuals in thoroughly pre-capitalist conditions, for instance in the Kingdom of the Franks and in the countries into which it dissolved. But they were few in number; they were clergymen, mostly monks; and their written performance was accessible to only an infinitesimal part of the population. No doubt strong individuals were occasionally able to develop unorthodox views and even to convey them to popular audiences. This however in general implied antagonizing a very strictly organized environment—from which at the same time it was difficult to get away—and risking the lot of the heretic. Even so it was hardly possible without the support or connivance of some great lord or chieftain, as the tactics of missionaries suffice to show. On the whole, therefore, intellectuals were well in hand, and kicking over the traces was no joke, even in times of exceptional disorganization and license, such as during the Black Death (in and after 1348).

But if the monastery gave birth to the intellectual of the medieval world, it was capitalism that let him loose and presented him with the printing press. The slow evolution of the lay intellectual was merely an aspect of this process; the coincidence of the emergence of humanism with the emergence of capitalism is very striking. The humanists were primarily philologists but—excellently illustrating a point made above—they quickly expanded into the fields of manners, politics, religion and philosophy. This was not alone due to the contents of the classic works which they interpreted along with their grammar—from the criticism of a text to the criticism of a society, the way is shorter than it seems. Nevertheless, the typical intellectual did not relish the idea of the stake which still awaited the heretic. As a rule, honors and comfort suited him a great deal better. And these were after all to be had only from princes, temporal or spiritual, though the humanists were the first intellectuals to have a public in the modern sense. The critical attitude grew stronger every day. But *social* criticism—beyond what was implied in certain attacks on the Catholic Church and in particular its head—did not flourish under such conditions.

Honors and emoluments can however be had in more than one way. Flattery and subservience are often less remunerative than are their opposites. This discovery was not made by the Aretino[5] but no mortal ever surpassed him in exploiting it. Charles V was a devoted husband but, during his campaigns which kept him from home for many months at a time, he lived the life of a gentleman of his time and class. Very well, the public—and what particularly mattered to Charles, his empress—need never know, provided arguments of the right kind and weight were duly handed to the great critic of politics and morals. Charles paid up. But the point is that this was not simple blackmail which in general benefits one party only and inflicts uncompensated loss on the other. Charles knew why he paid though doubtless it would have been possible to secure silence by cheaper if more drastic methods. He did not display resentment. On the contrary he even went out of his way to honor the man. Obviously he wanted more than silence and, as a matter of fact, he received full value for his gifts.

3. In a sense, therefore, the Aretino's pen was indeed stronger than the sword. But, perhaps through ignorance, I do not know of comparable instances of that type for the next hundred and fifty years,[6] during which intellectuals do not seem to have played any great role outside and independently of the established professions, mainly the law and the church. Now this setback roughly coincides with the setback in capitalist evolution which in most countries of continental Europe occurred in that troubled period. And the subsequent recovery of capitalist enterprise was similarly shared by the intellectuals. The cheaper book, the cheap newspaper or pamphlet, together with the

---

[5] Pietro Aretino, 1492-1556.

[6] In England, however, the scope and importance of pamphleteering increased greatly in the seventeenth century.

widening of the public that was in part their product but partly an independent phenomenon due to the access of wealth and weight which came to the industrial bourgeoisie and to the incident increase in the political importance of an anonymous public opinion—all these boons, as well as increasing freedom from restraint, are by-products of the capitalist engine.

In the first three-quarters of the eighteenth century the individual patron was slow to lose the paramount importance in the intellectual's career that he had held at the beginning. But in the peak successes at least, we clearly discern the growing importance of the new element— the support of the collective patron, the bourgeois public. In this as in every other respect, Voltaire affords an invaluable instance. His very superficiality that made it possible for him to cover everything from religion to Newtonian optics, allied to indomitable vitality and an insatiable curiosity, a perfect absence of inhibitions, an unerring instinct for and a wholesale acceptance of the humors of his time, enabled that uncritical critic and mediocre poet and historian to fascinate—and to sell. He also speculated, cheated, accepted gifts and appointments, but there was always the independence founded on the solid base of his success with the public. Rousseau's case and type, though entirely different, would be still more instructive to discuss.

In the last decades of the eighteenth century a striking episode displayed the nature of the power of a free-lance intellectual who has nothing to work with but the socio-psychological mechanism called Public Opinion. This happened in England, the country that was then farthest advanced on the road of capitalist evolution. John Wilkes' attacks on the political system of England, it is true, were launched under uniquely favorable circumstances; moreover, it cannot be said that he actually upset the Earl of Bute's government which never had any chance and was bound to fall for a dozen other reasons; but Wilkes' *North Briton* was nevertheless the last straw that broke . . . Lord Bute's political back. No. 45 of the *North Briton* was the first discharge in a campaign that secured the abolition of general warrants and made a great stride toward the freedom of the press and of elections. This does not amount to making history or to creating the conditions for a change in social institutions, but it does amount to playing, say, the role of a midwife's assistant.[7] The inability of Wilkes' enemies to thwart him is the most significant fact

[7] I do not fear that any historian of politics will find that I have exaggerated the importance of Wilkes' success. But I do fear objection to my calling him a free lance and to the implication that he owed everything to the collective, and nothing to any individual patron. In his beginnings he was no doubt encouraged by a *coterie*. On examination it will however be conceded, I think, that this was not of decisive importance and that all the support and all the money and honors he got afterwards were but a consequence of and tribute to previous success and to a position independently acquired with the public.

about it all. They evidently had all the power of organized government at their command. Yet something drove them back.

In France, the years preceding the revolution and the revolution itself brought the rabble-raising tabloid (Marat, Desmoulins), which however did not, like ours, completely jettison style and grammar. But we must hurry on. The Terror and, more systematically, the First Empire put an end to this. Then followed a period, interrupted by the rule of the *roi bourgeois,* of more or less resolute repression that lasted until the Second Empire felt compelled to loosen the reins—about the middle sixties. In central and southern Europe this period also lasted about as long, and in England analogous conditions prevailed from the beginning of the revolutionary wars to Canning's accession to power.

4. How impossible it is to stem the tide within the framework of capitalist society is shown by the failure of the attempts—some of them prolonged and determined—made during that period by practically all European governments to bring the intellectuals to heel. Their histories were nothing but so many different versions of Wilkes exploits. In capitalist society—or in a society that contains a capitalist element of decisive importance—any attack on the intellectuals must run up against the private fortresses of bourgeois business which, or some of which, will shelter the quarry. Moreover such an attack must proceed according to bourgeois principles of legislative and administrative practice which no doubt may be stretched and bent but will checkmate prosecution beyond a certain point. Lawless violence the bourgeois stratum may accept or even applaud when thoroughly roused or frightened, but only temporarily. In a purely bourgeois regime like that of Louis Philippe, troops may fire on strikers, but the police cannot round up intellectuals or must release them forthwith; otherwise the bourgeois stratum, however strongly disapproving some of their doings, will rally behind them because the freedom it disapproves cannot be crushed without also crushing the freedom it approves.

Observe that I am not crediting the bourgeoisie with an unrealistic dose of generosity or idealism. Nor am I unduly stressing what people think and feel and want—on the importance of which I almost, though not quite, agree with Marx. In defending the intellectuals as a group —not of course every individual—the bourgeoisie defends itself and its scheme of life. Only a government of non-bourgeois nature and non-bourgeois creed—under modern circumstances only a socialist or fascist one—is strong enough to discipline them. In order to do that it would have to change typically bourgeois institutions and drastically reduce the individual freedom of *all* strata of the nation. And such a government is not likely—it would not even be able—to stop short of private enterprise.

From this follows both the unwillingness and the inability of the capitalist order to control its intellectual sector effectively. The unwillingness in question is unwillingness to use methods consistently that are uncongenial to the mentality shaped by the capitalist process; the inability is the inability to do so within the frame of institutions shaped by the capitalist process and without submitting to non-bourgeois rule. Thus, on the one hand, freedom of public discussion involving freedom to nibble at the foundations of capitalist society is inevitable in the long run. On the other hand, the intellectual group cannot help nibbling, because it lives on criticism and its whole position depends on criticism that stings; and criticism of persons and of current events will, in a situation in which nothing is sacrosanct, fatally issue in criticism of classes and institutions.

5. A few strokes will complete the modern picture. There are the increasing means. There is the increase in the standard of life and in the leisure of the masses that changed and is still changing the composition of the collective patron for the tastes of whom the intellectuals have to provide. There was and is the further cheapening of the book and newspaper and the large-scale newspaper concern.[8] There is now the radio. And there was and is the tendency toward complete removal of restraints, steadily breaking down those short-run attempts at resistance by which bourgeois society proves itself so incompetent and occasionally so childish a disciplinarian.

[8] The emergence and the career up to date of the large-scale newspaper concern illustrate two points which I am anxious to stress: the manifold aspects, relations and effects of *every* concrete element of the social pattern that preclude simple and one-way propositions, and the importance of distinguishing short-run and long-run phenomena for which different, sometimes opposite, propositions hold true. The *large*-scale newspaper concern is in most cases simply a capitalist business enterprise. This does not *imply* that it espouses capitalist or any other class interests. It *may* do so, but only from one or more of the following motives, the limited importance of which is obvious: because it is subsidized by a capitalist group for the very purpose of advocating its interests or views—the larger the concern and its sales, the less important this element; because it intends to sell to a public of bourgeois tastes—this, very important until about 1914, now increasingly cuts the other way; because advertisers prefer to use a congenial medium—but mostly they take a very businesslike view of the matter; because the owners insist on a certain course irrespective of their interest in sales—to a certain extent, they do and especially did, but experience teaches that they do not hold out if the conflict with their pecuniary interest in sales is too severe. In other words, the large-scale newspaper concern is a most powerful tool for raising the position and increasing the influence of the intellectual group, but it is even now not completely in its control. It means employment and a wider public, but it also means "strings." These are mainly of importance in the short run; in fighting for greater freedom to do as he pleases, the individual journalist may easily meet defeat. But this short-run aspect—and the group's recollection of past conditions—are what enters the intellectual's mind and what determines the colors of the picture of slavery and martyrdom he draws for the public. In reality, it should be a picture of conquest. Conquest and victory are in this, as in so many other cases, a mosaic composed of defeats.

There is, however, another factor. One of the most important features of the later stages of capitalist civilization is the vigorous expansion of the educational apparatus and particularly of the facilities for higher education. This development was and is no less inevitable than the development of the largest-scale industrial unit,[9] but, unlike the latter, it has been and is being fostered by public opinion and public authority so as to go much further than it would have done under its own steam. Whatever we may think of this from other standpoints and whatever the precise causation, there are several consequences that bear upon the size and attitude of the intellectual group.

First, inasmuch as higher education thus increases the supply of services in professional, quasi-professional and in the end all "white-collar" lines beyond the point determined by cost-return considerations, it may create a particularly important case of sectional unemployment.

Second, along with or in place of such unemployment, it creates unsatisfactory conditions of employment—employment in substandard work or at wages below those of the better-paid manual workers.

Third, it may create unemployability of a particularly disconcerting type. The man who has gone through a college or university easily becomes psychically unemployable in manual occupations without necessarily acquiring employability in, say, professional work. His failure to do so may be due either to lack of natural ability—perfectly compatible with passing academic tests—or to inadequate teaching; and both cases will, absolutely and relatively, occur more frequently as ever larger numbers are drafted into higher education and as the required amount of teaching increases irrespective of how many teachers and scholars nature chooses to turn out. The results of neglecting this and of acting on the theory that schools, colleges and universities are just a matter of money, are too obvious to insist upon. Cases in which among a dozen applicants for a job, all formally qualified, there is not one who can fill it satisfactorily, are known to everyone who has anything to do with appointments—to everyone, that is, who is himself qualified to judge.

[9] At present this development is viewed by most people from the standpoint of the ideal of making educational facilities of any type available to all who can be induced to use them. This ideal is so strongly held that any doubts about it are almost universally considered to be nothing short of indecent, a situation not improved by the comments, all too often flippant, of dissentients. Actually, we brush here against a set of extremely complex problems of the sociology of education and educational ideals which we cannot attack within the limits of this sketch. This is why I have confined the above paragraph to two incontestable and noncommittal trivialities that are all we want for the purpose in hand. But of course they do not dispose of the larger problems which must be left aside to testify to the incompleteness of my exposition.

All those who are unemployed or unsatisfactorily employed or unemployable drift into the vocations in which standards are least definite or in which aptitudes and acquirements of a different order count. They swell the host of intellectuals in the strict sense of the term whose numbers hence increase disproportionately. They enter it in a thoroughly discontented frame of mind. Discontent breeds resentment. And it often rationalizes itself into that social criticism which as we have seen before is in any case the intellectual spectator's typical attitude toward men, classes and institutions especially in a rationalist and utilitarian civilization. Well, here we have numbers; a well-defined group situation of proletarian hue; and a group interest shaping a group attitude that will much more realistically account for hostility to the capitalist order than could the theory—itself a rationalization in the psychological sense—according to which the intellectual's righteous indignation about the wrongs of capitalism simply represents the logical inference from outrageous facts and which is no better than the theory of lovers that their feelings represent nothing but the logical inference from the virtues of the beloved.[10] Moreover our theory also accounts for the fact that this hostility increases, instead of diminishing, with every achievement of capitalist evolution.

Of course, the hostility of the intellectual group—amounting to moral disapproval of the capitalist order—is one thing, and the general hostile atmosphere which surrounds the capitalist engine is another thing. The latter is the really significant phenomenon; and it is not simply the product of the former but flows partly from independent sources, some of which have been mentioned before; so far as it does, it is raw material for the intellectual group to work on. There are give-and-take relations between the two which it would require more space to unravel than I can spare. The general contours of such an analysis are however sufficiently obvious and I think it safe to repeat that the role of the intellectual group consists primarily in stimulating, energizing, verbalizing and organizing this material and only secondarily in adding to it. Some particular aspects will illustrate the principle.

6. Capitalist evolution produces a labor movement which obviously is not the creation of the intellectual group. But it is not surprising that such an opportunity and the intellectual demiurge should find each other. Labor never craved intellectual leadership but intellectuals invaded labor politics. They had an important contribution to make:

[10] The reader will observe that any such theories would be unrealistic even if the facts of capitalism or the virtues of the beloved were actually all that the social critic or the lover believes them to be. It is also important to note that in the overwhelming majority of cases both critics and lovers are obviously sincere; neither psycho-sociological nor psycho-physical mechanisms enter as a rule into the limelight of the Ego, except in the mask of sublimations.

they verbalized the movement, supplied theories and slogans for it
—class war is an excellent example—made it conscious of itself and
in doing so changed its meaning. In solving this task from their own
standpoint, they naturally radicalized it, eventually imparting a revolutionary bias to the most bourgeois trade-union practices, a bias
most of the non-intellectual leaders at first greatly resented. But there
was another reason for this. Listening to the intellectual, the workman is almost invariably conscious of an impassable gulf if not of
downright distrust. In order to get hold of him and to compete with
non-intellectual leaders, the intellectual is driven to courses entirely
unnecessary for the latter who can afford to frown. Having no genuine
authority and feeling always in danger of being unceremoniously told
to mind his own business, he must flatter, promise and incite, nurse left
wings and scowling minorities, sponsor doubtful or submarginal cases,
appeal to fringe ends, profess himself ready to obey—in short, behave
toward the masses as his predecessors behaved first toward their ecclesiastical superiors, later toward princes and other individual patrons,
still later toward the collective master of bourgeois complexion.[11]
Thus, though intellectuals have not created the labor movement, they
have yet worked it up into something that differs substantially from
what it would be without them.

The social atmosphere, for the theory of which we have been gathering stones and mortar, explains why public policy grows more and
more hostile to capitalist interests, eventually so much so as to refuse
on principle to take account of the requirements of the capitalist
engine and to become a serious impediment to its functioning. The
intellectual group's activities have however a relation to anti-capitalist
policies that is more direct than what is implied in their share in verbalizing them. Intellectuals rarely enter professional politics and still
more rarely conquer responsible office. But they staff political bureaus,
write party pamphlets and speeches, act as secretaries and advisers,
make the individual politician's newspaper reputation which, though
it is not everything, few men can afford to neglect. In doing these
things they to some extent impress their mentality on almost everything that is being done.

The actual influence exerted varies greatly with the state of the
political game from mere formulation to making a measure politically
possible or impossible. But there is always plenty of scope for it. When
we say that individual politicians and parties are exponents of class
interests we are at best emphasizing one-half of the truth. The other
half, just as important if not more so, comes into view when we consider that politics is a profession which evolves interests of its own—
interests that may clash with as well as conform to the interests of the

[11] All this will be illustrated and further developed in Part V.

groups that a man or party "represents."[12] Individual and party opinion is, more than anything else, sensitive to those factors in the political situation that directly affect the career or the standing of the individual or party. Some of these are controlled by the intellectual group in much the same sense as is the moral code of an epoch that exalts the cause of some interests and puts the cause of others tacitly out of court.

Finally, that social atmosphere or code of values affects not only policies—the spirit of legislation—but also administrative practice. But again there is also a more direct relation between the intellectual group and bureaucracy. The bureaucracies of Europe are of pre- and extra-capitalist origin. However much they may have changed in composition as the centuries rolled on, they never identified themselves wholly with the bourgeoisie, its interests or its scheme of values, and never saw much more in it than an asset to be managed in the interest of the monarch or of the nation. Except for inhibitions due to professional training and experience, they are therefore open to conversion by the modern intellectual with whom, through a similar education, they have much in common,[13] while the tinge of gentility that in many cases used to raise a barrier has been fading away from the modern civil servant during the last decades. Moreover, in times of rapid expansion of the sphere of public administration, much of the additional personnel required has to be taken directly from the intellectual group—witness this country.

[12] This of course is just as true of the intellectuals themselves with respect to the class from which they come or to which, economically and culturally, they belong. The subject will be taken up again in ch. xxiii.

[13] For examples see ch. xxvi.

CHAPTER XIV

DECOMPOSITION

1. Faced by the increasing hostility of the environment and by the legislative, administrative and judicial practice born of that hostility, entrepreneurs and capitalists—in fact the whole stratum that accepts the bourgeois scheme of life—will eventually cease to function. Their standard aims are rapidly becoming unattainable, their efforts futile. The most glamorous of these bourgeois aims, the foundation of an industrial dynasty, has in most countries become unattainable already, and even more modest ones are so difficult to attain that they may cease to be thought worth the struggle as the permanence of these conditions is being increasingly realized.

Considering the role of bourgeois motivation in the explanation of the economic history of the last two or three centuries, its smothering by the unfavorable reactions of society or its weakening by disuse no doubt constitutes a factor adequate to explain a flop in the capitalist process—should we ever observe it as a permanent phenomenon—and one that is much more important than any of those that are presented by the Theory of Vanishing Investment Opportunity. It is hence interesting to observe that that motivation not only is threatened by forces external to the bourgeois mind but that it also tends to die out from internal causes. There is of course close interdependence between the two. But we cannot get at the true diagnosis unless we try to disentangle them.

One of those "internal causes" we have already met with. I have dubbed it Evaporation of the Substance of Property. We have seen that, normally, the modern businessman, whether entrepreneur or mere managing administrator, is of the executive type. From the logic of his position he acquires something of the psychology of the salaried employee working in a bureaucratic organization. Whether a stockholder or not, his will to fight and to hold on is not and cannot be what it was with the man who knew ownership and its responsibilities in the fullblooded sense of those words. His system of values and his conception of duty undergo a profound change. Mere stockholders of course have ceased to count at all—quite independently of the clipping of their share by a regulating and taxing state. Thus the modern corporation, although the product of the capitalist process, socializes the bourgeois mind; it relentlessly narrows the scope of capitalist motivation; not only that, it will eventually kill its roots.[1]

[1] Many people will deny this. This is due to the fact that they derive their impression from past history and from the slogans generated by past history during

2. Still more important however is another "internal cause," viz., the disintegration of the bourgeois family. The facts to which I am referring are too well known to need explicit statement. To men and women in modern capitalist societies, family life and parenthood mean less than they meant before and hence are less powerful molders of behavior; the rebellious son or daughter who professes contempt for "Victorian" standards is, however incorrectly, expressing an undeniable truth. The weight of these facts is not impaired by our inability to measure them statistically. The marriage rate proves nothing because the term Marriage covers as many sociological meanings as does the term Property, and the kind of alliance that used to be formed by the marriage contract may completely die out without any change in the legal construction or in the frequency of the contract. Nor is the divorce rate more significant. It does not matter how many marriages are dissolved by judicial decree—what matters is how many lack the content essential to the old pattern. If in our statistical age readers insist on a statistical measure, the proportion of marriages that produce no children or only one child, though still inadequate to quantify the phenomenon I mean, might come as near as we can hope to come to indicating its numerical importance. The phenomenon by now extends, more or less, to all classes. But it first appeared in the bourgeois (and intellectual) stratum and its symptomatic as well as causal value for our purposes lies entirely there. It is wholly attributable to the rationalization of everything in life, which we have seen is one of the effects of capitalist evolution. In fact, it is but one of the results of the spread of that rationalization to the sphere of private life. All the other factors which are usually adduced in explanation can be readily reduced to that one.

As soon as men and women learn the utilitarian lesson and refuse to take for granted the traditional arrangements that their social environment makes for them, as soon as they acquire the habit of weighing the individual advantages and disadvantages of any prospective course of action—or, as we might also put it, as soon as they introduce into their private life a sort of inarticulate system of cost accounting —they cannot fail to become aware of the heavy personal sacrifices that family ties and especially parenthood entail under modern conditions and of the fact that at the same time, excepting the cases of farmers and peasants, children cease to be economic assets. These sacrifices do not consist only of the items that come within the reach of the measuring rod of money but comprise in addition an indefinite

which the institutional change brought about by the big corporation had not yet asserted itself. Also they may think of the scope which corporate business used to give for illegal satisfactions of the capitalist motivation. But that would cut my way: the fact that personal gain beyond salary and bonus cannot, in corporate business, be reaped by executives except by illegal or semi-illegal practices shows precisely that the structural idea of the corporation is averse to it.

amount of loss of comfort, of freedom from care, and opportunity to enjoy alternatives of increasing attractiveness and variety—alternatives to be compared with joys of parenthood that are being subjected to a critical analysis of increasing severity. The implication of this is not weakened but strengthened by the fact that the balance sheet is likely to be incomplete, perhaps even fundamentally wrong. For the greatest of the assets, the contribution made by parenthood to physical and moral health—to "normality" as we might express it —particularly in the case of women, almost invariably escapes the rational searchlight of modern individuals who, in private as in public life, tend to focus attention on ascertainable details of immediate utilitarian relevance and to sneer at the idea of hidden necessities of human nature or of the social organism. The point I wish to convey is, I think, clear without further elaboration. It may be summed up in the question that is so clearly in many potential parents' minds: "Why should we stunt our ambitions and impoverish our lives in order to be insulted and looked down upon in our old age?"

While the capitalist process, by virtue of the psychic attitudes it creates, progressively dims the values of family life and removes the conscientious inhibitions that an old moral tradition would have put in the way toward a different scheme of life, it at the same time implements the new tastes. As regards childlessness, capitalist inventiveness produces contraceptive devices of ever-increasing efficiency that overcome the resistance which the strongest impulse of man would otherwise have put up. As regards the style of life, capitalist evolution decreases the desirability of, and provides alternatives to, the bourgeois family home. I have previously adverted to the Evaporation of Industrial Property; I have now to advert to the Evaporation of Consumers' Property.

Until the later decades of the nineteenth century, the town house and the country place were everywhere not only pleasant and convenient shells of private life on the higher levels of income, but they were indispensable. Not only hospitality on any scale and in any style, but even the comfort, dignity, repose and refinement of the family depended upon its having an adequate *foyer* of its own that was adequately staffed. The arrangements summarized by the term Home were accordingly accepted as a matter of course by the average man and woman of bourgeois standing, exactly as they looked upon marriage and children—the "founding of a family"—as a matter of course.

Now, on the one hand, the amenities of the bourgeois home are becoming less obvious than are its burdens. To the critical eye of a critical age it is likely to appear primarily as a source of trouble and expense which frequently fail to justify themselves. This would be so even independently of modern taxation and wages and of the attitude of modern household personnel, all of which are typical results of the capitalist process and of course greatly strengthen the case against what in the near future will be almost universally recognized as an outmoded and uneconomical way of life. In this respect as in others we are living in a transitional stage. The average family of bourgeois standing tends to reduce the difficulties of running the big house and the big country place by substituting for it small and mechanized establishments plus a maximum of outside service and outside life—hospitality in particular being increasingly shifted to the restaurant or club.

On the other hand, the home of the old type is no longer an indispensable requirement of comfortable and refined living in the bourgeois sphere. The apartment house and the apartment hotel represent a rationalized type of abode and another style of life which when fully developed will no doubt meet the new situation and provide all the essentials of comfort and refinement. To be sure, neither that style nor its shell are fully developed anywhere as yet and they proffer cost advantage only if we count in the trouble and annoyance incident to running a modern home. But other advantages they proffer already —the facility of using to the full the variety of modern enjoyments, of travel, of ready mobility, of shifting the load of the current little things of existence to the powerful shoulders of highly specialized organizations.

It is easy to see how this in turn bears, in the upper strata of capitalist society, upon the problems of the child. Again there is interaction: the passing of the spacious home—in which alone the rich life of a numerous family can unfold[2]—and the increasing friction with which it functions supply another motive for avoiding the cares of parenthood; but the decline of philoprogenitivity in turn renders the spacious home less worth while.

I have said that the new style of bourgeois life does not as yet offer any decisive cost advantage. But this refers only to the current or prime costs of servicing the wants of private life. As to overhead, even the purely pecuniary advantage is obvious already. And inasmuch as the outlay on the most durable elements of home life—especially the house, the pictures, the furniture—used to be financed mainly from previous earnings we may say that the need for accumulation of "consumers' capital" is drastically reduced by that process. This does not mean of course that demand for "consumers' capital" is at present, even relatively, smaller than it was; the increasing demand for durable consumers' goods from small and medium incomes more than counterbalances this effect. But it does mean that, so far as the hedonistic component in the pattern of acquisitive motives is concerned, the desirability of incomes beyond a certain level is reduced. In order to satisfy

---

[2] Modern relations between parents and children are of course partly conditioned by the crumbling of that steady frame of family life.

himself of this, the reader need only visualize the situation in a thoroughly practical spirit: the successful man or couple or the "society" man or couple who can pay for the best available accommodation in hotel, ship and train, and for the best available qualities of the objects of personal consumption and use—which qualities are increasingly being turned out by the conveyor of mass production[3]—will, things being what they are, as a rule have all they want with any intensity *for themselves*. And it is easy to see that a budget framed on those lines will be far below the requirements of a "seignioral" style of life.

3. In order to realize what all this means for the efficiency of the capitalist engine of production we need only recall that the family and the family home used to be the mainspring of the typically bourgeois kind of profit motive. Economists have not always given due weight to this fact. When we look more closely at their idea of the self-interest of entrepreneurs and capitalists we cannot fail to discover that the results it was supposed to produce are really not at all what one would expect from the rational self-interest of the detached individual or the childless couple who no longer look at the world through the windows of a family home. Consciously or unconsciously they analyzed the behavior of the man whose views and motives are shaped by such a home and who means to work and to save primarily for wife *and children*. As soon as these fade out from the moral vision of the businessman, we have a different kind of *homo oeconomicus* before us who cares for different things and acts in different ways. For him and from the standpoint of his individualistic utilitarianism, the behavior of that old type would in fact be completely irrational. He loses the only sort of romance and heroism that is left in the unromantic and unheroic civilization of capitalism—the heroism of *navigare necesse est, vivere non necesse est*.[4] And he loses the capitalist ethics that enjoins working for the future irrespective of whether or not one is going to harvest the crop oneself.

The last point may be put more tellingly. In the preceding chapter it was observed that the capitalist order entrusts the long-run interests of society to the upper strata of the bourgeoisie. They are really entrusted to the family motive operative in those strata. The bourgeoisie worked primarily in order to invest, and it was not so much a standard of consumption as a standard of accumulation that the bourgeoisie struggled for and tried to defend against governments that took the

---

[3] Effects on consumers' budgets of the increasing eligibility of mass-produced articles are enhanced by the price difference between them and the corresponding custom-made articles which increases owing to the increase in wages *pari passu* with the decrease in the relative desirability of the latter; the capitalist process democratizes consumption.

[4] "Seafaring is necessary, living is not necessary." Inscription on an old house in Bremen.

short-run view.[5] With the decline of the driving power supplied by the family motive, the businessman's time-horizon shrinks, roughly, to his life expectation. And he might now be--less willing than he was to fulfill that function of earning, saving and investing even if he saw no reason to fear that the results would but swell his tax bills. He drifts into an anti-saving frame of mind and accepts with an increasing readiness anti-saving *theories* that are indicative of a short-run *philosophy*.

But anti-saving theories are not all that he accepts. With a different attitude to the concern he works for and with a different scheme of private life he tends to acquire a different view of the values and standards of the capitalist order of things. Perhaps the most striking feature of the picture is the extent to which the bourgeoisie, besides educating its own enemies, allows itself in turn to be educated by them. It absorbs the slogans of current radicalism and seems quite willing to undergo a process of conversion to a creed hostile to its very existence. Haltingly and grudgingly it concedes in part the implications of that creed. This would be most astonishing and indeed very hard to explain were it not for the fact that the typical bourgeois is rapidly losing faith in his own creed. And this again becomes fully understandable as soon as we realize that the social conditions which account for its emergence are passing.

This is verified by the very characteristic manner in which particular capitalist interests and the bourgeoisie as a whole behave when facing direct attack. They talk and plead—or hire people to do it for them; they snatch at every chance of compromise; they are ever ready to give in; they never put up a fight under the flag of their own ideals and interests—in this country there was no real resistance anywhere against the imposition of crushing financial burdens during the last decade or against labor legislation incompatible with the effective management of industry. Now, as the reader will surely know by this time, I am far from overestimating the political power of either big business or the bourgeoisie in general. Moreover, I am prepared to make large allowances for cowardice. But still, means of defense were not entirely lacking as yet and history is full of examples of the success of small groups who, believing in their cause, were resolved to stand by their guns. The only explanation for the meekness we observe is that the bourgeois order no longer makes any sense to the bourgeoisie itself and that, when all is said and nothing is done, it does not really care.

Thus the same economic process that undermines the position of the bourgeoisie by decreasing the importance of the functions of entre-

[5] It has been said that in economic matters "the state can take the longer view." But excepting certain matters outside of party politics such as conservation of natural resources, it hardly ever does.

preneurs and capitalists, by breaking up protective strata and institutions, by creating an atmosphere of hostility, also decomposes the motor forces of capitalism from within. Nothing else shows so well that the capitalist order not only rests on props made of extra-capitalist material but also derives its energy from extra-capitalist patterns of behavior which at the same time it is bound to destroy.

We have rediscovered what from different standpoints and, so I believe, on inadequate grounds has often been discovered before: there is inherent in the capitalist system a tendency toward self-destruction which, in its earlier stages, may well assert itself in the form of a tendency toward retardation of progress.

I shall not stay to repeat how objective and subjective, economic and extra-economic factors, reinforcing each other in imposing accord, contribute to that result. Nor shall I stay to show what should be obvious and in subsequent chapters will become more obvious still, viz., that those factors make not only for the destruction of the capitalist but for the emergence of a socialist civilization. They all point in that direction. The capitalist process not only destroys its own institutional framework but it also creates the conditions for another. Destruction may not be the right word after all. Perhaps I should have spoken of transformation. The outcome of the process is not simply a void that could be filled by whatever might happen to turn up; things and souls are transformed in such a way as to become increasingly amenable to the socialist form of life. With every peg from under the capitalist structure vanishes an impossibility of the socialist plan. In both these respects Marx's *vision* was right. We can also agree with him in linking the particular social transformation that goes on under our eyes with an economic process as its prime mover. What our analysis, if correct, disproves is after all of secondary importance, however essential the role may be which it plays in the socialist credo. In the end there is not so much difference as one might think between saying that the decay of capitalism is due to its success and saying that it is due to its failure.

But our answer to the question that heads this part posits far more problems than it solves. In view of what is to follow in this book, the reader should bear in mind:

First, that so far we have not learned anything about the kind of socialism that may be looming in the future. For Marx and for most of his followers—and this was and is one of the most serious shortcomings of their doctrine—socialism meant just one definite thing. But the definiteness really goes no further than nationalization of industry would carry us and with this an indefinite variety of economic and cultural possibilities will be seen to be compatible.

Second, that similarly we know nothing as yet about the precise way by which socialism may be expected to come except that there must be a great many possibilities ranging from a gradual bureaucratization to the most picturesque revolution. Strictly speaking we do not even know whether socialism will actually come to stay. For to repeat: perceiving a tendency and visualizing the goal of it is one thing and predicting that this goal will actually be reached and that the resulting state of things will be workable, let alone permanent, is quite another thing. Before humanity chokes (or basks) in the dungeon (or paradise) of socialism it may well burn up in the horrors (or glories) of imperialist wars.[6]

Third, that the various components of the tendency we have been trying to describe, while everywhere discernible, have as yet nowhere fully revealed themselves. Things have gone to different lengths in different countries but in no country far enough to allow us to say with any confidence precisely how far they will go, or to assert that their "underlying trend" has grown too strong to be subject to anything more serious than temporary reverses. Industrial integration is far from being complete. Competition, actual and potential, is still a major factor in any business situation. Enterprise is still active, the leadership of the bourgeois group still the prime mover of the economic process. The middle class is still a political power. Bourgeois standards and bourgeois motivations though being increasingly impaired are still alive. Survival of traditions—and family ownership of controlling parcels of stock—still make many an executive behave as the owner-manager did of old. The bourgeois family has not yet died; in fact, it clings to life so tenaciously that no responsible politician has as yet dared to touch it by any method other than taxation. From the standpoint of immediate practice as well as for the purposes of short-run forecasting—and in these things, a century is a "short run"[7]—all this surface may be more important than the tendency toward another civilization that slowly works deep down below.

[6] Written in the summer of 1935.

[7] This is why the facts and arguments presented in this and the two preceding chapters do not invalidate my reasoning about the possible economic results of another fifty years of capitalist evolution. The thirties may well turn out to have been the last gasp of capitalism—the likelihood of this is of course greatly increased by the current war. But again they may not. In any case there are no *purely economic* reasons why capitalism should not have another successful run which is all I wished to establish.

PART III

Can Socialism Work?

CHAPTER XV

CLEARING DECKS

C AN socialism work? Of course it can. No doubt is possible about that once we assume, first, that the requisite stage of industrial development has been reached and, second, that transitional problems can be successfully resolved. One may, of course, feel very uneasy about these assumptions themselves or about the questions whether the socialist form of society can be expected to be democratic and, democratic or not, how well it is likely to function. All that will be discussed later on. But if we accept these assumptions and discard these doubts the answer to the remaining question is clearly Yes.

Before I attempt to prove it, I should like to clear some obstacles from our way. We have so far been rather careless about certain definitions and we must make up for it now. We shall simply envisage two types of society and mention others only incidentally. These types we will call Commercial and Socialist.

Commercial society is defined by an institutional pattern of which we need only mention two elements: private property in means of production and regulation of the productive process by private contract (or management or initiative). Such a type of society is not as a rule purely bourgeois, however. For as we have seen in Part II an industrial and commercial bourgeoisie will in general not be able to exist except in symbiosis with a non-bourgeois stratum. Nor is commercial society identical with capitalist society. The latter, a special case of the former, is defined by the additional phenomenon of credit creation—by the practice, responsible for so many outstanding features of modern economic life, of financing enterprise by bank credit, i.e., by money (notes or deposits) manufactured for that purpose. But since commercial society, as an alternative to socialism, in practice always appears in the particular form of capitalism, it will make no great difference if the reader prefers to keep to the traditional contrast between capitalism and socialism.

By socialist society we shall designate an institutional pattern in which the control over means of production and over production itself is vested with a central authority—or, as we may say, in which, as a matter of principle, the economic affairs of society belong to the public and not to the private sphere. Socialism has been called an intellectual Proteus. There are many ways of defining it—many acceptable ways, that is, besides the silly ones such as that socialism means bread for all—and ours is not necessarily the best. But there are some points about it which it may be well for us to notice, braving the danger of an indictment on the score of pedantry.

Our definition excludes guild socialism, syndicalism and other types. This is because what may be termed Centralist Socialism seems to me to hold the field so clearly that it would be waste of space to consider other forms. But if we adopt this term in order to indicate the only kind of socialism we shall consider, we must be careful to avoid a mis-understanding. The term centralist socialism is only intended to ex-clude the existence of a plurality of units of control such that each of them would on principle stand for a distinct interest of its own, in particular the existence of a plurality of autonomous territorial sectors that would go far toward reproducing the antagonisms of capitalist society. This exclusion of sectional interests may well be thought unrealistic. Nonetheless it is essential.

But our term is not intended to suggest centralism either in the sense that the central authority, which we shall alternatively call Central Board or Ministry of Production, is necessarily absolute or in the sense that all the initiative that pertains to the executive proceeds from it alone. As regards the first point, the board or ministry may have to submit its plan to a congress or parliament. There may also be a supervising and checking authority—a kind of *cour des comptes* that could conceivably even have the right to veto particular decisions. As regards the second point, some freedom of action must be left, and almost any amount of freedom might be left, to the "men on the spot," say, the managers of the individual industries or plants. For the moment, I will make the bold assumption that the rational amount of freedom is experimentally found and actually granted so that ef-ficiency suffers neither from the unbridled ambitions of subordinates nor from the piling up on the desk of the minister of reports and unanswered questions—nor from orders of the latter suggestive of Mark Twain's rules about the harvesting of potatoes.

I have not separately defined collectivism or communism. The former term I shall not use at all and the latter only incidentally with reference to groups that call themselves so. But if I had to use them I should make them synonymous with socialism. Analyzing historical usage, most writers have tried to give them distinct meanings. It is true that the term communist has fairly consistently been chosen to denote ideas more thoroughgoing or radical than others. But then, one of the classic documents of socialism is entitled the "Communist" Manifesto. And the difference of principle has never been fundamental —what there is of it is no less pronounced within the socialist camp than it is as between it and the communist one. Bolsheviks call them-selves communists and at the same time the true and only socialists. Whether or not the true and only ones, they are certainly socialists.

I have avoided the terms state ownership of, or property in, natural resources, plant and equipment. This point is of some importance in the methodology of the social sciences. There are no doubt concepts that bear no relation to any particular epoch or social world, such as want or choice or economic good. There are others which, while in their everyday meaning they do bear such a relation, have been refined by the analyst to the point of losing it. Price or cost may serve as examples.[1] But there are still others which by virtue of their nature cannot stand transplantation and always carry the flavor of a particular institutional framework. It is extremely dangerous, in fact it amounts to a distortion of historical description, to use them beyond the social world or culture whose denizens they are. Now ownership or property —also, so I believe, taxation—are such denizens of the world of commercial society, exactly as knights and fiefs are denizens of the feudal world.

But so is the state. We might of course define it by the criterion of sovereignty and then speak of a socialist state. But if there is to be meat in the concept and not merely legal or philosophic gas, the state should not be allowed to intrude into discussions of either feudal or socialist society, neither of which did or would display that dividing line between the private and the public sphere from which the better part of its meaning flows. To conserve that meaning with all its wealth of functions, methods and attitudes, it seems best to say that the state, the product of the clashes and compromises between feudal lords and bourgeoisie, will form part of the ashes from which the socialist phoenix is to rise. Therefore, I did not use it in my definition of socialism. Of course socialism may come about by an act of the state. But there is no inconvenience that I can see in saying that the state dies in this act—as has been pointed out by Marx and repeated by Lenin.

In one respect, finally, our definition agrees with all the others that I have ever come across, viz., in that it turns on an exclusively economic point. Every socialist wishes to revolutionize society from the economic angle and all the blessings he expects are to come through a change in economic institutions. This of course implies a theory about social causation—the theory that the economic pattern is the really operative element in the sum total of the phenomena that we call society. Two remarks, however, suggest themselves.

First, it has been pointed out in the preceding part with reference to capitalism, and must now be pointed out with reference to socialism, that neither for us, the observers, nor for the people that are to put their trust in socialism, is the economic aspect the only or even

[1] Price, in modern theory, is defined as a mere coefficient of transformation. Cost, in the sense of opportunity cost, is a general logical category. We shall however soon return to this.

the most important one. In defining as I did, I did not intend to deny that. And in fairness to all the civilized socialists whom I have ever met or read, it should be stated that the same holds true for them: that in stressing the economic element because of the causative importance their creed attributes to it, they do not mean to suggest that nothing is worth struggling for except beefsteaks and radios. There are indeed insufferable stick-in-the-muds who mean precisely that. And many who are not stick-in-the-muds will nevertheless, in the hunt for votes, emphasize the economic promise because of its immediate appeal. In doing so they distort and degrade their creed. We will not do the same. Instead we will keep in mind that socialism aims at higher goals than full bellies, exactly as Christianity means more than the somewhat hedonistic values of heaven and hell. First and foremost, socialism means a new cultural world. For the sake of it, one might conceivably be a fervent socialist even though believing that the socialist arrangement is likely to be inferior as to economic performance.[2] Hence no merely economic argument for or against can ever be decisive, however successful in itself.

But second—what cultural world? We might try to answer this question by surveying the actual professions of accredited socialists in order to see whether a type emerges from them. At first sight, the material seems to be abundant. Some socialists are ready enough, with folded hands and the smile of the blessed on their lips, to chant the canticle of justice, equality, freedom in general and freedom from "the exploitation of man by man" in particular, of peace and love, of fetters broken and cultural energies unchained, of new horizons opened, of new dignities revealed. But that is Rousseau adulterated with some Bentham. Others simply voice the interests and appetites of the radical wing of trade unionism. Still others, however, are remarkably reticent. Because they despise cheap slogans but cannot think of anything else? Because, though they do think of something else, they doubt its popular appeal? Because they know that they differ hopelessly with their comrades?

So we cannot proceed on this line. Instead we have to face what I shall refer to as the Cultural Indeterminateness of Socialism. In fact, according to our definition as well as to most others, a society may be fully and truly socialist and yet be led by an absolute ruler or be organized in the most democratic of all possible ways; it may be aristocratic or proletarian; it may be a theocracy and hierarchic or atheist or indifferent as to religion; it may be much more strictly disciplined than men are in a modern army or completely lacking in discipline; it may be ascetic or eudemonist in spirit; energetic or slack; thinking only of the future or only of the day; warlike and nationalist or peace-

[2] The reverse is also true of course: one might concede the economic claims made on behalf of socialism and yet hate it on cultural grounds.

ful and internationalist; equalitarian or the opposite; it may have
the ethics of lords or the ethics of slaves; its art may be subjective or
objective;[3] its forms of life individualistic or standardized; and—
what for some of us would by itself suffice to command our allegiance
or to arouse our contempt—it may breed from its supernormal or
from its subnormal stock and produce supermen or submen accordingly.

Why is this so? Well, the reader may have his choice. He may say
either that Marx is wrong and that the economic pattern does not
determine a civilization or else that the complete economic pattern
would determine it but that, without the aid of further economic
data and assumptions, the element that constitutes socialism in our
sense does not. We should not have fared any better with capitalism,
by the way, had we tried to reconstruct its cultural world from nothing
but the facts embodied in our definition of it. We have in this case
no doubt an impression of determinateness and find it possible to
reason on tendencies in capitalist civilization. But this is only because
we have a historic reality before us that supplies us with all the additional data we need and *via facti* excludes an infinite number of
possibilities.

We have, however, used the word determinateness in a rather strict
and technical sense and, moreover, with reference to a whole cultural
world. Indeterminateness in this sense is no absolute bar to attempts
at discovering certain features or tendencies that the socialist arrangement as such may be more likely to produce than others, especially features of, and tendencies in, particular spots of the cultural
organism. Nor is it impossible to frame reasonable additional assumptions. This much is obvious from the above survey of possibilities.
If, for instance, we believe as many socialists do—wrongly, as I think
—that wars are nothing but one of the forms of the conflict of capitalist interests, it readily follows that socialism would be pacifist and
not warlike. Or if we assume that socialism evolves along with, and
is inseparable from, a certain type of rationalism we shall conclude
that it is likely to be irreligious if not anti-religious. We shall ourselves try our hand at this game here and there, although in the main
we had better yield the floor to the only truly great performer in that
field, Plato. But all this does not do away with the fact that socialism
is indeed a *cultural* Proteus and that its cultural possibilities can be
made more definite only if we resign ourselves to speaking of special
cases within the socialist genus—each of which to be sure will be
the only true one for the man who stands for it but any one of which
may be in store for us.

[3] Paradoxical as it sounds, individualism and socialism are not necessarily opposites. One may argue that the socialist form of organization will guarantee "truly"
individualistic realization of personality. This would in fact be quite in the
Marxian line.

CHAPTER XVI

THE SOCIALIST BLUEPRINT

First of all we must see whether or not there is anything wrong with the pure logic of a socialist economy. For although no proof of the soundness of that logic will ever convert anyone to socialism or, in fact, prove much for socialism as a practical proposition, proof of logical unsoundness or even failure in an attempt to prove logical soundness would in itself suffice to convict it of inherent absurdity.

More precisely, our question may be formulated as follows: given a socialist system of the kind envisaged, is it possible to derive, from its data and from the rules of rational behavior, uniquely determined decisions as to what and how to produce or, to put the same thing into the slogan of exact economics, do those data and rules, under the circumstances of a socialist economy, yield equations which are independent, compatible—i.e., free from contradiction—and sufficient in number to determine uniquely the unknowns of the problem before the central board or ministry of production?

1. The answer is in the affirmative. There is nothing wrong with the pure logic of socialism. And this is so obvious that it would not have occurred to me to insist on it were it not for the fact that it has been denied and the still more curious fact that orthodox socialists, until they were taught their business by economists of strongly bourgeois views and sympathies, failed to produce an answer that would meet scientific requirements.

The only authority standing for denial that we need to mention is Professor L. von Mises.[1] Starting from the proposition that rational economic behavior presupposes rational cost calculations, hence prices of cost factors, hence markets which price them, he concluded that in a socialist society, since there would be no such markets, the beacon lights of rational production would be absent so that the system would have to function in a haphazard manner if at all. To this and similar criticisms or perhaps to some doubts of their own, the accredited exponents of socialist orthodoxy had at first not much to oppose except the argument that the socialist management would be able to start from the system of values evolved by its capitalist predecessor—which is no doubt relevant for a discussion of practical difficulties but not at all for the question of principle—or a paean on the

[1] His paper, published in 1920, is now available in English; see *Collectivist Economic Planning* (F. A. von Hayek, ed., 1935). Also see his *Gemeinwirtschaft*, English translation under the title *Socialism* (1937).

miraculous glories of their heaven, in which it would be easy to dispense altogether with capitalist tricks like cost rationality and in which comrades would solve all problems by helping themselves to the bounties pouring forth from social stores. This amounts to accepting the criticism, and some socialists actually seem to do so even today.

The economist who settled the question in a manner that left little to do except elaboration and the clearing up of points of secondary importance, was Enrico Barone to whose argument I refer readers who want a rigorous demonstration.[2] Here a brief sketch will suffice.

Viewed from the economists' standpoint, production—including transportation and all operations incident to marketing—is nothing but the rational combination of the existing "factors" within the constraints imposed by technological conditions: In a commercial society, the task of combining factors involves buying or hiring them, and those individual incomes which are typical of such a society emerge in this very process of buying or hiring. That is to say, the production and the "distribution" of the social product are but different aspects of one and the same process that affects both simultaneously. Now the most important logical—or purely theoretical—difference between commercial and socialist economy is that in the latter this is no longer so. Since *prima facie* there are no market values of means of production and, what is still more important, since the principles of socialist society would not admit of making them the criterion of distribution even if they did exist, the distributive automatism of commercial society is lacking in a socialist one. The void has to be filled by a political act, let us say by the constitution of the commonwealth. Distribution thus becomes a distinct operation and, in logic at least, is completely severed from production. This political act or decision would have to result from, and in turn go a long way toward determining, the economic and cultural character

[2] Upward of a dozen economists had hinted at the solution before Barone. Among them were such authorities as F. von Wieser (in his *Natural Value*, 1893, German original 1889) and Pareto (*Cours d'Économie politique*, vol. ii, 1897). Both perceived the fact that the fundamental logic of economic behavior is the same in both commercial and socialist society from which the solution follows. But Barone, a follower of Pareto, was the first to work it out. See his papers entitled "Il Ministro della Produzione nello Stato Collettivista," *Giornale degli Economisti*, 1908; English translation included in the volume *Collectivist Economic Planning* mentioned in the preceding note.

It is neither possible nor necessary to do justice to the rich crop of later work. I will only mention, as particularly important in one way or another; Fred M. Taylor, "The Guidance of Production in a Socialist State," *American Economic Review*, March 1929; K. Tisch, *Wirtschaftsrechnung und Verteilung im . . . sozialistischen Gemeinwesen*, 1932; H. Zassenhaus, "Theorie der Planwirtschaft," *Zeitschrift für Nationalökonomie*, 1934; especially Oskar Lange, "On the Economic Theory of Socialism," *Review of Economic Studies*, 1936/7, republished as a book in Lange and Taylor, same title, 1938; and A. P. Lerner whose articles will be referred to in a later footnote.

of the society, its behavior, aims and achievements; but it would be completely arbitrary when viewed from the economic standpoint. As has been pointed out before, the commonwealth may adopt an equalitarian rule—and this again in any of the many meanings that may be associated with equalitarian ideals—or admit inequalities to any desired degree. It might even distribute with a view to producing maximum performance in any desired direction—a particularly interesting case. It may study the wishes of individual comrades or resolve to give them what some authority or other thinks best for them; the slogan "to everyone according to his needs" might carry either meaning. But *some* rule must be established. For our purpose it will be sufficient to consider a very special case.

2. Suppose then that the ethical persuasion of our socialist commonwealth is thoroughly equalitarian but at the same time prescribes that comrades should be free to choose as they please among all the consumers' goods which the ministry is able and willing to produce— the community may of course refuse to produce certain commodities, alcoholic beverages for instance. Furthermore let us assume that the particular equalitarian ideal adopted is satisfied by handing out to every person—children and possibly other individuals counting for fractional persons as the competent authority may decide—a voucher representing his or her claim to a quantity of consumers' goods equal to the social product available in the current period of account divided by the number of claimants, all vouchers to become valueless at the end of that period. These vouchers can be visualized as claims to the Xth part of all food, clothing, household goods, houses, motorcars, movie plays and so on that have been or are being produced for consumption (for the purpose of being delivered to consumers) during the period under consideration. It is only to avoid a complex and unnecessary mass of exchanges that would otherwise have to take place among the comrades, that we express the claims not in goods but by equal amounts of conveniently chosen but meaningless units— we can call them simply units, or moons or suns or even dollars— and rule that units of each good will be handed over against the surrender of a stated number of them. These "prices" charged by the social stores would under our assumptions have always to fulfill the condition that, each of them multiplied by the existing quantity of the commodity to which it refers, they add up to the otherwise arbitrary total of the comrades' claims. But the ministry need not fix the individual "prices" except by way of initial suggestions. Given the tastes and the equal "dollar incomes," comrades will reveal, by their reaction to these initial suggestions, at what prices they are ready to take the whole social product save those articles that nobody cares to have at all, and the ministry will then have to accept those prices if it wishes to have the stores cleared. This will accordingly be done

and the principle of equal shares will be thus carried out in a very plausible sense and in a uniquely determined way.

But of course this presupposes that a definite quantity of every good has already been produced. The real problem, the solvability of which has been denied, is precisely how this can be done rationally, i.e., in a way which will result in a maximum of consumers' satisfaction[3] subject to the limits imposed by the available resources, the technological possibilities and the rest of the environmental conditions. It is clear that decision on the plan of production by, say, a majority vote of the comrades would entirely fail to fulfill this[4] requirement because in this case certainly some people and possibly all the people would not get what they want and what it would still be possible to give them without reducing the satisfaction of others. It is, however, equally clear that economic rationality in this sense can be attained in another way. For the theorist this follows from the elementary proposition that consumers in evaluating ("demanding") consumers' goods *ipso facto* also evaluate the means of production which enter into the production of those goods. For the layman proof of the possibility of a rational plan of production in our socialist society can be supplied as follows.

3. To facilitate matters we will assume that means of production are present in given and, for the moment, unalterable quantities. Now let the central board resolve itself into a committee on a particular industry or, still better, let us set up an authority for each industry that is to manage it and to cooperate with the central board which controls and coordinates all these industrial managers or managing boards. This the central board does by allocating productive resources —all of which are under its control—to these industrial managements according to certain rules. Suppose the board rules that industrial managements can have any quantities of producers' goods and services they choose to call for subject to three conditions. First, they must produce as economically as possible. Second, they are required to transfer to the central board, for every unit of each producer's good and service called for, a stated number of those consumers' dollars which they have acquired by previous deliveries of consumers' goods— we might just as well say that the central board declares itself ready to "sell" to any industrial management unlimited quantities of producers' goods and services at stated "prices." Third, the managements

---

[3] If modern theorists should object to this turn of phrase, let me entreat them to consider the amount of entirely unnecessary circumlocution that more correct phrasing would involve without offering, for the purposes of this argument, any compensatory advantage.

[4] This is not to say that it would not fulfill requirements from the standpoint of another definition of rationality. No assertion is being made here about how the arrangement under discussion compares with others. Something will be said about this presently.

are required to call for and to use such quantities as (and not less than), producing in the most economical manner, they can use without having to "sell" any part of their products for less "dollars" than they have to transfer to the central board for the corresponding amounts of means of production. In more technical language, this condition means that production in all lines should be such as to make "prices" equal (not merely proportional) to marginal costs.[5]

[5] This principle, which follows from the general logic of choice, was not universally accepted until Mr. A. P. Lerner stressed it and fought for it in a number of notes and papers, mostly in the *Review of Economic Studies* (also in the *Economic Journal*, September 1937), which constitute an important contribution to the theory of the socialist economy and to which I take this opportunity of drawing the reader's attention. It is also correct, as a proposition of that logic of choice, to say that the above condition should prevail over the rule of equating prices to total cost per unit whenever it conflicts with it. But the relation between them has been somewhat obscured by a confusion of different things, and calls for some clarification.

The concept of marginal cost, meaning the increment of total cost that must be incurred if production is to be increased by a small amount, is indeterminate as long as we do not relate it to a definite period of time. Thus, if the question is whether or not to transport an additional passenger by a train that would run in any case, marginal cost to be considered might be zero and at all events is very small. This may be expressed by saying that, from the standpoint of a very short period—an hour or a day, or even a week—practically everything is overhead, even lubricants and coal, and that overhead does not enter into marginal cost. But the longer the period envisaged the more cost elements enter marginal cost, first all that are usually comprised in the concept of prime cost and after them more and more of what the businessman calls overhead, until, for the very long run or from the standpoint of planning an as yet non-existent industrial unit, nothing (or practically nothing) is left in the category of overhead and everything including depreciation has to be taken into account in figuring out marginal cost, so far as this principle is not modified, in the case of some factors such as a railroad track, by the technological fact that they are available or usable only in very big units ("indivisibility"). Marginal costs should hence always be distinguished from (marginal) prime costs.

Now we often associate the condition under discussion with the rule that the socialist—just like the capitalist—managements should, at any point of time, let bygones be bygones if they are to act rationally; that is to say that in their decisions they are not to take account of the book values of existing investments. But this is only a rule for short-run behavior in a given situation. It does not mean that they are to neglect *ex ante* those elements that *will* crystallize into fixed costs or overhead. To neglect these would spell irrational behavior with respect to the labor hours and units of natural resources that go into the production of the overhead, whenever there is an alternative use for them. But to take account of them will in general imply equating prices to total cost per unit of product as long as things develop according to plans, and since exceptions are mainly due to the technological obstacle to rationality represented by indivisibility or to deviations of the actual course of events from the plans, the logic of these plans is after all not badly expressed by the latter principle. Though in a short-run situation it may be the most rational thing to do, it is yet never part of that logic to operate an industry at a deficit. This is important to note for two reasons.

First, it has been denied. It has even been suggested that welfare would (i.e., in the long run) be increased if prices were always equated to *short-run* marginal costs

The task of each industrial board is then uniquely determined. Exactly as today every firm in a perfectly competitive industry knows what and how much to produce and how to produce it as soon as technical possibilities, reactions of consumers (their tastes and incomes) and prices of means of production are given, so the industrial managements in our socialist commonwealth would know what to produce, how to produce and what factor quantities to "buy" from the central board as soon as the latter's "prices" are published and as soon as the consumers have revealed their "demands."

In a sense these "prices," unlike the "prices" of consumers' goods, are unilaterally set by the central board. We may also say however that industrial managers display a uniquely determined "demand" for the producers' goods much as consumers do for consumers' goods. All we still need to complete our proof is a rule, conforming to the maximum criterion, for that price-fixing activity of the central board. But this rule is obvious. The board has simply to set a single price on every kind and quality of producers' goods—if the board discriminates, i.e., charges different prices for the same kind and quality to different managements, this would in general[6] have to be justified on non-economic grounds—and to see to it that that price exactly "clears the market," i.e., that no unused quantities of producers' goods remain on its hands and that no additional quantities are called at those "prices." This rule will normally suffice to insure rational cost accounting, hence economically rational allocation of productive resources—for the former is nothing but a method of insuring and verifying the latter—hence rationality of the plan of production in socialist societies. Proof follows from the consideration that as long as this rule is being observed no element of productive resources can be diverted to any other line of production without causing the destruction of as much (or more) consumers' values, expressed in terms of consumers' dollars, as that element would add in its new employ-

excluding depreciation and that overhead (say, the cost of a bridge) should be financed by taxation. Our rule, as given in the text, does not mean this, and it would not be a rational thing to do.

Second, in a decree of March 1936 the Russian central authority, abolishing for a number of industries the system of subsidies till then in force, prescribed that prices should be regulated so as to equate average total cost per unit plus an addition for accumulation. For the first part of the rule it may be said that, though not strictly correct, it differs less from the correct one than incorrect formulations of the latter might lead one to suppose; for the latter, that the obvious objection to it is much weakened as soon as we take into account the conditions or necessities of rapid development—the reader will recall the argument submitted in Part II for the capitalist case—and that it is quite conceivable that the Soviet government was right *both* in embarking upon its policy of subsidies, which amounted to financing investment at a loss, and in partly abolishing the practice in 1936.

[6] There are exceptions to this which are of importance but do not affect the drift of our argument.

ment. This amounts to saying that production is being carried, in all directions open in the general conditions of the society's environment, as far as and no farther than it rationally can be, and completes our case for the rationality of socialist planning in a stationary process of economic life in which everything is correctly foreseen and repeats itself and in which nothing happens to upset the plan.

4. But no great difficulties arise if we go beyond the precincts of the theory of the stationary process and admit the phenomena incident to industrial change. So far as economic logic is concerned, it cannot be held that socialism of the kind envisaged, while theoretically capable of coping with the recurrent tasks of the administration of a stationary economy, would necessarily fail in the solution of the problems presented by "progress." We shall see later why it is nevertheless important for the success of a socialist society that it should embark upon its career not only as richly endowed as possible by its capitalist predecessor—with experience and techniques as well as with resources —but also after the latter has sown its wild oats, done its work and is approaching a stationary state. But the reason for it is not in any inability of ours to devise a rational and uniquely determined course for the socialist society to take whenever the opportunity for an improvement in the industrial apparatus presents itself.

Suppose that a new and more efficient piece of machinery has been designed for the productive process of industry X. In order to exclude the problems incident to the financing of investment—to be considered presently—and to isolate a distinct set of phenomena, we will assume that the new machine can be produced by the same plants which thus far produced the less efficient one and at exactly the same costs in terms of productive resources. The management of industry X, in obedience to the first clause of its instruction—viz., the rule to produce as economically as possible—will adopt the new machine and thus produce the same output with a smaller amount of means of production than heretofore. Consequently it would henceforth be in a position to transfer to the ministry or central board an amount of consumers' dollars smaller than the amount received from consumers. Call the difference as you please, for instance D, or a shovel, or "profits." The management would, it is true, violate the condition set by the third clause of its instruction if it realized that "profit"; and if it obeys that clause and immediately produces the greater amount now required in order to satisfy that condition, those profits will never emerge. But their potential existence in the calculations of the management is quite sufficient to make them fill the only function they would have under our assumption, viz., the function of indicating, in a uniquely determined manner, the direction and extent of the reallocation of resources that it is now rational to carry out.

If, at a time when the available resources of the society are fully employed in the task of providing a given level of consumption, an improvement—such as a new bridge or a new railway—which requires the use of additional factors or, as we may also say, additional investment suggests itself, the comrades would either have to work beyond the hours which so far we have assumed to be fixed by law or to restrict their consumption or both. In this case our assumptions, framed for the purpose of solving the fundamental problem in the simplest possible way, preclude an "automatic" solution, i.e., a decision at which the central board and the industrial managements could arrive merely by passively following, within the three rules, the guidance of objective indications. But this of course is a disability of our schema and not of the socialist economy. All we have to do if we wish to have such an automatic solution is to repeal the law invalidating all claims to consumers' goods that are not used during the period for which they are issued, to renounce the principle of absolute equality of incomes and to grant power to the central board to offer premiums for overtime and—what shall we call it?—well, let us say saving. The condition that possible improvements or investments be undertaken to such an extent that the least tempting one of them would yield a "profit" equal to the premiums which have to be offered in order to call forth the amounts of overtime or saving (or both) required for it, then uniquely determines all the new variables that our problem introduces provided overtime and saving are in the relevant interval single-valued functions of the respective premiums.[7] The "dollars" that are handed out in discharge of the latter may conveniently be assumed to be additional to the income dollars issued before. The readjustments this would impose in various directions need not detain us.

But this argument about investment makes it still clearer that the schema which seemed best adapted to our particular purpose is neither the only possible blueprint of a socialist economy, nor necessarily the one that would recommend itself to a socialist society. Socialism need not be equalitarian but no amount of inequality of *incomes* that we could reasonably expect a socialist society to tolerate is likely to produce the rate of investment that capitalist society produces in the average of cyclical phases. Even capitalist inequalities are not sufficient for that and they have to be reinforced by corporate accumulation and "created" bank credit, methods which are not particularly automatic or uniquely determined either. If, therefore, a socialist society

---

[7] The problem, it should be observed, only arises with *new* investment. Such investment as is currently needed in order to keep a stationary process going can and would be provided for exactly as are all other cost items. In particular, there would be no interest. I may take the opportunity to observe that the attitude of socialists toward the phenomenon of interest is not uniform. St. Simon admitted it almost as a matter of course. Marx excluded it from socialist society. Some modern socialists again admit it. Russian practice admits it.

desires to achieve a similar or even greater rate of real investment—of course it need not—methods other than saving would have to be resorted to. Accumulation out of "profits" which could be allowed to materialize instead of remaining potential only or, as suggested above, something analogous to credit creation would be quite feasible. It would be much more natural however to leave the matter to the central board and the congress or parliament who between them could settle it as part of the social budget; while the vote on the "automatic" part of the society's economic operations would be purely formal or perhaps supervisory in character, the vote on the investment item—at least on its amount—would involve a real decision and stand on a par with the vote on army estimates and so on. Coordination of this decision with the "automatic" decisions about the quantities and qualities of individual consumers' goods would not present any insurmountable difficulties. But in accepting this solution we should renounce allegiance to the basic principle of our schema in a very important point.

Other features of our blueprint can be altered even within its general framework. For example, with a conditional exception as to overtime, I have not left it to the individual comrades to decide how much work they are going to do, though as voters and in other ways they may have as much influence on this decision as they have on the distribution of incomes and so on. Nor have I allowed them more freedom of choice of occupation than the central board, within the requirements of its general plan, may be able and willing to grant them. The arrangement may be visualized by means of the analogy with compulsory military service. Such a plan comes fairly close to the slogan: "to everyone according to his need, everyone to contribute according to his aptitude"—or at all events it could, with only minor modifications, be made to conform to it. But instead we may also leave it to the individual comrades to decide how much and what kind of work they are to do. Rational allocation of the working force would then have to be attempted by a system of inducements—premiums again being offered, in this case not only for overtime but for all work, so as to secure everywhere the "offer" of labor of all types and grades appropriate to the structure of consumers' demand and to the investment program. These premiums would have to bear an obvious relation to the attractiveness or irksomeness of each job and to the skill that must be acquired in order to fill it, hence also to the wage schedule of capitalist society. Though the analogy between the latter and such a socialist system of premiums should not be pushed too far, we might speak of a "labor market." Insertion of this piece of mechanism would of course make a great deal of difference to our blueprint. But it would not affect the determinateness of the socialist system. Its formal rationality would in fact stand out still more strongly.

5. So would that family likeness between commercial and socialist economy which the reader cannot have failed to notice all along. Since this resemblance seems to have given pleasure to non-socialists and some socialists and to have annoyed other socialists, it is just as well to restate explicitly in what it consists and to what it is due. It will then be seen how little reason there is for either the pleasure or the annoyance. In trying to construct a rational schema of a socialist economy we have made use of mechanisms and concepts traditionally specified by terms that are familiar to us from our discussions of the processes and problems of capitalist economy. We have described a mechanism which is immediately understood as soon as we utter the words "market," "buying and selling," "competing" and so on. We seem to have used, or barely avoided using, such terms savoring of capitalism as prices, costs, incomes and even profits while rent, interest, wages and others, money among them, have, as it were, hovered about our path.

Let us consider what to most socialists would certainly seem to be one of the worst cases, that of rent, meaning thereby returns from the productive use of natural agents, let us say "land." Our schema evidently cannot imply that ground rent would be paid to any landholders. What then does it imply? Simply that any kind of land which is not plentiful beyond all requirements in the calculable future must be used economically or allocated rationally exactly like labor or any other type of productive resources, and that for this purpose it must receive an index of economic significance with which any new use that may suggest itself must be compared and by means of which the land enters the social bookkeeping process. If this were not done the commonwealth would be behaving irrationally. But no concession to capitalism or to the spirit of capitalism is implied in doing it. All that is commercial or capitalist about ground rent, in both its economic and its sociological associations, and all that can possibly be sympathetic to the advocate of private property (private income, the landlord and so on) has been completely removed.

The "incomes" with which we endowed the comrades at the start are not wages. In fact they would on analysis be seen to be composites of disparate economic elements of which one only could be linked to marginal productivity of labor. The premiums which we introduced later have more to do with the wages of capitalist society. But the counterpart of the latter really exists nowhere except in the books of the central board and again consists in a mere index of significance associated, for the purposes of rational allocation, with every type and grade of labor—an index from which has vanished a whole bundle of meanings that pertain to the capitalist world. In passing, we may observe that since we can call as we please the units into which we split the vouchers that represent the comrade's claims to consumers' goods, we can also call them hours of labor. And since the total number of these units is—within the limits set by convenience—no less arbitrary we could make it equal to the hours actually worked, adjusting all kinds and grades of labor to some standard quality in the Ricardo-Marxian way. Finally our commonwealth can adopt, just as well as any other, the principle that "incomes" should be proportional to the hours of standard work contributed by each comrade. Then we should have a system of labor notes. And the interesting point about it is that barring technical difficulties which do not concern us now such a system would prove quite workable. But it is easy to see why even then these "incomes" would not be "wages." It is no less obvious that the workability of such an arrangement does not prove anything for the labor theory of value.

It is hardly necessary to perform the same operation on profits, interest, prices and costs. The cause of that family likeness is by now clearly visible without doing so: our socialism borrows nothing from capitalism, but capitalism borrows much from the perfectly general logic of choice. Any rational behavior must of course display certain formal similarities with any other rational behavior, and it so happens that in the sphere of economic behavior the molding influence of mere rationality goes pretty far, at least with regard to the pure theory of it. The concepts which express the behaviorist pattern are then drenched with all the particular meanings of a historical epoch and will tend to retain, in the layman's mind, the colors thus acquired. If our historical acquaintance with economic phenomena had been made in socialist environments, we should now seem to be borrowing socialist concepts when analyzing a capitalist process.

So far, there is nothing for capitalist-minded economists to congratulate themselves on in the discovery that socialism could after all only use capitalist mechanisms and categories. There should be as little reason for socialists to object. For only the most naïve mind can feel disappointed at the fact that the socialist miracle does not create a logic of its own, and only the crudest and most stupid variants of the socialist creed can be endangered by any demonstration to that effect—those variants according to which the capitalist process is nothing but a wild jumble without any logic or order at all. Reasonable people of both persuasions can agree on such resemblance as there is and remain just as far apart as ever. But an objection on the score of terminology might remain: it may be argued that it is not convenient to use terms loaded with adventitious yet very important meaning which not everyone can be trusted to discard. Moreover, we must not forget that one may accept the result arrived at about the essential sameness of the economic logic of socialist and commercial production and yet object to the particular schema or model by means of which we have arrived at it (see below).

This is not all however. Some socialist as well as non-socialist economists have been not only willing but anxious to recognize a particularly strong family likeness between a socialist economy of the type envisaged and a commercial economy of the perfectly competitive type. We might almost speak of a school of socialist thought that tends to glorify perfect competition and to advocate socialism on the ground that it offers the only method by which the results of perfect competition can be attained in the modern world. The tactical advantages to be reaped by placing oneself on this standpoint are indeed obvious enough to explain what at first sight looks like surprising broad-mindedness. A competent socialist who sees as clearly as any other economist all the weaknesses of Marxian and of popular arguments can thus admit whatever he feels should be admitted without compromising his convictions because the admissions refer to a historical stage that (so far as it ever did exist) is safely dead and buried; he is enabled, by judiciously confining his condemnatory verdict to the non-competitive case, to lend qualified support to some indictments, such as that in modern capitalism production is for profit and not for the consumption of the people, which otherwise would be merely silly; and he can baffle and puzzle good bourgeois by telling them that socialism will only do what they really wanted all along and what their own economic ulemas always taught them. But the analytic advantages of stressing that family likeness are not equally great.[8]

As we have already seen, the bloodless concept of perfect competition that economic theory has framed for its purposes turns on whether or not individual firms can, by their single-handed action, influence the prices of their products and of their cost factors. If they cannot—that is, if each firm is a mere drop in an ocean and therefore has to accept the prices that rule in the market—the theorist speaks of perfect competition. And it can be shown that in this case the mass effect of the passive reaction of all individual firms will result in market prices and volumes of output displaying certain formal properties that are similar to those of the indices of economic significance and volumes of output in our blueprint of a socialist economy. However, in all that really matters—in the principles governing the formation of incomes, the selection of industrial leaders, the allocation of initiative and responsibility, the definition of success and failure—in everything that constitutes the physiognomy of competitive capitalism, the blueprint is the very opposite of perfect competition and much further removed from it than from the big-business type of capitalism.

[8] See ch. viii.

Though I do not think therefore that our blueprint can be objected to on the ground that it is borrowed from commercialism or that it wastes socialist oil in order to anoint that unholy thing, I am yet much in sympathy with those socialists who object to it on other grounds. I have, it is true, pointed out myself that the method of constructing a "market" of consumers' goods and of orienting production according to the indications derived from it will come nearer than any other, for instance the method of decision by majority vote, to giving each individual comrade what he wants—there exists no more democratic institution than a market—and that in this sense it will result in a "maximum of satisfaction." But this maximum is only a short-run one[9] and, moreover, is relative to the actual desires of the comrades as they are felt at the moment. Only outright beefsteak socialism can be content with a goal such as this. I cannot blame any socialist for despising it and dreaming of new cultural forms for the human clay, perhaps of a new clay withal; the real promise of socialism, if any, lies that way. Socialists who are of this mind may still allow their commonwealth to be guided by the comrades' actual tastes in matters that present no other than the hedonist aspect. But they will adopt a Gosplan not only, as we conditionally did ourselves, for their investment policy but for all purposes that do present other aspects. They may still let the comrades choose as they like between peas and beans. They may well hesitate as to milk and whisky and as to drugs and improvement of housing. And they will not allow comrades to choose between loafing and temples—if the latter be allowed to stand for what Germans inelegantly but tellingly call objective (manifestations of) culture.

6. It is therefore necessary to ask whether, if we jettison our "markets," rationality and determinateness do not go overboard also. The answer is obvious. There would have to be an authority to do the evaluating, i.e., to determine the indices of significance for all consumers' goods. Given its system of values, that authority could do this in a perfectly determined manner exactly as a Robinson Crusoe can.[10] And the rest of the planning process could then run its course, much as it did in our original blueprint. The vouchers, prices, and the abstract units would still serve the purposes of control and cost calculation, although they would lose their affinity to disposable income and *its* units. All the concepts that derive from the general logic of economic action would turn up again.

Any kind of centralist socialism, therefore, can successfully clear the first hurdle—logical definiteness and consistency of socialist plan-

---

[9] It *is* however a provable maximum and as such establishes the economic rationality of that type of socialism exactly as the competitive maximum establishes the rationality of competitive economy. And in neither case does this mean very much.

[10] This is perhaps why Marx showed considerable interest in Crusoe economics.

ning—and we may as well negotiate the next one at once. It consists of the "practical impossibility" on which, it seems, most anti-socialist economists are at present inclined to retire after having accepted defeat on the purely logical issue. They hold that our central board would be confronted with a task of unmanageable complication,[11] and some of them add that in order to function the socialist arrangement would presuppose a wholesale reformation of souls or of behavior—whichever way we prefer to style it—which historical experience and common sense prove to be out of the question. Deferring consideration of the latter point we can easily dispose of the former.

First, a glance at our solution of the theoretical problem will satisfy the reader that it is eminently operational; that is to say, it not only establishes a logical possibility but in doing so also shows the steps by which this possibility can be realized in practice. This holds even if, in order to face the issue squarely, we require that the plan of production be built up *ab ovo*, i.e., without any previous experience as to quantities and values and on no other basis to start from than a survey of the available resources and technologies and a general knowledge about what kind of people the comrades are. Moreover it must be borne in mind that under modern conditions a socialist economy requires the existence of a huge bureaucracy or at least social conditions favorable to its emergence and functioning. This requirement constitutes one of the reasons why the economic problems of socialism should never be discussed without reference to given states of the social environment or to historical situations. Such an administrative apparatus may or may not deserve all the derogatory comments which some of us are in the habit of passing upon bureaucracy—we shall presently comment upon it ourselves—but just now we are not concerned with the question how well or ill it may be expected to fulfill its task; all that matters is that, if it exists at all, there is no reason to believe that it will break down under the task.

In any normal situation it would command information sufficient to enable it to come at first throw fairly close to the correct quantities of output in the major lines of production, and the rest would be a matter of adjustments by informed trial and error. So far there is in this respect no very fundamental difference[12] between socialist and commercial economies either as to the problems which the theorist meets in showing how an economic system proceeds to a state that could be "rational" or "optimal" in the sense of fulfilling certain

---

[11] This is the line taken by most authors of non-socialist persuasion who accept the logical credentials of socialism. Professors Robbins and von Hayek may be mentioned as the chief authorities for this view.

[12] Some writers seem to imply that the process by which equilibrium is reached would be the *same* as in a state of perfect competition. That is not so however. Step-by-step adjustment in reaction to price changes alone might easily miss the goal altogether. This is why in the text I spoke of "informed" trial and error.

maximum conditions, or as to the problems which managers have to meet in actual practice. If we admit previous experience to start from as most socialists do and especially Karl Kautsky always did, the task is of course greatly simplified, particularly if that experience is of the big-business type.

But something else follows, secondly, from another inspection of our blueprint: solution of the problems confronting the socialist management would be not only just as possible as is the practical solution of the problems confronting commercial managements: it would be easier. Of this we can readily convince ourselves by observing that one of the most important difficulties of running a business—the difficulty which absorbs most of the energy of a successful business leader —consists in the uncertainties surrounding every decision. A very important class of these consists in turn in the uncertainties about the reaction of one's actual and potential competitors and about how general business situations are going to shape. Although other classes of uncertainties would no doubt persist in a socialist commonwealth, these two can reasonably be expected to vanish almost completely. The managements of socialized industries and plants would be in a position to know exactly what the other fellows propose to do and nothing would prevent them from getting together for concerted action.[13] The central board could, and to a certain extent would unavoidably, act as a clearing house of information and as a coordinator of decisions—at least as much as an all-embracing cartel bureau would. This would immensely reduce the amount of work to be done in the workshops of managerial brains and much less intelligence would be necessary to run such a system than is required to steer a concern of any importance through the waves and breakers of the capitalist sea. This suffices to establish our proposition.

[13] So far as this is being done in capitalist economies, it is a most important step toward socialism. In fact, it progressively reduces the difficulties of transition and is in itself a symptom of the advent of the transitional stage. To fight this tendency unconditionally is tantamount to fighting socialism.

CHAPTER XVII

COMPARISON OF BLUEPRINTS

I. A Preliminary Point

THE reader who has followed so far will naturally expect me to embark upon a comparative appraisal of the socialist plan. Perhaps it would be wise to disappoint that expectation. For nobody who is not completely lacking in a sense of responsibility can fail to see that comparison between a system which we have lived with and a system which as yet is but a mental image—no socialist will accept the Russian experience as a full-weight realization—must be extremely hazardous. But we will take the risk, bearing in mind all the time that beyond the realm of fact and argument over which we are going to travel there is the realm of individual preferences, convictions, evaluations into which we cannot enter. And we will improve our chances of success by severely restricting our goal and frankly recognizing difficulties and pitfalls.

In particular, we shall not compare the cultural worlds of commercial and socialist society. What I have called the cultural indeterminateness of socialism is in itself sufficient to bar the attempt. But we have also another reason for refraining. Even if socialist civilization meant just one definite pattern, comparative appraisal would still be a doubtful matter. There are idealists and monomaniacs who can see no difficulty in it and gaily adopt for a standard of comparison some feature which they value to the exclusion of everything else and which they expect their socialism to display. But if we resolved to do better than that and, so far as our vision may reach, to see all the facets of a civilization in the light that is born and dies with it, we should instantly discover that every civilization is a world unto itself, and incommensurable with every other.

There is one point however that bears upon comparison of actual and possible cultural achievement and yet comes within the scope of our type of analysis. It is often claimed that the socialist plan, by removing economic care from the shoulders of the individual, will release incalculable cultural energies that now go to waste in the struggle for daily bread. To some extent this is true—any "planned" society may do that as, for other reasons and in other respects, it also may smother cultural possibilities. It might be objected that public authorities as we know them are hardly up to the responsibility of discovering and nursing talent to the stage of fruition, and that there is no sound reason to believe that they would have appreciated Van Gogh any sooner than capitalist society did. But this objection misses the point. For public authority need not go as far as this. All that is necessary is that Van Gogh gets his "income" as everyone else does and that he is not worked too hard; this would suffice in any normal case—though, when I come to think of it, I am no longer sure whether it would have sufficed in the case of Van Gogh—to give the necessary opportunity for the assertion of creative ability.

But another objection carries more weight. In this matter as in others the advocate of socialism is likely to overlook—often he is passionately resolved not to admit—the degree to which certain ideals of his are satisfied in the modern world. Capitalism provides, to a much greater extent than most of us believe, the ladders for talent to climb. There is an element of truth in the brutal slogan of the typical bourgeois which many worthy men find so irritating, viz., that those who cannot climb by these ladders are not worth troubling about. The ladders may not be up to any standard we choose to set, but it cannot be said that they do not exist. Not only does modern capitalism systematically proffer means to shelter and nurse almost any kind of ability in the early stages of its development—so much so that in some lines the difficulty is not how to find the means for talent but how to find anything that has any claim to be called a talent for the means proffered—but by the very law of its structure it tends to send up the able individual and, much more effectively, the able family. Thus, though there may be social losses[1] particularly in the class of semi-pathological genius, it is not likely that they are very great.

II. A Discussion of Comparative Efficiency

Let us stay however within the economic sphere though I hope I have made it quite clear that I do not attribute to it more than secondary importance.

1. The restrictions of our scope are most obvious and hence the pitfalls least dangerous at the first step which is still concerned with nothing but blueprints. Again deferring discussion of transitional difficulties, to be dealt with separately, and provisionally assuming that they have been successfully overcome, we need only glance at the implications of our proof of the possibility and practicability of the socialist schema in order to realize that there is a strong case for believing in its superior economic efficiency.

That superiority need be proved only with respect to big-business

---

[1] Instances overstate by inference, even if they do not vanish on investigation as they often do. Moreover, some of those losses occur independently of the particular organization of society; not every such loss in the capitalist arrangement is also a loss through the capitalist arrangement.

or "monopolistic" capitalism because superiority over "competitive" capitalism then follows *a fortiori*. This is evident from our analysis in Chapter VIII. Many economists, on the strength of the fact that under completely unrealistic conditions all sorts of flattering propositions can be established about competitive capitalism, have acquired a habit of extolling it at the expense of its "monopolistic" successor. I wish to repeat therefore that even if those eulogies were entirely justified—which they are not—and if the theorist's perfect competition had ever been realized in the field of industry and transportation—which it never was—finally, if all the accusations ever leveled against big business were entirely justified—which is far from being the case—it would still be a fact that the actual efficiency of the capitalist engine of production in the era of the largest-scale units has been much greater than in the preceding era of small or medium-sized ones. This is a matter of statistical record. But if we recall the theoretical explanation of that fact, we further realize that the increasing size of units of control and all the business strategy that went with it were not only unavoidable incidents but to a considerable extent also conditions of the achievement reflected in that record; in other words, that the technological and organizational possibilities open to firms of the type which is compatible with approximately perfect competition could never have produced similar results. How modern capitalism would work under perfect competition is hence a meaningless question. Therefore, quite apart from the fact that socialism will inherit a "monopolistic" and not a competitive capitalism, we need not trouble about the competitive case except incidentally.

Economic efficiency of a system we will reduce to productive efficiency. Even the latter is by no means easy to define. The two alternatives to be compared must of course[2] be referred to the same point of time—past, present or future. But this is not enough. For the relevant question is not what, *ex visu* of a given point of time, socialist management could do with the capitalist apparatus existing at that point of time—this is for us not much more interesting than what socialist management could do with a given stock of consumers' goods—but what productive apparatus would exist or would have existed had a socialist instead of the capitalist management presided over its construction. The mass of information about our actual and potential productive resources that has been accumulated during the last twenty years, however valuable it may be for other purposes, thus lends but little aid in the struggle with our difficulty. And all

[2] This rule should be self-evident, yet it is frequently violated. For instance, the economic performance of Soviet Russia at the present time is often compared with that of the tsarist regime at the threshold of the First World War. But the lapse of a quarter of a century has robbed such a comparison of all significance. The only comparison that could possibly be significant would be with the values on an extrapolated trend based upon the figures for, say, 1890-1914.

we can do is to list such differences between the mechanisms of the economic engines of socialist and of commercial society as we may nevertheless perceive, and to appraise their importance as best we can.

We will postulate that the number, quality, tastes and age distribution of the population at the time of comparison be the same in both cases. Then we shall call that system relatively more efficient which we see reason to expect would *in the long run* produce the larger stream of consumers' goods per equal unit of time.[3]

2. This definition requires comment. It will be seen that it does not identify economic efficiency with economic welfare or with given degrees of satisfaction of wants. Even if *any* conceivable socialist economy were sure to be in our sense less efficient than *any* conceivable commercial economy, the majority of people—all in fact for whom the typical socialist cares—might still be "better off" or "happier" or "more content" in the former than in the latter. My first and main reply is that relative efficiency retains independent meaning even in such cases and that in all cases it will be an important consideration. But secondly I do not think that we lose much by adopting a criterion that neglects those aspects. This however is a very debatable matter on which it is just as well to be a little more explicit.

To begin with, convinced socialists will derive satisfaction from the mere fact of living in a socialist society.[4] Socialist bread may well

[3] Since the capitalist and the socialist streams of real income will to some extent consist of different commodities and contain the commodities common to both in somewhat different proportions—though in the absence of additional hypotheses about the change in the distribution of spendable incomes it is impossible to estimate the importance of the difference—comparison raises delicate questions of theory. If more wine and less bread are produced in the capitalist than would be produced in the socialist society, which of the streams is the larger? In any attempt to answer such a question, the difficulties incident to comparing income streams in the same social framework from one year to the next (to constructing any index of total output, that is) are met on a greatly magnified scale. For our purpose, however, the following definition sufficiently meets the *theoretical* problem: one of the streams shall be called larger than the other if, and only if, it yields a greater monetary total than the other, whichever of the two price systems is used in the evaluation of both. If one stream yields a higher figure when both are evaluated by means of, say, the capitalist price system, and at the same time a smaller figure when both are evaluated at the socialist price system, then we call them equal just as if they actually yielded equal totals with both price systems—which simply means that we trust that the difference will in general not be very significant in that case. The *statistical* problem is of course not solved by this definition, because we cannot have the two streams before us at the same time.

The reason why the words *in the long run* have been inserted in the sentence of the text should be obvious from our analysis in ch. vii.

[4] We are in fact sometimes invited to overlook admitted shortcomings of the socialist plan for the sake of the privilege of becoming members of a socialist society. This argument, frankly formulating as it does the truly socialist feeling, is by no means as unreasonable as it may sound. It really renders all other arguments superfluous.

taste sweeter to them than capitalist bread simply because it is socialist bread, and it would do so even if they found mice in it. If, moreover, the particular socialist system adopted happens to agree with one's moral principles as for instance equalitarian socialism would with the moral principles of many socialists, this fact and the consequent gratification of one's sense of justice will of course be listed among that system's titles to superiority. For the working of the system such moral allegiance is by no means indifferent; its importance even for efficiency in our sense will have to be noticed later. But beyond that all of us had better admit that our phraseology about justice and so on reduces largely to whether we like a certain form of society or not.

There seems however to be a purely economic argument in favor of equalitarian socialism or any socialism the structure of which admits of greater equality of incomes. Those economists at least who feel no compunction about treating satisfactions of wants as measurable quantities and about comparing and adding the satisfactions of different persons have a right to argue that a given stock or stream of consumers' goods will in general produce the maximum of satisfaction if equally distributed. An equalitarian system as efficient as its commercial counterpart will hence run at a higher level of welfare. Even a somewhat less efficient equalitarian system might do so. Most modern theorists would discard this argument on the grounds that satisfactions are not measurable or that comparison and addition of the satisfactions of different people are meaningless. We need not go so far. It is sufficient to point out that the equalitarian argument is particularly open to the objection raised in our analysis of monopolistic practice: the problem is not how to distribute a quantity given independently of the principles of income distribution. Wage incomes might well be higher in a commercial society admitting unrestricted inequalities than the equal incomes would be in equalitarian socialism. So long as it is not made reasonably certain that the socialist engine of production would be at least nearly as efficient as the commercial engine is or was or can be expected to be at the time of the comparison, the argument about distribution remains inconclusive—question-begging in fact—even if we choose to accept it.[5] And as soon as the question of productive efficiency is settled the distributive argument will in most cases be superfluous; unless it be based exclusively on moral ideals, it will turn the balance only in borderline cases.

3. There is still another reason why similar levels of productive

[5] The argument we thus discard may be made to read that other things being equal the socialist maximum is greater than the competitive maximum. Owing to the purely formal nature of both maxima however there is no point in comparing them, as should be obvious from previous considerations.

efficiency might be associated with different levels of welfare. Most socialists will hold that a given national income would go further in socialist than it goes in capitalist society because the former would make a more economical use of it. These economies follow from the fact that certain types of society may, by virtue of their organization, be indifferent or adverse to purposes to which other types, also by virtue of their organization, allocate considerable parts of their resources. A pacifist socialism for instance would economize on armaments, an atheist one on churches, and both might therefore have more hospitals instead. This is so, of course. But since it involves valuations which cannot with confidence be attributed to socialism in general—though they could be to many individual socialists—it does not concern us here.

Almost any socialist society—not the Platonic type though—would surely realize another type of economy, viz., the economy from the elimination of the leisure class, the "idle rich." Since from the socialist standpoint it is quite proper to neglect the satisfactions accruing to the individuals belonging to this group and to evaluate its cultural functions at zero—though civilized socialists always save their faces by adding: in the world of today—there is obviously a net gain to be made by the socialist regime. How much do we lose by using an efficiency test which neglects this?

Of course, modern taxation of incomes and inheritance is rapidly reducing the problem to quantitative insignificance, even independently of the fiscal methods applied in financing the current war. But this taxation itself is the expression of an anti-capitalist attitude and possibly the forerunner of complete elimination of the typically capitalist income brackets. We must therefore put our question for a capitalist society not yet attacked at its economic roots. For this country, it seems reasonable to select the data of 1929.[6]

Let us define rich people as those who have incomes of $50,000 and over. In 1929, they received about 13 billion dollars out of a national total of about 93 billions.[7] From these 13 billions we have to deduct taxes, savings, and gifts for public purposes, because the elimination of these items would not constitute economies for the socialist regime; it is only the expenditure of rich people for their own consumption that would be "saved" in the proper sense of the word.[8]

[6] The United States is the country that qualifies best 'for this test, In most European countries the problem would be complicated, at least for the nineteenth century or even until 1914, by the presence of high incomes which were of pre-capitalist origin but had been swelled by capitalist evolution.

[7] See H. G. Moulton, M. Levin, and C. A. Warburton, *America's Capacity to Consume* (1934), p. 206. These figures are admittedly extremely rough. They include incomes from occupations and investments, also from sales of property and imputed returns from owned homes.

[8] It will be seen that the fact that the socialist authority would presumably use those savings and gifts for different purposes does not affect the argument.

This expenditure cannot be estimated with any accuracy. All we can hope for is an idea about the orders of magnitude involved. Since most economists who have been willing to take the risk guessed at less than one-third of the 13 billions, it will be fairly safe to say that this expenditure did not amount to more than $4\frac{1}{3}$ billions or to about 4.6 per cent of the total national income. Now this 4.6 per cent includes all of the consumers' expenditure from the higher business and professional incomes, so that the idle rich cannot have absorbed more than 1 or 2 per cent at the outside. And, so far as the family motive is still alive, not even all of that can be considered irrelevant to performance conducive to the efficiency of the economic engine.

Some readers will no doubt feel that the $50,000 limit is unduly high. It is clear of course that more could be economized by eliminating or reducing to a subsistence level the incomes of all the people who are, economically speaking, idle whether rich or poor.[9] Still more could be economized, so one would think, by rationalizing the distribution of all higher incomes so as to bring them into closer correspondence with performance. But arguments to be submitted in the next section suggest that the high hopes entertained on that score are likely to meet with disappointment.

I do not wish however to insist. For if the reader should attach greater importance to these economies than I think justified, the conclusion we are going to arrive at will apply only *a fortiori*.

III. The Case for the Superiority of the Socialist Blueprint

Thus our criterion of superiority or inferiority after all covers more ground than it seems to. But if we stand by it, what is that strong case for the superiority of the socialist blueprint of which I spoke before?

The reader who has perused the analysis in Chapter VIII may well wonder. Most of the arguments usually advanced in support of the socialist and against the capitalist regime, as we have seen, fail as soon as proper account is taken of the conditions created for business by a rapid rate of progress. Some of those arguments, on closer inspection, even turn out to cut the other way. Much of what is

---

[9] It should however be noted that an income consisting exclusively of returns on investments is no indication of the economic idleness of its receiver, because his work may be embodied in his investments. The classroom illustration of this will serve as well as a longer argument could: suppose a man reclaims a piece of land by the work of his hands; the return he will thereafter receive is a "return on an appliance made by man" or, as economists call it, a quasi-rent. If the improvement is permanent, it will become undistinguishable from the rent of land proper and hence look like the very incarnation of unearned income whereas in reality it is a form of wages if we define wages as returns attributable to personal productive exertions. Generalizing, we may say that effort may be undergone in order to secure revenues which may, but need not, take the form of wages.

being considered pathological is seen to be physiological—to fulfill important functions in the process of creative destruction. Many wastes carry compensations that sometimes completely, in other cases partly, invalidate the inference. Socially irrational allocation of resources is not nearly as frequent or important as it is made out to be. In some cases, moreover, it is no less likely to occur in a socialist economy. Excess capacity, also partly inevitable in a socialist economy, will often bear an interpretation which rebuts criticism. And even unrelieved blemishes are after all but incidents of an achievement that is great enough to cover a multitude of sins.

The answer to our question follows from the last paragraph of the preceding chapter. It might be of doubtful validity as long as capitalist evolution is in full swing but it will be decisive as soon as it *permanently* slackens down, whether from reasons inherent in or external to its economic mechanism.

There are cases in which capitalist industries are so circumstanced that prices and output become theoretically indeterminate. They may occur, though they do not always occur, whenever there is oligopoly. In a socialist economy everything—limiting cases without practical importance alone excepted—is uniquely determined. But even when there exists a theoretically determined state it is much more difficult and expensive to reach in the capitalist economy than it would be in the socialist economy. In the former endless moves and counter-moves are necessary and decisions have to be taken in an atmosphere of uncertainty that blunts the edge of action, whereas that strategy and that uncertainty would be absent from the latter. That this applies not only to "monopolistic" capitalism but, though for other reasons, still more to the competitive species is shown by the hog-cycle case[10] and by the behavior of more or less perfectly competitive industries in general depressions or in vicissitudes of their own.

But this means more than it seems to mean at first sight. Those determinate solutions of the problems of production are rational or optimal from the standpoint of given data, and anything that shortens, smoothens or safeguards the road that leads to them is bound to save human energy and material resources, and to reduce the costs at which a given result is attained. Unless the resources thus saved are completely wasted, efficiency in our sense must necessarily increase.

Under this heading some of the sweeping indictments of the capitalist system which have been glanced at above acquire a qualified justification. As an instance, take excess capacity. It is not true that it would be entirely absent in socialism; it would be absurd for the central board to insist on full utilization of a new railroad through as yet unsettled country. Nor is it true that excess capacity spells loss in all cases. But there are types of excess capacity which do spell loss

10 See ch. viii.

and can be avoided by a socialist management, the chief case being
that of reserve capacity for the purpose of economic warfare. Whatever the importance of the particular case—I do not think it is very
considerable—it shows up a point to which I have already adverted:
there are things which within the conditions of capitalist evolution
are, or may be, perfectly rational and even necessary and therefore
need not, *ex visu* of the capitalist order, constitute blemishes at all;
nor need they constitute weaknesses of "monopolistic" as against competitive capitalism if they are associated, as conditions, with achievements of the former that are out of the reach of the latter; but even
if that be so they may yet constitute weaknesses as against the
socialist blueprint.

This is particularly true of most of the phenomena that make up
the mechanism of trade cycles. Capitalist enterprise does not lack
regulators, some of which may well be met with again in the practice
of the ministry of production. But the planning of progress, in particular the systematic coordination and orderly distribution in time
of new ventures in all lines, would be incomparably more effective
in preventing bursts at some times and depressive reactions at others
than any automatic or manipulative variations of the rate of interest
or the supply of credit can be. In fact, it would eliminate the cause
of the cyclical ups and downs whereas in the capitalist order it is
only possible to mitigate them. And the process of discarding the
obsolete that in capitalism—especially in competitive capitalism—
means temporary paralysis and losses that are in part functionless,
could be reduced to what "discarding the obsolete" actually conveys
to the layman's mind within a comprehensive plan providing in advance for the shifting to other uses of the non-obsolete complements
of the obsolete plants or pieces of equipment. Concretely: a crisis
centering in the cotton industry may in the capitalist order put a stop
to residential construction; in the socialist order it may of course
also happen that the production of cotton goods has to be drastically
curtailed at short notice, though it is not so likely to happen; but
this would be a reason to speed up residential construction instead
of stopping it.

Whatever the economic goals desired by whoever is in the position
to give effect to his desires, socialist management could attain them
with less disturbance and loss without necessarily incurring the disadvantages that would attend attempts at planning progress within
the framework of capitalist institutions. One aspect of this might
be expressed by saying that the socialist management could steer a
course approximating the long-run trend of output, thus developing
a tendency which as we have seen is not foreign to big-business policy.
And the whole of our argument might be put in a nutshell by saying
that socialization means a stride beyond big business on the way that

has been chalked out by it or, what amounts to the same thing, that socialist management may conceivably prove as superior to big-business capitalism as big-business capitalism has proved to be to the kind of competitive capitalism of which the English industry of a hundred years ago was the prototype. It is quite possible that future generations will look upon arguments about the inferiority of the socialist plan as we look upon Adam Smith's arguments about joint-stock companies which, also, were not simply false.

Of course, all that I have said so far refers exclusively to the logic of blueprints, hence to "objective" possibilities which socialism in practice may be quite unable to realize. But as a matter of blueprint logic it is undeniable that the socialist blueprint is drawn at a higher level of rationality. This, I believe, is the correct way of putting the matter. It is not a case of rationality versus irrationality. The farmer whose reaction to hog and fodder prices produces the hog cycle is, individually and from the standpoint of the moment, acting perfectly rationally. So is the management of a concern that maneuvers in an oligopolistic situation. So is the firm that expands in the boom and restricts in recession. It is the kind and scope of rationality that makes the difference.

This is certainly not all that can be adduced on behalf of the socialist plan. But so far as the pure logic of a socialist economy is concerned, most arguments that are not provably wrong are in fact implied in the one submitted.

An example of the first importance is afforded by unemployment. We have seen in Part II that, as regards the interest of the unemployed themselves, capitalist society in any stage sufficiently advanced to offer a chance for successful socialization need and presumably will not leave very much to be desired. But concerning the loss to society the preceding argument implies that in a socialist society unemployment will be less, mainly in consequence of the elimination of depressions, and that where it does occur, mainly in consequence of technological improvement, the ministry of production will be in a position—whatever it may actually do—to redirect the men to other employments which, if the planning lives up to its possibilities at all, might in each case be waiting for them.

A minor advantage that is also implied in the superior rationality of the socialist plan results from the fact that in the capitalist order improvements occur as a rule in individual concerns and take time and meet resistance in spreading. If the pace of progress is rapid, there is often a large number of firms that cling to old methods or are otherwise of substandard efficiency. In the socialist order every improvement could theoretically be spread by decree and substandard practice could be promptly eliminated. I call this a minor advantage because capitalism as a rule also deals pretty efficiently with the inefficient. Of course, the likelihood of this particular advantage, whether great or small, being realized by a bureaucracy is another matter; a decent bureaucracy may always be relied on to bring all its members up to *its* standard, but this says nothing about what this standard itself will be. That possible superiorities might in practice turn into actual inferiorities must be kept in mind throughout.

Again, managers or owner-managers of small or medium-sized concerns are as a rule primarily either engineers or salesmen or organizers and, even if good men, rarely do all things equally well. We often find that even successful businesses are indifferently managed in some respect or other—witness the reports of efficiency experts— and their leaders are therefore partially misplaced. The socialist economy could, as modern largest-scale business does, use them to fuller advantage by using them exclusively in what they really know how to do. But obvious considerations that need not detain us will not allow us to entertain high hopes on that score.

There is however an advantage of prime importance that is not visible in our blueprint as drawn. The outstanding feature of commercial society is the division between the private and the public sphere—or, if you prefer, the fact that in commercial society there is a private sphere which contains so much more than either feudal or socialist society allocates to it. This private sphere is distinct from the public sphere not only conceptually but also actually. The two are to a great extent manned by different people—the history of local self-government offering the most conspicuous exception—and organized as well as run on different and often conflicting principles, productive of different and often incompatible standards.

Friction can only temporarily be absent from such an arrangement the paradoxical nature of which would be a source of wonder to us if we were not so accustomed to it. As a matter of fact, friction was present long before it developed into antagonism in consequence of the wars of conquest waged upon the bourgeois domain with ever-increasing success by the men of the public sphere. This antagonism entails struggle. Most activities of the state in the economic field then appear in the light that is well characterized by the old bourgeois economist's phrase, government *interference*. These activities do in fact interfere in every sense of the word, especially in the sense that they hamper and paralyze the private engine of production. It cannot be urged that they are frequently successful, even in increasing productive efficiency. But as far as they are, the central board's activity would stand a still greater chance of being so, whereas the costs and losses incident to the struggle as such would be entirely avoided in the socialist case. And these losses are considerable, especially if we count in all the worry caused by incessant inquiries and prosecutions and the consequent discouraging effects on the energies that propel business.

One element of these costs should be mentioned specifically. It consists in the absorption of ability in merely protective activities. A considerable part of the total work done by lawyers goes into the struggle of business with the state and its organs. It is immaterial whether we call this vicious obstruction of the common good or defense of the common good against vicious obstruction. In any case the fact remains that in socialist society there would be neither need nor room for this part of legal activity. The resulting saving is not satisfactorily measured by the fees of the lawyers who are thus engaged. That is inconsiderable. But not inconsiderable is the social loss from such unproductive employment of many of the best brains. Considering how terribly rare good brains are, their shifting to other employments might be of more than infinitesimal importance.

The friction or antagonism between the private and the public sphere was intensified from the first by the fact that, ever since the princes' feudal incomes ceased to be of major importance, the state has been living on a revenue which was being produced in the private sphere for private purposes and had to be deflected from these purposes by political force.[11] On the one hand, taxation is an essential attribute of commercial society—or, if we accept the conception of the state alluded to in the first chapter, of the state—and, on the other hand, it is almost inevitably[12] in the nature of an injury to the productive process. Until 1914 roughly—if we agree to consider modern times only—that injury was confined within narrow bounds. But since then taxes have grown, by degrees, into the dominant item of business and family budgets and into a major factor in the explanation of unsatisfactory economic performance. Moreover, in order to wrench ever-increasing amounts from an unwilling organism, a huge administrative apparatus has come into existence that does nothing but struggle with the bourgeoisie for every dollar of its revenue. That organism has in response developed organs of defense and does an immense amount of work in self-protection.

Nothing else brings out so well the wastes that result from the conflict of structural principles in a social body. Modern capitalism relies on the profit principle for its daily bread yet refuses to allow it to prevail. No such conflict, consequently no such wastes, would exist in socialist society. Since it would control all sources of revenue, taxes could vanish with the state or, if my conception of the state does not command approval, with the bourgeois state. For, as a

[11] The theory which construes taxes on the analogy of club dues or of the purchase of the services of, say, a doctor only proves how far removed this part of the social sciences is from scientific habits of mind.

[12] Exceptions exist, but they do not matter for practical purposes.

matter of common sense, it would be clearly absurd for the central board to pay out incomes first and, after having done so, to run after the recipients in order to recover part of them. If radicals were not so fond of chivying the bourgeois that they cannot see anything wrong in taxes except that they are too low, it would have been recognized before this that here we have got hold of one of the most significant titles to superiority that can be advanced in favor of the socialist plan.

CHAPTER XVIII

THE HUMAN ELEMENT

A WARNING

IT IS quite likely that many opponents of socialism will accept the result we have just arrived at. But their assent will mostly take the following form: "Oh well, of course, if you had demigods to direct the socialist engine and archangels to man it, all that might well be so. But the point is that you have not and that, human nature being what it is, the capitalist alternative with its pattern of motivations and its distribution of responsibilities and rewards after all offers, though not the best conceivable, yet the best practicable arrangement."

And there is something to this reply. On the one hand, we have now to guard not only against the dangers that lurk in any attempt to compare a given reality with an *idea*, but also against the error or trick inherent in any comparison of a given reality with an *ideal*.[1] On the other hand, though I think I have made it abundantly clear that in the nature of things there never can be a general case for socialism but only a case with reference to given social conditions and given historical stages, this relativity becomes much more important now than it was as long as we moved among blueprints.

I. THE HISTORICAL RELATIVITY OF THE ARGUMENT

To illustrate this point by an analogy. In feudal society, much of what all of us, the staunchest supporters of private property included,

[1] An idea or schema or model or blueprint also embodies an ideal, but only in the logical sense; such an ideal means only absence of non-essentials—the unadulterated design as we might say. Of course it remains a debatable question exactly what should be included in it and what should, in consequence, be regarded as deviation. Though this should be a question of analytic technique, love and hate may enter into it nevertheless: socialists will tend to include in the blueprint of capitalism as many traits as possible that are felt to be derogatory; anti-socialists will do the same to the socialist blueprint; and both parties will try to "whitewash" their own by listing as many "blemishes" as possible among unessential, hence by implication avoidable, deviations. Even if they agree in any given case to label certain phenomena as deviations, they may still disagree as to the degree to which their own system and that of their opponents are liable to deviate. For instance, bourgeois economists will tend to attribute to "political interference" whatever they themselves do not like about capitalism while socialists will hold that these politics are the inevitable outcome of capitalist processes and situations created by the way in which the capitalist engine works. Although I recognize all these difficulties, I do not think that they affect my exposition which, as the professional reader will notice, has been framed so as to avoid them.

now think of as the exclusive domain of public administration was managed by means of an arrangement that to us looks as if those public functions had been made the objects of private ownership and the sources of private gain; every knight or lord in a hierarchy of liege relations held his fief for profit and not as a payment for the services he rendered *in managing it*. The now so-called public functions connected with it were but a reward for services rendered to some superior liege. Even this does not quite express the matter: he held his fief because, being a knight or lord, he was entitled to hold one whatever he did or did not do. This state of things people who lack the historical dimension are prone to look upon as a compound of "abuses." But that is nonsense. Under the circumstances of its own epoch—like every bit of institutional framework, feudalism survived what was truly "its" epoch—this arrangement was the only feasible one and it embodied the only method by which those public functions could be discharged. If Karl Marx had put in appearance, say, in the fourteenth century and if he had been so foolish as to advocate another method of public administration, then he would have laid himself open to the reply that such a system was an admirable device for getting done what without it could not have been done at all and in particular that "human nature being what it is" the profit motive was indispensable for the functioning of public administration; its elimination would in fact have spelled chaos and could have been well described as an impracticable dream.

Similarly, at the time when the English textile mill was the high spot of capitalist economy—up to 1850, say—socialism was not a practical proposition and no sensible socialist would hold now or did hold then that it was. The master's eye that makes the cattle fat and turns sand to gold, the goose that lays the golden eggs and other such homely phrases then were but the expression, by and for simple and slow-witted people, of an undeniable truth. I submit to socialist friends that there is a better way of encountering them than sneering —sneering in the hope that the opponent, a vain and touchy intellectual like themselves, will cease to argue as soon as he perceives that he may encounter ridicule: it is better to recognize the rightful claim of those geese within their proper historical setting and confine denial to other historical settings. We shall then at least face the relevant question—to wit, how much there is to them now—and still retain plenty of parking space for our disagreements.

Since we must visualize a definite pattern of capitalism if comparison of capitalist reality with socialist chances of success is to have any meaning, let us choose the capitalism of our own epoch, that is to say, big-business capitalism *in fetters*. And let us observe first, that though this defines an epoch and a pattern it does not define any particular date, not even in terms of decades, because the question how far the pattern of fettered capitalism has developed and stabilized its features at any given time, say at present, would still have to wait upon factual investigation; second, that for this part of our argument it becomes irrelevant whether those fetters, whatever they are, have been evolved by the capitalist process itself or may be looked upon as something imposed upon it by an agency that stands outside of it; third, that though we are now going to deal with somewhat more practical problems—namely, how far socialism can be expected to reap the harvest that is potentially present in its blueprint—we shall still be speaking of chances only and that assumptions will have to step in to remedy our ignorance about what kind of socialism will be our fate.

II. ABOUT DEMIGODS AND ARCHANGELS

Returning to our bourgeois who talked about demigods and archangels, we can easily dispose of the first; no demigods will be required to direct the socialist engine because, as we have seen before, the task to be solved will—once transitional difficulties have been disposed of—be not only no more difficult but easier than the task that faces a captain of industry in the modern world. The archangels stand for the well-known proposition that the socialist form of existence presupposes an ethical level that men as they are cannot be expected to reach.

Socialists have themselves to blame if arguments of this type ever carried weight with their opponents. They talked about the horrors of capitalist oppression and exploitation which had only to be removed in order to reveal human nature in all its beauty right away or, at all events, in order to start a process of education that would reform human souls so as to lead up to the ethical level required.[2] Thus they laid themselves open not only to the charge of flattering the masses to a ridiculous degree but also to the charge of espousing a Rousseauism which should be sufficiently exploded by now. But it is not at all necessary to do that. A good common-sense case can be made out without it.

For this purpose, let us adopt a distinction that proves useful though psychologists may object to it. First, a given set of propensities to feel and to act may be altered by changes in the social environment while the fundamental pattern underlying it ("human nature") remains what it is. We will call this Change by Reconditioning. Second, still within that fundamental pattern, reconditioning may impinge on propensities to feel and to act which, though ultimately amenable to change by environmental alterations—particularly if

---

[2] Among Neo-Marxists the chief sinner was Max Adler (not to be confused with the two other Viennese Adlers who hold a prominent place in the history of Austrian socialism, Victor Adler, the great organizer and leader of the party, and his son, Fritz Adler, the murderer of Prime Minister Count Stürgkh).

these alterations are carried out rationally—yet resist for a time and create trouble as long as they do. This fact we may associate with the term Habits. Third, the fundamental pattern itself may be changed either within the same stock of human material or by means of eliminating refractory elements of it; human nature is certainly malleable to some extent particularly in groups whose composition may be changed. How far this malleability goes is a question for serious research and not one that can be usefully dealt with in the platform style by reckless assertion or equally reckless denial. But we need not commit ourselves either way, because no such fundamental reform of the human soul would now be necessary in order to make socialism work.

Of this we can easily satisfy ourselves. We can first exclude the agrarian sector which could be expected to offer the most serious difficulties. Our socialism would still be socialism if the socialist management confined itself to a kind of agrarian planning that would only in degree differ from the practice that is already developing. Settling a plan of production; rationalizing location (land use); supplying farmers with machinery, seeds, stock for breeding purposes, fertilizers and so on; fixing prices of products and buying them from farmers at these prices—this is all that would be necessary and yet it would leave the agrarian world and its attitudes substantially intact. There are other possible courses. But what matters to us is that there is one which could be followed with very little friction and could be followed indefinitely without impairing the claim of the society to being called socialist.

Second, there is the world of the laborer and of the clerk. No reform of souls, no painful adaptation would be required of them. Their work would remain substantially what it is—and it would, with an important qualification to be added later, turn out similar attitudes and habits. From his work the laborer or clerk would return to a home and to pursuits which socialist fancy may denote as it pleases—he may, for instance, play proletarian football whereas now he is playing bourgeois football—but which would still be the same kind of home and the same kind of pursuits. No great difficulties need arise in that quarter.

Third, there is the problem of the groups that not unnaturally expect to be the victims of the socialist arrangement—the problem, roughly speaking, of the upper or leading stratum. It cannot be settled according to that hallowed doctrine which has become an article of faith much beyond the socialist camp, viz., the doctrine that this stratum consists of nothing but overfed beasts of prey whose presence in their economic and social positions is explicable only by luck and ruthlessness and who fill no other "function" than to withhold from the working masses—or the consumers, as the case may be—the fruits of their toil; that these beasts of prey, moreover, bungle their own game by incompetence and (to add a more modern touch) produce depressions by their habit of hoarding the greater part of their loot; and that the socialist community need not bother about them beyond seeing to it that they are promptly ousted from those positions and prevented from committing acts of sabotage. Whatever the political and, in the case of the subnormal, the psycho-therapeutic virtues of this doctrine, it is not even good socialism. For any civilized socialist will, when on his good behavior and intending to be taken seriously by serious people, admit many facts about the quality and the achievements of the bourgeois stratum which are incompatible with such a doctrine, and go on to argue that its upper ranks are not going to be victimized at all but that, on the contrary, they too are to be freed from the shackles of the system which oppresses them morally no less than it oppresses the masses economically. From this standpoint which agrees with the teaching of Karl Marx, the way is not so very far to the conclusion that a cooperation of the bourgeois elements may make all the difference between success and failure for the socialist order.

The problem, then, posits itself like this. Here is a class which, by virtue of the selective process of which it is the result, harbors human material of supernormal quality[3] and hence is a national asset which it is rational for any social organization to use. This alone implies more than refraining from exterminating it. Moreover, this class is fulfilling vital functions that will have to be fulfilled also in socialist

[3] See ch. vi. More precisely, the modal individual in the bourgeois class is superior as to intellectual and volitional aptitudes to the modal individual in any other of the classes of industrial society. This has never been established statistically, and hardly ever can be, but it follows from an analysis of that process of social selection in capitalist society. The nature of the process also determines the sense in which the term superiority is to be understood. By similar analysis of other social environments, it can be shown that the same holds true for all ruling classes about which we have historical information. That is to say, it can be shown in all cases, first, that human molecules rise and fall within the class into which they are born, in a manner which fits the hypothesis that they do so because of their relative aptitudes; and it can also be shown, second, that they rise and fall across the boundary lines of their class in the same manner. This rise and fall into higher and lower classes as a rule takes more than one generation. These molecules are therefore families rather than individuals. And this explains why observers who focus attention on individuals so frequently fail to find any relation between ability and class position and are inclined to go so far as to contrast them. For individuals do start so differently handicapped that, excepting cases of unusual personal achievement, that relation, which moreover refers to a mode only and leaves room for many exceptions, reveals itself much less clearly if we neglect to survey the whole chain of which each individual is a link. These indications do not of course establish my point but only suggest how I should go about establishing it if it were possible to do so within the frame of this book. I may nowever refer the reader to my "Theorie der sozialen Klassen im ethnisch homogenen Milieu," *Archiv für Sozialwissenschaft*, 1927.

society. We have seen that it has been and is causally associated with practically all the cultural achievements of the capitalistic epoch and with as much of its economic achievements as is not accounted for by the growth of the laboring population—with all the increase, that is, in what is usually called the productivity of labor (product per man-hour).[4] And this achievement has been in turn causally associated with a system of prizes and penalties of unique efficiency that socialism is bound to abolish. Therefore the question is, on the one hand, whether the bourgeois stock can be harnessed into the service of socialist society and, on the other hand, whether those of the functions discharged by the bourgeoisie which socialism must take away from it can be discharged by other agents or by other than bourgeois methods, or by both.

III. The Problem of Bureaucratic Management

Rational exploitation of the bourgeois stock is doubtless the problem which a socialist regime will find the most difficult of all, and it would take some optimism to aver that it will be successfully solved. This however is due not primarily to the difficulties inherent in it but rather to the difficulty socialists will experience in recognizing its importance and in facing it in a reasonable frame of mind. The doctrine about the nature and the functions of the capitalist class that has been alluded to above is in itself a symptom of a strong aversion to doing so and may be looked upon as a psycho-technic preparation for refusing to do so. Nor is this surprising. Whether a free lance or a party executive or a civil servant, the individual socialist looks upon the advent of socialism, naïvely but naturally, as synonymous with *his* advent to power. Socialization means to him that "we" are going to take over. Displacement of existing managements is an important, perhaps the most important, part of the show. And I confess that in conversing with militant socialists I have often felt some doubt as to whether some or even most of them would care for a socialist regime, however perfect in other respects, if it were to be run by other people. I must add at once that the attitude of others was irreproachable.[5]

In itself, successful solution of the problem requires above all that the bourgeois stock be allowed to do the work it is qualified to do by aptitude and tradition, and hence that a method of selection for managerial positions be adopted which is based upon fitness and does not differentiate against the ex-bourgeois. Such methods are conceivable and some of them may even compare favorably with

[4] As pointed out in the first Part, this has been recognized by Marx himself, in a *locus classicus* of the Communist Manifesto.

[5] On this, see the comments on the deliberations of the German Committee on Socialization, ch. xxiii, p. 300.

the capitalist method as it works in the era of the big corporation. However, to be allowed to do one's work involves more than appointment to an appropriate place. When so appointed, one must also be given freedom to act under one's own responsibility. And this raises the question of that Bureaucratization of Economic Life which constitutes the theme of so many anti-socialist homilies.

I for one cannot visualize, in the conditions of modern society, a socialist organization in any form other than that of a huge and all-embracing bureaucratic apparatus. Every other possibility I can conceive would spell failure and breakdown. But surely this should not horrify anyone who realizes how far the bureaucratization of economic life—of life in general even—has gone already and who knows how to cut through the underbrush of phrases that has grown up around the subject. As in the case of "monopoly" these phrases derive much of their hold on our minds from their historical source. In the epoch of rising capitalism the bourgeoisie asserted itself primarily through a struggle with territorial powers represented by, and acting through, a monarchist bureaucracy. And most of what the merchant and the manufacturer felt to be irksome or silly interference associated itself in the collective mind of the capitalist class with this bureaucracy or civil service. Such an association is an extremely durable thing; this particular one proved so durable that even socialists themselves are afraid of the bugbear and often go out of their way to assure us that nothing is further removed from their plans than the idea of a bureaucratic regime.[6]

We shall see in the next part that bureaucracy is not an obstacle to democracy but an inevitable complement to it. Similarly it is an inevitable complement to modern economic development and it will be more than ever essential in a socialist commonwealth. But recognition of the inevitability of comprehensive bureaucratization does not solve the problems that arise out of it, and it is just as well to use this opportunity to state what they consist of.

The elimination of the profit and loss motive that is often exclusively stressed is not the essential point. Moreover, responsibility in the sense of having to pay for one's mistakes with one's own money is passing anyhow (though not as quickly as wishful thinking would have us believe) and the kind of responsibility that exists in the large-scale corporation could no doubt be reproduced in a socialist society (see below). Nor is the method of selecting leading executives which is peculiar to a bureaucracy or civil service necessarily so inefficient as it is often made out to be. Civil service rules of ap-

[6] In Russia there is an additional reason for such professions. The bugbear became a scapegoat which all the leaders, but especially Trotsky, knew how to use. Rightly banking on the thoughtlessness of both the domestic and the foreign public, they simply laid at the door of "bureaucracy" anything in Russia that they felt to be short of admirable.

pointment and promotion are not without an appreciable measure of rationality. Also they sometimes work better in practice than they appear on paper: in particular, the element of the corporate opinion of the service about a given man may, if given adequate weight, do much toward favoring ability—at least ability of a certain type.[7]

Much more important is another point. The bureaucratic method of transacting business and the moral atmosphere it spreads doubtless often exert a depressing influence on the most active minds. Mainly, this is due to the difficulty, inherent in the bureaucratic machine, of reconciling individual initiative with the mechanics of its working. Often the machine gives little scope for initiative and much scope for vicious attempts at smothering it. From this a sense of frustration and of futility may result which in turn induces a habit of mind that revels in blighting criticism of the efforts of others. This need not be so; many bureaucracies gain on closer acquaintance with their work. But it is difficult to avoid and there is no simple recipe for doing so.

It is not difficult however to insert the stock of bourgeois extraction into its proper place within that machine and to reshape its habits of work. We shall see later that, at least in the case of socialization in the fullness of time, the conditions for moral acceptance of the socialist order of things and for a transfer of loyalties to it are likely to be met, and that there need be no commissars to thwart and to insult. Rational treatment of the ex-bourgeois elements with a view to securing a maximum of performance from them will then not require anything that is not just as necessary in the case of managerial personnel of any other extraction. The question what this rational treatment implies has been so reasonably and so undemagogically answered by some socialist authorities that a very brief survey of the important points will suffice.

We had better recognize from the start that exclusive reliance on a purely altruistic sense of duty is as unrealistic as would be a wholesale denial of its importance and its possibilities. Even if full allowance be made for the various elements that are cognate to sense of duty, such as the satisfaction derived from working and directing, some system of rewards at least in the form of social recognition and prestige would presumably prove advantageous. On the one one hand, common experience teaches that it is difficult to find a man or woman, however high-minded, whose altruism or sense of duty functions in complete independence of at least that kind of self-interest or, if you prefer, of his or her vanity or desire for self-assertion. On the other hand, it is clear that the attitude which underlies this often pathetically obvious fact is more deeply rooted than the capitalist system and belongs to the logic of life within any social group.

[7] See below, ch. xxiv.

Hence it cannot be disposed of by phrases about the pest of capitalism that infects souls and distorts their "natural" propensities. It is however quite easy to deal with this type of individual egotism so as to exploit it for the service of society. And a socialist community is in a particularly favorable position to do this.

In capitalist society, social recognition of performance or social prestige carries a strongly economic connotation both because pecuniary gain is the typical index of success, according to capitalist standards, and because most of the paraphernalia of social prestige—in particular, that most subtle of all economic goods, Social Distance—have to be bought. This prestige or distinction value of private wealth has of course always been recognized by economists. John Stuart Mill, no wizard in foresight or insight, saw it. And it is clear that among the incentives to supernormal performance this is one of the most important.

It has been shown in Part II that capitalist evolution itself tends to weaken that motive for desiring wealth along with all the others. Socialism will hence require not nearly as great a revaluation of the values of life in what now forms the uppermost stratum as it would have done a hundred years ago. Moreover the prestige motive, more than any other, can be molded by simple reconditioning: successful performers may conceivably be satisfied nearly as well with the privilege—if granted with judicious economy—of being allowed to stick a penny stamp on their trousers as they are by receiving a million a year. Nor would that be irrational. For, assuming that the penny stamp will impress the environment sufficiently to induce it to behave deferentially toward the wearer, it will give him many of the advantages for the sake of which he at present prizes the million a year. This argument loses nothing by the fact that such a practice would only revive a device which in the past has been widely used with excellent results. Why not? Trotsky himself accepted the Order of the Red Flag.

As regards preferential treatment in terms of real income it should be observed first of all that to a certain extent it is a matter of rational behavior toward the existing stock of social resources quite independently of the stimulus aspect. Just as race horses and prize bulls are the grateful recipients of attentions which it would be neither rational nor possible to bestow on every horse and bull, so the supernormal human performer has to be accorded preferential treatment if the rules of economic rationality are to prevail. Of course they need not. The community may elect to give effect to ideals that preclude this and to refuse to look upon men as they would upon machines. And all that an economist is entitled to say about it is that the community should not act in ignorance of the fact that those ideals cost something. The point is of considerable importance.

Many incomes high enough to evoke adverse comment do not give their receivers more than the conditions of life and work—distance and freedom from minor worries included—that are sufficient to keep them fit for the kind of thing they are doing.

So far as that point is taken account of, it will simultaneously solve, at least in part, the problem of providing purely economic stimuli. But I think that, again as a matter of rationality, the socialist community stands to gain considerably by going much beyond the limits that are imposed by the race horse or machine aspect. Once more the reason for this flows, on the one hand, from observation of behavior and, on the other, from analysis of the economy and civilization of capitalism which fails to support the view that the urge which society may exploit by preferential treatment is a product of capitalist conditions. This urge is a propeller of socially valuable effort. If it is denied all chance of satisfaction, results will be somewhat smaller than they could be although it is impossible to say by how much and although the importance of this element will be the smaller the more stationary the economic process when socialism takes over.

This does not mean that in order to do justice to the possibilities of stimulation of this kind, nominal incomes would have to go to anything like their present heights. At present, they include taxes, savings and so on. The elimination of these items would in itself suffice to reduce drastically the figures that are so offensive to the petty-bourgeois mentality of our time. Moreover, as we have seen before, the people in the upper income brackets are being increasingly trained to more modest ideas and in fact are losing most of the motives—other than the prestige motive—for desiring those levels of income that used to support expenditure on the seignorial scale; their ideas will be still more modest by the time socialism can be expected to be a success.

Naturally, economic pharisees would still throw up their hands in holy horror. For their benefit, I beg to point out that devices are ready at hand to placate their scruples. These devices have emerged in the capitalist world but have been greatly developed in Russia. Essentially they amount to a combination of payments in kind with a liberal provision in money for what are supposed to be expenses of the proper discharging of certain duties. In most countries the higher ranks of the civil service are no doubt very modestly paid, often irrationally so, and the great political offices mostly carry decorously small money salaries. But at least in many cases this is partly, in some cases very amply, compensated not only by honors but also by official residences staffed at the public expense, allowances for "official" hospitality, the use of admiralty and other yachts, special

provisions for service on international commissions or in the headquarters of an army and so on.

IV. SAVING AND DISCIPLINE

Finally, what about the functions at present discharged by the
bourgeoisie that the socialist regime is bound to take away from it?
Under this heading we shall discuss Saving and Discipline.

As regards the first—a function almost entirely discharged by the
bourgeoisie and especially its higher ranks—I am not going to argue
that saving is unnecessary or anti-social. Nor am I going to ask the
reader to rely on the individual comrades' propensity to save. Their
contribution need not be neglected but it would be inadequate unless
the socialist economy is to be thought of as quasi-stationary. Much
more effectively, as we have seen, the central authority can do all
that is now being done through private saving by directly allocating
part of the national resources to the production of new plant and
equipment. The Russian experience may be inconclusive on many
points, but it is conclusive on this. Hardships and "abstinence" have
been imposed such as no capitalist society could ever have enforced.
In a more advanced stage of economic development it would not, in
order to secure progress at the capitalist rate, be necessary to impose
nearly as much. When a quasi-stationary stage has been reached by
the capitalist predecessor, even voluntary saving may be sufficient.
The problem, though always solvable, again shows that different
situations require different socialisms and that the idyllic type can
be successful only if economic progress is held to be of no account,
in which case the economic criterion ceases to be relevant, or if economic progress though appreciated for the past is held to have gone
far enough to be of no account for the future.

As regards discipline: there is an obvious relation between the
efficiency of the economic engine and the authority over employees
which, by means of the institutions of private property and "free"
contracting, commercial society vests with the bourgeois employer.
This is not simply a privilege conferred upon Haves in order to
enable them to exploit Have-nots. Behind the private interest immediately concerned there is the social interest in the smooth running
of the productive apparatus. Opinions may differ fairly as to how far
in a given situation the latter is actually served by the former and
as to the extent of functionless hardship which the method of entrust-
ing the social interest to the self-interest of employers used to inflict
on the underdog. But historically there cannot be any difference of
opinion either as to the existence of that social interest or as to the
general effectiveness of that method which moreover, during the
epoch of intact capitalism, was evidently the only possible one. Hence
we have two questions to answer. Will that social interest persist

in the socialist environment? If so, can the socialist plan supply the required amount of authority whatever it may be?

It will be convenient to replace the term authority by its complement, authoritarian discipline, which is taken to mean the habit, inculcated by agents other than the disciplined individuals themselves, of obeying orders and of accepting supervision and criticism. From this we distinguish self-discipline—noting that, in part at least, it is due to previous, even ancestral, exposure to the disciplining influence of authority—and group discipline which is the result of the pressure of group opinion on every member of the group and similarly due, in part, to authoritarian training undergone in the past.

Now there are two facts that may be expected to make for stricter self-discipline and group discipline in the socialist order. The case has, like so many others, been all but spoiled by foolish idealizations —the absurd picture of workers who are supposed to arrive by means of intelligent discussion (when resting from pleasant games) at decisions which they then arise to carry out in joyful emulation. But things of this sort should not blind us to facts and inferences from facts that lend support to favorable expectations of a more reasonable nature.

First, the socialist order presumably will command that moral allegiance which is being increasingly refused to capitalism. This, it need hardly be emphasized, will give the workman a healthier attitude toward his duties than he possibly can have under a system he has come to disapprove. Moreover his disapproval is largely the result of the influences to which he is exposed. He disapproves because he is told to do so. His loyalty and his pride in good performance are being systematically talked out of him. His whole outlook on life is being warped by the class-war complex. But what on a previous occasion I have called the vested interest in social unrest will to a large extent disappear—or be made to disappear as we shall presently see—along with all other vested interests. Of course, against this must be set the removal of the disciplining influence exerted by the responsibility for one's own economic fate.

Second, one of the chief merits of the socialist order consists in the fact that it shows up the nature of economic phenomena with unmistakable clearness whereas in the capitalist order their faces are covered by the mask of the profit interest. We may think as we please about the crimes and follies which socialists hold are perpetrated behind that mask but we cannot deny the importance of the mask itself. For instance, in a socialist society nobody could possibly doubt that what a nation gets out of international trade is the imports and that the exports are the sacrifice which must be undergone in order to procure the imports, whereas in commercial society this common-sense view is as a rule completely hidden from the man in the street who therefore cheerfully supports policies that are to his disadvantage. Or whatever else the socialist management may bungle, it certainly will not pay any premium to anybody for the express purpose of inducing him *not* to produce. Or nobody will be able to get away with nonsense about saving. Far beyond the matter in hand, economic policy will therefore be rationalized and some of the worst sources of waste will be avoided simply because the economic significance of measures and processes will be patent to every comrade. Among other things, every comrade will realize the true significance of restiveness at work and especially of strikes. It does not matter in the least that he will not on that account *ex post facto* condemn the strikes of the capitalist period, provided he comes to the conclusion that strikes would "now" be nothing else but anti-social attacks upon the nation's welfare. If he struck all the same, he would do so with a bad conscience and meet public disapproval. There would no longer be, in particular, any well-meaning bourgeois of both sexes who think it frightfully exciting to applaud strikers and strike leaders.

V. Authoritarian Discipline in Socialism; a Lesson from Russia

But those two facts carry us beyond an inference to the effect that as far as they go there might be more self-discipline and more group discipline in socialist society, hence less need for authoritarian discipline than there is in the society of fettered capitalism. They also suggest that, whenever needed, authoritarian enforcement of discipline will prove an easier task.[8] Before giving the reasons for believing this I must give the reasons for believing that socialist society will not be able to dispense with authoritarian discipline.

First of all, so far as self-discipline and group discipline are, at least to a considerable extent, the result of previous, possibly ancestral, training provided by authoritarian discipline, they will wear away if that training is discontinued for a sufficient length of time, quite irrespective of whether or not the socialist order provides additional reasons for conserving the required type of behavior that may appeal to the rational consideration or the moral allegiance of individuals or groups. Such reasons and their acceptance are important factors

---

[8] The importance of this, if it can be established as a reasonable expectation to entertain at least for some types of the socialist pattern, can hardly be exaggerated. It is not only that discipline improves the quality and, if required, the quantity of the labor hours. Irrespective of this, discipline is an economizing factor of the first order. It lubricates the wheels of the economic engine and greatly reduces waste and total effort per unit of performance. The efficiency of planning as well as of current management in particular may be raised to a level far above anything that is feasible under present conditions.

in inducing people to submit to the training and to a system of sanctions rather than in enabling them to keep up to the mark of themselves. This aspect gains weight if we reflect that we are considering discipline in the drab routine of everyday life, unglorified by enthusiasm, irksome in some if not in all details, and that the socialist order will remove, to say the least, some of the pressure of the survival motive which largely motivates self-discipline in capitalist society.

Second, closely allied to the necessity of incessant training of the normal is the necessity of dealing with the subnormal performer. This term does not refer to isolated pathological cases but to a broad fringe of perhaps 25 per cent of the population. So far as subnormal performance is due to moral or volitional defects, it is perfectly unrealistic to expect that it will vanish with capitalism. The great problem and the great enemy of humanity, the subnormal, will be as much with us as he is now. He can hardly be dealt with by *unaided* group discipline alone—although of course the machinery of authoritarian discipline can be so constructed as to work, partly at least, through the group of which the subnormal is an element.

Third, though the vested interest in social unrest may be expected to disappear in part, there is reason to believe that it will not disappear entirely. Stirring up trouble and putting monkey wrenches into the works will still mean a career or the short cut to a career; it will no less than now be the natural reaction of both idealists and self-seekers displeased with their position or with things in general. Moreover there will be plenty to fight about in socialist society. After all, only one of all the great sources of controversy will be eliminated. Beyond the obvious likelihood of the partial survival of sectional interests—geographical and industrial—there may be clashes of opinion for instance about the relative weight to be attributed to immediate enjoyment versus the welfare of future generations, and a management that espouses the cause of the latter might well be faced by an attitude not entirely dissimilar to the present attitude of labor and of the public in general toward big business and its policy of accumulation. Last but not least, recalling what has been said on the subject of the cultural indeterminateness of socialism, we shall have to realize that many of the great issues of national life will be as open as ever and that there is little reason to expect that men will cease to fight over them.

Now, in appraising the ability of socialist management to cope with the difficulties that may arise under these three heads, we must bear in mind that the comparison is with capitalism as it is today or even with capitalism as it may be expected to function in a still more advanced stage of disintegration. When discussing the importance, so completely overlooked by many economists since the

time of Jeremy Bentham, of unquestioning subordination within
the individual firm,[9] we saw that capitalist evolution tends to wear
away its socio-psychological bases. The workman's readiness to obey
orders was never due to a rational conviction of the virtues of capitalist society or to a rational perception of any advantages accruing
to him personally. It was due to discipline inculcated by the feudal
predecessor of his bourgeois master. To this master the proletariat
transferred part of that respect—by no means all of it—that their
ancestors in all normal cases bore to their feudal lords, whose descendants also made things a lot easier for the bourgeoisie by staying
in political power for the greater part of capitalist history.

By fighting the protecting stratum, by accepting equality in the
political sphere, by teaching the laborers that they were just as valuable citizens as anyone else, the bourgeoisie forfeited that advantage.
For a time, enough authority remained to veil the gradual but
incessant change that was bound to dissolve the discipline in the
factory. By now, most of it is gone. Gone are most of the means of
maintaining discipline, and, even more, the power to use them.
Gone is the moral support of the community that used to be extended to the employer struggling with infractions of discipline.
Gone finally is—largely in consequence of the withdrawal of that
support—the old attitude of governmental agencies; step by step
we can trace the way that led from backing the master to neutrality,
through the various *nuances* of neutrality to backing the workman's
right to being considered an equal partner in a bargain, and from
this to backing the trade union against both employers and individual
workmen.[10] The picture is completed by the attitude of the hired
business executive who, knowing that if he claimed to be fighting
for a public interest he would not even rouse indignation but only
hilarity, concludes that it is more pleasant to be commended for
progressiveness—or to go on holiday—than to incur obloquy or
danger by doing what nobody admits to be his duty.

Considering this state of things, we need not project the tendencies

[9] See ch. xi, p. 127.
[10] Toleration amounting to encouragement of such practices as picketing may
serve as a useful landmark in a process that has not run a straight-line course.
Legislation, still more administrative practice, in this country is particularly interesting because the problems involved have been brought out with unequaled
emphasis owing to the fact that change, after having been long delayed, has been
crowded into so short a time. The absence of any awareness that there may be
other social interests for government to take care of in its attitude to labor
problems than the short-run interest of the working class is as characteristic as is
the half-hearted but significant adoption of class-war tactics. Much of this can
be explained by a peculiar political configuration and by the peculiarly American
impossibility of corralling the proletariat into an effective organization in any
other way. But the illustrative value of the American labor situation is not substantially impaired thereby.

inherent in it very far ahead in order to visualize situations in which *socialism might be the only means of restoring social discipline.* But it is clear in any case that the advantages which a socialist management will command in this respect are so considerable as to weigh heavily in the balance of productive efficiencies.

First, the socialist management will have at its disposal many more tools of authoritarian discipline than any capitalist management can ever have again. The threat of dismissal is practically the only one that is left—agreeable to the Benthamite idea of a contract to be rationally entered into and dissolved by social equals—and the handle of even that tool is so framed as to cut the hand that attempts to use it. But threat of dismissal by the socialist management may mean the threat of withholding sustenance that cannot be secured by an alternative employment. Moreover, whereas in capitalist society it must as a rule be dismissal or nothing—because public opinion on principle disapproves of the very idea of one party to a contract disciplining the other—the socialist management may be able to apply that threat to any degree that may seem rational and to apply other sanctions as well. Among the less drastic of the latter are some which a capitalist management cannot use because of its lack of moral authority. In a new social atmosphere, mere admonition may have an effect which it could not possibly have now.

Second, the socialist management will find it much easier to use whatever tools of authoritarian discipline it may have. There will be no government to interfere. Intellectuals as a group will no longer be hostile and those individuals who are will be restrained by a society that once more believes in its own standards. Such a society will in particular be firm in its guidance of the young. And, to repeat, public opinion will no longer countenance what it will consider semicriminal practice. A strike would be mutiny.

Third, there will be infinitely more motive for the managing group to uphold authority than there is for government in capitalist democracy. At present the attitude of governments toward business is akin to the attitude which in political life we associate with opposition: it is critical, checking and fundamentally irresponsible. That could not be so in socialism. The ministry of production will be responsible for the functioning of the engine. To be sure that responsibility would be political only and good oratory might possibly cover many sins. Nevertheless the opposition interest of government will of necessity be eliminated, and a strong motive for successful operation will be substituted for it. Economic necessities will no longer be a laughing matter. Attempts at paralyzing operations and at setting people against their work will amount to attacking the government. And it can reasonably be expected to react to this.

Again, as in the case of saving, the various objections that may be raised against generalizations from Russian experience do not impair the value of its lessons in a matter which in a more mature or otherwise more nearly normal socialist society should present less and not more difficulties. On the contrary, we can hardly hope for a better illustration of the main points of the above argument.

The Bolshevik Revolution of 1917 completed the disorganization of the small but highly concentrated industrial proletariat of Russia. The masses got out of hand entirely and gave effect to their conception of the new order of things by innumerable strikes of the holiday-making type and by taking possession of the factories.[11] Management by workmen's councils or by trade unions was the order of the day and was accepted by many leaders as a matter of course. A minimum of influence was with difficulty secured for engineers and for the Supreme Council by a compromise arrived at early in 1918, the thoroughly unsatisfactory working of which was one of the major motives for embarking upon the New Economic Policy in 1921. Trade unions then for a time relapsed into something like the functions and attitudes they have in a severely fettered capitalism. But the first Five-Year Plan (1928) changed all that; by 1932 the industrial proletariat was more in hand than it had been under the last Tsar. Whatever else the bolsheviks may have failed in, they have certainly succeeded in this respect ever since. The way in which this was done is highly instructive.

The trade unions were not suppressed. On the contrary they were fostered by the government: membership increased by leaps and bounds and was nearly 17 millions as early as 1932. But from exponents of group interests and obstacles to discipline and performance they developed into exponents of the social interests and into tools of discipline and performance, acquiring an attitude so completely different from that which is associated with trade unions in capitalist countries that some western laborites refused to recognize them as trade unions at all. They no longer opposed the hardships incident to the pace of industrialization. They readily stood for extension of the working day without additional remuneration. They dropped the principle of equal wages and espoused a system of premiums and other inducements to effort, *Stakhanovism* and the rest of it. They recognized—or submitted to—the manager's right to dismiss workmen *at will*, discouraged "democratic meetingism"—the practice of the workmen's discussing the orders received and executing them only after approval—and, cooperating with "comrades' courts" and "purge commissions," adopted rather strong lines against the slacker and the

---

[11] Such breakdowns of discipline so far have occurred in most historical cases. For instance, they were the immediate cause of the failure of the quasi-socialist experiments tried in Paris during the revolution of 1848.

subnormal. Nothing was heard any more of the right to strike and to control production.

Now ideologically there was no difficulty at all about this. We may smile at the quaint terminology which labeled as counterrevolutionary and contrary to Marx's teaching everything that did not quite agree with the government's interest in the full utilization of labor. But there is in fact nothing anti-socialist in that attitude: it is only logical that with class warfare the obstructionist practices should pass away and the character of collective agreements should change. Critics are wrong to overlook the amount of self-discipline and group discipline which the system was able to release and which fully bears out the expectations we have formed on the subject. At the same time it is no less wrong to overlook the part played in the achievement, such as it is, by the authoritarian kind of discipline which powerfully supports and no less powerfully supplements the other kinds.

The individual trade unions as well as their central organ, the General Council, have been subjected to the control of the government and of the Communist party. What used to be described as the labor opposition in the latter has been suppressed, and labor leaders who persisted in recognizing a distinct interest of the workmen have been removed from their positions. Thus, ever since the governmental reorganization in 1921, certainly since 1929, trade unions have hardly been in a position to say or do anything that might run counter to the wishes of the ruling set. They have become organs of authoritarian discipline—which fact well illustrates a point made before.

Again, inasmuch as the modern workman's unhealthy attitude to his work is due to the influences to which he is exposed, it is essential to notice the tremendous difference it makes if sense of duty and pride in performance are incessantly being talked into him instead of being incessantly talked out of him. The fact that the Russian state, unlike the capitalist state, is in a position to enforce, in the teaching and guiding of the young, conformity with its ends and structural ideas immeasurably increases its ability to create an atmosphere favorable to factory discipline. Intellectuals are evidently not at liberty to tamper with it. And there is no public opinion to encourage infractions.

Finally, dismissal spelling privation, shifts amounting to deportation, "visits" by shock brigades and occasionally also by comrades of the Red Army are, whatever their legal construction, practically independent means in the hands of the government by which to safeguard performance. There is motive to use them and, as a matter of universally admitted fact, they have been unflinchingly used. Sanctions which no capitalist employer would think of applying even if he had the power frown sternly from behind all gentler psycho-technics.

The sinister connotations of all this are not essential to our argument. There is nothing sinister in what I am trying to convey. The cruelties to individuals and whole groups are largely attributable to the unripeness of the situation, to the circumstances of the country and to the quality of its ruling personnel. In other circumstances, in other stages of development and with other ruling personnel they will not be necessary. If it should prove unnecessary to apply any sanctions at all, so much the better. The point is that at least one socialist regime has actually been able to foster group discipline and to impose authoritarian discipline. It is the principle that matters and not the particular forms in which it was turned into practice.

Thus, even apart from the merits or demerits of blueprints, comparison with fettered capitalism does not turn out unfavorably for the socialist alternative. It must be emphasized again that we have been talking—though in a sense different from that which was relevant to our discussion of the blueprint—of possibilities only. Many assumptions are necessary in order to turn them into certainties or even practical likelihoods, and it is no doubt just as legitimate to adopt other assumptions that would yield different results. In fact, we need only assume that the ideas prevail which constitute what I have termed idyllic socialism in order to convince ourselves of the likelihood of complete and even ludicrous failure. This would not even be the worst possible outcome. Failure so patent as to be ludicrous could be remedied. Much more insidious as well as likely is failure not so complete which political psycho-technics could make people believe to be a success. Moreover, deviations from the blueprint of the engine and from the principles of running the system are of course no less likely than they are in commercial society but they may prove to be more serious and less self-corrective. But if the reader glances once more over the steps of our argument he will, I think, be able to satisfy himself that the objections which have their roots in this class of considerations do not substantially impair our case—or that, more precisely, they are objections not to socialism *per se*, as defined for our purpose, but to the features particular types of socialism may present. It does not follow from them that it is nonsense or wickedness to fight for socialism. It only follows that fighting for socialism means no determinate thing unless it is coupled with a perception of what kind of socialism will work. Whether such a socialism is compatible with what we usually mean by democracy is another question.

CHAPTER XIX

TRANSITION

I. Two Different Problems Distinguished

IT IS, I believe, recognized by everybody and in particular by all orthodox socialists that the transition from the capitalist to the socialist order will always raise problems *sui generis* whatever the conditions under which it may take place. But the nature and extent of the difficulties to be expected differ so greatly according to the stage of the capitalist evolution at which the transition is to be made and according to the methods which the socializing group is able and willing to use that it will be convenient to construct two different cases in order to typify two different sets of circumstances. This device is all the more easy to apply because there is an obvious connection between the When and the How. Nevertheless both cases will be dealt with in reference to fully developed and "fettered" capitalism only—I shall not waste space on the possibilities or impossibilities presented by any earlier stages. Bearing this in mind, we shall call them the cases of mature and premature socialization.

Most of the argument of Part II may be summed up in the Marxian proposition that the economic process tends to socialize *itself*—and also the human soul. By this we mean that the technological, organizational, commercial, administrative and psychological prerequisites of socialism tend to be fulfilled more and more. Let us again visualize the state of things which looms in the future if that trend be projected. Business, excepting the agrarian sector, is controlled by a small number of bureaucratized corporations. Progress has slackened and become mechanized and planned. The rate of interest converges toward zero, not temporarily only or under the pressure of governmental policy, but permanently owing to the dwindling of investment opportunities. Industrial property and management have become depersonalized—ownership having degenerated to stock and bond holding, the executives having acquired habits of mind similar to those of civil servants. Capitalist motivation and standards have all but wilted away. The inference as to the transition to a socialist regime in such fullness of time is obvious. But two points deserve to be mentioned.

First, different people—different socialists even—will differ from one another both in the degree of approximation to that state which will be satisfactory to them and in their diagnosis of the degree of approximation which has been actually reached at any given time.

This is quite natural because the progress toward socialism which is inherent in the capitalist process goes on by slow degrees and will never pass any traffic light that, recognizable to all, would show beyond the possibility of doubt exactly when the road is open. Room for honest difference of opinion is greatly increased by the additional fact that the required conditions of success do not necessarily evolve *pari passu*. For instance, it might be plausibly argued that in 1913 the industrial structure of this country, taken by itself, was more nearly "ripe" than that of Germany. Yet few people will doubt that, had the experiment been made in both countries, the chances of success would have been infinitely greater with the state-broken Germans, led and disciplined as they were by the best bureaucracy the world has ever seen and by her excellent trade unions. But beyond honest differences of opinion—including those that are explainable on differences of temperament similar to those which will make equally competent and honest doctors differ as to the advisability of an operation—there will always be a suspicion, often but too well founded, that the one party to the discussion does not and will never want to admit maturity because it does not really want socialism and that the other party will, for reasons that may or may not spring from idealistic bases, assume maturity under any circumstances whatsoever.

Second, even supposing that an unmistakable state of maturity be reached, transition will still require distinct action and still present a number of problems.

The capitalist process shapes things and souls for socialism. In the limiting case it might do this so completely that the final step would not be more than a formality. But even then the capitalist order would not of itself turn into the socialist order; such a final step, the official adoption of socialism as the community's law of life, would still have to be taken, say, in the form of a constitutional amendment. In practice however people will not wait for the limiting case to emerge. Nor would it be rational for them to do so, for maturity may to all intents and purposes be reached at a time when capitalist interests and attitudes have not yet completely vanished from every nook and cranny of the social structure. And then the passing of the constitutional amendment would be more than a formality. There would be some resistance and some difficulties to overcome. Before considering these, let us introduce another distinction.

Fundamentally, things and souls shape themselves for socialism automatically, i.e., independently of anyone's volition and of any measures taken to that effect. But among other things that process also produces such volition and hence such measures—enactments, administrative actions and so on. The sum total of these measures is part of the policy of socialization which therefore must be thought of as covering a long stretch of time, at all events many decades. But its history naturally divides into two segments separated by the act of adopting and organizing the socialist regime. Before that act, the policy of socialization is—no matter whether intentionally or unintentionally—preparatory, after that act it is constitutive. The former segment will come in for only a short discussion at the end of this chapter. Now we are going to concentrate on the latter.

II. Socialization in a State of Maturity

In the case of mature socialization the difficulties with which it will be the first task of "socialization after the act" to deal are not only not insurmountable but not even very serious. Maturity implies that resistance will be weak and that cooperation will be forthcoming from the greater part of *all* classes—one symptom of which will be precisely the possibility of carrying adoption by a constitutional amendment, i.e., in a peaceful way without a break in legal continuity. *Ex hypothesi* people will understand the nature of the step and even most of those who do not like it will give it a *tolerari posse*. Nobody will be bewildered or feel that the world is crashing about his ears.

Even so, of course, it is not entirely off the cards that there might be revolution. But there is not much danger of this. Not only will complete or approximate absence of organized resistance on the one hand and of violent excitement on the other reduce the opportunity for a revolutionary drive, but also there will be a group of experienced and responsible men ready to put their hands to the helm, both able and willing to keep up discipline and to use rational methods that will minimize the shock. They will be assisted by well-trained public and business bureaucracies which are in the habit of accepting orders from the legal authority whatever it is and who are not very partial to capitalist interests anyway.

To begin with, we will simplify the transitional problems before the new ministry or central board in the same way in which we have already simplified their permanent problems, i.e., by assuming that they will leave farmers substantially alone. This will not only eliminate a difficulty that might well prove fatal—for nowhere else is the property interest so alive as it is among farmers or peasants; the agrarian world is not everywhere peopled by *Russian* peasants—but also bring additional support, for nobody hates large-scale industry and the specifically capitalist interest as much as the farmer does. The board may also be expected to conciliate small men of other types: around the socialized industries the small craftsman might, for a time at least, be allowed to do his jobs for profit, and the small independent retailer to sell as the tobacconist does today in countries where tobacco and tobacco products are monopolized by the state. On the other end of the scale, the personal interests of the man whose work counts individually—the executive type, let us say—

could easily be taken care of, on the lines indicated before, so as to avoid any serious hitch in the running of the economic engine. Drastic assertion of equalitarian ideals of course might spoil everything.

What about the capitalist interest? In the fullness of time, as indicated above, we may roughly equate it to the interest of stock and bond holders—the latter standing also for holders of mortgages and insurance policies. For the socialist who knows nothing except the Holy Writ and who thinks of this group as composed of a small number of immensely rich idlers there would be a surprise in store: at maturity this group might possibly comprise a majority of the electorate which then would look with little favor on proposals for the confiscation of their claims however small individually. But never mind whether or not the socialist regime could or "should" expropriate them without indemnity. All that matters to us is that it would be under no economic necessity to do so and that, if it should decide for confiscation, this would be the community's free choice, in obedience, say, to the ethical principles it might adopt, and not because there is no other way. For payment of the interest on bonds and mortgages as far as owned by individuals plus payment of claims from insurance contracts plus payment, in lieu of dividends, of interest on bonds to be issued to former stockholders by the central board—so that these stockholders while losing their voting power would still retain an income roughly equal to a suitably chosen average of past dividends—would not, as a glance at the relevant statistics will show, constitute an unbearable burden. So far as the socialist commonwealth continues to make use of private savings it obviously might be policy to shoulder it. Limitation in time could be achieved either by turning all these payments into terminable annuities or else by an appropriate use of income and inheritance taxes that might thus render their last service before disappearing forever.

This, I think, sufficiently characterizes a feasible method of "socialization after the act" that, under the circumstances envisaged, might be expected to perform the task of transition firmly, safely and gently with a minimum of loss of energy and of injury to cultural and economic values. The managements of large-scale concerns would be replaced only in cases in which there are specific reasons for replacement. If at the moment of transition there are still private partnerships among the firms to be socialized, they would be first transformed into companies and then socialized in the same way as others. Foundation of new firms would of course be prohibited. The structure of intercorporate relations—holding companies in particular—would be rationalized, i.e., reduced to those relations that serve administrative efficiency. Banks would all be turned into branch offices of the central institution and in this form might still retain not only some of their mechanical functions—part at least of the social bookkeeping would almost necessarily devolve upon them—but possibly also some power over industrial managements that might take the form of power to grant and to refuse "credits"; if so, the central bank might be left independent of the ministry of production itself and become a sort of general supervisor.

Thus, the central board going slowly at first and gradually taking up the reins without a jerk, the economic system would have time to settle down and find its bearings while the minor problems incident to transition could be solved one by one. Little adjustment of production would be necessary at the beginning—a matter of 5 per cent of total output at the outside. For unless equalitarian ideas assert themselves much more strongly than I have assumed, the structure of demand will not be very materially affected. Transfer of men, lawyers for instance, to other employments would, it is true, be on a somewhat larger scale because there are functions to be served in capitalist industry which will no longer have to be served in the socialist economy. But this too would not create any serious difficulty. The larger problems of the elimination of subnormal units of production, of further concentration on the best opportunities, of locational rationalization with the incidental redistribution of the population, of standardization of consumers' and producers' goods and so on would or, at all events, need not emerge before the system has digested the organic change and is running smoothly on the old lines. Of socialism of this type it may without absurdity be expected that it would in time realize all the possibilities of superior performance inherent in its blueprint.

III. Socialization in a State of Immaturity

1. No such prognosis is possible in the second case, the case of premature adoption of the principle of socialism. It may be defined as transition from the capitalist to the socialist order occurring at a time when it has become possible for socialists to gain control of the central organs of the capitalist state while nevertheless both things and souls are as yet unprepared. We are not, let me repeat, going to discuss situations so immature that the hope of success would seem fantastic to any sane person and the attempt at conquering power could not be more than a ridiculous *Putsch*. Hence I am not going to argue that immature socialization must unavoidably end in complete discomfiture or that the resulting arrangement is bound to break down. I am still envisaging fettered capitalism of the present-day type with reference to which the problem can at least be reasonably raised. In such a setting it is even likely to be raised sooner or later. The long-run situation becomes more and more favorable to socialist ambitions. It is still more important that short-run situations may occur—the German situation in 1918 and 1919 is a good example; some people would also point to the American situation in 1932—in

which temporary paralysis of the capitalist strata and their organs offers tempting opportunities.

2. Just what this unpreparedness or immaturity of things and souls means, the reader can easily realize by turning to the picture of a mature situation that has been drawn a few pages back. Nevertheless I wish to add a few touches for the particular case of this country in 1932.

A period of vigorous—though, in terms of rates of change, not abnormal—industrial activity had preceded a depression the very violence of which testified to the extent of the necessary adjustments to the results of "progress." That progress, in the leading lines, was obviously not completed—it is enough to point to the fields of rural electrification, of the electrification of the household, to all the new things in chemistry and to the possibilities opening up in the building industry. Hence considerable loss in entrepreneurial energy, in productive efficiency and in the future welfare of the masses could have been confidently predicted from bureaucratizing socialization. It is amusing to realize that the general opinion which in the hysteria of the depression the intellectuals of socialist leanings were able to impart to the public was exactly the opposite. This however is more germane to the diagnosis of the social psychology of that situation than to its economic interpretation.

Immaturity also showed in the industrial and commercial organization. Not only was the number of small and medium-sized firms still very considerable and their cooperation in trade associations and so on far from perfect, but the development of big business itself, though the subject of much uncritical wonder and hostility, had not gone nearly far enough to make it safe and easy to apply our method of socialization. If we draw the line of large-scale business at firms having 50 million dollars of assets, then only 53.3 per cent of the national total was owned by large corporations, only 36.2 per cent if we exclude finance and public utilities and only 46.3 per cent in the division of manufactures.[1] But corporations smaller than this will not in general lend themselves easily to socialization and cannot be expected to work on under it in their existing form. If nevertheless we descend to a 10-million-dollar limit, we still find no more than 67.5, 52.7 and 64.5 per cent, respectively. The mere task of "taking over" an organism structured like this would have been formidable. The still more formidable task of making it function and of improving it would have had to be faced without an experienced bureaucracy and with a labor force so imperfectly organized and, in part, so questionably led as to be likely to get out of hand.

Souls were still more unprepared than things. In spite of the shock

[1] See W. L. Crum, "Concentration of Corporate Control," *Journal of Business*, vol. viii, p. 275.

imparted by the depression, not only business people but a very large part of the workmen and farmers thought and felt in the terms of the bourgeois order and did not *really* have a clear conception of any alternative; for them the conception of socialization and even of much less than this was still "un-American." There was no efficient socialist party, in fact no quantitatively significant support for any of the official socialist groups excepting the communists of Stalinist persuasion. The farmers disliked socialism, though every trouble was taken to reassure them, only a shade less than they disliked big business in general or railroads in particular. While support would have been weak and much of it either blatantly interested or else lukewarm, resistance would have been strong. It would have been the resistance of people who honestly felt that what they were doing nobody, least of all the state, could do as well and that in resisting they were fighting not for their interests only but also for the common good—for the absolute light against absolute darkness. The American bourgeoisie was losing its vitality but had not lost it completely. It would have resisted with a clear conscience and would have been in a position to refuse both assent and cooperation. One symptom of the situation would have been the necessity to use force not against isolated individuals but against groups and classes; another would have been the impossibility of carrying adoption of the socialist principle by constitutional amendment, i.e., without break in legal continuity: the new order would have had to be established by revolution, more likely than not by a sanguinary one. This particular example of an immature situation may be open to the objection that it comes within the category of absurdly hopeless cases. But the picture combines and illustrates the main features presented by every immature socialization and will hence serve for the purposes of a discussion of the general case.

This case is of course the one contemplated by orthodox socialists, most of whom would be unable to put up with anything less fascinating than the spectacular slaying of the capitalist dragon by the proletarian St. George. It is not however because of that unfortunate survival of early bourgeois revolutionary ideology that we are going to survey the consequences which follow from the combination of political opportunity and economic unpreparedness but because the problems characteristic of the act of socialization as usually understood arise only in this case.

3. Suppose then that the Revolutionary People—in the Bolshevist Revolution this became a sort of official title like Most Christian King—have conquered the central offices of the government, the non-socialist parties, the non-socialist press, etc., and installed their men. The personnel of these offices as well as the personnel of the industrial and commercial concerns is partly goaded into—*ex hypothesi*—

unwilling cooperation and partly replaced by the labor leaders and by the intellectuals who rush from the café to these offices. To the new central board we shall concede two things: a red army strong enough to quell open resistance and to repress excesses—wild socializations in particular[2]—by firing impartially to right and left, and sense enough to leave peasants or farmers alone in the way indicated above. No assumption is made as to the degree of rationality or humanity in the treatment dealt out to the members of what had been the ruling strata. In fact, it is difficult to see how any but the most ruthless treatment could be possible under the circumstances. People who know that their action is felt to be nothing else but vicious aggression by their opponents and that they are in danger of meeting the fate of Karl Liebknecht and Rosa Luxemburg will soon be driven to courses violent beyond any original intention. They will hardly be able to help behaving with criminal ferocity toward opponents whom they will look upon as ferocious criminals—those opponents that still stand for the old order and those opponents that form the new leftist party which cannot fail to emerge. Neither violence nor sadism will solve problems however. What is the central board to do except complain about sabotage and call for additional powers in order to deal with conspirators and wreckers?

The first thing which must be done is to bring about inflation. The banks must be seized and combined or coordinated with the treasury, and the board or ministry must create deposits and banknotes using traditional methods as much as possible. I believe inflation to be unavoidable because I have still to meet the socialist who denies that in the case under discussion the socialist revolution would at least temporarily paralyze the economic process or that in consequence the treasury and the financial centers would for the moment be short of ready means. The socialist system of bookkeeping and income units not being as yet in working order, nothing remains except a policy analogous to that of Germany during and after the First World War or that of France during and after the revolution of 1789, notwithstanding the fact that in those cases it was precisely the unwillingness to break with the system of private property and with the methods of commercial society that enforced inflation for so considerable a time; for "the day after the socialist revolution" when nothing would be in shape, this difference does not matter.

It should be added however that besides necessity there is another motive to embark upon this course. Inflation is in itself an excellent means of smoothing certain transitional difficulties and of effecting partial expropriation. As regards the first, it is for instance evident

[2] Wild socializations—a term that has acquired official standing—are attempts by the workmen of each plant to supersede the management and to take matters into their own hands. They are the nightmare of every responsible socialist.

that a drastic increase in money wage rates will for a time avail to ward off possible outbreaks of rage at the fall in real wage rates that, temporarily at least, would have to be imposed. As regards the second, inflation expropriates the holder of claims in terms of money in a delightfully simple way. The board might even make matters easier for itself by paying owners of real capital—factories and so on—any amount of indemnities if it resolves at the same time that these shall become valueless before long. Finally, it must not be forgotten that inflation would powerfully ram such blocks of private business as may have to be left standing for the moment. For, as Lenin has pointed out, nothing disorganizes like inflation: "in order to destroy bourgeois society you must debauch its money."

4. The second thing to do is of course to socialize. Discussion of transitional problems starts from the old controversy waged among socialists themselves—more precisely between socialists and what are more properly called laborites—on full or one-stroke versus partial or gradual socialization. Many socialists seem to think it due to the purity of the Faith and the true belief in the efficacy of the socialist grace to champion the former under any circumstances and to despise weak-kneed laborites who on this point as on others are much hampered by most inconvenient traces of a sense of responsibility. But I am going to vote for the true believers.[3] We are not now discussing transitional policy in a capitalist system; that is another problem to be touched upon presently when we shall see that gradual socialization *within the framework of capitalism* is not only possible but even the most obvious thing to expect. We are discussing the completely different transitional policy which is to be pursued *after* a socialist regime has been set up by a political revolution.

In this case, even if there be no more than the inevitable minimum of excesses and if a strong hand impose comparatively orderly procedure, it is difficult to imagine a stage in which some of the great industries are socialized whereas others are expected to work on as if nothing had happened. Under a revolutionary government which would have to live up to at least some of the ideas propagated in the days of irresponsibility, any remaining private industries may well cease to function. I am not thinking primarily of the obstruction that might be expected from the entrepreneurs and from capitalist interests in general. Their power is being exaggerated now and would largely cease to exist under the eyes of commissars. And it is not the bourgeois way to refuse to fulfill current duties; the bourgeois way is to cling to them. Resistance there would be, but it would be resistance in the political sphere and outside of the factory rather than resistance within

[3] Scripture does not support them clearly however. If the reader will look up the *Communist Manifesto* he will find a most disconcerting "by degrees" planted right in the most relevant passage.

it. Unsocialized industries would cease to function simply because they
would be prevented from functioning in their own way—the only one
in which capitalist industry can function—by the supervising commissars and by the humor of both their workmen and the public.

But this argument covers only the cases of large-scale industries and
of those sectors which can be easily molded into large-scale units of
control. It does not completely cover all the ground between the
agrarian sphere which we have excluded and the large-scale industries. On that ground, consisting mainly of small or medium-sized
business, the central board could presumably maneuver as expediency
might dictate and in particular advance and retire according to
changing conditions. This would still be full socialization within our
meaning of the term.

One point remains to be added. It should be obvious that socialization in any situation immature enough to require revolution not only
in the sense of a break in legal continuity but also in the sense of a
subsequent reign of terror cannot benefit, either in the short or in the
long run, anyone except those who engineer it. To work up enthusiasm
about it and to glorify the courage of risking all that it might entail
may be one of the less edifying duties of the professional agitator. But
as regards the academic intellectual, the only courage that can possibly
reflect any credit on him is the courage to criticize, to caution and to
restrain.

IV. SOCIALIST POLICY BEFORE THE ACT; THE ENGLISH EXAMPLE

But must we really conclude that, now and for another fifty or one
hundred years, serious socialists cannot do anything except to preach
and wait? Well, the fact that this is more than can be expected of any
party that wants to keep any members, and all the arguments—and
sneers—that flow from this all-too-human source, should not be allowed
to blot out the other fact that there is a weighty argument for this
conclusion. It might even be argued quite logically that socialists
have an interest to further the development that works for them,
hence to unfetter capitalism rather than to fetter it still more.

I do not think however that this means there is nothing for socialists
to do, at all events under the conditions of our own time. Though attempts to establish socialism now would, for most of the great nations
and many small ones, undoubtedly amount to courting failure—failure of socialism as such perhaps, but certainly failure of the socialist
groups responsible for the plunge, while another group not necessarily
socialist in the usual sense might then easily walk away with their
clothes—and though in consequence a policy of socialization after the
act probably is a very doubtful matter, a policy of socialization before
the act offers much better chances. Like other parties, but with a
clearer perception of the goal, socialists can take a hand in it without

compromising ultimate success. All that I wish to say on this question will stand out best in the garb of a particular example.

All the features we could wish our example to display are presented by modern England. On the one hand, her industrial and commercial structure is obviously not ripe for successful one-stroke socialization, in particular because concentration of corporate control has not gone far enough. In conformity with this, neither managements nor capitalists nor workmen are ready to accept it—there is a lot of vital "individualism" left, enough at any rate to put up a fight and to refuse cooperation. On the other hand there has been, roughly since the beginning of the century, a perceptible slackening of entrepreneurial effort which among other things produced the result that state leadership and state control in important lines, production of electric power for instance, have been not only approved but demanded by *all* parties. With more justice than anywhere else it might be argued that capitalism has done by far the greater part of its work. Moreover, English people on the whole have become state-broken by now. English workmen are well organized and as a rule responsibly led. An experienced bureaucracy of irreproachable cultural and moral standards could be trusted to assimilate the new elements required for an extension of the sphere of the state. The unrivaled integrity of the English politician and the presence of a ruling class that is uniquely able and civilized make many things easy that would be impossible elsewhere. In particular this ruling group unites in the most workable proportions adherence to formal tradition with extreme adaptability to new principles, situations and persons. It wants to rule but it is quite ready to rule on behalf of changing interests. It manages industrial England as well as it managed agrarian England, protectionist England as well as free-trade England. And it possesses an altogether unrivaled talent for appropriating not only the programs of oppositions but also their brains. It assimilated Disraeli who elsewhere would have become another Lassalle. It would have, if necessary, assimilated Trotsky himself or rather, as in that case he would assuredly have been, the Earl of Prinkipo K.G.

In such conditions a policy of socialization is conceivable that, by carrying out an extensive program of nationalization, might on the one hand accomplish a big step toward socialism and, on the other hand, make it possible to leave untouched and undisturbed for an indefinite time all interests and activities not included in that program. In fact, these could be freed from many fetters and burdens, fiscal and other, which hamper them now.

The following departments of business activity could be socialized without serious loss of efficiency or serious repercussions on the departments that are to be left to private management. The question of indemnities could be settled on the lines suggested in our discussion of mature socialization; with modern rates of income tax and death duties this would not be a serious matter.

First the banking apparatus of England is no doubt quite ripe for socialization. The Bank of England is little more than a treasury department, in fact less independent than a well-ordered socialist community may well wish its financial organ to be. In commercial banking, concentration and bureaucratization seem to have done full work. The big concerns could be made to absorb as much of independent banking as there is left to absorb and then be merged with the Bank of England into the National Banking Administration, which could also absorb savings banks, building societies and so on without any customer becoming aware of the change except from his newspaper. The gain from rationalizing coordination of services might be substantial. From the socialist standpoint, there would also be a gain in the shape of an increase in the government's influence on non-nationalized sectors.

Second, the insurance business is an old candidate for nationalization and has to a large extent become mechanized by now. Integration with at least some of the branches of social insurance may prove feasible; selling costs of policies could be considerably reduced and socialists might again rejoice in the access of power that control over the funds of insurance companies would give to the state.

Third, few people would be disposed to make great difficulties over railroads or even over trucking. Inland transportation is in fact the most obvious field for successful state management.

Fourth, nationalization of mining, in particular coal mining, and of the coal and tar products down to and including benzol, and also of the trade in coal and in those products might even result in an immediate gain in efficiency and prove a great success if labor problems can be dealt with satisfactorily. From the technological and commercial standpoint, the case seems clear. But it seems equally clear that, private enterprise having been active in the chemical industry, no such success can with equal confidence be expected from an attempt to go beyond the limit indicated.

Fifth, the nationalization of the production, transmission and distribution of electric current being substantially completed already, all that remains to be said under this head is that the electro-technical industry is a typical instance of what may still be expected from private enterprise—which shows how little sense, economically speaking, there is in standing either for general socialization or against any. But the case of power production also shows the difficulty of working a socialized industry for profit which nevertheless would be an essential condition of success if the state is to absorb so great a part of the nation's economic life and still fulfill all the tasks of the modern state.

Sixth, socialization of the iron and steel industry will be felt to be a much more controversial proposition than any made so far. But this industry has certainly sown its wild oats and can be "administered" henceforth—the administration including, of course, a huge research department. Some gains would result from coordination. And there is hardly much danger of losing the fruits of any entrepreneurial impulses.

Seventh, with the possible exception of the architects' share in the matter, the building and building material industries could, I believe, be successfully run by a public body of the right kind. So much of it already is regulated, subsidized and controlled in one way or another that there even might be a gain in efficiency—more than enough, perhaps, to compensate for the sources of loss that might be opened up.

This is not necessarily all. But any step beyond this program would have to justify itself by special, mostly non-economic reasons—the armament or key industries, movies, shipbuilding, trade in foodstuffs being possible instances. At any rate, those seven items are enough to digest for quite a time to come, enough also to make a responsible socialist, if he gets so much done, bless his work and accept the concessions that it would at the same time be rational to make outside of the nationalized sector. If he insists also on nationalizing land—leaving, I suppose, the farmer's status as it is—i.e., transferring to the state all that remains of ground rents and royalties, I have no objection to make as an economist.[4]

The present war will of course alter the social, political and economic data of our problem. Many things will become possible, many others impossible, that were not so before. A few pages at the end of this book will briefly deal with this aspect. But it seems to me essential, for the sake of clarity of political thought, to visualize the problem irrespective of the effects of the war. Otherwise its nature can never stand out as it should. Therefore I leave this chapter, both in form and in content, exactly as I wrote it in the summer of 1938.

[4] This is no place for airing personal preferences. Nevertheless I wish it to be understood that the above statement is made as a matter of professional duty and does not imply that I am in love with that proposal which, were I an Englishman, I should on the contrary oppose to the best of my ability.

PART IV

Socialism and Democracy

CHAPTER XX

THE SETTING OF THE PROBLEM

I. The Dictatorship of the Proletariat

NOTHING is so treacherous as the obvious. Events during the past twenty or twenty-five years have taught us to see the problem that lurks behind the title of this part. Until about 1916 the relation between socialism and democracy would have seemed quite obvious to most people and to nobody more so than to the accredited exponents of socialist orthodoxy. It would hardly have occurred to anyone to dispute the socialists' claim to membership in the democratic club. Socialists themselves of course—except a few syndicalist groups—even claimed to be the only true democrats, the exclusive sellers of the genuine stuff, never to be confused with the bourgeois fake.

Not only was it natural for them to try to enhance the values of their socialism by the values of democracy; but they had also a theory to offer that proved to their satisfaction that the two were indissolubly wedded. According to this theory, private control over the means of production is at the bottom both of the ability of the capitalist class to exploit labor and of its ability to impose the dictates of its class interest upon the management of the political affairs of the community; the political power of the capitalist class thus appears to be but a particular form of its economic power. The inferences are, on the one hand, that there cannot be democracy so long as that power exists—that mere political democracy is of necessity a sham—and, on the other hand, that the elimination of that power will at the same time end the "exploitation of man by man" and bring about the "rule of the people."

This argument is essentially Marxian of course. Precisely because it follows logically—tautologically in fact—from the definitions of terms in the Marxian schema, it will have to share the fate of the latter and in particular the fate of the doctrine of "exploitation of man by man."[1] What seems to me a more realistic analysis of the relation between socialist groups and the democratic creed will presently be offered. But we also want a more realistic theory of the relation that may exist between socialism and democracy themselves, that is to say, of the relation that may exist, independently of wishes and

---

[1] The fact that individual and group-wise power cannot be defined in purely economic terms—as Marx's theory of social classes defines it—is however a still more fundamental reason why this argument is inacceptable.

slogans, between the socialist order as we have defined it and the *modus operandi* of democratic government. In order to solve this problem we must first inquire into the nature of democracy. Another point however calls for immediate clarification.

Socialism in being might be the very ideal of democracy. But socialists are not always so particular about the way in which it is to be brought into being. The words Revolution and Dictatorship stare us in the face from sacred texts, and many modern socialists have still more explicitly testified to the fact that they have no objection to forcing the gates of the socialist paradise by violence and terror which are to lend their aid to more democratic means of conversion. Marx's own position concerning this matter is no doubt capable of an interpretation that will clear him in the eyes of democrats. In Part I it was shown how his views on revolution and evolution may be reconciled. Revolution need not mean an attempt by a minority to impose its will upon a recalcitrant people; it may mean no more than the removal of obstructions opposed to the will of the people by outworn institutions controlled by groups interested in their preservation. The dictatorship of the proletariat will bear a similar interpretation. In support, I may again point to the wording of the relevant passages in the *Communist Manifesto* where Marx talks about wresting things from the bourgeoisie "by degrees" and about the disappearance of class distinctions "in the course of development"—phrases which, the emphasis on "force" notwithstanding, seem to point toward a procedure that might come within the meaning of democracy as ordinarily understood.[2]

But the grounds for this interpretation, which all but reduces the famous social revolution and the no less famous dictatorship to agitatorial flourishes intended to fire the imagination, are not quite conclusive. Many socialists who were, and many others who declared themselves to be, disciples of Marx were of a different opinion. Yielding to the authority of the true scribes and pharisees who should know the Law better than I do, and to an impression based upon perusal of the volumes of the *Neue Zeit*, I must admit the possibility that, if he had had to choose, Marx might have put socialism above the observance of democratic procedure.

In that case he would no doubt have declared, as so many have done after him, that he was not really deviating from the truly democratic path because in order to bring true democracy to life it is necessary to remove the poisonous fumes of capitalism that asphyxiate it. Now for the believer in democracy, the importance of observing democratic procedure obviously increases in proportion to the importance of the point at issue. Hence its observance never needs to

[2] In ch. xxv I shall return to the question of how the problem of democracy presented itself to Marx personally.

be more jealously watched and more carefully safeguarded by all available guarantees than in the case of fundamental social reconstruction. Whoever is prepared to relax this requirement and to accept either frankly undemocratic procedure or some method of securing formally democratic decision by undemocratic means, thereby proves conclusively that he values other things more highly than he values democracy. The thoroughgoing democrat will consider any such reconstruction as vitiated in its roots, however much he might approve of it on other grounds. To try to force the people to embrace something that is believed to be good and glorious but which they do not actually want—even though they may be expected to like it when they experience its results—is the very hall mark of anti-democratic belief. It is up to the casuist to decide whether an exception may be made for undemocratic acts that are perpetrated for the *sole* purpose of realizing true democracy, provided they are the only means of doing so. For this, even if granted, does not apply to the case of socialism which, as we have seen, is likely to become democratically possible precisely when it can be expected to be practically successful.

In any case however it is obvious that any argument in favor of shelving democracy for the transitional period affords an excellent opportunity to evade all responsibility for it. Such provisional arrangements may well last for a century or more and means are available for a ruling group installed by a victorious revolution to prolong them indefinitely or to adopt the forms of democracy without the substance.

II. The Record of Socialist Parties

As soon as we turn to an examination of the records of socialist parties, doubts will inevitably arise about the validity of their contention that they have uniformly championed the democratic creed.

In the first place, there is the great socialist commonwealth that is ruled by a party in a minority and does not offer any chance to any other. And the representatives of that party, assembled in their eighteenth congress, listened to reports and unanimously passed resolutions without anything resembling what we should call a discussion. They wound up by voting—as officially stated—that "the Russian people [?], in unconditional devotion to the party of Lenin-Stalin and to the great Leader, accept the program of the grand works which has been sketched in that most sublime document of our epoch, the report of comrade Stalin, in order to fulfill it unwaveringly" and that "our Bolshevik Party enters, under the leadership of the genius of the great Stalin, upon a new phase of development."[3] That, and single-

[3] I do not know Russian. The above passages have been translated faithfully from the German newspaper that used to be published in Moscow and are open to possible objections against its translation of the Russian text, though that news-

candidate elections, complemented by demonstration trials and GPU methods, may no doubt constitute "the most perfect democracy in the world," if an appropriate meaning be assigned to that term—but it is not exactly what most Americans would understand by it.

Yet in essence and principle at least, this commonwealth is a socialist one, and so were the short-lived creations of this type of which Bavaria and especially Hungary were the scenes. Now there are no doubt socialist groups which to this day consistently keep to what in this country is meant by Democratic Ideals; they include for instance the majority of English socialists, the socialist parties in Belgium, the Netherlands and the Scandinavian countries, the American party led by Mr. Norman Thomas, and German groups in exile. From their standpoint as well as from the standpoint of the observer it is tempting to deny that the Russian system constitutes "true" socialism and to hold that, in this respect at least, it is an aberration. But what does "true" socialism mean except "the socialism which we like"? Hence what do such statements signify except recognition of the fact that there are forms of socialism which do not command the allegiance of all socialists and which include non-democratic ones? That a socialist regime may be non-democratic is indeed undeniable, as we have seen before, on the purely logical ground that the defining feature of socialism does not imply anything about political procedure. As far as that goes the only question is whether and in what sense it *can* be democratic.

In the second place, those socialist groups that have consistently upheld the democratic faith never had either a chance or a motive for professing any other. They lived in environments that would have strongly resented undemocratic talk and practice and in fact always turned against syndicalists. In some cases they had every reason to espouse democratic principles that sheltered them and their activity. In other cases most of them were satisfied with the results, political and other, that advance on democratic lines promised to yield. It is easy to visualize what would have happened to the socialist parties of, say, England or Sweden if they had displayed serious symptoms of anti-democratic propensities. They at the same time felt that they were steadily growing in power and that responsible office was slowly coming to them of itself. When it came, it satisfied them. Thus, in professing allegiance to democracy, they simply did the obvious thing all along. The fact that their policy did not give pleasure to Lenin does not prove that, had he been situated as they were, he would have behaved differently. In Germany where the party developed still better but where until 1918 the avenue to political responsibility seemed to be blocked, socialists, facing a strong and hostile state and

paper was of course in no position to publish anything that was not fully approved by the authorities.

having to rely for protection on bourgeois sympathies and on the power of trade unions that were at best semi-socialistic, were still less free to deviate from the democratic creed, since by doing so they would only have played into the hands of their enemies.[4] To call themselves social *democrats* was for them a matter of common prudence.

But, in the third place, the test cases that turned out favorably are few and not very convincing.[5] It is true in a sense that in 1918 the Social Democratic party of Germany had a choice, that it decided for democracy, and (if this is a proof of democratic faith) that it put down the communists with ruthless energy. But the party split on the issue. It lost heavily from its left wing and the seceding dissenters have more, not less, claim to the badge of socialism than those who stayed. Many of the latter moreover, though submitting to party discipline, disapproved. And many of those who approved did so merely on the ground that, from the summer of 1919 at least, chances of succeeding in more radical (i.e., in this case, anti-democratic) courses had become negligible and that, in particular, a leftist policy in Berlin would have meant serious danger of secession in the Rhineland and the countries south of the Main even if it had not met smashing defeat immediately. Finally, to the majority, or at all events to the trade-union element in it, democracy gave everything they really cared for, including office. They had no doubt to share the spoils with the Centrist (Catholic) party. But the bargain was satisfactory to both. Presently the socialists did indeed become vociferously democratic. This however was when an opposition associated with an anti-democratic creed began to rise against them.

I am not going to blame German Social Democrats for the sense of responsibility they displayed or even for the complacency with which they settled down in the comfortable armchairs of officialdom. The second is a common human failing, the first was entirely to their credit as I shall try to show in the last part of this book. But it takes some optimism to cite them as witnesses for the unswerving allegiance of socialists to democratic procedure. Nor can I think of any better test case—unless indeed we agree to accept the Russian and Hungarian cases both of which present the crucial combination of a possibility of the conquest of power with the impossibility of doing so by democratic means. Our difficulty is well illustrated by the Austrian case, the importance of which is enhanced much beyond the importance of the country by the exceptional standing of the leading (Neo-Marxist) group. The Austrian socialists did adhere to democracy in 1918 and

---

[4] These situations will be more fully discussed in Part V.

[5] We are going to confine ourselves to the attitudes of socialist parties in national politics. Their practice and that of trade unions concerning non-socialist or non-union workmen is of course still less convincing.

1919 when it was not yet, as it soon afterwards became, a matter of self-defense. But during the few months when monopolization of power seemed within their reach, the position of many of them was not unequivocal. At that time Fritz Adler referred to the majority principle as the fetishism of the "vagaries of arithmetics" (*Zufall der Arithmetik*) and many others shrugged their shoulders at democratic rules of procedure. Yet these men were regular party members and not communists. When bolshevism ruled in Hungary, the question of the course to choose became burning. Nobody can have followed the discussion of that epoch without realizing that the sense of the party was not badly rendered by the formula: "We do not particularly relish the prospect of having to go left [= adopt soviet methods]. But if go we must, then we shall go all of us."[6] This appraisal both of the country's general situation and of the party danger was eminently reasonable. So was the inference. Ardent loyalty to democratic principles, however, was not conspicuous in either. Conversion came to them eventually. But it did not come from repentance, it came in consequence of the Hungarian counter-revolution.

Please do not think that I am accusing socialists of insincerity or that I wish to hold them up to scorn either as bad democrats or as unprincipled schemers and opportunists. I fully believe, in spite of the childish Machiavellism in which some of their prophets indulge, that fundamentally most of them always have been as sincere in their professions as any other men. Besides, I do not believe in insincerity in social strife, for people always come to think what they want to think and what they incessantly profess. As regards democracy, socialist parties are presumably no more opportunists than are any others; they simply espouse democracy if, as, and when it serves their ideals and interests and not otherwise. Lest readers should be shocked and think so immoral a view worthy only of the most callous of political practitioners, we will at once make a mental experiment that will at the same time yield the starting point of our inquiry into the nature of democracy.

III. A Mental Experiment

Suppose that a community, in a way which satisfies the reader's criteria of democracy, reached the decision to persecute religious dissent. The instance is not fanciful. Communities which most of us would readily recognize as democracies have burned heretics at the stake—the republic of Geneva did in Calvin's time—or otherwise per-

---

[6] In plain English, this saying of one of the more prominent leaders meant that they fully realized the risk involved in staging bolshevism in a country entirely dependent on capitalist powers for its food and with French and Italian troops practically at its door, but that, if pressure from Russia via Hungary should become too great, they would not split the party but would try to lead the whole flock into the bolshevik camp.

secuted them in a manner repulsive to our moral standards—colonial Massachusetts may serve as an example. Cases of this type do not cease to be relevant if they occur in non-democratic states. For it is naïve to believe that the democratic process completely ceases to work in an autocracy or that an autocrat never wishes to act according to the will of the people or to give in to it. Whenever he does, we may conclude that similar action would have been taken also if the political pattern had been a democratic one. For instance, at least the earlier persecutions of the Christians were certainly approved by Roman public opinion and presumably would have been no milder if Rome had been a pure democracy.[7]

Witch hunting affords another example. It grew out of the very soul of the masses and was anything but a diabolical invention of priests and princes who, on the contrary, suppressed it as soon as they felt able to do so. The Catholic Church, it is true, punished witchcraft. But if we compare the measures actually taken with those taken against heresy, where Rome meant business, we immediately have the impression that in the matter of witchcraft the Holy See gave in to public opinion rather than instigated it. The Jesuits fought witch hunting, at first unsuccessfully. Toward the end of the seventeenth and in the eighteenth centuries—that is to say, when monarchic absolutism was fully established on the continent—governmental prohibitions eventually prevailed. The curiously cautious way in which so strong a ruler as the Empress Maria Theresa went about prohibiting the practice clearly shows that she knew she was fighting the will of her people.

Finally, to choose an example that has some bearing on modern issues, anti-Semitism has been one of the most deep-seated of all popular attitudes in most nations in which there was, relative to total population, any considerable number of Jews. In modern times this attitude has in part given way under the rationalizing influence of capitalist evolution, but enough has remained of it to assure popular success to any politician who cared to appeal to it. Most of the anticapitalist movements of our time other than straight socialism have in fact learned the lesson. In the Middle Ages however, it is not too much to say that the Jews owed their survival to the protection of the

[7] An example will illustrate the kind of evidence there is for this statement. Suetonius in his biography of Nero (*De vita Cæsarum, liber VI*) first relates those acts of the latter's reign which he, Suetonius, considered to be partly blameless and partly even commendable (*partim nulla reprehensione, partim etiam non mediocri laude digna*) and then his misdeeds (*probra ac scelera*). The Neronian persecution of the Christians he noted not under the second but under the first heading in the midst of a list of rather meritorious administrative measures (*afflicti suppliciis Christiani, genus hominum superstitionis novæ ac maleficæ*). There is no reason to suppose that Suetonius expressed anything but the opinion (and, by inference, the will) of the people. In fact it is not far-fetched to suspect that Nero's motive was to please the people.

church and of the princes who sheltered them in the face of popular opposition and in the end emancipated them.[8]

Now for our experiment. Let us transport ourselves into a hypothetical country that, in a democratic way, practices the persecution of Christians, the burning of witches, and the slaughtering of Jews. We should certainly not approve of these practices on the ground that they have been decided on according to the rules of democratic procedure. But the crucial question is: would we approve of the democratic constitution itself that produced such results in preference to a non-democratic one that would avoid them? If we do not, we are behaving exactly as fervent socialists behave to whom capitalism is worse than witch hunting and who are therefore prepared to accept non-democratic methods for the purpose of suppressing it. As far as that goes we and they are in the same boat. There are ultimate ideals and interests which the most ardent democrat will put above democracy, and all he means if he professes uncompromising allegiance to it is that he feels convinced that democracy will guarantee those ideals and interests such as freedom of conscience and speech, justice, decent government and so on.

The reason why this is so is not far to seek. Democracy is a political *method*, that is to say, a certain type of institutional arrangement for arriving at political—legislative and administrative—decisions and hence incapable of being an end in itself, irrespective of what decisions it will produce under given historical conditions. And this must be the starting point of any attempt at defining it.

Whatever the distinctive trait of the democratic method may be, the historical examples we have just glanced at teach us a few things about it that are important enough to warrant explicit restatement.

First, these examples suffice to preclude any attempt at challenging the proposition just stated, viz., that, being a political method, democracy cannot, any more than can any other method, be an end in itself. It might be objected that as a matter of logic a method as such can be an absolute ideal or ultimate value. It can. No doubt one might conceivably hold that, however criminal or stupid the thing that democratic procedure may strive to accomplish in a given historical pattern, the will of the people must prevail, or at all events that it must not be opposed except in the way sanctioned by democratic principles. But it seems much more natural in such cases to speak of the rabble instead of the people and to fight its criminality or stupidity by all the means at one's command.

Second, if we agree that unconditional allegiance to democracy can

[8] The protective attitude of the popes may be instanced by the bull *Etsi Judæis* (1120) the repeated confirmation of which by the successors of Calixtus II proves both the continuity of that policy and the resistance it met. The protective attitude of the princes will be readily understood if it be pointed out that expulsions or massacres of Jews meant loss of much-needed revenue to them.

be due only to unconditional allegiance to certain interests or ideals which democracy is expected to serve, our examples also preclude the objection that though democracy may not be an absolute ideal in its own right, it is yet a vicarious one by virtue of the fact that it will necessarily, always and everywhere, serve certain interests or ideals for which we do mean to fight and die unconditionally. Obviously that cannot be true.[9] No more than any other political method does democracy always produce the same results or promote the same interests or ideals. Rational allegiance to it thus presupposes not only a schema of hyper-rational values but also certain states of society in which democracy can be expected to work in ways we approve. Propositions about the working of democracy are meaningless without reference to given times, places and situations[10] and so, of course, are anti-democratic arguments.

This after all is only obvious. It should not surprise, still less shock, anyone. For it has nothing to do with the fervor or dignity of democratic conviction in any given situation. To realize the relative validity of one's convictions and yet stand for them unflinchingly is what distinguishes a civilized man from a barbarian.

IV. In Search of a Definition

We have a starting point from which to proceed with our investigation. But a definition that is to serve us in an attempt to analyze the relations between democracy and socialism is not yet in sight. A few preliminary difficulties still bar the outlook.

It would not help us much to look up Aristotle who used the term in order to designate one of the deviations from his ideal of a well-ordered commonwealth. But some light may be shed on our difficulties by recalling the meaning we have attached to the term Political Method. It means the method a nation uses for arriving at decisions. Such a method we ought to be able to characterize by indicating by whom and how these decisions are made. Equating "making decisions" to "ruling," we might then define democracy as Rule by the People. Why is that not sufficiently precise?

It is not because it covers as many meanings as there are combinations between all the possible definitions of the concept "people" (*demos,* the Roman *populus*) and all the possible definitions of the concept "to rule" (*kratein*), and because these definitions are not independent of the argument about democracy. As regards the first concept, the *populus* in the constitutional sense may exclude slaves

---

[9] In particular it is not true that democracy will always safeguard freedom of conscience better than autocracy. Witness the most famous of all trials. Pilate was, from the standpoint of the Jews, certainly the representative of autocracy. Yet he tried to protect freedom. And he yielded to a democracy.

[10] See below, ch. xxiii.

completely and other inhabitants partially; the law may recognize any number of *status* between slavery and full or even privileged citizenship. And irrespective of legal discrimination, different groups considered themselves as the People at different times.[11]

Of course we might say that a democratic society is one that does not thus differentiate, at least in matters concerning public affairs, such as the franchise. But, first, there have been nations that practiced discrimination of the kind alluded to and nevertheless displayed most of those characteristics which are usually associated with democracy. Second, discrimination can never be entirely absent. For instance, in no country, however democratic, is the right to vote extended below a specified age. If, however, we ask for the rationale of this restriction we find that it also applies to an indefinite number of inhabitants above the age limit. If persons below the age limit are not allowed to vote, we cannot call a nation undemocratic that for the same or analogous reasons excludes other people as well. Observe: it is not relevant whether we, the observers, admit the validity of those reasons or of the practical rules by which they are made to exclude portions of the population; all that matters is that the society in question admits it. Nor should it be objected that, while this may apply to exclusions on grounds of personal unfitness (e.g., "age of discretion"), it does not apply to wholesale exclusion on grounds that have nothing to do with the ability to make an intelligent use of the right to vote. For fitness is a matter of opinion and of degree. Its presence must be established by some set of rules. *Without absurdity or insincerity* it is possible to hold that fitness is measured by one's ability to support oneself. In a commonwealth of strong religious conviction it may be held—again without any absurdity or insincerity—that dissent disqualifies or, in an anti-feminist commonwealth, sex. A race-conscious nation may associate fitness with racial considerations.[12] And so on. The salient point, to repeat, is not what *we* think about any or all of these possible disabilities. The salient point is that, given appropriate views on those and similar subjects, disqualifications on grounds of economic status, religion and sex will enter into the same class with disqualifications which

[11] See, e.g., the definition given by Voltaire in his *Letters Concerning the English Nation* (published in English, 1733; reprint of the first edition published by Peter Davies, 1926, p. 49): "the most numerous, the most useful, even the most virtuous, and consequently the most venerable part of mankind, consisting of those who study the laws and the sciences; of traders, of artificers, in a word, of all who were not tyrants; that is, those who are call'd the people." At present "people" is likely to mean the "masses," but Voltaire's concept comes nearer to identifying that people·for which the Constitution of this country was written.

[12] Thus the United States excludes Orientals and Germany excludes Jews from citizenship; in the southern part of the United States Negroes are also often deprived of the vote.

we all of us consider compatible with democracy. We may disapprove of them to be sure. But if we do so we should in good logic disapprove of the theories about the importance öf property, religion, sex, race and so on, rather than call such societies undemocratic. Religious fervor for instance is certainly compatible with democracy however we define the latter. There is a type of religious attitude to which a heretic seems worse than a madman. Does it not follow that the heretic should be barred from participation in political decisions as is the lunatic.[13] Must we not leave it to every *populus* to define himself?

This inescapable conclusion is usually evaded by introducing additional assumptions into the theory of the democratic process, some of which will be discussed in the next two chapters. Meanwhile we will merely note that it clears much mist from the road. Among other things it reveals the fact that the relation between democracy and liberty must be considerably more complex than we are in the habit of believing.

Still more serious difficulties arise with respect to the second element that enters into the concept of democracy, the *kratein*. The nature and the *modus operandi* of any "rule" are always difficult to explain. Legal powers never guarantee the ability to use them yet are important pegs as well as fetters; traditional prestige always counts for something but never for everything; personal success and, partly independent of success, personal weight act and are reacted upon by both the legal and the traditional components of the institutional pattern. No monarch or dictator or group of oligarchs is ever absolute. They rule not only subject to the data of the national situation but also subject to the necessity of acting with some people, of getting along with others, of neutralizing still others and of subduing the rest. And this may be done in an almost infinite variety of ways each of which will determine what a given formal arrangement really means either for the nation in which it obtains or for the scientific observer; to speak of monarchy as if it meant a definite thing spells dilettantism. But if it is the people, however defined, who are to do the *kratein*, still another problem emerges. How is it technically possible for "people" to rule?

There is a class of cases in which this problem does not arise, at least not in an acute form. In small and primitive communities with a simple social structure[14] in which there is not much to disagree

13 To the bolshevik any non-bolshevik is in the same category. Hence the rule of the Bolshevik party would not *per se* entitle us to call the Soviet Republic un-democratic. We are entitled to call it so only if the Bolshevik party itself is managed in an undemocratic manner—as obviously it is.

14 Smallness of numbers and local concentration of the people are essential. Primitivity of civilization and simplicity of structure are less so but greatly facilitate the functioning of democracy.

on, it is conceivable that all the individuals who form the people as defined by the constitution actually participate in all the duties of legislation and administration. Certain difficulties may still remain even in such cases and the psychologist of collective behavior would still have something to say about leadership, advertising and other sources of deviation from the popular ideal of a democracy. Nevertheless there would be obvious sense in speaking of the will or the action of the community or the people as such—of government by the people—particularly if the people arrive at political decisions by means of debates carried out in the physical presence of all, as they did, for instance, in the Greek *polis* or in the New England town meeting. The latter case, sometimes referred to as the case of "direct democracy," has in fact served as a starting point for many a political theorist.

In all other cases our problem does arise but we might. dispose of it with comparative ease provided we are prepared to drop government by the people and to substitute for it government approved by the people. There is much to be said for doing this. Many of the propositions we usually aver about democracy will hold true for all governments that command the general allegiance of a large majority of their people or, better still, of a large majority of every class of their people. This applies in particular to the virtues usually associated with the democratic method: human dignity, the contentment that comes from the feeling that by and large things political do conform to one's ideas of how they should be, the coordination of politics with public opinion, the citizen's attitude of confidence in and cooperation with government, the reliance of the latter on the respect and support of the man in the street—all this and much besides which to many of us will seem the very esssence of democracy is quite satisfactorily covered by the idea of government approved by the people. And since it is obvious that excepting the case of "direct democracy" the people as such can never actually rule or govern, the case for this definition seems to be complete.

All the same we cannot accept it. Instances abound—perhaps they are the majority of historical cases—of autocracies, both *dei gratia* and dictatorial, of the various monarchies of non-autocratic type, of aristocratic and plutocratic oligarchies, which normally commanded the unquestioned, often fervent, allegiance of an overwhelming majority of all classes of their people and which, considering their environmental conditions, did very well in securing what most of us believe the democratic method should secure. There is point in emphasizing this and in recognizing the large element of democracy —in this sense—that entered into those cases. Such an antidote to the cult of mere forms, of mere phraseologies even, would indeed be highly desirable. But this does not alter the fact that by accepting this solution we should lose the phenomenon we wish to identify: democracies would be merged in a much wider class of political arrangement which contains individuals of clearly non-democratic complexion.

Our failure teaches us one thing however. Beyond "direct" democracy lies an infinite wealth of possible forms in which the "people" may partake in the business of ruling or influence or control those who actually do the ruling. None of these forms, particularly none of the workable ones, has any obvious or exclusive title to being described as Government by the People if these words are to be taken in their natural sense. If any of them is to acquire such a title it can do so only by virtue of an arbitrary convention defining the meaning to be attached to the term "to rule." Such a convention is always possible of course: the people never actually rule but they can always be made to do so by definition.

The legal "theories" of democracy that evolved in the seventeenth and eighteenth centuries were precisely intended to provide such definitions as would link certain actual or ideal forms of government to the ideology of the Rule by the People. Why this ideology should have imposed itself is not difficult to understand. At that time, with the nations of western Europe at least, the trappings of God-ordained authority were rapidly falling from the shoulders of royalty[15]—the process set in much earlier of course—and, as a matter of both ethical and explanatory principle, the Will of the People or the Sovereign Power of the People stood out as the substitute most acceptable to a mentality which, while prepared to drop that particular *charisma* of ultimate authority, was not prepared to do without any.

The problem being thus set, the legal mind ransacked the lumber room of its constructs in search for tools by which to reconcile that supreme postulate with existing political patterns. Fictitious contracts of subjection to a prince[16] by which the sovereign people was supposed to have bargained away its freedom or power, or no less fictitious contracts by which it delegated that power, or some of it, to chosen representatives, were substantially what the lumber room supplied. However well such devices may have served certain practical purposes, they are utterly valueless for us. They are not even defensible from a legal standpoint.

For in order to make sense at all the terms delegation and repre-

[15] Sir Robert Filmer's *Patriarcha* (published 1680) may be looked upon as the last important exposition of the doctrine of divine right in English political philosophy.

[16] Those contracts were *fictiones juris et de jure*. But there was one realistic analogy for them, viz., the voluntary and contractual subjection of a freeholder to a medieval lord extensively practiced between the sixth and twelfth centuries. The freeholder accepted the jurisdiction of the lord and certain economic obligations. He gave up his status as a fully free man. In exchange he received the lord's protection and other advantages.

sentation must refer not to the individual citizens—that would be the doctrine of the medieval estates—but to the people as a whole. The people as such, then, would have to be conceived as delegating its power to, say, a parliament that is to represent it. But only a (physical or moral) person can legally delegate or be represented. Thus the American colonies or states that sent delegates to the continental congresses which met from 1774 on in Philadelphia—the so-called "revolutionary congresses"—were in fact represented by these delegates. But the people of those colonies or states were not, since a people as such has no legal personality: to say that it delegates powers to, or is represented by, a parliament is to say something completely void of legal meaning.[17] What, then, is a parliament? The answer is not far to seek: it is an organ of the state exactly as the government or a court of justice is. If a parliament represents the people at all, it must do so in another sense which we have still to discover.

However, these "theories" about the sovereignty of the people and about delegation and representation reflect something more than an ideological postulate and a few pieces of legal technique. They complement a sociology or social philosophy of the body politic that, partly under the influence of the revival of Greek speculations on the subject, partly under the influence of the events of the time,[18] took shape and reached its apogee toward the end of the eighteenth century and actually tried to solve the problem. Though such general terms are never adequate or strictly correct, I will risk describing it—in the usual way—as fundamentally rationalist, hedonist and individualist: the happiness, defined in hedonic terms, of individuals endowed with a clear perception—or amenable to education that will impart clear perception—both of this end and of the appropriate means, was conceived as the meaning of life and the grand principle of action in the private as well as in the political sphere. We may just as well designate this sociology or social philosophy, the product of early capitalism, by the term introduced by John Stuart Mill, Utilitarianism. According to it, behavior conforming to that principle was not merely the only rational and justifiable but *ipso*

[17] Similarly, there is no legal sense in describing a public prosecution as a case of "the People versus So-and-so." The prosecuting legal person is the state.

[18] This is particularly obvious in England and especially in the case of John Locke. As a political philosopher he simply pleaded, in the guise of general argument, against James II and for his Whig friends who made themselves responsible for the "glorious" revolution. This accounts for the success of a line of reasoning that without this practical connotation would have been beneath contempt. The end of government is the good of the people and this good consists in the protection of private property which is why men "enter into society." For this purpose they meet and make an Original Contract of submission to a common authority. This contract is broken, property and liberty endangered and resistance justified when, to put it frankly, Whig aristocrats and London merchants think they are.

facto also the "natural" one. This proposition is the bridge between the otherwise very different theories of Bentham and Rousseau's *contrat social*—names that may serve us for beacons in what for the rest must be left in darkness here.

If such desperate brevity does not prevent readers from following my argument, the bearing of this philosophy on the subject of democracy should be clear. It evidently yielded, among other things, a theory of the nature of the state and the purposes for which the state exists. Moreover, by virtue of its emphasis on the rational and hedonistic individual and his ethical autonomy it seemed to be in a position to teach the only right political methods for running that state and for achieving those purposes—the greatest happiness for the greatest number and that sort of thing. Finally, it provided what looked like a rational foundation for belief in the Will of the People (*volonté générale*) and in the advice that sums up all that democracy meant to the group of writers who became known as Philosophical Radicals:[19] educate the people and let them vote freely.

Adverse criticism of this construction arose almost immediately as a part of the general reaction against the rationalism of the eighteenth century that set in after the revolutionary and Napoleonic Wars. Whatever we may think about the merits or demerits of the movement usually dubbed Romanticism, it certainly conveyed a deeper understanding of pre-capitalist society and of historical evolution in general and thus revealed some of the fundamental errors of utilitarianism and of the political theory for which utilitarianism served as base. Later historical, sociological, biological, psychological and economic analysis proved destructive to both and today it is difficult to find any student of social processes who has a good word for either. But strange though it may seem, action continued to be taken on that theory all the time it was being blown to pieces. The more untenable it was being proved to be, the more completely it dominated official phraseology and the rhetoric of the politician. This is why in the next chapter we must turn to a discussion of what may be termed the Classical Doctrine of Democracy.

But no institution or practice or belief stands or falls with the theory that is at any time offered in its support. Democracy is no exception. It is in fact possible to frame a theory of the democratic process that takes account of all the realities of group-wise action and of the public mind. This theory will be presented in Chapter XXII and then we shall at last be able to say how democracy may be expected to fare in a socialist order of things.

[19] For general orientation see especially, Kent, *The Philosophical Radical*; Graham Wallas, *The Life of Francis Place*; Leslie Stephen, *The English Utilitarians*.

CHAPTER XXI

THE CLASSICAL DOCTRINE OF DEMOCRACY

I. The Common Good and the Will of the People

THE eighteenth-century philosophy of democracy may be couched in the following definition: the democratic method is that institutional arrangement for arriving at political decisions which realizes the common good by making the people itself decide issues through the election of individuals who are to assemble in order to carry out its will. Let us develop the implications of this.

It is held, then, that there exists a Common Good, the obvious beacon light of policy, which is always simple to define and which every normal person can be made to see by means of rational argument. There is hence no excuse for not seeing it and in fact no explanation for the presence of people who do not see it except ignorance—which can be removed—stupidity and anti-social interest. Moreover, this common good implies definite answers to all questions so that every social fact and every measure taken or to be taken can unequivocally be classed as "good" or "bad." All people having therefore to agree, in principle at least, there is also a Common Will of the people (= will of all reasonable individuals) that is exactly coterminous with the common good or interest or welfare or happiness. The only thing, barring stupidity and sinister interests, that can possibly bring in disagreement and account for the presence of an opposition is a difference of opinion as to the speed with which the goal, itself common to nearly all, is to be approached. Thus every member of the community, conscious of that goal, knowing his or her mind, discerning what is good and what is bad, takes part, actively and responsibly, in furthering the former and fighting the latter and all the members taken together control their public affairs.

It is true that the management of some of these affairs requires special aptitudes and techniques and will therefore have to be entrusted to specialists who have them. This does not affect the principle, however, because these specialists simply act in order to carry out the will of the people exactly as a doctor acts in order to carry out the will of the patient to get well. It is also true that in a community of any size, especially if it displays the phenomenon of division of labor, it would be highly inconvenient for every individual citizen to have to get into contact with all the other citizens on every issue in order to do his part in ruling or governing. It will be more convenient to reserve only the most important decisions for the individual citizens to pronounce upon—say by referendum—and to deal with the rest through a committee appointed by them—an assembly or parliament whose members will be elected by popular vote. This committee or body of delegates, as we have seen, will not represent the people in a legal sense but it will do so in a less technical one—it will voice, reflect or represent the will of the electorate. Again as a matter of convenience, this committee, being large, may resolve itself into smaller ones for the various departments of public affairs. Finally, among these smaller committees there will be a general-purpose committee, mainly for dealing with current administration, called cabinet or government, possibly with a general secretary or scapegoat at its head, a so-called prime minister.[1]

As soon as we accept all the assumptions that are being made by this theory of the polity—or implied by it—democracy indeed acquires a perfectly unambiguous meaning and there is no problem in connection with it except how to bring it about. Moreover we need only forget a few logical qualms in order to be able to add that in this case the democratic arrangement would not only be the best of all conceivable ones, but that few people would care to consider any other. It is no less obvious however that these assumptions are so many statements of fact every one of which would have to be proved if we are to arrive at that conclusion. And it is much easier to disprove them.

There is, first, no such thing as a uniquely determined common good that all people could agree on or be made to agree on by the force of rational argument. This is due not primarily to the fact that some people may want things other than the common good but to the much more fundamental fact that to different individuals and groups the common good is bound to mean different things. This fact, hidden from the utilitarian by the narrowness of his outlook on the world of human valuations, will introduce rifts on questions of principle which cannot be reconciled by rational argument because ultimate values—our conceptions of what life and what society should be—are beyond the range of mere logic. They may be bridged by compromise in some cases but not in others. Americans who say, "We want this country to arm to its teeth and then to fight for what we conceive to be right all over the globe" and Americans who say, "We want this country to work out its own problems which is the only way it can serve humanity" are facing irreducible differences of ultimate values which compromise could only maim and degrade.

Secondly, even if a sufficiently definite common good—such as for

[1] The official theory of the functions of a cabinet minister holds in fact that he is appointed in order to see to it that in his department the will of the people prevails.

instance the utilitarian's maximum of economic satisfaction[2]—proved acceptable to all, this would not imply equally definite answers to individual issues. Opinions on these might differ to an extent important enough to produce most of the effects of "fundamental" dissension about ends themselves. The problems centering in the evaluation of present versus future satisfactions, even the case of socialism versus capitalism, would be left still open, for instance, after the conversion of every individual citizen to utilitarianism. "Health" might be desired by all, yet people would still disagree on vaccination and vasectomy. And so on.

The utilitarian fathers of democratic doctrine failed to see the full importance of this simply because none of them seriously considered any substantial change in the economic framework and the habits of bourgeois society. They saw little beyond the world of an eighteenth-century ironmonger.

But, third, as a consequence of both preceding propositions, the particular concept of the will of the people or the *volonté générale* that the utilitarians made their own vanishes into thin air. For that concept presupposes the existence of a uniquely determined common good discernible to all. Unlike the romanticists the utilitarians had no notion of that semi-mystic entity endowed with a will of its own —that "soul of the people" which the historical school of jurisprudence made so much of. They frankly derived their will of the people from the wills of individuals. And unless there is a center, the common good, toward which, in the long run at least, *all* individual wills gravitate, we shall not get that particular type of "natural" *volonté générale*. The utilitarian center of gravity, on the one hand, unifies individual wills, tends to weld them by means of rational discussion into the will of the people and, on the other hand, confers upon the latter the exclusive ethical dignity claimed by the classic democratic creed. *This creed does not consist simply in worshiping the will of the people as such* but rests on certain assumptions about the "natural" object of that will which object is sanctioned by utilitarian reason. Both the existence and the dignity of this kind of *volonté générale* are gone as soon as the idea of the common good fails us. And both the pillars of the classical doctrine inevitably crumble into dust.

II. THE WILL OF THE PEOPLE AND INDIVIDUAL VOLITION

Of course, however conclusively those arguments may tell against this particular conception of the will of the people, they do not debar

---

[2] The very meaning of "greatest happiness" is open to serious doubt. But even if this doubt could be removed and definite meaning could be attached to the sum total of economic satisfaction of a group of people, that maximum would still be relative to given situations and valuations which it may be impossible to alter, or compromise on, in a democratic way.

us from trying to build up another and more realistic one. I do not intend to question either the reality or the importance of the socio-psychological facts we think of when speaking of the will of a nation. Their analysis is certainly the prerequisite for making headway with the problems of democracy. It would however be better not to retain the term because this tends to obscure the fact that as soon as we have severed the will of the people from its utilitarian connotation we are building not merely a different theory of the same thing, but a theory of a completely different thing. We have every reason to be on our guard against the pitfalls that lie on the path of those de-fenders of democracy who while accepting, under pressure of accu-mulating evidence, more and more of the facts of the democratic process, yet try to anoint the results that process turns out with oil taken from eighteenth-century jars.

But though a common will or public opinion of some sort may still be said to emerge from the infinitely complex jumble of individual and group-wise situations, volitions, influences, actions and reactions of the "democratic process," the result lacks not only rational unity but also rational sanction. The former means that, though from the standpoint of analysis, the democratic process is not simply chaotic—for the analyst nothing is chaotic that can be brought within the reach of explanatory principles—yet the results would not, except by chance, be meaningful in themselves—as for instance the realization of any definite end or ideal would be. The latter means, since *that* will is no longer congruent with any "good," that in order to claim ethical dignity for the result it will now be necessary to fall back upon an unqualified confidence in democratic forms of government as such—a belief that in principle would have to be independent of the desirability of results. As we have seen, it is not easy to place one-self on that standpoint. But even if we do so, the dropping of the utilitarian common good still leaves us with plenty of difficulties on our hands.

In particular, we still remain under the practical necessity of at-tributing to the will of the *individual* an independence and a rational quality that are altogether unrealistic. If we are to argue that the will of the citizens *per se* is a political factor entitled to respect, it must first exist. That is to say, it must be something more than an indeter-minate bundle of vague impulses loosely playing about given slogans and mistaken impressions. Everyone would have to know definitely what he wants to stand for. This definite will would have to be imple-mented by the ability to observe and interpret correctly the facts that are directly accessible to everyone and to sift critically the informa-tion about the facts that are not. Finally, from that definite will and from these ascertained facts a clear *and prompt* conclusion as to particu-lar issues would have to be derived according to the rules of logical inference—with so high a degree of general efficiency moreover that one man's opinion could be held, without glaring absurdity, to be roughly as good as every other man's.[3] And all this the modal citizen would have to perform for himself and independently of pressure groups and propaganda,[4] for volitions and inferences that are imposed upon the electorate obviously do not qualify for ultimate data of the democratic process. The question whether these conditions are fulfilled to the extent required in order to make democracy work should not be answered by reckless assertion or equally reckless denial. It can be answered only by a laborious appraisal of a maze of conflicting evidence.

Before embarking upon this, however, I want to make quite sure that the reader fully appreciates another point that has been made already. I will therefore repeat that even if the opinions and desires of individual citizens were perfectly definite and independent data for the democratic process to work with, and if everyone acted on them with ideal rationality and promptitude, it would not necessarily follow that the political decisions produced by that process from the raw material of those individual volitions would represent anything that could in any convincing sense be called the will of the people. It is not only conceivable but, whenever individual wills are much divided, very likely that the political decisions produced will not conform to "what people really want." Nor can it be replied that, if

[3] This accounts for the strongly equalitarian character both of the classical doctrine of democracy and of popular democratic beliefs. It will be pointed out later on how Equality may acquire the status of an ethical postulate. As a factual statement about human nature it cannot be true in any conceivable sense. In recognition of this the postulate itself has often been reformulated so as to mean "equality of opportunity." But, disregarding even the difficulties inherent in the word opportunity, this reformulation does not help us much because it is actual and not potential equality of performance in matters of political behavior that is required if each man's vote is to carry the same weight in the decision of issues.

It should be noted in passing that democratic phraseology has been instrumental in fostering the association of inequality of any kind with "injustice" which is so important an element in the psychic pattern of the unsuccessful and in the arsenal of the politician who uses him. One of the most curious symptoms of this was the Athenian institution of ostracism or rather the use to which it was sometimes put. Ostracism consisted in banishing an individual by popular vote, not necessarily for any particular reason: it sometimes served as a method of eliminating an uncomfortably prominent citizen who was felt to "count for more than one."

[4] This term is here being used in its original sense and not in the sense which it is rapidly acquiring at present and which suggests the definition: propaganda is any statement emanating from a source that we do not like. I suppose that the term derives from the name of the committee of cardinals which deals with matters concerning the spreading of the Catholic faith, the *congregatio de propaganda fide*. In itself therefore it does not carry any derogatory meaning and in particular it does not imply distortion of facts. One can make propaganda, for instance, for a scientific method. It simply means the presentation of facts and arguments with a view to influencing people's actions or opinions in a definite direction.

not exactly what they want, they will get a "fair compromise." This may be so. The chances for this to happen are greatest with those issues which are quantitative in nature or admit of gradation, such as the question how much is to be spent on unemployment relief provided everybody favors some expenditure for that purpose. But with qualitative issues, such as the question whether to persecute heretics or to enter upon a war, the result attained may well, though for different reasons, be equally distasteful to all the people whereas the decision imposed by a non-democratic agency might prove much more acceptable to them.

An example will illustrate. I may, I take it, describe the rule of Napoleon, when First Consul, as a military dictatorship. One of the most pressing political needs of the moment was a religious settlement that would clear the chaos left by the revolution and the directorate and bring peace to millions of hearts. This he achieved by a number of master strokes, culminating in a concordat with the pope (1801) and the "organic articles" (1802) that, reconciling the irreconcilable, gave just the right amount of freedom to religious worship while strongly upholding the authority of the state. He also reorganized and refinanced the French Catholic church, solved the delicate question of the "constitutional" clergy, and most successfully launched the new establishment with a minimum of friction. If ever there was any justification at all for holding that the people actually want something definite, this arrangement affords one of the best instances in history. This must be obvious to anyone who looks at the French class structure of that time and it is amply borne out by the fact that this ecclesiastical policy greatly contributed to the almost universal popularity which the consular regime enjoyed. But it is difficult to see how this result could have been achieved in a democratic way. Anti-church sentiment had not died out and was by no means confined to the vanquished Jacobins. People of that persuasion, or their leaders, could not possibly have compromised to that extent.[5] On the other end of the scale, a strong wave of wrathful Catholic sentiment was steadily gaining momentum. People who shared that sentiment, or leaders dependent on their good will, could not possibly have stopped at the Napoleonic limit; in particular, they could not have dealt so firmly with the Holy See for which moreover there would have been no motive to give in, seeing which way things were moving. And the will of the peasants who more than anything else wanted their priests, their churches and processions would have been paralyzed by the very natural fear that the revolutionary settlement of the land question might be endangered once the clergy—the bishops especially—were in the saddle again. Deadlock or interminable struggle, engendering

---

[5] The legislative bodies, cowed though they were, completely failed in fact to support Napoleon in this policy. And some of his most trusted paladins opposed it.

increasing irritation, would have been the most probable outcome of any attempt to settle the question democratically. But Napoleon was able to settle it reasonably, precisely because all those groups which could not yield their points of their own accord were at the same time able and willing to accept the arrangement if imposed.

This instance of course is not an isolated one.[6] If results that prove in the long run satisfactory to the people at large are made the test of government *for* the people, then government *by* the people, as conceived by the classical doctrine of democracy, would often fail to meet it.

III. HUMAN NATURE IN POLITICS

It remains to answer our question about the definiteness and independence of the voter's will, his powers of observation and interpretation of facts, and his ability to draw, clearly and promptly, rational inferences from both. This subject belongs to a chapter of social psychology that might be entitled Human Nature in Politics.[7]

During the second half of the last century, the idea of the human personality that is a homogeneous unit and the idea of a definite will that is the prime mover of action have been steadily fading—even before the times of Théodule Ribot and of Sigmund Freud. In particular, these ideas have been increasingly discounted in the field of social sciences where the importance of the extra-rational and irrational element in our behavior has been receiving more and more attention, witness Pareto's *Mind and Society*. Of the many sources of the evidence that accumulated against the hypothesis of rationality, I shall mention only two.

The one—in spite of much more careful later work—may still be associated with the name of Gustave Le Bon, the founder or, at any

[6] Other instances could in fact be adduced from Napoleon's practice. He was an autocrat who, whenever his dynastic interests and his foreign policy were not concerned, simply strove to do what he conceived the people wanted or needed. This is what the advice amounted to which he gave to Eugène Beauharnais concerning the latter's administration of northern Italy.

[7] This is the title of the frank and charming book by one of the most lovable English radicals who ever lived, Graham Wallas. In spite of all that has since been written on the subject and especially in spite of all the detailed case studies that now make it possible to see so much more clearly, that book may still be recommended as the best introduction to political psychology. Yet, after having stated with admirable honesty the case against the uncritical acceptance of the classical doctrine, the author fails to draw the obvious conclusion. This is all the more remarkable because he rightly insists on the necessity of a scientific attitude of mind and because he does not fail to take Lord Bryce to task for having, in his book on the American commonwealth, professed himself "grimly" resolved to see some blue sky in the midst of clouds of disillusioning facts. Why, so Graham Wallas seems to exclaim, what should we say of a meteorologist who insisted from the outset that he saw some blue sky? Nevertheless in the constructive part of his book he takes much the same ground.

rate, the first effective exponent of the psychology of crowds (*psychologie des foules*).[8] By showing up, though overstressing, the realities of human behavior when under the influence of agglomeration—in particular the sudden disappearance, in a state of excitement, of moral restraints and civilized modes of thinking and feeling, the sudden eruption of primitive impulses, infantilisms and criminal propensities—he made us face gruesome facts that everybody knew but nobody wished to see and he thereby dealt a serious blow to the picture of man's nature which underlies the classical doctrine of democracy and democratic folklore about revolutions. No doubt there is much to be said about the narrowness of the factual basis of Le Bon's inferences which, for instance, do not fit at all well the normal behavior of an English or Anglo-American crowd. Critics, especially those to whom the implications of this branch of social psychology were uncongenial, did not fail to make the most of its vulnerable points. But on the other hand it must not be forgotten that the phenomena of crowd psychology are by no means confined to mobs rioting in the narrow streets of a Latin town. Every parliament, every committee, every council of war composed of a dozen generals in their sixties, displays, in however mild a form, some of those features that stand out so glaringly in the case of the rabble, in particular a reduced sense of responsibility, a lower level of energy of thought and greater sensitiveness to non-logical influences. Moreover, those phenomena are not confined to a crowd in the sense of a physical agglomeration of many people. Newspaper readers, radio audiences, members of a party even if not physically gathered together are terribly easy to work up into a psychological crowd and into a state of frenzy in which attempt at rational argument only spurs the animal spirits.

The other source of disillusioning evidence that I am going to mention is a much humbler one—no blood flows from it, only nonsense. Economists, learning to observe their facts more closely, have begun to discover that, even in the most ordinary currents of daily life, their consumers do not quite live up to the idea that the economic textbook used to convey. On the one hand their wants are nothing like as definite and their actions upon those wants nothing like as rational and prompt. On the other hand they are so amenable to the influence of advertising and other methods of persuasion that producers often seem to dictate to them instead of being directed by them. The technique of successful advertising is particularly instructive. There is indeed nearly always some appeal to reason. But mere assertion, often repeated, counts more than rational argument and so does the direct

---

[8] The German term, *Massenpsychologie*, suggests a warning: the psychology of crowds must not be confused with the psychology of the masses. The former does not necessarily carry any class connotation and in itself has nothing to do with a study of the ways of thinking and feeling of, say, the working class.

attack upon the subconscious which takes the form of attempts to evoke and crystallize pleasant associations of an entirely extra-rational, very frequently of a sexual nature.

The conclusion, while obvious, must be drawn with care. In the ordinary run of often repeated decisions the individual is subject to the salutary and rationalizing influence of favorable and unfavorable experience. He is also under the influence of relatively simple and unproblematical motives and interests which are but occasionally interfered with by excitement. Historically, the consumers' desire for shoes may, at least in part, have been shaped by the action of producers offering attractive footgear and campaigning for it; yet at any given time it is a genuine want, the definiteness of which extends beyond "shoes in general" and which prolonged experimenting clears of much of the irrationalities that may originally have surrounded it.[9] Moreover, under the stimulus of those simple motives consumers learn to act upon unbiased expert advice about some things (houses, motorcars) and themselves become experts in others. It is simply not true that housewives are easily fooled in the matter of foods, *familiar* household articles, wearing apparel. And, as every salesman knows to his cost, most of them have a way of insisting on the exact article they want.

This of course holds true still more obviously on the producers' side of the picture. No doubt, a manufacturer may be indolent, a bad judge of opportunities or otherwise incompetent; but there is an effective mechanism that will reform or eliminate him. Again Taylorism rests on the fact that man may perform simple handicraft operations for thousands of years and yet perform them inefficiently. But neither the intention to act as rationally as possible nor a steady pressure toward rationality can seriously be called into question at whatever level of industrial or commercial activity we choose to look.[10]

And so it is with most of the decisions of daily life that lie within the little field which the individual citizen's mind encompasses with a full sense of its reality. Roughly, it consists of the things that directly concern himself, his family, his business dealings, his hobbies, his friends and enemies, his township or ward, his class, church, trade union or any other social group of which he is an active member—

[9] In the above passage irrationality means failure to act rationally upon a given wish. It does not refer to the reasonableness of the wish itself in the opinion of the observer. This is important to note because economists in appraising the extent of consumers' irrationality sometimes exaggerate it by confusing the two things. Thus, a factory girl's finery may seem to a professor an indication of irrational behavior for which there is no other explanation but the advertiser's arts. Actually, it may be all she craves for. If so her expenditure on it may be ideally rational in the above sense.

[10] This level differs of course not only as between epochs and places but also, at a given time and place, as between different industrial sectors and classes. There is no such thing as a universal pattern of rationality.

the things under his personal observation, the things which are familiar to him independently of what his newspaper tells him, which he can directly influence or manage and for which he develops the kind of responsibility that is induced by a direct relation to the favorable or unfavorable effects of a course of action.

Once more: definiteness and rationality in thought and action[11] are not guaranteed by this familiarity with men and things or by that sense of reality or responsibility. Quite a few other conditions which often fail to be fulfilled would be necessary for that. For instance, generation after generation may suffer from irrational behavior in matters of hygiene and yet fail to link their sufferings with their noxious habits. As long as this is not done, objective consequences, however regular, of course do not produce subjective experience. Thus it proved unbelievably hard for humanity to realize the relation between infection and epidemics: the facts pointed to it with what to us seems unmistakable clearness; yet to the end of the eighteenth century doctors did next to nothing to keep people afflicted with infectious disease, such as measles or smallpox, from mixing with other people. And things must be expected to be still worse whenever there is not only inability but reluctance to recognize causal relations or when some interest fights against recognizing them.

Nevertheless and in spite of all the qualifications that impose themselves, there is for everyone, within a much wider horizon, a narrower field—widely differing in extent as between different groups and individuals and bounded by a broad zone rather than a sharp line—which is distinguished by a sense of reality or familiarity or responsibility. And this field harbors relatively definite individual volitions. These may often strike us as unintelligent, narrow, egotistical; and it may not be obvious to everyone why, when it comes to political decisions, we should worship at their shrine, still less why we should feel bound to count each of them for one and none of them for more than one. If, however, we do choose to worship we shall at least not find the shrine empty.[12]

[11] Rationality of thought and rationality of action are two different things. Rationality of thought does not always guarantee rationality of action. And the latter may be present without any conscious deliberation and irrespective of any ability to formulate the rationale of one's action correctly. The observer, particularly the observer who uses interview and questionnaire methods, often overlooks this and hence acquires an exaggerated idea of the importance of irrationality in behavior. This is another source of those overstatements which we meet so often.

[12] It should be observed that in speaking of definite and genuine volitions I do not mean to exalt them into ultimate data for all kinds of social analysis. Of course they are themselves the product of the social process and the social environment. All I mean is that they may serve as data for the kind of special-purpose analysis which the economist has in mind when he derives prices from tastes or wants that are "given" at any moment and need not be further analyzed each time. Similarly we may for our purpose speak of genuine and definite volitions that at

Now this comparative definiteness of volition and rationality of behavior does not suddenly vanish as we move away from those concerns
of daily life in the home and in business which educate and discipline
us. In the realm of public affairs there are sectors that are more
within the reach of the citizen's mind than others. This is true, first,
of local affairs. Even there we find a reduced power of discerning
facts, a reduced preparedness to act upon them, a reduced sense of
responsibility. We all know the man—and a very good specimen he
frequently is—who says that the local administration is not his business and callously shrugs his shoulders at practices which he would
rather die than suffer in his own office. High-minded citizens in a
hortatory mood who preach the responsibility of the individual voter
or taxpayer invariably discover the fact that this voter does not feel
responsible for what the local politicians do. Still, especially in communities not too big for personal contacts, local patriotism may be
a very important factor in "making democracy work." Also, the problems of a town are in many respects akin to the problems of a manufacturing concern. The man who understands the latter also understands, to some extent, the former. The manufacturer, grocer or
workman need not step out of his world to have a rationally defensible
view (that may of course be right or wrong) on street cleaning or
town halls.

Second, there are many national issues that concern individuals and
groups so directly and unmistakably as to evoke volitions that are
genuine and definite enough. The most important instance is afforded
by issues involving immediate and personal pecuniary profit to individual voters and groups of voters, such as direct payments, protective duties, silver policies and so on. Experience that goes back to
antiquity shows that by and large voters react promptly and rationally
to any such chance. But the classical doctrine of democracy evidently
stands to gain little from displays of rationality of this kind. Voters
thereby prove themselves bad and indeed corrupt judges of such issues,[13] and often they even prove themselves bad judges of their own

---

any moment are given independently of attempts to manufacture them, although
we recognize that these genuine volitions themselves are the result of environmental
influences in the past, propagandist influences included. This distinction between
genuine and manufactured will (see below) is a difficult one and cannot be applied
in all cases and for all purposes. For our purpose however it is sufficient to point
to the obvious common-sense case which can be made for it.

[13] The reason why the Benthamites so completely overlooked this is that they
did not consider the possibilities of mass corruption in modern capitalism. Committing in their political theory the same error which they committed in their economic theory, they felt no compunction about postulating that "the people" were
the best judges of their own individual interests and that these must necessarily
coincide with the interests of all the people taken together. Of course this was
made easier for them because actually though not intentionally they philosophized
in terms of bourgeois interests which had more to gain from a parsimonious state
than from any direct bribes.

long-run interests, for it is only the short-run promise that tells politically and only short-run rationality that asserts itself effectively.

However, when we move still farther away from the private concerns of the family and the business office into those regions of national and international affairs that lack a direct and unmistakable link with those private concerns, individual volition, command of facts and method of inference soon cease to fulfill the requirements of the classical doctrine. What strikes me most of all and seems to me to be the core of the trouble is the fact that the sense of reality[14] is so completely lost. Normally, the great political questions take their place in the psychic economy of the typical citizen with those leisure-hour interests that have not attained the rank of hobbies, and with the subjects of irresponsible conversation. These things seem so far off; they are not at all like a business proposition; dangers may not materialize at all and if they should they may not prove so very serious; one feels oneself to be moving in a fictitious world.

This reduced sense of reality accounts not only for a reduced sense of responsibility but also for the absence of effective volition. One has one's phrases, of course, and one's wishes and daydreams and grumbles; especially, one has one's likes and dislikes. But ordinarily they do not amount to what we call a will—the psychic counterpart of purposeful responsible action. In fact, for the private citizen musing over national affairs there is no scope for such a will and no task at which it could develop. He is a member of an unworkable committee, the committee of the whole nation, and this is why he expends less disciplined effort on mastering a political problem than he expends on a game of bridge.[15]

The reduced sense of responsibility and the absence of effective volition in turn explain the ordinary citizen's ignorance and lack of judgment in matters of domestic and foreign policy which are if anything more shocking in the case of educated people and of people who are successfully active in non-political walks of life than it is with uneducated people in humble stations. Information is plentiful and readily available. But this does not seem to make any difference. Nor should we wonder at it. We need only compare a lawyer's attitude to his brief and the same lawyer's attitude to the statements of political fact presented in his newspaper in order to see what is the matter. In

[14] William James' "pungent sense of reality." The relevance of this point has been particularly emphasized by Graham Wallas.

[15] It will help to clarify the point if we ask ourselves why so much more intelligence and clear-headedness show up at a bridge table than in, say, political discussion among non-politicians. At the bridge table we have a definite task; we have rules that discipline us; success and failure are clearly defined; and we are prevented from behaving irresponsibly because every mistake we make will not only immediately tell but also be immediately allocated to us. These conditions, by their failure to be fulfilled for the political behavior of the ordinary citizen, show why it is that in politics he lacks all the alertness and the judgment he may display in his profession.

the one case the lawyer has qualified for appreciating the relevance of his facts by years of purposeful labor done under the definite stimulus of interest in his professional competence; and under a stimulus that is no less powerful he then bends his acquirements, his intellect, his will to the contents of the brief. In the other case, he has not taken the trouble to qualify; he does not care to absorb the information or to apply to it the canons of criticism he knows so well how to handle; and he is impatient of long or complicated argument. All of this goes to show that without the initiative that comes from immediate responsibility, ignorance will persist in the face of masses of information however complete and correct. It persists even in the face of the meritorious efforts that are being made to go beyond presenting information and to teach the use of it by means of lectures, classes, discussion groups. Results are not zero. But they are small. People cannot be carried up the ladder.

Thus the typical citizen drops down to a lower level of mental performance as soon as he enters the political field. He argues and analyzes in a way which he would readily recognize as infantile within the sphere of his real interests. He becomes a primitive again. His thinking becomes associative and affective.[16] And this entails two further consequences of ominous significance.

First, even if there were no political groups trying to influence him, the typical citizen would in political matters tend to yield to extra-rational or irrational prejudice and impulse. The weakness of the rational processes he applies to politics and the absence of effective logical control over the results he arrives at would in themselves suffice to account for that. Moreover, simply because he is not "all there," he will relax his usual moral standards as well and occasionally give in to dark urges which the conditions of private life help him to repress. But as to the wisdom or rationality of his inferences and conclusions, it may be just as bad if he gives in to a burst of generous indignation. This will make it still more difficult for him to see things in their correct proportions or even to see more than one aspect of one thing at a time. Hence, if for once he does emerge from his usual vagueness and does display the definite will postulated by the classical doctrine of democracy, he is as likely as not to become still more unintelligent and irresponsible than he usually is. At certain junctures, this may prove fatal to his nation.[17]

[16] See ch. xii.

[17] The importance of such bursts cannot be doubted. But it is possible to doubt their genuineness. Analysis will show in many instances that they are induced by the action of some group and do not spontaneously arise from the people. In this case they enter into a (second) class of phenomena which we are about to deal with. Personally, I do believe that genuine instances exist. But I cannot be sure that more thorough analysis would not reveal some psycho-technical effort at the bottom of them.

Second, however, the weaker the logical element in the processes of the public mind and the more complete the absence of rational criticism and of the rationalizing influence of personal experience and responsibility, the greater are the opportunities for groups with an ax to grind. These groups may consist of professional politicians or of exponents of an economic interest or of idealists of one kind or another or of people simply interested in staging and managing political shows. The sociology of such groups is immaterial to the argument in hand. The only point that matters here is that, Human Nature in Politics being what it is, they are able to fashion and, within very wide limits, even to create the will of the people. What we are confronted with in the analysis of political processes is largely not a genuine but a manufactured will. And often this artefact is all that in reality corresponds to the *volonté générale* of the classical doctrine. So far as this is so, the will of the people is the product and not the motive power of the political process.

The ways in which issues and the popular will on any issue are being manufactured is exactly analogous to the ways of commercial advertising. We find the same attempts to contact the subconscious. We find the same technique of creating favorable and unfavorable associations which are the more effective the less rational they are. We find the same evasions and reticences and the same trick of producing opinion by reiterated assertion that is successful precisely to the extent to which it avoids rational argument and the danger of awakening the critical faculties of the people. And so on. Only, all these arts have infinitely more scope in the sphere of public affairs than they have in the sphere of private and professional life. The picture of the prettiest girl that ever lived will in the long run prove powerless to maintain the sales of a bad cigarette. There is no equally effective safeguard in the case of political decisions. Many decisions of fateful importance are of a nature that makes it impossible for the public to experiment with them at its leisure and at moderate cost. Even if that is possible, however, judgment is as a rule not so easy to arrive at as it is in the case of the cigarette, because effects are less easy to interpret.

But such arts also vitiate, to an extent quite unknown in the field of commercial advertising, those forms of political advertising that profess to address themselves to reason. To the observer, the anti-rational or, at all events, the extra-rational appeal and the defenselessness of the victim stand out more and not less clearly when cloaked in facts and arguments. We have seen above why it is so difficult to impart to the public unbiased information about political problems and logically correct inferences from it and why it is that information and arguments in political matters will "register" only if they link up with the citizen's preconceived ideas. As a rule, however, these ideas are not definite enough to determine particular conclusions. Since they can themselves be manufactured, effective political argument almost inevitably implies the attempt to twist existing volitional premises into a particular shape and not merely the attempt to implement them or to help the citizen to make up his mind.

Thus information and arguments that are really driven home are likely to be the servants of political intent. Since the first thing man will do for his ideal or interest is to lie, we shall expect, and as a matter of fact we find, that effective information is almost always adulterated or selective[18] and that effective reasoning in politics consists mainly in trying to exalt certain propositions into axioms and to put others out of court; it thus reduces to the psycho-technics mentioned before. The reader who thinks me unduly pessimistic need only ask himself whether he has never heard—or said himself—that this or that awkward fact must not be told publicly, or that a certain line of reasoning, though valid, is undesirable. If men who according to any current standard are perfectly honorable or even high-minded reconcile themselves to the implications of this, do they not thereby show what they think about the merits or even the existence of the will of the people?

There are of course limits to all this.[19] And there is truth in Jefferson's dictum that in the end the people are wiser than any single individual can be, or in Lincoln's about the impossibility of "fooling all the people all the time." But both dicta stress the long-run aspect in a highly significant way. It is no doubt possible to argue that given time the collective psyche will evolve opinions that not infrequently strike us as highly reasonable and even shrewd. History however consists of a succession of short-run situations that may alter the course of events for good. If all the people can in the short run be "fooled" step by step into something they do not really want, and if this is not an exceptional case which we could afford to neglect, then no amount of retrospective common sense will alter the fact that in reality they neither raise nor decide issues but that the issues that shape their fate are normally raised and decided for them. More than anyone else the lover of democracy has every reason to accept this fact and to clear his creed from the aspersion that it rests upon make-believe.

IV. REASONS FOR THE SURVIVAL OF THE CLASSICAL DOCTRINE

But how is it possible that a doctrine so patently contrary to fact should have survived to this day and continued to hold its place in

---

[18] Selective information, if in itself correct, is an attempt to lie by speaking the truth.

[19] Possibly they might show more clearly if issues were more frequently decided by referendum. Politicians presumably know why they are almost invariably hostile to that institution.

the hearts of the people and in the official language of governments? The refuting facts are known to all; everybody admits them with perfect, frequently with cynical, frankness. The theoretical basis, utilitarian rationalism, is dead; nobody accepts it as a correct theory of the body politic. Nevertheless that question is not difficult to answer.

First of all, though the classical doctrine of collective action may not be supported by the results of empirical analysis, it is powerfully supported by that association with religious belief to which I have adverted already. This may not be obvious at first sight. The utilitarian leaders were anything but religious in the ordinary sense of the term. In fact they believed themselves to be anti-religious and they were so considered almost universally. They took pride in what they thought was precisely an unmetaphysical attitude and they were quite out of sympathy with the religious institutions and the religious movements of their time. But we need only cast another glance at the picture they drew of the social process in order to discover that it embodied essential features of the faith of protestant Christianity and was in fact derived from that faith. For the intellectual who had cast off his religion the utilitarian creed provided a substitute for it. For many of those who had retained their religious belief the classical doctrine became the political complement of it.[20]

Thus transposed into the categories of religion, this doctrine—and in consequence the kind of democratic persuasion which is based upon it—changes its very nature. There is no longer any need for logical scruples about the Common Good and Ultimate Values. All this is settled for us by the plan of the Creator whose purpose defines and sanctions everything. What seemed indefinite or unmotivated before is suddenly quite definite and convincing. The voice of the people that is the voice of God for instance. Or take Equality. Its very meaning is in doubt, and there is hardly any rational warrant for exalting it into a postulate, so long as we move in the sphere of empirical analysis. But Christianity harbors a strong equalitarian element. The Redeemer died for all: He did not differentiate between individuals of different social status. In doing so, He testified to the intrinsic value of the individual soul, a value that admits of no gradations. Is not this a sanction—and, as it seems to me, the only possible sanction[21]—of "everyone to count for one, no one to count for more

[20] Observe the analogy with socialist belief which also is a substitute for Christian belief to some and a complement of it to others.

[21] It might be objected that, however difficult it may be to attach a *general* meaning to the word Equality, such meaning can be unraveled from its context in most if not all cases. For instance, it may be permissible to infer from the circumstances in which the Gettysburg address was delivered that by the "proposition that all men are created free and equal," Lincoln simply meant equality of legal status versus the kind of inequality that is implied in the recognition of slavery. This meaning would be definite enough. But if we ask why that proposi-

than one"—a sanction that pours super-mundane meaning into articles of the democratic creed for which it is not easy to find any other? To be sure this interpretation does not cover the whole ground. However, so far as it goes, it seems to explain many things that otherwise would be unexplainable and in fact meaningless. In particular, it explains the believer's attitude toward criticism: again, as in the case of socialism, fundamental dissent is looked upon not merely as error but as sin; it elicits not merely logical counterargument but also moral indignation.

We may put our problem differently and say that democracy, when motivated in this way, ceases to be a mere method that can be discussed rationally like a steam engine or a disinfectant. It actually becomes what from another standpoint I have held it incapable of becoming, viz., an ideal or rather a part of an ideal schema of things. The very word may become a flag, a symbol of all a man holds dear, of everything that he loves about his nation whether rationally contingent to it or not. On the one hand, the question how the various propositions implied in the democratic belief are related to the facts of politics will then become as irrelevant to him as is, to the believing Catholic, the question how the doings of Alexander VI tally with the supernatural halo surrounding the papal office. On the other hand, the democrat of this type, while accepting postulates carrying large implications about equality and brotherliness, will be in a position also to accept, in all sincerity, almost any amount of deviations from them that his own behavior or position may involve. That is not even illogical. Mere distance from fact is no argument against an ethical maxim or a mystical hope.

Second, there is the fact that the forms and phrases of classical democracy are for many nations associated with events and developments in their history which are enthusiastically approved by large majorities. Any opposition to an established regime is likely to use these forms and phrases whatever its meaning and social roots may be.[22] If it prevails and if subsequent developments prove satisfactory, then these forms will take root in the national ideology.

The United States is the outstanding example. Its very existence as a sovereign state is associated with a struggle against a monarchial and aristocratic England. A minority of loyalists excepted, Americans

---

tion should be morally and politically binding and if we refuse to answer "Because every man is by nature exactly like every other man," then we can only fall back upon the divine sanction supplied by Christian belief. This solution is conceivably implied in the word "created."

[22] It might seem that an exception should be made for oppositions that issue into frankly autocratic regimes. But even most of these rose, as a matter of history, in democratic ways and based their rule on the approval of the people. Caesar was not killed by plebeians. But the aristocratic oligarchs who did kill him also used democratic phrases.

had, at the time of the Grenville administration, probably ceased to look upon the English monarch as *their* king and the English aristocracy as *their* aristocracy. In the War of Independence they fought what in fact as well as in their feeling had become a foreign monarch and a foreign aristocracy who interfered with their political and economic interests. Yet from an early stage of the troubles they presented their case, which really was a national one, as a case of the "people" versus its "rulers," in terms of inalienable Rights of Man and in the light of the general principles of classical democracy. The wording of the Declaration of Independence and of the Constitution adopted these principles. A prodigious development followed that absorbed and satisfied most people and thereby seemed to verify the doctrine embalmed in the sacred documents of the nation.

Oppositions rarely conquer when the groups in possession are in the prime of their power and success. In the first half of the nineteenth century, the oppositions that professed the classical creed of democracy rose and eventually prevailed against governments some of which—especially in Italy—were obviously in a state of decay and had become bywords of incompetence, brutality and corruption. Naturally though not quite logically, this redounded to the credit of that creed which moreover showed up to advantage when compared with the benighted superstitions sponsored by those governments. Under these circumstances, democratic revolution meant the advent of freedom and decency, and the democratic creed meant a gospel of reason and betterment. To be sure, this advantage was bound to be lost and the gulf between the doctrine and the practice of democracy was bound to be discovered. But the glamour of the dawn was slow to fade.

Third, it must not be forgotten that there are social patterns in which the classical doctrine will actually fit facts with a sufficient degree of approximation. As has been pointed out, this is the case with many small and primitive societies which as a matter of fact served as a prototype to the authors of that doctrine. It may be the case also with societies that are not primitive provided they are not too differentiated and do not harbor any serious problems. Switzerland is the best example. There is so little to quarrel about in a world of peasants which, excepting hotels and banks, contains no great capitalist industry, and the problems of public policy are so simple and so stable that an overwhelming majority can be expected to understand them and to agree about them. But if we can conclude that in such cases the classical doctrine approximates reality we have to add immediately that it does so not because it describes an effective mechanism of political decision but only because there are no great decisions to be made. Finally, the case of the United States may again be invoked in order to show that the classical doctrine sometimes appears to fit facts even in a society that is big and highly differentiated and in which there are great issues to decide provided the sting is taken out of them by favorable conditions. Until this country's entry into the First World War, the public mind was concerned mainly with the business of exploiting the economic possibilities of the environment. So long as this business was not seriously interfered with nothing mattered fundamentally to the average citizen who looked on the antics of politicians with good-natured contempt. Sections might get excited over the tariff, over silver, over local misgovernment, or over an occasional squabble with England. The people at large did not care much, except in the one case of serious disagreement which in fact produced national disaster, the Civil War.

And fourth, of course, politicians appreciate a phraseology that flatters the masses and offers an excellent opportunity not only for evading responsibility but also for crushing opponents in the name of the people.

CHAPTER XXII

ANOTHER THEORY OF DEMOCRACY

I. COMPETITION FOR POLITICAL LEADERSHIP

I THINK that most students of politics have by now come to accept the criticisms leveled at the classical doctrine of democracy in the preceding chapter. I also think that most of them agree, or will agree before long, in accepting another theory which is much truer to life and at the same time salvages much of what sponsors of the democratic method really mean by this term. Like the classical theory, it may be put into the nutshell of a definition.

It will be remembered that our chief troubles about the classical theory centered in the proposition that "the people" hold a definite and rational opinion about every individual question and that they give effect to this opinion—in a democracy—by choosing "representatives" who will see to it that that opinion is carried out. Thus the selection of the representatives is made secondary to the primary purpose of the democratic arrangement which is to vest the power of deciding political issues in the electorate. Suppose we reverse the roles of these two elements and make the deciding of issues by the electorate secondary to the election of the men who are to do the deciding. To put it differently, we now take the view that the role of the people is to produce a government, or else an intermediate body which in turn will produce a national executive[1] or government. And we define: the democratic method is that institutional arrangement for arriving at political decisions in which individuals acquire the power to decide by means of a competitive struggle for the people's vote.

Defense and explanation of this idea will speedily show that, as to both plausibility of assumptions and tenability of propositions, it greatly improves the theory of the democratic process.

First of all, we are provided with a reasonably efficient criterion by which to distinguish democratic governments from others. We have seen that the classical theory meets with difficulties on that score because both the will and the good of the people may be, and in many historical instances have been, served just as well or better by govern-

---

[1] The insincere word "executive" really points in the wrong direction. It ceases however to do so if we use it in the sense in which we speak of the "executives" of a business corporation who also do a great deal more than "execute" the will of stockholders.

ments that cannot be described as democratic according to any accepted usage of the term. Now we are in a somewhat better position partly because we are resolved to stress a *modus procedendi* the presence or absence of which it is in most cases easy to verify.[2]

For instance, a parliamentary monarchy like the English one fulfills the requirements of the democratic method because the monarch is practically constrained to appoint to cabinet office the same people as parliament would elect. A "constitutional" monarchy does not qualify to be called democratic because electorates and parliaments, while having all the other rights that electorates and parliaments have in parliamentary monarchies, lack the power to impose their choice as to the governing committee: the cabinet ministers are in this case servants of the monarch, in substance as well as in name, and can in principle be dismissed as well as appointed by him. Such an arrangement may satisfy the people. The electorate may reaffirm this fact by voting against any proposal for change. The monarch may be so popular as to be able to defeat any competition for the supreme office. But since no machinery is provided for making this competition effective the case does not come within our definition.

Second, the theory embodied in this definition leaves all the room we may wish to have for a proper recognition of the vital fact of leadership. The classical theory did not do this but, as we have seen, attributed to the electorate an altogether unrealistic degree of initiative which practically amounted to ignoring leadership. But collectives act almost exclusively by accepting leadership—this is the dominant mechanism of practically any collective action which is more than a reflex. Propositions about the working and the results of the democratic method that take account of this are bound to be infinitely more realistic than propositions which do not. They will not stop at the execution of a *volonté générale* but will go some way toward showing how it emerges or how it is substituted or faked. What we have termed Manufactured Will is no longer outside the theory, an aberration for the absence of which we piously pray; it enters on the ground floor as it should.

Third, however, so far as there are genuine group-wise volitions at all—for instance the will of the unemployed to receive unemployment benefit or the will of other groups to help—our theory does not neglect them. On the contrary we are now able to insert them in exactly the role they actually play. Such volitions do not as a rule assert themselves directly. Even if strong and definite they remain latent, often for decades, until they are called to life by some political leader who turns them into political factors. This he does, or else his agents do it for him, by organizing these volitions, by working them up and by including eventually appropriate items in his competitive offering. The interaction between sectional interests and public opin-

2 See however the fourth point below.

ion and the way in which they produce the pattern we call the political situation appear from this angle in a new and much clearer light.

Fourth, our theory is of course no more definite than is the concept of competition for leadership. This concept presents similar difficulties as the concept of competition in the economic sphere, with which it may be usefully compared. In economic life competition is never completely lacking, but hardly ever is it perfect.[3] Similarly, in political life there is always some competition, though perhaps only a potential one, for the allegiance of the people. To simplify matters we have restricted the kind of competition for leadership which is to define democracy, to free competition for a free vote. The justification for this is that democracy seems to imply a recognized method by which to conduct the competitive struggle, and that the electoral method is practically the only one available for communities of any size. But though this excludes many ways of securing leadership which should be excluded,[4] such as competition by military insurrection, it does not exclude the cases that are strikingly analogous to the economic phenomena we label "unfair" or "fraudulent" competition or restraint of competition. And we cannot exclude them because if we did we should be left with a completely unrealistic ideal.[5] Between this ideal case which does not exist and the cases in which all competition with the established leader is prevented by force, there is a continuous range of variation within which the democratic method of government shades off into the autocratic one by imperceptible steps. But if we wish to understand and not to philosophize, this is as it should be. The value of our criterion is not seriously impaired thereby.

Fifth, our theory seems to clarify the relation that subsists between democracy and individual freedom. If by the latter we mean the existence of a sphere of individual self-government the boundaries of which are historically variable—*no* society tolerates absolute freedom even of conscience and of speech, *no* society reduces that sphere to zero—the question clearly becomes a matter of degree. We have seen that the democratic method does not necessarily guarantee a greater amount of individual freedom than another political method would permit in similar circumstances. It may well be the other way round. But there is still a relation between the two. If, on principle at least,

[3] In Part II we had examples of the problems which arise out of this.

[4] It also excludes methods which should not be excluded, for instance, the acquisition of political leadership by the people's tacit acceptance of it or by election *quasi per inspirationem*. The latter differs from election by voting only by a technicality. But the former is not quite without importance even in modern politics; the sway held by a party boss *within his party* is often based on nothing but tacit acceptance of his leadership. Comparatively speaking however these are details which may, I think, be neglected in a sketch like this.

[5] As in the economic field, *some* restrictions are implicit in the legal and moral principles of the community.

everyone is free to compete for political leadership[6] by presenting himself to the electorate, this will in most cases though not in all mean a considerable amount of freedom of discussion *for all*. In particular it will normally mean a considerable amount of freedom of the press. This relation between democracy and freedom is not absolutely stringent and can be tampered with. But, from the standpoint of the intellectual, it is nevertheless very important. At the same time, it is all there is to that relation.

Sixth, it should be observed that in making it the primary function of the electorate to produce a government (directly or through an intermediate body) I intended to include in this phrase also the function of evicting it. The one means simply the acceptance of a leader or a group of leaders, the other means simply the withdrawal of this acceptance. This takes care of an element the reader may have missed. He may have thought that the electorate controls as well as installs. But since electorates normally do not control their political leaders in any way except by refusing to reelect them or the parliamentary majorities that support them, it seems well to reduce our ideas about this control in the way indicated by our definition. Occasionally, spontaneous revulsions occur which upset a government or an individual minister directly or else enforce a certain course of action. But they are not only exceptional, they are, as we shall see, contrary to the spirit of the democratic method.

Seventh, our theory sheds much-needed light on an old controversy. Whoever accepts the classical doctrine of democracy and in consequence believes that the democratic method is to guarantee that issues be decided and policies framed according to the will of the people must be struck by the fact that, even if that will were undeniably real and definite, decision by simple majorities would in many cases distort it rather than give effect to it. Evidently the will of the majority is the will of the majority and not the will of "the people." The latter is a mosaic that the former completely fails to "represent." To equate both by definition is not to solve the problem. Attempts at real solutions have however been made by the authors of the various plans for Proportional Representation.

These plans have met with adverse criticism on practical grounds. It is in fact obvious not only that proportional representation will offer opportunities for all sorts of idiosyncrasies to assert themselves but also that it may prevent democracy from producing efficient governments and thus prove a danger in times of stress.[7] But before con-

---

[6] Free, that is, in the same sense in which everyone is free to start another textile mill.

[7] The argument against proportional representation has been ably stated by Professor F. A. Hermens in "The Trojan Horse of Democracy," *Social Research*, November 1938.

cluding that democracy becomes unworkable if its principle is carried out consistently, it is just as well to ask ourselves whether this principle really implies proportional representation. As a matter of fact it does not. If acceptance of leadership is the true function of the electorate's vote, the case for proportional representation collapses because its premises are no longer binding. The principle of democracy then merely means that the reins of government should be handed to those who command more support than do any of the competing individuals or teams. And this in turn seems to assure the standing of the majority system within the logic of the democratic method, although we might still condemn it on grounds that lie outside of that logic.

II. The Principle Applied

The theory outlined in the preceding section we are now going to try out on some of the more important features of the structure and working of the political engine in democratic countries.

1. In a democracy, as I have said, the primary function of the elector's vote is to produce government. This may mean the election of a complete set of individual officers. This practice however is in the main a feature of local government and will be neglected henceforth.[8] Considering national government only, we may say that producing government practically amounts to deciding who the leading man shall be.[9] As before, we shall call him Prime Minister.

There is only one democracy in which the electorate's vote does this directly, viz., the United States.[10] In all other cases the electorate's

[8] This we shall do for simplicity's sake only. The phenomenon fits perfectly into our schema.

[9] This is only approximately true. The elector's vote does indeed put into power a group that in all normal cases acknowledges an individual leader but there are as a rule leaders of second and third rank who carry political guns in their own right and whom the leader has no choice but to put into appropriate offices. This fact will be recognized presently.

Another point must be kept in mind. Although there is reason to expect that a man who rises to a position of supreme command will in general be a man of considerable personal force, whatever else he may be—to this we shall return later on—it does not follow that this will always be the case. Therefore the term "leader" or "leading man" is not to imply that the individuals thus designated are necessarily endowed with qualities of leadership or that they always do give any personal leads. There are political situations favorable to the rise of men deficient in leadership (and other qualities) and unfavorable to the establishment of strong individual positions. A party or a combination of parties hence may occasionally be acephalous. But everyone recognizes that this is a pathological state and one of the typical causes of defeat.

[10] We may, I take it, disregard the electoral college. In calling the President of the United States a prime minister I wish to stress the fundamental similarity of his position to that of prime ministers in other democracies. But I do not wish to minimize the differences, although some of them are more formal than real. The least important of them is that the President also fulfills those largely cere-

vote does not directly produce government but an intermediate organ, henceforth called parliament,[11] upon which the government-producing function devolves. It might seem easy to account for the adoption or rather the evolution of this arrangement, both on historical grounds and on grounds of expediency, and for the various forms it took in different social patterns. But it is not a logical construct; it is a natural growth the subtle meanings and results of which completely escape the official, let alone legal, doctrines.

How does a parliament produce government? The most obvious method is to elect it or, more realistically, to elect the prime minister and then to vote the list of ministers he presents. This method is rarely used.[12] But it brings out the nature of the procedure better than any of the others. Moreover, these can all be reduced to it, because the man who becomes prime minister is in all normal cases the one whom parliament would elect. The way in which he is actually appointed to office, by a monarch as in England, by a President as in France or by a special agency or committee as in the Prussian Free State of the Weimar period, is merely a matter of form.

The classical English practice is this. After a general election the victorious party normally commands a majority of seats in Parliament and thus is in a position to carry a vote of want of confidence against everyone except its own leader who in this negative way is designated "by Parliament" for national leadership. He receives his commission from the monarch—"kisses hands"—and presents to him his list of ministers of which the list of cabinet ministers is a part. In this he includes, first, some party veterans who receive what might be called

---

monial functions of, say, the French presidents. Much more important is it that he cannot dissolve Congress—but neither could the French Prime Minister do so. On the other hand, his position is stronger than that of the English Prime Minister by virtue of the fact that his leadership is independent of his having a majority in Congress—at least legally; for as a matter of fact he is checkmated if he has none. Also, he can appoint and dismiss cabinet officers (almost) at will. The latter can hardly be called ministers in the English sense of the word and are really no more than the word "secretary" conveys in common parlance. We might say, therefore, that in a sense the President is not only prime minister but sole minister, unless we find an analogy between the functions of an English Cabinet minister and the functions of the managers of the administration's forces in Congress.

There is no difficulty about interpreting and explaining these and many other peculiarities in this or any other country that uses the democratic method. But in order to save space we shall mainly think of the English pattern and consider all other cases as more or less important "deviations" on the theory that thus far the logic of democratic government has worked itself out most completely in the English practice though not in its legal forms.

[11] It will be recalled that I have defined parliament as an organ of the state. Although that was done simply for reasons of formal (legal) logic this definition fits in particularly well with our conception of the democratic method. Membership in parliament is hence an office.

[12] For example, it was adopted in Austria after the breakdown in 1918.

complimentary office; secondly, the leaders of the second rank, those men on whom he counts for the current fighting in Parliament and who owe their preferment partly to their positive political value and partly to their value as potential nuisances; third, the rising men whom he invites to the charmed circle of office in order to "extract the brains from below the gangway"; and sometimes, fourth, a few men whom he thinks particularly well qualified to fill certain offices.[13] But again, in all normal cases this practice will tend to produce the same result as election by Parliament would. The reader will also see that where, as in England, the prime minster has the actual power to dissolve ("to go to the country"), the result will to some extent approximate the result we should expect from direct election of the cabinet by the electorate so long as the latter supports him.[14] This may be illustrated by a famous instance.

2. In 1879, when the Beaconsfield (Disraeli) government, after almost six years of prosperous tenure of power culminating in the spectacular success of the Congress of Berlin,[15] was on all ordinary counts entitled to expect a success at the polls, Gladstone suddenly roused the country by a series of addresses of unsurpassable force (Midlothian campaign) which played up Turkish atrocities so successfully as to place him on the crest of a wave of popular enthusiasm *for him personally*. The official party had nothing to do with it. Several of its leaders in fact disapproved. Gladstone had resigned the

[13] To lament, as some people do, how little fitness for office counts in these arrangements is beside the point where description is concerned; it is of the essence of democratic government that political values should count primarily and fitness only incidentally. See below, ch. xxiii.

[14] If, as was the case in France, the prime minister has no such power, parliamentary *coteries* acquire so much independence that this parallelism between acceptance of a man by parliament and acceptance of the same man by the electorate is weakened or destroyed. This is the situation in which the parlor game of parliamentary politics runs riot. From our standpoint this is a deviation from the design of the machine. Raymond Poincaré was of the same opinion.

Of course, such situations also occur in England. For the Prime Minister's power to dissolve—strictly, his power to "advise" the monarch to dissolve the House of Commons—is inoperative either if his party's inner circle sets its face against it or if there is no chance that elections will strengthen his hold upon Parliament. That is to say, he may be stronger (though possibly still weak) in Parliament than he is in the country. Such a state of things tends to develop with some regularity after a government has been in power for some years. But under the English system this deviation from design cannot last very long.

[15] I do not mean that the temporary settlement of the questions raised by the Russo-Turkish War and the acquisition of the perfectly useless island of Cyprus were in themselves such masterpieces of statesmanship. But I do mean that from the standpoint of domestic politics they were just the kind of showy success that would normally flatter the average citizen's vanity and would greatly enhance the government's prospects in an atmosphere of jingo patriotism. In fact it was the general opinion that Disraeli would have won if he had dissolved immediately on returning from Berlin.

leadership years before and tackled the country single-handed. But when the liberal party under this impetus had won a smashing victory, it was obvious to everyone that he had to be again accepted as the party leader—nay, that he had become the party leader by virtue of his national leadership and that there simply was no room for any other. He came into power in a halo of glory.

Now this instance teaches us a lot about the working of the democratic method. To begin with, it must be realized that it is unique only in its dramatic quality, but in nothing else. It is the oversized specimen of a normal genus. The cases of both Pitts, Peel, Palmerston, Disraeli, Campbell Bannerman and others differ from it only in degree.

First, as to the Prime Minister's political leadership.[16] Our example shows that it is composed of three different elements which must not be confused and which in every case mix in different proportions, the mixture then determining the nature of every individual Prime Minister's rule. On the face of it, he comes into office as the leading

[16] It is characteristic of the English way of doing things that official recognition of the existence of the Prime Minister's office was deferred until 1907, when it was allowed to appear in the official order of precedence at court. But it is as old as democratic government. However, since democratic government was never introduced by a distinct act but slowly evolved as part of a comprehensive social process, it is not easy to indicate even an approximate birthday or birth period. There is a long stretch that presents embryonic cases. It is tempting to date the institution from the reign of William III, whose position, so much weaker than that of the native rulers had been, seems to give color to the idea. The objection to this however is not so much that England was no "democracy" then—the reader will recall that we do not define democracy by the extent of the franchise—as that, on the one hand, the embryonic case of Danby had occurred under Charles II and that, on the other hand, William III never reconciled himself to the arrangement and kept certain matters successfully in his own hands. We must not of course confuse prime ministers with mere advisers, however powerful with their sovereign and however firmly entrenched in the very center of the public power plant they may be—such men as Richelieu, Mazarin or Strafford for instance. Godolphin and Harley under Queen Anne were clearly transitional cases. The first man to be universally recognized at the time and by political historians was Sir Robert Walpole. But he as well as the Duke of Newcastle (or his brother Henry Pelham or both jointly) and in fact all the leading men down to Lord Shelburne (including the elder Pitt who even as foreign secretary came very near to fulfilling our requirements *in substance*) lack one or another of the characteristics. The first full-fledged specimen was the younger Pitt.

It is interesting to note that what his own time recognized in the case of Sir Robert Walpole (and later in that of Lord Carteret [Earl of Granville]) was not that here was an organ essential to democratic government that was breaking through atrophic tissues. On the contrary, public opinion felt it to be a most vicious cancer the growth of which was a menace to the national welfare and to democracy—"sole minister" or "first minister" was a term of opprobrium hurled at Walpole by his enemies. This fact is significant. It not only indicates the resistance new institutions usually meet with. It also indicates that this institution was felt to be incompatible with the classic doctrine of democracy which in fact has no place for political leadership in our sense, hence no place for the realities of the position of a prime minister.

man of his party *in Parliament*. As soon as installed however, he becomes in a sense the leader *of Parliament*, directly of the house of which he is a member, indirectly also of the other. This is more than an official euphemism, more also than is implied in his hold upon his own party. He acquires influence on, or excites the antipathy of, the other parties and individual members of the other parties as well, and this makes a lot of difference in his chances of success. In the limiting case, best exemplified by the practice of Sir Robert Peel, he may coerce his own party by means of another. Finally, though in all normal cases he will also be the head of his party in *the country*, the well-developed specimen of the prime ministerial genus will have a position in the country distinct from what he automatically acquires by heading the party organization. He will lead party opinion creatively—shape it—and eventually rise toward a formative leadership of public opinion beyond the lines of party, toward national leadership that may to some extent become independent of mere party opinion. It is needless to say how very personal such an achievement is and how great the importance of such a foothold outside of both party and Parliament. It puts a whip into the hand of the leader the crack of which may bring unwilling and conspiring followers to heel, though its thong will sharply hit the hand that uses it unsuccessfully.

This suggests an important qualification to our proposition that in a parliamentary system the function of producing a government devolves upon parliament. Parliament does normally decide who will be Prime Minister, but in doing so it is not completely free. It decides by acceptance rather than by initiative. Excepting pathological cases like the French *chambre*, the wishes of members are not as a rule the ultimate data of the process from which government emerges. Members are not only handcuffed by party obligations. They also are driven by the man whom they "elect"—driven to the act of the "election" itself exactly as they are driven by him once they have "elected" him. Every horse is of course free to kick over the traces and it does not always run up to its bit. But revolt or passive resistance against the leader's lead only shows up the normal relation. And this normal relation is of the essence of the democratic method. Gladstone's personal victory in 1880 is the answer to the official theory that Parliament creates and cashiers government.[17]

[17] Gladstone himself upheld that theory strongly. In 1874, when defeated at the polls, he still argued for meeting Parliament because it was up to Parliament to pass the sentence of dismissal. This of course means nothing at all. In the same way he studiously professed unbounded deference to the crown. One biographer after another has marveled at this courtly attitude of the great democratic leader. But surely Queen Victoria showed better discernment than did those biographers if we may judge from the strong dislike which she displayed for Gladstone from 1879 on and which the biographers attribute simply to the baleful influence of Disraeli. Is it really necessary to point out that professions of deference may mean

3. Next, as to the nature and role of the cabinet.[18] It is a curiously double-faced thing, the joint product of Parliament and Prime Minister. The latter designates its members for appointment, as we have seen, and the former accepts but also influences his choice. Looked at from the party's standpoint it is an assemblage of subleaders more or less reflecting its own structure. Looked at from the Prime Minister's standpoint it is an assemblage not only of comrades in arms but of party men who have their own interests and prospects to consider— a miniature Parliament. For the combination to come about and to work it is necessary for prospective cabinet ministers to make up their minds—not necessarily from enthusiastic love—to serve under Mr. X and for Mr. X to shape his program so that his colleagues in the cabinet will not too often feel like "reconsidering their position," as official phraseology has it, or like going on a sitdown strike. Thus the cabinet—and the same applies to the wider ministry that comprises also the political officers not in the cabinet—has a distinct function in the democratic process as against Prime Minister, party, Parliament and electorate. This function of intermediate leadership is associated with, but by no means based upon, the current business transacted by the individual cabinet officers in the several departments to which they are appointed in order to keep the leading group's hands on the bureaucratic engine. And it has only a distant relation, if any, with "seeing to it that the will of the people is carried out in each of them." Precisely in the best instances, the people are presented with results they never thought of and would not have approved of in advance.

4. Again, as to Parliament. I have both defined what seems to me to be its primary function and qualified that definition. But it might be objected that my definition fails to do justice to its other functions. Parliament obviously does a lot of other things besides setting up and pulling down governments. It legislates. And it even administers. For although every act of a parliament, except resolutions and declara-

---

two different things? The man who treats his wife with elaborate courtliness is not as a rule the one to accept comradeship between the sexes on terms of equality. As a matter of fact, the courtly attitude is precisely a method to evade this.

[18] Still more than the evolution of the prime minister's office, that of the cabinet is blurred by the historical continuity that covers changes in the nature of an institution. To this day the English cabinet is legally the operative part of the Privy Council, which of course was an instrument of government in decidedly predemocratic times. But below this surface an entirely different organ has evolved. As soon as we realize this we find the task of dating its emergence somewhat easier than we found the analogous task in the case of the prime minister. Though embryonic cabinets existed in the time of Charles II (the "cabal" ministry was one, and the committee of four that was formed in connection with Temple's experiment was another), the Whig "junto" under William III is a fair candidate for first place. From the reign of Anne on only minor points of membership or functioning remain to disagree on.

tions of policy, makes "law" in a formal sense, there are many acts which must be considered as administrative measures. The budget is the most important instance. To make it is an administrative function. Yet in this country it is drawn up by Congress. Even where it is drawn up by the minister of finance with the approval of the cabinet, as it is in England, Parliament has to vote on it and by this vote it becomes an act of Parliament. Does not this refute our theory?

When two armies operate against each other, their individual moves are always centered upon particular objects that are determined by their strategical or tactical situations. They may contend for a particular stretch of country or for a particular hill. But the desirability of conquering that stretch or hill must be derived from the strategical or tactical purpose, which is to beat the enemy. It would be obviously absurd to attempt to derive it from any extra-military properties the stretch or hill may have. Similarly, the first and foremost aim of each political party is to prevail over the others in order to get into power or to stay in it. Like the conquest of the stretch of country or the hill, the decision of the political issues is, from the standpoint of the politician, not the end but only the material of parliamentary activity. Since politicians fire off words instead of bullets and since those words are unavoidably supplied by the issues under debate, this may not always be as clear as it is in the military case. But victory over the opponent is nevertheless the essence of both games.[19]

Fundamentally, then, the current production of parliamentary decisions on national questions is the very method by which Parliament keeps or refuses to keep a government in power or by which Parliament accepts or refuses to accept the Prime Minister's leadership.[20] With the exceptions to be noticed presently, *every* vote is a vote of confidence or want of confidence, and the votes that are technically so called merely bring out *in abstracto* the essential element that is

[19] Sometimes politicians do emerge from phraseological mists. To cite an example to which no objection can be raised on the score of frivolity: no lesser politician than Sir Robert Peel characterized the nature of his craft when he said after his parliamentary victory over the Whig government on the issue of the latter's policy in Jamaica: "Jamaica was a good horse to start." The reader should ponder over this.

[20] This of course applies to the pre-Vichy French and pre-Fascist Italian practice just as much as to the English practice. It may however be called in question in the case of the United States where defeat of the administration on a major issue does not entail resignation of the President. But this is merely due to the fact that the Constitution, which embodies a different political theory, did not permit parliamentary practice to develop according to its logic. In actual fact this logic did not entirely fail to assert itself. Defeats on major issues, though they cannot displace the President, will in general so weaken his prestige as to oust him from a position of leadership. For the time being this creates an abnormal situation. But whether he wins or loses the subsequent presidential election, the conflict is then settled in a way that does not fundamentally differ from the way in which an English Prime Minister deals with a similar situation when he dissolves Parliament.

common to all. Of this we can satisfy ourselves by observing that the initiative in bringing up matters for parliamentary decision as a rule lies with the government or else with the opposition's shadow cabinet and not with private members.

It is the Prime Minister who selects from the incessant stream of current problems those which he is going to make parliamentary issues, that is to say, those on which his government proposes to introduce bills or, if he is not sure of his ground, at least resolutions. Of course every government receives from its predecessor a legacy of open questions which it may be unable to shelve; others are taken up as a matter of routine politics; it is only in the case of the most brilliant achievement that a Prime Minister is in a position to impose measures about a political issue which he has created himself. In any case however the government's choice or lead, whether free or not, is the factor that dominates parliamentary activity. If a bill is brought in by the opposition, this means that it is offering battle: such a move is an attack which the government must either thwart by purloining the issue or else defeat. If a major bill that is not on the governmental menu is brought in by a group of the governmental party, this spells revolt and it is from this angle and not from the extra-tactical merits of the case that it is looked upon by the ministers. This even extends to the raising of a debate. Unless suggested or sanctioned by the government, these are symptoms of the government forces' getting out of hand. Finally, if a measure is carried by inter-party agreement, this means a drawn battle or a battle avoided on strategical grounds.[21]

5. The exceptions to this principle of governmental leadership in "representative" assemblies only serve to show how realistic it is. They are of two kinds.

First, no leadership is absolute. Political leadership exerted according to the democratic method is even less so than are others because of that competitive element which is of the essence of democracy. Since theoretically every follower has the right of displacing his leader and since there are nearly always some followers who have a real

[21] Another highly significant piece of English technique may be mentioned in this connection. A major bill is or was usually not proceeded with if the majority for it fell to a very low figure on the second reading. This practice first of all recognized an important limitation of the majority principle as actually applied in well-managed democracies: it would not be correct to say that in a democracy the minority is always compelled to surrender. But there is a second point. While the minority is not always compelled to yield to the majority on the particular issue under debate, it is practically always—there were exceptions even to this—compelled to yield to it on the question whether the cabinet is to stay in power. Such a vote on the second reading of a major government measure may be said to combine a vote of confidence with a vote for shelving a bill. If the contents of the bill were all that mattered there would hardly be any sense in voting for it if it is not to make the statute book. But if Parliament is primarily concerned with keeping the cabinet in office, then such tactics become at once understandable.

chance of doing so, the private member and—if he feels that he could do with a bigger hat—the minister within and without the inner circle steers a middle course between an unconditional allegiance to the leader's standard and an unconditional raising of a standard of his own, balancing risks and chances with a nicety that is sometimes truly admirable.[22] The leader in turn responds by steering a middle course between insisting on discipline and allowing himself to be thwarted. He tempers pressure with more or less judicious concessions, frowns with compliments, punishments with benefits. This game results, according to the relative strength of individuals and their positions, in a very variable but in most cases considerable amount of freedom. In particular, groups that are strong enough to make their resentment felt yet not strong enough to make it profitable to include their protagonists and their programs in the governmental arrangement will in general be allowed to have their way in minor questions or, at any rate, in questions which the Prime Minister can be induced to consider as of minor or only sectional importance. Thus, groups of followers or even individual members may occasionally have the opportunity of carrying bills of their own and still more indulgence will of course be extended to mere criticism or to failure to vote mechanically for every government measure. But we need only look at this in a practical spirit in order to realize, from the limits that are set to the use of this freedom, that it embodies not the principle of the working of a parliament but deviations from it.

Second, there are cases in which the political engine fails to absorb certain issues either because the high commands of the government's and the opposition's forces do not appreciate their political values or because these values are in fact doubtful.[23] Such issues may then be taken up by outsiders who prefer making an independent bid for power to serving in the ranks of one of the existing parties. This of course is perfectly normal politics. But there is another possibility. A man may feel so strongly about a particular question that he may enter the political arena merely in order to have it solved in his way and without harboring any wish to start in on a normal political

[22] One of the most instructive examples by which the above can be illustrated is afforded by the course taken by Joseph Chamberlain with respect to the Irish question in the 1880's. He finally outmaneuvered Gladstone, but he started the campaign while officially an ardent adherent. And the case is exceptional only in the force and brilliance of the man. As every political captain knows, only mediocrities can be counted on for loyalty. That is why some of the greatest of those captains, Disraeli for instance, surrounded themselves by thoroughly second-rate men.

[23] An issue that has never been tried out is the typical instance of the first class. The typical reasons why a government and the shadow cabinet of the opposition may tacitly agree to leave an issue alone in spite of their realizing its potentialities are technical difficulty of handling it and the fear that it will cause sectional difficulties.

career. This however is so unusual that it is difficult to find instances
of first-rank importance of it. Perhaps Richard Cobden was one. It is
true that instances of second-rank importance are more frequent,
especially instances of the crusader type. But nobody will hold that
they are anything but deviations from standard practice.

We may sum up as follows. In observing human societies we do
not as a rule find it difficult to specify, at least in a rough common-
sense manner, the various ends that the societies under study struggle
to attain. These ends may be said to provide the rationale or meaning
of corresponding individual activities. But it does not follow that
the social meaning of a type of activity will necessarily provide the
motive power, hence the explanation of the latter. If it does not, a
theory that contents itself with an analysis of the social end or need to
be served cannot be accepted as an adequate account of the activities
that serve it. For instance, the reason why there is such a thing as economic activity is of course that people want to eat, to clothe themselves and so on. To provide the means to satisfy those wants is the
social end or meaning of production. Nevertheless we all agree that
this proposition would make a most unrealistic starting point for a
theory of economic activity in commercial society and that we shall
do much better if we start from propositions about profits. Similarly,
the social meaning or function of parliamentary activity is no doubt
to turn out legislation and, in part, administrative measures. But in
order to understand how democratic politics serve this social end, we
must start from the competitive struggle for power and office and
realize that the social function is fulfilled, as it were, incidentally—
in the same sense as production is incidental to the making of profits.

6. Finally, as to the role of the electorate, only one additional point
need be mentioned. We have seen that the wishes of the members of
a parliament are not the ultimate data of the process that produces
government. A similar statement must be made concerning the electorate. Its choice—ideologically glorified into the Call from the People—does not flow from its initiative but is being shaped, and the
shaping of it is an essential part of the democratic process. Voters do
not decide issues. But neither do they pick their members of parliament from the eligible population with a perfectly open mind. In
all normal cases the initiative lies with the candidate who makes a
bid for the office of member of parliament and such local leadership
as that may imply. Voters confine themselves to accepting this bid in
preference to others or refusing to accept it. Even most of those exceptional cases in which a man is *genuinely* drafted by the electors
come into the same category for either of two reasons: naturally a
man need not bid for leadership if he has acquired leadership already;
or it may happen that a local leader who can control or influence
the vote but is unable or unwilling to compete for election himself

designates another man who then may seem to have been sought out by the voters acting on their own initiative.

But even as much of electoral initiative as acceptance of one of the competing candidates would in itself imply is further restricted by the existence of parties. A party is not, as classical doctrine (or Edmund Burke) would have us believe, a group of men who intend to promote public welfare "upon some principle on which they are all agreed." This rationalization is so dangerous because it is so tempting. For all parties will of course, at any given time, provide themselves with a stock of principles or planks and these principles or planks may be as characteristic of the party that adopts them and as important for its success as the brands of goods a department store sells are characteristic of it and important for its success. But the department store cannot be defined in terms of its brands and a party cannot be defined in terms of its principles. A party is a group whose members propose to act in concert in the competitive struggle for political power. If that were not so it would be impossible for different parties to adopt exactly or almost exactly the same program. Yet this happens as everyone knows. Party and machine politicians are simply the response to the fact that the electoral mass is incapable of action other than a stampede, and they constitute an attempt to regulate political competition exactly similar to the corresponding practices of a trade association. The psycho-technics of party management and party advertising, slogans and marching tunes, are not accessories. They are of the essence of politics. So is the political boss.

CHAPTER XXIII

THE INFERENCE

I. Some Implications of the Preceding Analysis

THE theory of competitive leadership has proved a satisfactory interpretation of the facts of the democratic process. So we shall naturally use it in our attempt to unravel the relation between democracy and a socialist order of things. As has been stated before, socialists claim not only compatibility; they claim that democracy implies socialism and that there cannot be true democracy except in socialism. On the other hand, the reader cannot but be familiar with at least some of the numerous pamphlets that have been published in this country during the last few years in order to prove that a planned economy, let alone full-fledged socialism, is completely incompatible with democracy. Both standpoints are of course easy to understand from the psychological background of the contest and from the natural wish of both parties to it to secure the support of a people the great majority of whom fervently believes in democracy. But suppose we ask: where lies the truth?

Our analysis in this and preceding parts of this book readily yields an answer. Between socialism as we defined it and democracy as we defined it there is no necessary relation: the one can exist without the other. At the same time there is no incompatibility: in appropriate states of the social environment the socialist engine can be run on democratic principles.

But observe that these simple statements depend upon our view about what socialism and democracy are. Therefore they mean not only less than, but also something different from, what either party to the contest has in mind. For this reason and also because behind the question of mere compatibility there inevitably arises the further question whether the democratic method will work more or less effectively in a socialist as compared with a capitalist regime, we have still a lot of explaining to do. In particular we must try to formulate the conditions under which the democratic method can be expected to give satisfaction. This will be done in the second section of this chapter. Now we shall look at some of the implications of our analysis of the democratic process.

First of all, according to the view we have taken, democracy does not mean and cannot mean that the people actually rule in any obvious sense of the terms "people" and "rule." Democracy means only that the people have the opportunity of accepting or refusing the men who are to rule them. But since they might decide this also in entirely undemocratic ways, we have had to narrow our definition by adding a further criterion identifying the democratic method, viz., free competition among would-be leaders for the vote of the electorate. Now one aspect of this may be expressed by saying that democracy is the rule of the politician. It is of the utmost importance to realize clearly what this implies.

Many exponents of democratic doctrine have striven hard to divest political activity of any professional connotation. They have held strongly, sometimes passionately, that politics ought not to be a profession and that democracy degenerates whenever it becomes one. But this is just ideology. It is true that, say, businessmen or lawyers may be elected to serve in parliament and even taken office occasionally and still remain primarily businessmen and lawyers. It is also true that many who become primarily politicians continue to rely on other activities for their livelihood.[1] But normally, personal success in politics, more than occasional rise to cabinet office in particular, will imply concentration of the professional kind and relegate a man's other activities to the rank of sidelines or necessary chores. If we wish to face facts squarely, we must recognize that, in modern democracies of any type other than the Swiss, politics will unavoidably be a career. This in turn spells recognition of a distinct professional interest in the individual politician and of a distinct group interest in the political profession as such. It is essential to insert this factor into our theory. Many a riddle is solved as soon as we take account of it.[2] Among other things we immediately cease to wonder why it is that politicians so often fail to serve the interest of their class or of the groups with which they are personally connected. Politically speaking, the man is still in the nursery who has not absorbed, so as never to forget, the saying attributed to one of the most successful politicians that ever lived: "What businessmen do not understand is that exactly as they are dealing in oil so I am dealing in votes."[3]

[1] Illustrations abound of course. A particularly instructive class are the lawyers in the French *chambre* and *sénat*. Some of the outstanding political leaders were also great *avocats*: think for instance of Waldeck-Rousseau and of Poincaré. But as a rule (and if we choose to neglect the cases in which lawyers' firms will miraculously run by themselves if one of their partners is a leading politician and enjoys frequent spells of political office) success at the bar and success in politics do not go together.

[2] It should be noticed how this argument links up with our analysis of the position and behavior of the intellectuals in ch. xiii, Section II.

[3] Such a view is sometimes disapproved of as frivolous or cynical. I think, on the contrary, that it is frivolous or cynical to render lip service to slogans for which in private one has nothing but an augur's smile. But it is just as well to point out that the view in question is not so derogatory to the politician as it

Let us note that there is no reason to believe that this will be either better or worse in a socialist organization of society. The doctor or engineer who means to fill the cup of his ambitions by means of success as a doctor or engineer will still be a distinct type of man and have a distinct pattern of interests; the doctor or engineer who means to work or reform the institutions of his country will still be another type and have another pattern of interests.

Second, students of political organization have always felt doubts concerning the administrative efficiency of democracy in large and complex societies. In particular it has been urged that, as compared with other arrangements, the efficiency of democratic government is inevitably impaired because of the tremendous loss of energy which the incessant battle in parliament and outside of it imposes upon the leading men. It is further impaired, for the same reason, by the necessity of bending policies to the exigencies of political warfare. Neither proposition is open to doubt. Both are but corollaries to our previous statement that the democratic method produces legislation and administration as by-products of the struggle for political office.

Visualize, for instance, the situation of a Prime Minister. Where governments are as unstable as they have been in France from 1871 to the breakdown in 1940, his attention must be almost monopolized by a task that is like trying to build a pyramid from billiard balls. Only men of quite unusual force under such conditions can have had any energy to spare for current administrative work on bills and so on; and only such exceptional men can have acquired any authority with their civil service subordinates who like everybody else knew that their chief would be out before long. Of course this is not anything like as bad in the English case. Unstable governmental combinations are exceptions, and normally a government can count on a life of about five or six years. Ministers can settle down in their offices and are not so easy to unhorse in Parliament. But this does not mean that they are exempt from fighting. There always is a current contest and if governments are not constantly on trial for their lives it is only because they are as a rule able to smother current attacks this side of the danger point. The Prime Minister has to watch his opponents all the time, to lead his own flock incessantly, to be ready to step into breaches that might open at any moment, to keep his hand on the measures under debate, to control his cabinet—all of which amounts to saying that, when Parliament is in session, he is

---

might seem. It does not exclude ideals or a sense of duty. The analogy with the businessman will again help to make this clear. As I have said in another place, no economist who knows anything about the realities of business life will hold for a moment that sense of duty and ideals about service and efficiency play no role in shaping businessmen's behavior. Yet the same economist is within his rights if he bases his explanation of that behavior on a schema that rests on the profit motive.

lucky if he has a couple of hours in the morning left for thinking things over and for real work. Individual miscarriages and defeats of a government as a whole are not infrequently due to physical exhaustion of the leading man or men.[4] How could he, so it might well be asked, undertake to lead and supervise an administrative organism that is to embrace all the problems of economic life?

But this wastage of governmental energy is not all. The incessant competitive struggle to get into office or to stay in it imparts to every consideration of policies and measures the bias so admirably expressed by the phrase about "dealing in votes." The fact that in a democracy government must attend primarily to the political values of a policy or a bill or an administrative act—that is to say, the very fact that enforces the democratic principle of the government's dependence upon the voting of parliament and of the electorate—is likely to distort all the pro's and con's. In particular, it forces upon the men at or near the helm a short-run view and makes it extremely difficult for them to serve such long-run interests of the nation as may require consistent work for far-off ends; foreign policy, for instance, is in danger of degenerating into domestic politics. And it makes it no less difficult to dose measures rationally. The dosing that a government decides on with an eye to its political chances is not necessarily the one that will produce the results most satisfactory to the nation.

Thus the prime minister in a democracy might be likened to a horseman who is so fully engrossed in trying to keep in the saddle that he cannot plan his ride, or to a general so fully occupied with making sure that his army will accept his orders that he must leave strategy to take care of itself. And this remains true (and must, in the case of some countries such as France and Italy, be frankly recognized as one of the sources from which anti-democratic feeling has spread) in spite of the facts that may be invoked in extenuation.

There is, to begin with, the fact that the instances in which those consequences show to an extent that may be felt to be unbearable can often be explained on the ground that the social pattern is not up to the task of working democratic institutions. As the examples of France and Italy show, this may happen in countries that are much more civilized than some which do succeed in that task. But neverthe-

[4] To give a portentous example: no student of the origins of the World War of 1914-1918 can fail to be struck by the passivity of the English government from the murder of the Archduke to the declarations of war. Not that no efforts were made to avoid the conflagration. But they were singularly ineffective and fell far short of what could have been done. It is of course possible to explain this on the theory that the Asquith government did not really wish to avoid the war. But if this theory be considered unsatisfactory, as I think it should be, then we are driven back upon another: it is just possible that the gentlemen on the treasury bench were so absorbed in their political game that they did not wake up to the dangers of the international situation until it was too late.

less the weight of the criticism is thereby reduced to the statement that the satisfactory working of the democratic method is contingent upon fulfillment of certain conditions—a subject that will be taken up presently.

Then there is the question of the alternative. These weaknesses are obviously not absent in non-democratic patterns. Paving one's way to a leading position, say, at a court, may absorb quite as much energy and distort one's views about issues quite as much as does the democratic struggle though that waste or distortion does not stand out so publicly. This amounts to saying that attempts at comparative appraisal of engines of government will have to take account of many other factors besides the institutional principles involved.

Moreover, some of us will reply to the critic that a lower level of governmental efficiency may be exactly what we want. We certainly do not want to be the objects of dictatorial efficiency, mere material for deep games. Such a thing as the Gosplan may at present be impossible in the United States. But does not this prove precisely that, just like the Russian Gosplan, its hypothetical analogue in this country would violate the spirit as well as the organic structure of the commonwealth?

Finally, something can be done to reduce the pressure on the leading men by appropriate institutional devices. The American arrangement for instance shows up to advantage on this point. The American "prime minister" must no doubt keep his eye on his political chessboard. But he need not feel responsible for every individual measure. And, not sitting in Congress, he is at least exempt from the physical strain this would involve. He has all the opportunity he wants to nurse his strength.

Third, our analysis in the preceding chapter brings into bold relief the problem of the quality of the men the democratic method selects for positions of leadership. The well-known argument about this hardly needs recalling: the democratic method creates professional politicians whom it then turns into amateur administrators and "statesmen." Themselves lacking all the acquirements necessary for dealing with the tasks that confront them, they appoint Lord Macaulay's "judges without law and diplomatists without French," ruining the civil service and discouraging all the best elements in it. Worse still, there is another point, distinct from any question of specialized competence and experience: the qualities of intellect and character that make a good candidate are not necessarily those that make a good administrator, and selection by means of success at the polls may work against the people who would be successes at the head of affairs. And even if the products of this selection prove successes in office these successes may well be failures for the nation. The politician who is a good tactician can successfully survive any number of administrative miscarriages.

Recognition of the elements of truth in all this should again be tempered by the recognition of the extenuating facts. In particular, the case for democracy stands to gain from a consideration of the alternatives: no system of selection whatever the social sphere—with the possible exception of competitive capitalism—tests exclusively the ability to perform and selects in the way a stable selects its Derby crack. Though to varying degrees, all systems put premiums on other qualities as well, qualities that are often inimical to performance. But we may perhaps go further than this. It is not quite true that in the average case political success proves nothing for a man or that the politician is nothing but an amateur. There is one very important thing that he knows professionally, viz., the handling of men. And, as a broad rule at least, the ability to win a position of political leadership will be associated with a certain amount of personal force and also of other aptitudes that will come in usefully in a prime minister's workshop. There are after all many rocks in the stream that carries politicians to national office which are not entirely ineffective in barring the progress of the moron or the windbag.

That in such matters general argument one way or another does not lead to a definite result is only what we should expect. It is much more curious and significant that factual evidence is not, at first sight at least, any more conclusive. Nothing is easier than to compile an impressive list of failures of the democratic method, especially if we include not only cases in which there was actual breakdown or national discomfiture but also those in which, though the nation led a healthy and prosperous life, the performance in the political sector was clearly substandard relative to the performance in others. But it is just as easy to marshal hardly less impressive evidence in favor of the politician. To cite one outstanding illustration: It is true that in antiquity war was not so technical an affair as it has become of late. Yet one would think that the ability to make a success at it had even then very little to do with the ability to get oneself elected to political office. All the Roman generals of the republican era however were politicians and all of them got their commands directly through the elective offices they held or had previously held. Some of the worst disasters were due to this. But on the whole, these politician-soldiers did remarkably well.

Why is that so? There can be only one answer to this question.

II. Conditions for the Success of the Democratic Method

If a physicist observes that the same mechanism works differently at different times and in different places, he concludes that its functioning depends upon conditions extraneous to it. We cannot but arrive at the same conclusion. And it is as easy to see what these conditions are as it was to see what the conditions were under which the classical doctrine of democracy might be expected to fit reality to an acceptable degree.

This conclusion definitely commits us to that strictly relativist view that has been indicated all along. Exactly as there is no case for or against socialism at all times and in all places, so there is no absolutely general case for or against the democratic method. And exactly as with socialism, this makes it difficult to argue by means of a *ceteris paribus* clause, for "other things" *cannot* be equal as between situations in which democracy is a workable, or the only workable, arrangement and situations in which it is not. Democracy thrives in social patterns that display certain characteristics and it might well be doubted whether there is any sense in asking how it would fare in others that lack those characteristics—or how the people in those other patterns would fare with it. The conditions which I hold must be fulfilled for the democratic method to be a success[5]—in societies in which it is possible for it to work at all—I shall group under four headings; and I shall confine myself to the great industrial nations of the modern type.

The first condition is that the human material of politics—the people who man the party machines, are elected to serve in parliament, rise to cabinet office—should be of sufficiently high quality. This means more than that individuals of adequate ability and moral character must exist in sufficient numbers. As has been pointed out before, the democratic method selects not simply from the population but only from those elements of the population that are available for the political vocation or, more precisely, that offer themselves for election. All methods of selection do this of course. All of them therefore may, according to the degree to which a given vocation attracts talent and character, produce in it a level of performance that is above or below the national average. But the competitive struggle for responsible office is, on the one hand, wasteful of personnel and energy. On the other hand, the democratic process may easily create conditions in the political sector that, once established, will repel most of the men who can make a success at anything else. For both these reasons, adequacy of material is particularly important for the success of democratic government. It is not true that in a democracy people always have the kind and quality of government they want or merit.

There may be many ways in which politicians of sufficiently good

[5] By "success" I mean no more than that the democratic process reproduce itself steadily without creating situations that enforce resort to non-democratic methods and that it cope with current problems in a way which all interests that count politically find acceptable in the long run. I do not mean that every observer, from his own individual standpoint, need approve of the results.

quality can be secured. Thus far however, experience seems to suggest that the only effective guarantee is in the existence of a social stratum, itself a product of a severely selective process, that takes to politics as a matter of course. If such a stratum be neither too exclusive nor too easily accessible for the outsider and if it be strong enough to assimilate most of the elements it currently absorbs, it not only will present for the political career products of stocks that have successfully passed many tests in other fields—served, as it were, an apprenticeship in private affairs—but it will also increase their fitness by endowing them with traditions that embody experience, with a professional code and with a common fund of views.

It is hardly mere coincidence that England, which is the only country to fulfill our condition completely, is also the only country to have a political society in this sense. Still more instructive is the case of Germany in the period of the Weimar Republic (1918-1933). As I hope to show in Part V, there was nothing about the German politicians of that period that would ordinarily be considered a glaring defect. The average member of parliament and the average prime and cabinet minister were honest, reasonable and conscientious. This applies to all parties. However, with due respect for the sprinkling of talent that showed here and there, though rarely in a position of or near high command, it must be added that most of them were distinctly below par, in some cases pitifully so. Obviously this cannot have been due to any lack of ability and energy in the nation as a whole. But ability and energy spurned the political career. And there was no class or group whose members looked upon politics as their predestined career. That political system missed fire for many reasons. But the fact that eventually it met smashing defeat at the hands of an anti-democratic leader is nevertheless indicative of the lack of inspiring democratic leadership.

The second condition for the success of democracy is that the effective range of political decision should not be extended too far. How far it can be extended depends not only on the general limitations of the democratic method which follow from the analysis presented in the preceding section but also on the particular circumstances of each individual case. To put this more concretely: the range does not only depend, for instance, on the kind and quantity of matters that can be successfully handled by a government subject to the strain of an incessant struggle for its political life; it also depends, at any given time and place, on the quality of the men who form that government and on the type of political machine and the pattern of public opinion they have to work with. From the standpoint of our theory of democracy it is not necessary to require, as it would be from the standpoint of the classical theory, that only such matters should be dealt with by the political apparatus which the people at large can fully understand and have a serious opinion about. But a less exacting requirement of the same nature still imposes itself. It calls for additional comment.

Of course there cannot be any legal limits to what a parliament, led by the prime minister, might subject to its decision, if need be, by means of a constitutional amendment. But, so Edmund Burke argued in discussing the behavior of the English government and Parliament with respect to the American colonies, in order to function properly that all-powerful parliament must impose limits upon itself. Similarly we may argue that, even within the range of matters that have to be submitted to parliamentary vote, it is often necessary for government and parliament to pass measures on which their decision is purely formal or, at most, of a purely supervisory nature. Otherwise the democratic method may turn out legislative freaks. Take for instance the case of so bulky and so technical a measure as a criminal code. The democratic method will apply to the question whether or not a country is to have such a codification at all. It will also apply to certain "issues" that the government may choose to select for political decision which is more than formal—for instance, whether certain practices of labor or employers' associations should or should not be considered criminal. But for the rest, government and parliament will have to accept the specialists' advice whatever they may think themselves. For crime is a complex phenomenon. The term in fact covers many phenomena that have very little in common. Popular slogans about it are almost invariably wrong. And a rational treatment of it requires that legislation in this matter should be protected from both the fits of vindictiveness and the fits of sentimentality in which the laymen in the government and in the parliament are alternatingly prone to indulge. This is what I meant to convey by stressing the limitations upon the *effective* range of political decision—the range within which politicians decide in truth as well as in form.

Again, the condition in question can indeed be fulfilled by a corresponding limitation of the activities of the state. But it would be a serious misunderstanding if the reader thought that such a limitation is necessarily implied. Democracy does not require that every function of the state be subject to its political method. For instance, in most democratic countries a large measure of independence from political agencies is granted to the judges. Another instance is the position held by the Bank of England until 1914. Some of its functions were in fact of a public nature. Nevertheless these functions were vested with what legally was just a business corporation that was sufficiently independent of the political sector to have a policy of its own. Certain federal agencies in this country are other cases in point. The Interstate Commerce Commission embodies an attempt to extend the sphere of public authority without extending the sphere of political decision. Or, to present still another example, certain of our states finance state universities "without any strings," that is to say, without interfering with what in some cases amounts to practically complete autonomy.

Thus, almost any type of human affairs may conceivably be made to enter the sphere of the state without becoming part of the material of the competitive struggle for political leadership beyond what is implied in passing the measure that grants the power and sets up the agency to wield it and the contact that is implied in the government's role of general supervisor. It is of course true that this supervision may degenerate into vitiating influence. The politician's power to appoint the personnel of non-political public agencies, if remorselessly used, will often suffice in itself to corrupt them. But that does not affect the principle in question.

As a third condition, democratic government in modern industrial society must be able to command, for all purposes the sphere of public activity is to include—no matter whether this be much or little—the services of a well-trained bureaucracy of good standing and tradition, endowed with a strong sense of duty and a no less strong *esprit de corps*. Such a bureaucracy is the main answer to the argument about government by amateurs. Potentially it is the only answer to the question so often heard in this country: democratic politics has proved itself unable to produce decent city government; how can we expect the nation to fare if everything, eventually including the whole of the productive process, is to be handed over to it? And finally, it is also the principal answer to the question about how our second condition can be fulfilled[6] whenever the sphere of public control is wide.

It is not enough that the bureaucracy should be efficient in current administration and competent to give advice. It must also be strong enough to guide and, if need be, to instruct the politicians who head the ministries. In order to be able to do this it must be in a position to evolve principles of its own and sufficiently independent to assert them. It must be a power in its own right. This amounts to saying that in fact though not in form appointment, tenure and promotion must depend largely—within civil service rules that politicians hesitate to violate—on its own corporate opinion in spite of all the clamor that is sure to arise whenever politicians or the public find themselves crossed by it as they frequently must.

Again, as in the case of the personnel of politics, the question of the

[6] Reference to some comments on the subject of bureaucracy in ch. xviii will convince the reader that, in all three respects, the answer provided by bureaucracy is not held to be ideal in any sense. On the other hand readers should not allow themselves to be unduly influenced by the associations the term carries in popular parlance. In any case that answer is the only realistic one.

available human material is all-important. Training though essential is quite secondary to this. And again, both requisite material and the traditional code necessary for the functioning of an official class of this kind can be most easily secured if there is a social stratum of adequate quality and corresponding prestige that can be drawn upon for recruits—not too rich, not too poor, not too exclusive, not too accessible. The bureaucracies of Europe, in spite of the fact that they have drawn enough hostile criticism to blur their records, exemplify very well what I am trying to convey. They are the product of a long development that started with the *ministeriales* of medieval magnates (originally serfs selected for administrative and military purposes who thereby acquired the status of petty nobles) and went on through the centuries until the powerful engine emerged which we behold today. It cannot be created in a hurry. It cannot be "hired" with money. But it grows everywhere, whatever the political method a nation may adopt. Its expansion is the one certain thing about our future.

The fourth set of conditions may be summed up in the phrase Democratic Self-control. Everybody will of course agree that the democratic method cannot work smoothly unless all the groups that count in a nation are willing to accept any legislative measure as long as it is on the statute book and all executive orders issued by legally competent authorities. But democratic self-control implies much more than this.

Above all, electorates and parliaments must be on an intellectual and moral level high enough to be proof against the offerings of the crook and the crank, or else men who are neither will be driven into the ways of both. Moreover, miscarriages that will discredit democracy and undermine allegiance to it may also occur if measures are passed without regard to the claims of others or to the national situation. The individual proposals for legislative reform or executive action must, as it were, be content to stand in an orderly breadline; they must not attempt to rush the shop. Recalling what has been said in the preceding chapter about the *modus operandi* of the democratic method, the reader will realize that this involves a lot of voluntary subordination.

In particular, politicians in parliament must resist the temptation to upset or embarrass the government each time they could do so. No successful policy is possible if they do this. This means that the supporters of the government must accept its lead and allow it to frame and act upon a program and that the opposition should accept the lead of the "shadow cabinet" at its head and allow it to keep political warfare within certain rules. Fulfillment of this requirement, habitual violation of which spells the beginning of the end of a democracy, will be seen to call for just the right amount—not too much, not too little—of traditionalism. To protect this traditionalism is in fact one of the purposes for which rules of parliamentary procedure and etiquette exist.

The voters outside of parliament must respect the division of labor between themselves and the politicians they elect. They must not withdraw confidence too easily between elections and they must understand that, once they have elected an individual, political action is his business and not theirs. This means that they must refrain from instructing him about what he is to do—a principle that has indeed been universally recognized by constitutions and political theory ever since Edmund Burke's time. But its implications are not generally understood. On the one hand, few people realize that this principle clashes with the classical doctrine of democracy and really spells its abandonment. For if the people are to rule in the sense of deciding individual issues, what could be more natural for them to do than to issue instructions to their representatives as the voters for the French States-General did in and before 1789? On the other hand, it is still less recognized that if the principle be accepted, not only instructions as formal as those French *cahiers* but also less formal attempts at restricting the freedom of action of members of parliament—the practice of bombarding them with letters and telegrams for instance—ought to come under the same ban.

We cannot enter into the various delicate problems which this raises concerning the true nature of democracy as defined by us. All that matters here is that successful democratic practice in great and complicated societies has invariably been hostile to political back-seat driving—to the point of resorting to secret diplomacy and lying about intentions and commitments—and that it takes a lot of self-control on the part of the citizen to refrain from it.

Finally, effective competition for leadership requires a large measure of tolerance for difference of opinion. It has been pointed out before that this tolerance never is and never can be absolute. But it must be possible for every would-be leader who is not lawfully excluded to present his case without producing disorder. And this may imply that people stand by patiently while somebody is attacking their most vital interests or offending their most cherished ideals— or as an alternative, that the would-be leader who holds such views restrains himself correspondingly. Neither is possible without genuine respect for the opinions of one's fellow citizens amounting to a willingness to subordinate one's own opinions.

Every system can stand deviating practice to a certain extent. But even the necessary minimum of democratic self-control evidently requires a national character and national habits of a certain type which have not everywhere had the opportunity to evolve and which the democratic method itself cannot be relied on to produce. And nowhere will that self-control stand tests beyond a varying degree of severity. In fact the reader need only review our conditions in order to satisfy himself that democratic government will work to full advantage only if all the interests that matter are practically unanimous not only in their allegiance to the country but also in their allegiance to the structural principles of the existing society. Whenever these principles are called in question and issues arise that rend a nation into two hostile camps, democracy works at a disadvantage. And it may cease to work at all as soon as interests and ideals are involved on which people refuse to compromise.

This may be generalized to read that the democratic method will be at a disadvantage in troubled times. In fact, democracies of all types recognize with practical unanimity that there are situations in which it is reasonable to abandon competitive and to adopt monopolistic leadership. In ancient Rome a non-elective office conferring such a monopoly of leadership in emergencies was provided for by the constitution. The incumbent was called *magister populi* or *dictator*. Similar provisions are known to practically all constitutions, our own included: the President of the United States acquires in certain conditions a power that makes him to all intents and purposes a dictator in the Roman sense, however great the differences are both in legal construction and in practical details. If the monopoly is effectively limited either to a definite time (as it originally was in Rome) or to the duration of a definite short-run emergency, the democratic principle of competitive leadership is merely suspended. If the monopoly, either in law or in fact, is not limited as to time—and if not limited as to time it will of course tend to become unlimited as to everything else—the democratic principle is abrogated and we have the case of dictatorship in the present-day sense.[7]

III. Democracy in the Socialist Order

1. In setting forth our conclusions we had better begin with the relation between democracy and the capitalist order of things.

The ideology of democracy as reflected by the classical doctrine rests on a rationalist scheme of human action and of the values of life. By virtue of a previous argument (Chapter XI) this fact would in itself suffice to suggest that it is of bourgeois origin. History clearly confirms this suggestion: historically, the modern democracy rose along with capitalism, and in causal connection with it. But the same

---

[7] In ancient Rome whose term we are in the habit of misusing, an autocracy developed that for several centuries displayed certain features not dissimilar to those of modern dictatorships though the analogy should not be pushed too far. But that autocracy did not make use of the republican office of dictator except in one case, that of G. Julius Caesar. Sulla's dictatorship was simply a temporary magistracy created for a definite purpose (constitutional reform). And there are no other but quite "regular" cases.

holds true for democratic practice: democracy in the sense of our theory of competitive leadership presided over the process of political and institutional change by which the bourgeoisie reshaped, and from its own point of view rationalized, the social and political structure that preceded its ascendancy: the democratic method was the political tool of that reconstruction. We have seen that the democratic method works, particularly well, also in certain extra- and pre-capitalist societies. But modern democracy is a product of the capitalist process.

Whether or not democracy is one of those products of capitalism which are to die out with it is of course another question. And still another is how well or ill capitalist society qualifies for the task of working the democratic method it evolved.

As regards the latter question, it is clear that capitalist society qualifies well in one respect. The bourgeoisie has a solution that is peculiar to it for the problem of how the sphere of political decision can be reduced to those proportions which are manageable by means of the method of competitive leadership. The bourgeois scheme of things limits the sphere of politics by limiting the sphere of public authority; its solution is in the ideal of the parsimonious state that exists primarily in order to guarantee bourgeois legality and to provide a firm frame for autonomous individual endeavor in all fields. If, moreover, account be taken of the pacific—at any rate, anti-militarist—and free-trade tendencies we have found to be inherent in bourgeois society, it will be seen that the importance of the role of political decision in the bourgeois state can, in principle at least, be scaled down to almost any extent that the disabilities of the political sector may require.

Now this kind of state has no doubt ceased to appeal to us. Bourgeois democracy is certainly a very special historical case and any claims that may be made on behalf of it are obviously contingent upon acceptance of standards which are no longer ours. But it is absurd to deny that this solution which we dislike is a solution and that bourgeois democracy is democracy. On the contrary, as its colors fade it is all the more important to recognize how colorful it was in the time of its vitality; how wide *and equal* the opportunities it offered to the families (if not to the individuals); how large the personal freedom it granted to those who passed its tests (or to their children). It is also important to recognize how well it stood, for some decades at least, the strain of uncongenial conditions and how well it functioned, when faced by demands that were outside of and hostile to the bourgeois interests.

Also in another respect capitalist society in its meridian qualified well for the task of making democracy a success. It is easier for a class whose interests are best served by being left alone to practice demo-

cratic self-restraint than it is for classes that naturally try to live on
the state. The bourgeois who is primarily absorbed in his private
concerns is in general—as long as these concerns are not seriously
threatened—much more likely to display tolerance of political differences and respect for opinions he does not share than any other type
of human being. Moreover so long as bourgeois standards are dominant in a society this attitude will tend to spread to other classes as
well. The English landed interest accepted the defeat of 1845 with
relatively good grace; English labor fought for the removal of disabilities but until the beginning of the present century was slow to
claim privileges. It is true that in other countries such self-restraint
was much less in evidence. These deviations from the principle were
not always serious or always associated with capitalist interests only.
But in some cases political life all but resolved itself into a struggle
of pressure groups and in many cases practices that failed to conform
to the spirit of the democratic method have become important enough
to distort its *modus operandi*. That there "cannot" be true democracy
in the capitalist order is nevertheless an obvious over-statement.[8]

In both respects however capitalism is rapidly losing the advantages it used to possess. Bourgeois democracy which is wedded to
that ideal of the state has for some time been working with increasing
friction. In part this was due to the fact that, as we have seen before,
the democratic method never works at its best when nations are much
divided on fundamental questions of social structure. And this difficulty in turn proved particularly serious, because bourgeois society
signally failed to fulfill another condition for making the democratic
method function. The bourgeoisie produced individuals who made a
success at political leadership upon entering a political class of non-
bourgeois origin, but it did not produce a successful political stratum
of its own although, so one should think, the third generations of
the industrial families had all the opportunity to form one. Why
this was so has been fully explained in Part II. All these facts together seem to suggest a pessimistic prognosis for this type of democracy. They also suggest an explanation of the apparent ease with
which in some cases it surrendered to dictatorship.

2. The ideology of classical socialism is the offspring of bourgeois
ideology. In particular, it fully shares the latter's rationalist and utilitarian background and many of the ideas and ideals that entered the

---

[8] What should be said is that there are some deviations from the principle of
democracy which link up with the presence of organized capitalist interests. But
thus corrected, the statement is true both from the standpoint of the classical and
from the standpoint of our own theory of democracy. From the first standpoint,
the result reads that the means at the disposal of private interests are often used in
order to thwart the will of the people. From the second standpoint, the result reads
that those private means are often used in order to interfere with the working of the
mechanism of competitive leadership.

classical doctrine of democracy. So far as this goes, socialists in fact experienced no difficulty whatever in appropriating this part of the bourgeois inheritance and in making out a case for the proposition that those elements of the classical doctrine which socialism is unable to absorb—the emphasis on protection of private property for instance—are really at variance with its fundamental principles. Creeds of this kind could survive even in entirely non-democratic forms of socialism and we may trust the scribes and pharisees to bridge by suitable phrases any gap there may be between creed and practice. But it is the practice that interests us—the fate of democratic practice as interpreted by the doctrine of competitive leadership. And so, since we have seen that non-democratic socialism is perfectly possible, the real question is again how well or ill socialism qualifies for the task of making the democratic method function should it attempt to do so.

The essential point to grasp is this. No responsible person can view with equanimity the consequences of extending the democratic method, that is to say the sphere of "politics," to all economic affairs. Believing that democratic socialism means precisely this, such a person will naturally conclude that democratic socialism must fail. But this does not necessarily follow. As has been pointed out before, extension of the range of public management does not imply corresponding extension of the range of political management. Conceivably, the former may be extended so as to absorb a nation's economic affairs while the latter still remains within the boundaries set by the limitations of the democratic method.

It does follow however that in socialist society these limitations will raise a much more serious problem. For socialist society lacks the automatic restrictions imposed upon the political sphere by the bourgeois scheme of things. Moreover, in socialist society it will no longer be possible to find comfort in the thought that the inefficiencies of political procedure are after all a guarantee of freedom. Lack of efficient management will spell lack of bread. However, the agencies that are to operate the economic engine—the Central Board we met in Part III as well as the subordinate bodies entrusted with the management of individual industries or concerns—may be so organized and manned as to be sufficiently exempt in the fulfillment of their current duties from interference by politicians or, for that matter, by fussing citizens' committees or by their workmen. That is to say, they may be sufficiently removed from the atmosphere of political strife as to display no inefficiencies other than those associated with the term Bureaucracy. And even these *can* be much reduced by an appropriate concentration of responsibility on individuals and by a system of well-chosen incentives and penalties, of which the methods of appointment and promotion are the most important part.

Serious socialists, when off the stump and in a responsible mood, have always been aware of this problem and also of the fact that "democracy" is no answer to it. An interesting illustration is afforded by the deliberations of the German Committee on Socialization (*Sozialisierungs Kommission*). In 1919, when the German Social Democratic party had definitely set its face against bolshevism, the more radical among its members still believed that some measure of socialization was imminent as a matter of practical necessity and a committee was accordingly appointed in order to define aims and to recommend methods. It did not consist exclusively of socialists but socialist influence was dominating. Karl Kautsky was chairman. Definite recommendations were made only about coal and even these, arrived at under the gathering clouds of anti-socialist sentiment, are not very interesting. All the more interesting are the views that emerged in discussion at the time when more ambitious hopes still prevailed. The idea that managers of plants should be elected by the workmen of the same plants was frankly and unanimously condemned. The workmen's councils that had grown up during the months of universal breakdown were objects of dislike and suspicion. The committee, trying to get away as far as possible from the popular ideas about Industrial Democracy,[9] did its best to shape them into an innocuous mold and cared little for developing their functions. All the more did it care for strengthening the authority and safeguarding the independence of the managerial personnel. Much thought was bestowed on how to prevent managers from losing capitalist vitality and sinking into bureaucratic ruts. In fact—if it be possible to speak of results of discussions that were soon to lose practical importance—these socialist managers would not have differed very much from their capitalist predecessors, and in many cases the same individuals would have been reappointed. We thus reach, by a different route, the conclusion already arrived at in Part III.

But we are now in a position to link up this conclusion with an answer to the problem of democracy in socialism. In a sense, of course, the present-day forms and organs of democratic procedure are as much the outgrowth of the structure and the issues of the bourgeois

[9] Industrial or Economic Democracy is a phrase that figures in so many quasi-utopias that it has retained very little precise meaning. Mainly, I think, it means two things: first, the trade-union rule over industrial relations; second, democratization of the monarchic factory by workmen's representation on boards or other devices calculated to secure them influence on the introduction of technological improvements, business policy in general and, of course, discipline in the plant in particular, including methods of "hiring and firing." Profit-sharing is a nostrum of a subgroup of schemes. It is safe to say that much of this economic democracy will vanish into thin air in a socialist regime. Nor is this so offensive as it may sound. For many of the interests this kind of democracy is intended to safeguard will then cease to exist.

world as is the fundamental principle of democracy itself. But this is no reason why they should have to disappear along with capitalism. General elections, parties, parliaments, cabinets and prime ministers may still prove to be the most convenient instruments for dealing with the agenda that the socialist order may reserve for political decision. The list of these agenda will be relieved of all those items that at present arise from the clash of private interests and from the necessity of regulating them. Instead there will be new ones. There will be such questions to decide as what the volume of investment should be or how existing rules for the distribution of the social product should be amended and so on. General debates about efficiency, investigation committees of the type of the English Royal Commissions would continue to fulfill their present functions.

Thus the politicians in the cabinet, and in particular the politician at the head of the Ministry of Production, would no doubt assert the influence of the political element, both by their legislative measures concerning the general principles of running the economic engine and by their power to appoint which could not be entirely absent or entirely formal. But they need not do so to an extent incompatible with efficiency. And the Minister of Production need not interfere more with the internal working of individual industries than English Ministers of Health or of War interfere with the internal working of their respective departments.

3. It goes without saying that operating socialist democracy in the way indicated would be a perfectly hopeless task except in the case of a society that fulfills all the requirements of "maturity" listed in Part III, including, in particular, the ability to establish the socialist order in a democratic way and the existence of a bureaucracy of adequate standing and experience. But a society that does fulfill these requirements—I shall not deal with any other—would first of all command an advantage of possibly decisive importance.

I have emphasized that democracy cannot be expected to function satisfactorily unless the vast majority of the people in all classes are resolved to abide by the rules of the democratic game and that this in turn implies that they are substantially agreed on the fundamentals of their institutional structure. At present the latter condition fails to be fulfilled. So many people have renounced, and so many more are going to renounce, allegiance to the standards of capitalist society that on this ground alone democracy is bound to work with increasing friction. At the stage visualized however, socialism may remove the rift. It may reestablish agreement as to the tectonic principles of the social fabric. If it does, then the remaining antagonisms will be exactly of the kind with which the democratic method is well able to cope.

It has also been pointed out in Part III that those remaining antagonisms will be further decreased in number and importance by the elimination of clashing capitalist interests. The relations between agriculture and industry, small-scale and large-scale industry, steel-producing and steel-consuming industries, protectionist and export industries will—or may—cease to be political questions to be settled by the relative weights of pressure groups and become technical questions to which technicians would be able to give unemotional and unequivocal answers. Though it may be utopian to expect that there would be no distinct economic interests or conflicts between them, and still more utopian to expect that there would be no non-economic issues to disagree about, a good case may be made out for expecting that the sum total of controversial matter would be decreased even as compared with what it was in intact capitalism. There would, for instance, be no silver men. Political life would be purified.

On the face of it, socialism has no obvious solution to offer for the problem solved in other forms of society by the presence of a political class of stable traditions. I have said before that there will be a political profession. There may evolve a political set, about the quality of which it is idle to speculate.

Thus far socialism scores. It might still be argued that this score can be easily balanced by the importance and likelihood of possible deviations. To some extent we have provided for this by insisting on economic maturity which among other things implies that no great sacrifices need be required of one generation for the benefit of a later one. But even if there is no necessity for sweating the people by means of a Gosplan, the task of keeping the democratic course may prove to be extremely delicate. Circumstances in which the individuals at the helm would normally succeed in solving it are perhaps no easier to imagine than circumstances in which, faced by a spectacle of paralysis spreading from the political sector all over the nation's economy, they might be driven into a course of action which must always have some temptation for men beholding the tremendous power over the people inherent in the socialist organization. After all, effective management of the socialist economy means dictatorship not *of* but *over* the proletariat in the factory. The men who are there so strictly disciplined would, it is true, be sovereign at the elections. But just as they may use this sovereignty in order to relax the discipline of the factory, so governments—precisely the governments which have the future of the nation at heart—may avail themselves of this discipline in order to restrict this sovereignty. As a matter of practical necessity, socialist democracy may eventually turn out to be more of a sham than capitalist democracy ever was.

In any case, that democracy will not mean increased personal freedom. And, once more, it will mean no closer approximation to the ideals enshrined in the classical doctrine.

PART V

A Historical Sketch of Socialist Parties

PROLOGUE

IT IS not for me to write a history of the socialist parties. Both the settings in which they rose and fell and the ways in which they grappled with their problems call for a larger canvas and a mightier brush than mine. Also, the time has not yet come to make the attempt: though the last twenty years have brought up many valuable monographs that shed all the light we need on particular situations or phases, a vast amount of research has still to be done before a history of modern socialism in action can be written that will meet the requirements of scholarship. But certain facts are necessary in order to complement and to put into the proper perspective much of what has been said in the preceding parts of this book. And some other points that have occurred to me from study or personal observation[1] I wish to present because they seem to be interesting on their own account. For this double purpose I have assembled the fragments that are to follow, in the hope that even fragments may indicate the contours of the whole.

Not every reader—not even every socialist reader—will approve of the central position this fragment gives to Marx and Marxism. I readily confess to personal bias in the matter. For me, the fascinating thing about socialist policy—the thing that gives it a special claim to attention and a dignity all its own that is both intellectual and moral—is its clear and close relation to a doctrinal basis. In principle at least, it is theory implemented by action or inaction turning on the true or false perception of a historical necessity. (See Part I.) Even considerations of expediency and mere tactics carry that *character indelebilis* and always have been discussed in the light of that principle. But all this is true only of the Marxian streak; no truer, of course, than it is, within the bourgeois compound, of the Benthamite radicals—the "philosophical" radicals as they were significantly called. All non-Marxian socialist groups are more or less like other groups and parties; only Marxists of pure persuasion consistently walked in the light of a doctrine that to them contained all answers to all questions. As will be seen, I do not admire this attitude unconditionally. It may well be called narrow and even naïve. But the doctrinaires of all types, whatever their practical disabilities, have certain esthetic qualities that raise them high above the common run of political practitioners. Also they command sources of strength which mere practitioners will never be able to understand.

[1] One of these points has been dealt with elsewhere. See ch xx.

CHAPTER XXIV

THE NONAGE

Sociaⅼist doctrines, in some of their roots presumably as old as articulate thought, were dreams, beautiful or hateful—impotent longings out of contact with social realities—so long as they lacked the means to convince anybody that the social process worked for the realization of socialism. Socialist effort amounted to preaching in the desert so long as it had no established contact with an existing or potential source of social power—to preaching of the Platonic type about which no politician need bother and which no observer of social processes need list among operative factors.

This is the gist of Marx's criticism of most of the socialists who preceded him or in his day offered competitive teaching, and the reason why he called them utopian. The point was not so much that many of their schemes were obviously freaks or otherwise below par intellectually, but that those schemes were essentially unimplemented and unimplementable. A few examples will illustrate this and will stand instead of a survey of a large body of literature. Also they will suffice to show how far Marx's judgment was wrong.

Sir Thomas More's (1478-1535) *Utopia,* read, admired and even copied right into the nineteenth century—witness the success of Cabet and of Bellamy—unfolds the picture of a frugal, moral and equalitarian society that was the exact opposite of English society in More's day. This ideal may be but the literary form of social criticism. Perhaps we need not accept it for a presentation of More's opinion about the aims of practical social planning. However, if it be understood in the latter sense—and so it was—the trouble with it does not lie in its impracticability. In some respects it is less impracticable than are certain present-day forms of idyllic socialism. For instance, it faces the question of authority and it frankly accepts the prospect—exalted no doubt into a virtue—of a modest standard of life. The real trouble is that there is no attempt to show how society is to evolve toward that ideal state (except possibly by conversion) or what the real factors are that might be worked upon in order to produce it. We can like or dislike the ideal. But we cannot do much about it. To put the practical dot on the i, there is nothing in it on which to found a party and to provide a program.

Another type may be instanced by Robert Owen's (1771-1858) socialism. A manufacturer and practical reformer, he was not content to conceive—or adopt—the idea of small self-sufficing communities, producing and consuming their means of livelihood according to communist principles in the word's boldest acceptance. He actually went about realizing it. First he hoped for government action, then he tried the effect of setting an example. So it might seem that the plan was more operational than More's: there was not only an ideal but also a bridge leading to it. Actually however that kind of bridge only serves to illustrate more precisely the nature of utopianism. For both government action and individual efforts are introduced as *dei ex machina*—the thing would have had to be done just because some agent thought it worth while. No social force working toward the goal was indicated or could have been indicated. No soil was provided for the rose trees—they were left to feed on beauty.[1]

The same applies to Proudhon's (1809-1865) anarchism, except that in his case definite economic error is much more in evidence than it is with most of the other classics of anarchism who despised economic argument and, whether stressing the ideal of free and stateless co-operation of individuals or the task of destruction to be accomplished in order to make way for it, avoided errors of reasoning largely by avoiding reasoning. Like "poet, lunatic and lover of imagination all compact," they were constitutionally unable to do anything except to upset socialist applecarts and to add to confusion in situations of revolutionary excitement. It is not difficult to sympathize with Marx's disgust, that sometimes was not unmixed with despair, at the doings of M. Bakunin.

But anarchism was utopianism with a vengeance. The pathological species has been mentioned only in order to make it quite clear that such revivals of fourteenth-century mentality should not be confused with the genuine brand of utopian socialism which St. Simon's (1760-1825) writings display at its best. There we find sense and responsibility coupled with considerable analytic power. The goal envisaged was not absurd or visionary. What was lacking was the way: again the only method suggested was government action—action by governments that at the time were essentially bourgeois.

If this view be accepted, the great break that put an end to the nonage of socialism must in fact be associated with the name and

[1] The same is true of the similar plan of Charles Fourier (1772-1837) which will not however be called socialist by everyone, since labor was to receive only 5/12 of the social product, the rest going to capital and management. Though in itself this was a meritorious attempt to take account of realities, it is amusing to note that labor would in that ideal state of things have done worse than it actually does in capitalist society. In prewar England for instance (see A. Bowley, *The Division of the Product of Industry*, 1921, p. 37), wages and salaries under £160 absorbed, in manufacturing and mining, 62 per cent of the value of net output or, counting in salaries above £160, 68 per cent. Of course Fourier's ideals were not primarily economic, but as far as they were, they illustrate well how large an element of ignorance about capitalist facts enters into reformist creeds.

work of Karl Marx. We may then date it, so far as in such matters dating is possible at all, by the issue of the *Manifesto of the Communist Party* (1848) or by the foundation of the First International (1864): it was in that period that both the doctrinal and the political criteria of seriousness were met. But, on the one hand, this achievement only summed up the developments of the centuries of nonage and, on the other hand, it formulated them in a particular way that perhaps was practically, but certainly was not logically, the only possible one. To some extent, therefore, the judgment passed by orthodox socialism on the men of the nonage must be revised.

First of all, if the socialist schemes of those centuries were dreams, most of them were rationalized dreams. And what individual thinkers more or less perfectly succeeded in rationalizing were not simply their individual dreams but the dreams of the non-ruling classes. Thus, those thinkers were not living completely in the clouds; they also helped to bring to the surface what slumbered below but was getting ready to wake up. In this respect even the anarchists, back to their medieval predecessors who flourished in many a convent and still more in the tertiary groups of the Franciscan Order, acquire a significance which Marxists usually do not accord to them. However contemptible their beliefs may seem to the orthodox socialist, much of the propelling force of socialism comes, even today, from those irrational longings of the hungry *soul*—not belly—which they voiced.[2]

Second, the socialist thinkers of the nonage provided many a brick and many a tool that proved useful later on. After all, the very idea of a socialist society was their creation, and it was owing to their efforts that Marx and his contemporaries were able to discuss it as a thing familiar to everyone. But many of the utopians went much further than that. They worked out details of the socialist plan or of certain variants of it, thereby formulating problems—however inadequately—and clearing much ground. Even their contribution to purely economic analysis cannot be neglected. It provided a much-needed leaven in an otherwise distressingly stodgy pudding. Much of it moreover was simply professional work that improved existing theory and, among other things, stood Marx in good stead. The English socialists and quasi-socialists who elaborated the labor theory of value—such men as William Thompson—afford the best example of this.

Third, not all of those whom Marxists include among the utopians

---

[2] That is why the trained socialist's endeavors to shake off what he himself admits to be nonsensical or visionary in the creed of the untutored believer can never be wholly successful. The popular appeal of socialism is due *not* to what can be rationally established about it, but precisely to those mystic heresies which bourgeois and socialist economists unite in· condemning. In trying to distance himself, the socialist not only is being ungrateful to the wave that carries him, but he is also courting the danger that its forces might be harnessed into other service.

lacked contact with mass movements. Some contact inevitably resulted from the fact that the social and economic conditions which set in motion the intellectual's pen will also set in motion some group or class of the people—peasants or artisans or agricultural laborers or simply the vagrants and the rabble. But many of the utopians established much closer contact. The demands of the peasants during the revolutions of the sixteenth century were already formulated by intellectuals, and coordination and cooperation steadily became closer as the centuries rolled on. "Gracchus" Babeuf, the leading spirit of the only purely socialist movement within the French Revolution, was considered of sufficient importance for the government to pay him the compliment of executing him in 1797. Again England best illustrates this development. We need only compare, from this angle, the history of the Leveller movement in the seventeenth and the Chartist movement in the nineteenth centuries. In the first case, Winstanley joined and led as an individual; in the second case, groups of intellectuals reacted in a body and though their cooperation tapered off into Christian Socialism, it was not merely an affair of the student's closet entirely divorced from a contemporaneous mass movement. In France, the best example is afforded by Louis Blanc's activities in 1848. In this as in other respects, therefore, utopian socialism differed from "scientific" socialism in degree rather than in kind: the relation of the socialists of the nonage to class movements was occasional and not as a rule a matter of fundamental principle, whereas with Marx and with post-Marxian socialism it became precisely a matter of fundamental principle and similar to the relation of a government to its standing army.

A very important point—I hope it will not prove a stumbling block—remains to be made. I have said that the doctrine which avers the presence of a tendency toward socialism,[3] and the permanent contact with an existing or potential source of social power—the two requisites of socialism as a serious political factor—were definitely established around the middle of the nineteenth century in a way that was logically not the only possible one. Marx and most of his contemporaries imparted a particular slant to their doctrine by holding that the laboring class was the only one to be actively associated with this tendency and that hence it was the only source of power for the socialist to tap. For them, socialism meant primarily liberation of labor from exploitation, and "the emancipation of the workers must be the task of the working class itself."

[3] For the precise meaning of this phrase the reader should again turn to our discussions in Parts I and II. Here it means two things: first, that real social forces, independent of desirabilities or undesirabilities, are making for socialism which therefore will increasingly acquire the character of a practical proposition; second, that this being so, there is *present* room for party activities on socialist lines. The latter point will be discussed in ch. xxv.

Now it is easy to understand why, as a practical proposition, the conquest of the labor interest should have appealed to Marx more than any other course, and why his doctrine should have been shaped accordingly. But the idea has become so firmly rooted, also in some non-socialist minds, as to blot out completely some facts which it takes a lot of trouble to explain away, viz., that the labor movement, though often allied with socialism, has remained distinct from it to this day, and that it proved by no means so easy for socialists to establish in the workers' world spheres of influence in which their creed is accepted as a matter of course. However we may interpret these facts, it should be clear that the labor movement is not essentially socialist, just as socialism is not necessarily laborite or proletarian. Nor is this surprising. For we have seen in Part II that though the capitalist process slowly socializes economic life and much besides, this spells transformation of the *whole* of the social organism *all* parts of which are equally affected. The real income and the social weight of the working class rise in this process, and capitalist society becomes more and more incapable of dealing with labor difficulties. But this is a poor substitute for the Marxian picture of labor being goaded into the grand revolution by increasingly intolerable suffering. If we discard this picture and realize that what actually increases is labor's stake in the capitalist system, we shall inevitably think less of the particular call addressed to the working class by the logic of evolution. Still less convincing is the role that Marxism assigns to the proletariat in the catastrophe of the social drama. There is little for it to do if the transformation is gradual. And if there be a grand revolution, the proletariat will simply be talked and bullied into consent. The spearhead will be formed by intellectuals assisted by the semi-criminal rabble. And Marx's ideas on the subject are nothing but "ideology"—just as utopian as any beliefs of the utopists.

Thus, while it remains substantially true that, unlike most of his predecessors, Marx intended to rationalize an existing movement and not a dream, and also that he and his successors actually gained partial control of that movement, the difference is smaller than Marxists would have us believe. There was, as we have seen, more of realism in the thought of the utopists, and there was more of unrealistic dreaming in Marx's thought than they admit.

In the light of this fact, we shall think better of the socialists of the nonage *because* they did not exclusively stress the proletarian aspect. In particular their appeal to governments or to classes other than the proletariat will appear to us less visionary and more realistic than it appeared to Marx. For the state, its bureaucracy and the groups that man the political engine are quite promising prospects for the socialist looking for his source of social power. As should be evident by now, they are likely to move in the desired direction with no less "dialectical" necessity than are the masses. And that excrescence of the bourgeois stratum which we shall term (*a potiori*) Fabian Socialism[4] is also suggestive. Marx's choice of social motive power thus produced a special case which, though practically the most important, yet stands logically on a par with others that are frauds and heresies to the orthodox.

[4] See ch. xxvi. Marxists will naturally reply that those phenomena are mere derivates of the genuine one, mere effects of the forward march of the proletariat. This is true if it means that the latter is one of the factors in the situation which produced and is producing the former. But taken in this sense, this proposition does not constitute an objection. If it means that there is a one-way or purely cause-effect relation between proletarian and state socialism, then it does constitute an objection but it is wrong. The socio-psychological process described in Part II will, without any pressure from below, produce state and Fabian socialism which *will even help to produce that pressure.* As we shall presently see, it is a fair question to ask where socialism would be without the fellow traveler. It is certain that socialism (as distinguished from the labor movement of the trade-union type) would be nowhere without the intellectual leader of bourgeois extraction.

CHAPTER XXV

THE SITUATION THAT MARX FACED

1. According to Engels, Marx in 1847 adopted the term "communist" in preference to the term "socialist," because socialism had by that time acquired a flavor of bourgeois respectability. However that may have been and however we choose to explain this fact if it was a fact—more than once we have seen good reason for interpreting socialism as a product of the bourgeois mentality—there cannot be any doubt that Marx and Engels themselves were typical bourgeois intellectuals. Exiles of bourgeois extraction and tradition—this formula accounts for a lot both in Marx's thought and in the policies and political tactics he recommended. The astounding thing is the extent to which his ideas prevailed.

First of all, the uprooted intellectual, with the formative experience of 1848 forever impressed upon his whole soul, cast off his own class and was cast off by it. Similarly uprooted intellectuals and, at one remove, the proletarian masses were henceforth all that was accessible to him and all he had to put his trust in. This explains the doctrine which, as we have seen in the preceding chapter, does stand in need of explanation, viz., that workers would "emancipate themselves."

Second, the same uprooted intellectual naturally became internationalist *in feeling*. This meant more than that the problems and vicissitudes of any particular country—even of individual national proletariats—did not primarily concern him and always remained on the periphery of his interests. It meant that it was so much easier for him to create the hypernational socialist religion and to conceive of an international proletariat the component parts of which were, in principle at least, much more closely wedded to each other than each of them was to its own co-nationals of a different class. Anyone could in cold logic have framed this obviously unrealistic conception and all that it implies for the interpretation of past history and for the views of Marxist parties on foreign policy. But then it would have had to contend with all the affective influences exerted by the national environments and could never have been passionately embraced by a man tied to a country by innumerable bonds. No such bonds existed for Marx. Having no country himself he readily convinced himself that the proletariat had none.

We shall presently see why—and how far—this teaching survived and what, under varying circumstances, it was made to mean. Marx himself no doubt accepted its non-interventionist and pacifist impli-cations. He certainly thought not only that "capitalist wars" were of no concern to the proletariat but also that they were the means of subjugating it still more completely. The concession he may be held to have made, i.e., that participation in the defense of one's own country against attack is not incompatible with the duties of the faithful, obviously was no more than a very necessary tactical device.

Third, whatever his doctrine may have been,[1] the uprooted bour-geois had democracy in his blood. That is to say, belief in that part of the bourgeois scheme of values which centers in democracy was for him not alone a matter of the rational perception of the condi-tions peculiar to the social pattern of his or any other time. Nor was it merely a matter of tactics. It is true that socialist activities (and his personal work) could not have been carried on, not with any comfort at all events, in any environment professing other than democratic principles as then understood. Save in very exceptional cases, every opposition must stand for freedom—which for him meant democracy—and throw itself on the mercy of "the people." Of course this element was and in some countries is even now very important. This is precisely, as I have pointed out, why democratic professions by socialist parties do not mean much until their political power becomes great enough to give them a choice of an alternative, and why they do not, in particular, avail to establish any fundamental relation between the logic of socialism and the logic of democracy. But it nevertheless seems safe to say that for Marx democracy was above discussion and any other political pattern below it. This much must be granted to the revolutionary of the 1848 type.[2] Of course it was out of the question for him to accept so important an article of the bourgeois faith as it stood. That would have uncovered a most inconveniently large expanse of common ground. But we have seen in the preceding part that he knew how to meet this difficulty by boldly claiming that only socialist democracy was true democracy and that bourgeois democracy was no democracy at all.

2. Such then was Marx's political *apriori*.[3] No need to emphasize that it was totally different from the *aprioris* of the average English socialist not only of his own but of any time—so different as to render mutual sympathy and even full mutual understanding almost impos-sible, quite irrespective of Hegelianism and other doctrinal barriers. The same difference will stand out still better if we compare Marx to

[1] See ch. xx and xxiii.

[2] The emotional attitude acquired in 1848 also made it quite impossible for him to understand, let alone to do justice to, the non-democratic regime that exiled him. Dispassionate analysis could not have failed to reveal its achievements and possibilities. But such analysis was in this case quite beyond his range.

[3] No language that I know officially admits this word as a noun. To make it one is however a very convenient solecism.

another German intellectual of very similar background, Ferdinand Lassalle (1825-1864). The scion of the same race, the product of the same stratum, molded by a closely similar cultural tradition, similarly conditioned by the experiences of 1848 and by the ideology of bourgeois democracy, Lassalle yet differs from Marx in a manner that cannot be explained wholly by the personal equation. Much more vital than this was the fact that Marx was an exile and Lassalle was not. Lassalle never cut himself off from his country or from classes other than the proletariat. He never was an internationalist like Marx. By proletariat he meant primarily the German proletariat. He had no objection to cooperation with the state that was. He did not object to personal contact with Bismarck or with the king of Bavaria. Such things are important, more important perhaps than the most profound doctrinal differences, important enough to produce different kinds of socialism and irreconcilable antagonisms.

Let us now take our stand on Marx's *apriori* and survey the political data that confronted him.

At first, the huge industrial masses of which Marx wrote and thought existed nowhere except in England. Even there, the chartist movement having petered out by the time he had found his bearings, the working class was becoming increasingly realistic and conservative. Disappointed by the failure of earlier radical activities, the men were turning away from flashy programs and from songs about their right to the total product. They soberly embarked upon an attempt to increase their share in it. The leaders were cautiously trying to establish, to buttress and to increase the legal status and the economic power of the trade unions within the political framework of bourgeois society. On principle as well as for obvious tactical considerations, they were bound to look upon revolutionary ideas or activities as a nuisance and as a stupid or frivolous sabotage of labor's serious business. Also, they concerned themselves with the upper stratum of the working class; for the lower, they harbored feelings that were akin to contempt.

In any case however, Marx and Engels, circumstanced as they were and being the types they were, could never have thought of going forth in order to organize the industrial proletariat, or any particular group of it, according to ideas of their own. All they could hope for was contact with leaders and with the union bureaucracy. Beholding, on the one hand, that attitude of the "respectable" workman and, on the other hand, the attitude of the (then) unorganizable mob of the big cities with which they hardly wished to act,[4] they faced a disagreeable dilemma. They could not fail to recognize the importance of the trade-union movement that was about to accomplish, step by

[4] Marxians are, it should be remembered, quite prone to speak of a proletarian mob (*Lumpenproletariat*).

step, the gigantic task of organizing the masses into something like an articulate class, that is to say, to solve the problem which they themselves felt to be the most important of all. But, being completely out of it and realizing the danger that this class might acquire bourgeois standing and adopt a bourgeois attitude, they were bound to dislike and to distrust the trade unions as much as they were disliked and distrusted—as far as they were noticed at all—by them. They were thus driven back upon the position that has become characteristic of classical socialism and that, though much reduced in importance, to this day expresses the fundamental antagonism between the socialist intellectuals and labor (which may in important cases be roughly equated to the antagonism between socialist parties and trade unions). For them, the trade-union movement was something to be converted to the doctrine of class war; as a means of such conversion, occasional cooperation with it was proper for the faithful whenever labor troubles radicalized the masses and sufficiently worried or excited trade-union officials to induce them to listen to the gospel. But so long as conversion was not complete and in particular so long as trade-union opinion remained on principle averse to revolutionary or simply to political action, the movement was not in a state of grace but on the contrary in error, misconceiving its own true ends, deluding itself with trivialities that were worse than futile; hence, except for the purpose of boring from within, the faithful had to keep aloof.

This situation changed even during Marx's and still more during Engels' lifetime. The growth of the industrial proletariat that eventually made it a power also on the Continent and the unemployment incident to the depressions of that period increased their influence with labor leaders though they never acquired any direct influence on the masses. To the end however it was mainly the intellectuals that supplied them the material to work with. But though their success in that quarter was considerable, the intellectuals gave them still more trouble than did the indifference, occasionally amounting to hostility, of the labor men. There was a fringe of socialist intellectuals that had no objection to identifying themselves either with the trade unions or with social reform of the bourgeois-radical or even the conservative type. And these of course dispensed a very different socialism which, holding out the promise of immediate benefit, was a dangerous competitor. There were moreover intellectuals, foremost among them Lassalle, who had conquered positions among the masses that were still more directly competitive. And finally there were intellectuals who went far enough as regards revolutionary ardor, but whom Marx and Engels quite rightly looked upon as the worst enemies of serious socialism—the "putschists" like Blanqui, the dreamers, the anarchists and so on. Doctrinal as well as tactical considerations rendered it imperative to meet all of these groups with an unflinching No.

3. That doctrinal background and that tactical situation made it extremely difficult for Marx to find answers for two vital questions which every follower or would-be follower was sure to ask: the question of the attitude toward the policies of the bourgeois parties and the question of the immediate program.

As regards the first, socialist parties could not be advised to watch bourgeois politics in silence. Their obvious task was to criticize capitalist society, to expose the masquerade of class interests, to point out how much better everything would be in the socialist paradise and to beat up for recruits: to criticize and to organize. However, a wholly negative attitude, though quite satisfactory as a principle, would have been impossible for any party of more than negligible political importance to keep up. It would inevitably have collided with most of the real desiderata of organized labor and, if persisted in for any length of time, would have reduced the followers to a small group of political ascetics. Considering the influence that Marx's teaching exerted, right up to 1914, on the great German party and on many smaller groups it is interesting to see how he dealt with this difficulty.

So far as he felt it possible to do so, he took the only position that was logically unimpeachable. Socialists must refuse to participate in the sham improvements by which the bourgeoisie tried to deceive the proletariat. Such participation—later dubbed Reformism—spelled lapse from the Faith, betrayal of the true aims, an insidious attempt to patch up what should be destroyed. Disciples like Bebel who made the pilgrimage to the shrine after having thus strayed from the right path were soundly rated. It is true that Marx and Engels themselves had at the time of their communist party of 1847 contemplated cooperation with left-wing bourgeois groups. Also, the Communist Manifesto recognized the necessity of occasional compromises and alliances, just as it allowed that tactics would have to differ according to the circumstances of time and place. So much was implied in the maxim enjoined upon the faithful to make use of all the antagonisms between the bourgeoisies of different countries and between bourgeois groups within every country—for this can hardly be done without a measure of cooperation with some of them. But all that only amounted to qualifying a principle in order to uphold it the more effectively. In each case, the exception had to be severely scrutinized, the presumption being always against it. Moreover, it was cooperation in certain definite emergencies, preferably revolutions, that was envisaged rather than more durable alliance involving understandings in the ordinary run of political life which might endanger the purity of the creed.

How Marxists should behave when confronted by a particular

policy of the bourgeois enemy that clearly benefits the proletariat, we may infer from the example set by the master himself in a very important instance. Free trade was one of the main planks in the platform of English liberalism. Marx was far too good an economist not to see what boon, in the circumstances of that time, it conferred upon the working class. The boon might be belittled, the motives of bourgeois free traders might be reviled. But that did not solve the problem, for surely socialists would have to support free trade, particularly in foodstuffs. Well, so they should but not of course because cheap bread was a boon—oh, no!—but because free trade would quicken the pace of social evolution, hence the advent of the social revolution. The tactical trick is admirable. The argument is moreover quite true and admits of application to a great many cases. The oracle did not say however what socialists should do about policies which, while also benefiting the proletariat, do not promote capitalist evolution—such as most measures of social betterment, social insurance and the like—or which, while promoting capitalist evolution, do not directly benefit the proletariat. But if the bourgeois camp should split upon such questions the road was clear by virtue of the precept to make use of capitalist dissensions. From this angle Marx would also have dealt with reforms sponsored, in opposition to the bourgeoisie by extra-bourgeois elements such as the landed aristocracy and gentry although, in his schema of things, there was no separate place for this phenomenon.

The second question was no less thorny. No party can live without a program that holds out the promise of immediate benefits. But in strict logic Marxism had no such program to offer. Anything positive done or to be done in the vitiated atmosphere of capitalism was *ipso facto* tainted. Marx and Engels were in fact worrying about this and always discouraged programs that involved constructive policy within the capitalist order and inevitably savored of bourgeois radicalism. However, when they themselves faced the problem in 1847, they resolutely cut the Gordian knot. The Communist Manifesto quite illogically lists a number of immediate objects of socialist policy, simply laying the socialist barge alongside the liberal liner.

Free education, universal suffrage, suppression of child labor, a progressive income tax, nationalization of land, banking and transportation, expansion of state enterprise, reclamation of waste lands, *compulsory industrial service for all,* the spreading out of industrial centers over the country—all this clearly measures the extent to which (at that time) Marx and Engels allowed themselves to be opportunist though they were inclined to deny the privilege to other socialists. For the striking thing about this program is the absence of any plank that we should recognize as typically or exclusively socialist if we met it in another entourage; any single one of them could figure in a non-

socialist program—even the nationalization of land has been advocated, on special grounds, by otherwise bourgeois writers—and most
of them are simply taken from the radical stockpot. This was of course
the only sensible thing to do. But all the same it was a mere make-
shift, obviously intended to serve no other purpose than that of
covering an embarrassing practical weakness. Had Marx been interested in those items for their own sake, he would have had no alternative but to coalesce with the radical wing of bourgeois liberalism. As
it was, they mattered little to him and he felt no obligation to make
any sacrifice for their sake; had the bourgeois radicals carried them
all, this would presumably have come to Marx as a very disagreeable
surprise.

4. The same principles, the same tactics and similar political data
produced the Inaugural Address to the International Workmen's Association (the "First International") in 1864. The foundation of the
latter meant indeed a great stride beyond the German *Arbeiterbil-
dungsverein* of 1847 or the little international group of the same year.
It was of course no organization of socialist parties—though for instance the two German ones joined, the Lassallean *Allgemeiner
Deutscher Arbeiterverein* speedily resigned—and still less an international organization of the proletariat. But labor groups from many
lands and of many types were actually represented and even English
trade unions showed interest enough to bear for a time, in a rather
noncommittal way and with an eye to possible immediate advantages,
with a somewhat uncongenial alliance. George Odger figured among
the founders.[5] The large claims made by the Association and some
of its historians concerning its role in the revolutionary movements
and the major labor troubles of the time will bear discounting. But
if it effected little and never led or controlled, it at least offered
unifying phraseology. And it established contacts that in the end
might have raised it, with the kind assistance of its bourgeois enemies
who were foolish enough to advertise for it, to a position of real importance. In the beginning all went fairly well and the first four
"congresses" were distinctly successful, certain unsocialist incidents,
such as the vote upholding the principle of inheritance, being tactfully overlooked by the orthodox members. Bakunin's invasion (1869)
and expulsion (1872) however dealt a blow from which the Association proved unable to recover though it lingered on till 1874.

Marx was from the first aware of the possibilities and of the dangers
inherent in that caravanserai which held intellectuals of doubtful
standing alongside of labor men obviously determined to use the

---

[5] He even acted as president of the International's council. That meant a lot,
since he had been one of the most prominent promoters of federation and amalga-
mation among trade unions, an organizer of the London Trade Council and a
leading officer of the reform league for the enfranchisement of urban workers.

Association or to disown it according to circumstances. They were the possibilities for which, and the dangers against which, he had always fought. The first task was to keep the organization together, the second to impart to it the Marxian slant, both to be solved in the face of the facts, that his personal followers were always a minority and that his influence on the other members was much smaller than might be inferred from his being drafted—or rather allowed—to make the program address. In consequence, this address contained concessions to un-Marxian views similar to those which Marx himself was shocked to find in the Gotha program of the German Social Democratic party (1875). Similarly, judicious maneuvering and compromise were much in evidence ever after—the sort of thing that once made Marx exclaim in semi-humorous despair: *"Je ne suis pas Marxiste."* But the meaning of compromise depends upon the man by whom, and the spirit in which, it is made. He who cares only for the trend may put up with many deviations. Evidently Marx trusted himelf to keep his trend steadily in view and to find his way back to it after each deviation. But we shall understand that he felt misgivings when he saw others playing the same game. There was thus more than mere egotism both in his tactical shuffling and in his venomous denunciations of other people's shuffling.

Of course both the tactics and the principle of what has ever since remained the classical policy of orthodox socialism are open to criticism. The tactical example set by Marx left followers free to justify practically any course of action or inaction by some move or dictum of the master. The principle has been denounced for pointing a way that led nowhere. All the more important is it to realize its rationale. Marx believed in the proletarian revolution. He also believed—though his own doctrine should have made him doubt this—that the right moment for it was not far off, just as most early Christians believed that the day of judgment was at hand. Therefore, his political method was indeed founded upon an error of diagnosis. Those intellectuals who extol his political acumen[6] fail entirely to see the amount of wishful thinking that entered into his practical judgment. But the facts within his horizon and his inferences from them being taken for granted, that method does follow as do his views on the subject of immediate results and on the table fellowship with bourgeois reformers. To found a homogeneous party based upon the organized proletariat of all countries that would march toward the goal without losing its revolutionary faith and getting its powder wet on the road was from that standpoint indeed the task of paramount importance compared with which everything else was nugatory.

[6] See for instance Benedetto Croce, *Materialismo Storico ed Economia Marxista,* translation by C. M. Meredith, 1914.

CHAPTER XXVI

FROM 1875 TO 1914

I. ENGLISH DEVELOPMENTS AND THE SPIRIT OF FABIANISM

THERE is some symbolic significance in these two dates. The year 1875 saw the birth of the first purely socialist party that was powerful enough to count as a factor in politics. This momentous event came to pass through the merger of the two German groups—Lassalle's group and another founded by Bebel and Liebknecht in 1869—into the Social Democratic Party which, though at the time (Gotha program) it made considerable concessions to Lassalle's creed,[1] eventually embraced Marxism (Erfurt program, 1891) and steadily fought its way to the proud position it held in 1914 when, like all socialist parties, it met the crisis of its fate.[2] Before commenting on the astounding development that brought a Marxist party, without any compromise involving sacrifice of principle, within sight of parliamentary leadership, we shall glance at the course of events in other countries and first at the English socialism of that period which on the surface offers so striking and instructive a contrast to it.

Below the surface, there are of course substantially similar social processes and, as parts of them, substantially similar labor movements. The differences between the English and the German cases as to tone, ideology and tactics are easily explained. Ever since the Owenite Grand National Consolidated Trade Union had broken down in 1834 or since chartism had ebbed away, the English labor movement had ceased to elicit any determined hostility. Some of its economic aims were espoused by the liberal and others by the conservative party.[3] The trade union acts of 1871, 1875 and 1876, for instance, were passed without anything that could have stung labor into militancy. Moreover, the battle for enfranchisement was fought out by non-socialist

---

[1] Lassalle's main nostrum was organization of the workmen into state-aided producers' cooperatives that were to compete with, and in the end to eliminate, private industry. This so obviously smacks of utopianism that it is not difficult to understand Marx's aversion.

[2] It then held 110 out of 397 seats in the Reichstag and, owing to the inability of the bourgeois groups to organize great homogeneous parties, this meant even more than the figure in itself suggests.

[3] The emergence of a pro-labor attitude in the conservative camp is particularly striking. On the one hand the group led by Lord Ashley, and on the other hand the Young England group (Disraeli's Tory Democracy) may be mentioned by way of illustration.

groups, the masses not having to do much except cheering and booing. In all this, the superior quality of the rank and file of English labor stands out well. So does the superior quality of English political society; after having proved itself able to avoid an analogon to the French Revolution and to eliminate the dangers threatening from dear bread, it then continued to know how to manage social situations of increasing difficulty and how to surrender with some grace—witness the Trades Disputes Act of 1906.[4] In consequence, the English proletariat took longer in becoming "class-conscious" or in getting to the landmark at which Keir Hardie was able to organize the Independent Labour Party (1893). But the rise of the New Unionism[5] eventually heralded a state of things that, barring verbalization, did not differ essentially from the German one.

The nature and extent of such difference as there was will stand out most clearly if for a moment we look at the group whose aims and methods express it to perfection, the Fabian Society. Marxists will smile contemptuously at what to them must seem to be a gross exaggeration of the importance of a small group of intellectuals which never wished to be anything else. In reality, the Fabians in England, or the attitudes they embodied, were just as important as were the Marxists in Germany.

The Fabians emerged in 1883, and remained for the whole of our

[4] It is difficult, at the present time, to realize how this measure must have struck people who still believed in a state and in a legal system that centered in the institution of private property. For in relaxing the law of conspiracy in respect to peaceful picketing—which practically amounted to legalization of trade-union action implying the threat of force—and in exempting trade-union funds from liability in actions for damages *for torts*—which practically amounted to enacting that trade unions could do no wrong—this measure in fact resigned to the trade unions part of the authority of the state and granted to them a position of privilege which the formal extension of the exemption to employers' unions was powerless to affect. Yet the bill was the result of the report of a Royal Commission set up in 1903 when the conservative party was in power. And the conservative leader (Balfour), in a speech on the third reading, accepted it without displaying any discomfort. The political situation in 1906 no doubt goes far to explain this attitude. But this does not invalidate my point.

[5] The New Unionism means the spread of regular and stable organizations which to the middle of the nineties were substantially confined to the skilled trades and had developed attitudes of professional pride and bourgeois respectability (some leaders of the eighties, like Crawford, frequently emphasized the gulf that separated the respectable people in the trade unions from the proletarian mass) to the more or less unskilled strata below them. These felt much less sure of their bargaining power and were hence more amenable to socialist propaganda and to the argument that strikes alone were unsafe weapons and that they should be supplemented by political action. There is thus an important link between that downward spread of unionism and the change in the trade unions' attitude toward political activity on the one hand and toward socialism on the other. It was then—a few years after the great dock strike of 1889—that trade-union congresses began to pass socialist resolutions.

period a small group of bourgeois intellectuals.[6] They hailed from Bentham and Mill and carried on their tradition. They entertained the same generous hopes for humanity as the philosophical radicals had before them. They went forth to work for rational reconstruction and improvement in the same spirit of practical progressivism.

They were careful about their facts which some of them took no end of trouble to collect by means of extensive research, and critical of arguments and measures. But they were quite uncritical as to the fundamentals, cultural and economic, of their aims. These they took for granted which is only another way of saying that, like good Englishmen, they took themselves for granted. They were unable to see the difference between a slum and the House of Lords. Why both of these were obviously "bad things," that's common sense, is it not? And greater economic equality or self-government in India or trade unions or free trade were no less obviously "good things," who could doubt it? All the thinking that was necessary was on how to clean up the bad things and on how to secure the good things; everything else was irritating futility. Single-minded devotion to public service was as much in evidence in all this as was intolerance of other views about individual and national values—in its way quite as pronounced as was that of the Marxists—and an element of petty-bourgeois resentment against everything aristocratic, including beauty.

At first there was nothing behind the Fabians. They set out to persuade whoever would listen. They lectured to working-class and to bourgeois crowds. They pamphleteered ably and extensively. They recommended or fought particular policies, plans and bills. The most important of all their avenues to influence however was their contact with individual "keymen," or rather with individuals in the entourage of political, industrial and labor leaders. Their country and their own social and political location in their country offered a unique opportunity for establishing and exploiting such contacts.

English political society does not always accept outsiders' advice but, much more than any other society, it is ready to listen to it. And some of the Fabians were not simply outsiders. A few were able to avail themselves of connections formed in Oxford and Cambridge students' unions and common rooms. They were not living, morally speaking, on another planet. Most of them were not straight enemies of the established order. All of them stressed willingness to cooperate much more than hostility. They were not out to found a party and greatly disliked the phraseology of class war and revolution. Whenever

[6] The group, which never numbered more than from 3000 to 4000 members, was really still smaller than its membership indicates. For the operative nucleus amounted to no more than 10 or 20 per cent of it. This nucleus was bourgeois in background and tradition and also in another respect: most of its members were economically independent at least in the sense that they had a bare competence to live on.

possible they preferred making themselves useful to making themselves a nuisance. And they had something to offer to the parliamentarian or administrator who often welcomed suggestions as to what should be done and how to do it.

A modern cabinet minister can in general find within the walls of his ministry most of the information and suggestions he needs. In particular, he can never suffer from lack of statistics. That was not so in the eighties and nineties. With rare exceptions, civil servants of all ranks knew their routine and little else. Outside of the lines of established policies the parliamentarian in office, still more the parliamentarian out of office, was often hard up for facts and ideas especially in the field of the "new" social problems. A group that had them in stock and was always willing to serve them up, neatly arranged and ready for use from the treasury or any other bench, was sure to have entrée, especially by the backdoor. The civil service accepted this. And not only that: being to a considerable extent in sympathy with at least the immediate aims of the Fabians, it allowed itself to be educated by them. The Fabians in turn also accepted this role of unofficial public servants. In fact, it suited them perfectly. They were not personally ambitious. They liked to serve behind the scene. Action through the bureaucracy whose growth in numbers and in power they foresaw and approved fitted in very well with the general scheme of their democratic state socialism.

But how—so Marx would have asked and so the little group of English Marxists (Hyndman's Democratic Federation, born in 1881) actually did ask—could that kind of achievement ever amount to anything if, indeed, it did not amount to conspiracy with the political exponents of the bourgeois interests? How could it be called socialist at all and, if so, was this not another edition of utopian socialism (in the Marxist sense defined above)? It is easy to visualize how perfectly nauseating Fabians and Marxists must have been to each other and how heartily they must have despised each other's illusions, though it was the practice of the Fabians to avoid the discussions of fundamental principles and tactics in which Marxists delighted and to bear with the latter in an attitude of slightly patronizing sympathy. Yet for the detached observer there is no difficulty in answering these questions.

Socialist endeavor of the Fabian type would not have amounted to anything at any other time. But it did amount to much during the three decades preceding 1914, because things and souls were ready for that kind of message and neither for a less nor for a more radical one. Formulation and organization of existing opinion were all that was needed in order to turn possibilities into articulate policy, and this "organizing formulation" the Fabians provided in a most workmanlike manner. They were reformers. The spirit of the times made socialists of them. They were genuine socialists because they aimed at helping in a fundamental reconstruction of society which in the end was to make economic care a public affair. They were voluntarist socialists and therefore they would at any earlier stage have come within the Marxian concept of utopists. But as it was, they had their bearings waiting for them so that the implications of that concept did not fit their case. From their standpoint it would have been nothing short of madness to rouse the bourgeois quarry into awareness of danger by talking about revolutions and class wars. The awakening of class consciousness was precisely what they wanted to avoid, at least at first, since it would have rendered impossible the peaceful but effective spread of their principles throughout the political and administrative organs of bourgeois society. When things had sufficiently matured, they did not hesitate to help the Independent Labour party into existence, to cooperate with (and on) the Labour Representation Committee of 1900, to start the trade unions on their political career, to shape the course of the Progressive party in the London County Council, to preach first municipal and then general socialism —and, eventually, the virtues of the soviet system.

No doubt there is a side to all this which it would be easy to make the subject of adverse comment. But, after all, if they never issued a resounding declaration of war *more Marxiano* and never told the quarry exactly what they were going to do to it, they also never undertook to protect it. Another criticism that might be leveled against the Fabians from the opposite standpoint, viz., that their modus procedendi courted the danger of getting stuck in the outlying defenses of the capitalist system and that it might never lead to the grand pitched battle, fails to take account of their peculiar attitude. On their behalf it can be replied that if, *par l'impossible,* their attack on the capitalist system succeeded in reforming it sufficiently without killing it, why, that would only be a matter for congratulation. And as to the pitched battle, they answered their revolutionary critics in advance by adopting, with singular felicity, the name of the Roman general who, for all his circumspection, did more than any of his impetuous predecessors had done toward driving Hannibal from Italy.

Thus, though it might be said with truth that, in the matter of class war as in others, Fabianism is the very opposite of Marxism, it might also be held that the Fabians were in a sense better Marxists than Marx was himself. To concentrate on the problems that are within practical politics, to move in step with the evolution of things social, and to let the ultimate goal take care of itself is really more in accord with Marx's fundamental doctrine than the revolutionary ideology he himself grafted upon it. To have no illusions about an imminent catastrophe of capitalism, to realize that socialization is a slow process which tends to transform the attitudes of *all* classes of society, even spells superiority in fundamental doctrine.

II. SWEDEN ON THE ONE HAND AND RUSSIA ON THE OTHER

Every country has its own socialism. But things did not differ greatly from the English paradigma in those continental countries whose contributions to humanity's fund of cultural values is so strikingly out of proportion to their size—the Netherlands and the Scandinavian countries in particular. Take Sweden for an instance. Like her art, her science, her politics, her social institutions and much besides, her socialism and her socialists owe their distinction not to any peculiar features of principle or intention, but to the stuff the Swedish nation is made of and to its exceptionally well-balanced social structure. That is why it is so absurd for other nations to try to copy Swedish examples; the only effective way of doing so would be to import the Swedes and to put them in charge.

The Swedes being the people they are and their social structure being what it is, we shall have no difficulty in understanding the two outstanding characteristics of their socialism. The socialist party, almost always ably and conscientiously led, grew slowly in response to a very normal social process, without any attempt to push ahead of normal development and to antagonize for the sake of antagonizing. Hence its rise to political power produced no convulsions. Responsible office came naturally to its leaders who were able to meet the leaders of other parties on terms of equality and largely on common ground: to this day, though a communist group has of course developed, the differences in current politics reduce to such questions as whether a few million kroner more or less should be spent on some social purpose accepted by all. And within the party, the antagonism between intellectuals and labor men only shows under the microscope precisely because, owing to the level of both, there is no great cultural gulf between them and because, the Swedish social organism producing a relatively smaller supply of unemployable intellectuals than do other social organisms, exasperated and exasperating intellectuals are not as numerous as they are elsewhere. This is sometimes described as the "enervating control" exerted by trade unions over the socialist movement in general and over the party in particular. To observers steeped in the phraseology of current radicalism, this may well seem so. But this diagnosis entirely fails to do justice to the social and racial environment of which not only the labor men but also the intellectuals are the products and which prevents both of them from exalting their socialism into a religion. Though room might be found in Marx's teaching for such patterns, the average Marxist cannot of course be expected to look with favor upon a socialist party of the Swedish type, or even to admit that it embodies a genuine case of socialist endeavor. Swedish socialists in turn were very lightly tinged with Marxism though they frequently used language that conformed to what was then considered socialist etiquette, especially in their international relations with other socialist groups.

On the other end of the scale, in Russia, we find a socialism that was almost purely Marxist and hence enjoyed that favor to the full, but is no less easy to understand from its environment. Tsarist Russia was an agrarian country of largely pre-capitalist complexion. The industrial proletariat, so far as it was accessible to the professional socialist, formed but a small part of the total population of about 150 millions.[7] The commercial and industrial bourgeoisie, correspondingly weak in numbers, was not much more efficient than was anyone else, though capitalist evolution fostered by the government was rapidly gathering momentum. Inserted into this structure was an intelligentsia whose ideas were as foreign to the soil as were the Paris dresses of Russian society women.

To many of the intellectuals, the form of government then prevailing—an absolute monarch (autocrator) heading a huge bureaucracy and allied with the landed aristocracy and the church—was of course abomination. And public opinion all over the world has accepted their reading of history. Even writers most hostile to the regime that followed upon that of the tsars invariably make haste to assure their readers that they are duly horrified at the monstrosity of tsarism. Thus the simple truth has been entirely lost in a maze of cant phrases. As a matter of fact, that form of government was no less appropriate to the social pattern that had produced it than was the parliamentary monarchy in England and the democratic republic in the United States. The performance of the bureaucracy, considering the conditions under which it had to work, was far above what the world has been made to believe; its social reforms, agrarian and other, and its halting steps toward a diluted type of constitutionalism were all that could have been expected in the circumstances. It was the imported radicalism and the group interest of the intellectuals that clashed with the spirit of the nation and not the tsarist monarchy which on the contrary had a strong hold upon the vast majority of all classes.

From this, two conclusions follow which at first sight seem paradoxical though no serious student of history will consider them so. On the one hand, any big or sudden move in the direction desired by those liberal lawyers, doctors, professors and civil servants that formed the Kadet party (the party of the Constitutional Democrats) was impossible not so much because their program was inacceptable to the monarchy as because they were so weak. Admitting them to power would have meant admitting an element that commanded not more but less support among the masses and was not more but less

[7] In 1905 factory employment amounted to about one million and a half.

in sympathy with their feelings and interests than were the groups that ran tsarism. There was no scope for a bourgeois regime let alone a socialist one. And there was no analogy between the French situation of 1789 and the Russian situation of 1905. The social structure that crumbled in 1789 was obsolete, stood in the way of almost everything that had any vitality in the nation, and was unable to cope with the fiscal, economic and social problems of the hour. This was not so in the Russia of 1905. There had been loss of prestige owing to the defeat suffered at the hands of Japan and there were disaffection and disorder in consequence. But the state proved itself equal to the tasks not only of suppressing the disorder but also of attacking the problems behind it. In France the result was Robespierre, in Russia it was Stolypin. This would not have been possible if the life had gone out of tsarism as it had gone out of the French *ancien régime*. There is no reason for assuming that, but for the strain the World War put upon the social fabric, the Russian monarchy would have failed to transform itself peacefully and successfully under the influence of, and in step with, the economic development of the country.[8]

---

[8] This analysis, of course, raises questions of great interest concerning the nature of what we are in the habit of calling historical necessity on the one hand and of the role in the historical process of the quality of individual leadership on the other. It would, I think, be difficult to hold that Russia was driven into the war by inexorable necessity. The interests at stake in the Serbian quarrel were not of vital importance, to say the least. The domestic situation in 1914 was not such as to enforce a policy of military aggression as a last resort. The former no doubt actuated nationalists, the latter some (not all) of the extreme reactionaries, and both a number of individuals and groups with axes to grind. But a modicum of common prudence and firmness in the last of the tsars could no doubt have averted participation in the war. It would have been more difficult, but it cannot be called impossible, to avert catastrophe later on when the situation had declared itself and when, after the battle of Gorlice, all hope for military success had gone. Even after the downfall of the monarchy, it is by no means certain that the Kerensky government could not have saved the situation by carefully husbanding its resources and refusing to yield to the importunity of the Allies instead of ordering that desperate last attack. But tsarist society before the bourgeois revolt, and bourgeois society after it, watched the approaching doom in a state of paralysis that was as unmistakable as it is difficult to explain. Now the presence of groupwise incompetence in the one camp and of ability and energy in the other cannot of course be attributed to chance. But in this case, the incompetence of the old regime merely amounted to its being not equal to a situation of complete disorganization and this situation could doubtless have been avoided.

The reader will hardly expect to find that my analysis of Russian socialism and its environmental conditions agrees with Trotsky's (*History of the Russian Revolution*, English translation by M. Eastman, 1934). All the more significant is the fact that the two do not differ *toto coelo* and that, in particular, Trotsky considered the question what would have happened if the revolutionary movement had impinged upon a "different tsar." It is true that he dismisses the obvious inference from considerations of that order. But he recognizes that the Marxist doctrine does not constrain us to neglect the element of personality, though he does not seem to admit the full importance of it for a diagnosis of the Russian revolution.

On the other hand, it was precisely because of the fundamental stability of the social structure that the intellectuals, who could not hope to prevail by anything like normal methods, were driven into a desperate radicalism and into courses of criminal violence. Theirs was the kind of radicalism whose intensity is in inverse proportion to its practical possibilities, the radicalism of impotence. Assassinations might be futile and productive of nothing but repression but there was not much else to do. The brutality of the methods of repression in turn produced retaliation and thus that tragedy unfolded, the tragedy of cruelty and crime incessantly reinforcing each other, which is all that the world saw and felt and which it diagnosed as we should expect.

Now Marx was no putschist. For some of the antics of Russian revolutionaries, especially for those of the Bakunin type, he harbored as much hatred as is compatible with contempt. Moreover, he should have seen—perhaps he did see—that the social and economic structure of Russia failed to fulfill every one of the conditions which according to his own doctrine are essential for the success and even for the emergence of his type of socialism. But if, on logical grounds, this should have prevented the Russian intellectuals from embracing his teaching, we shall understand readily why, on the contrary, it was a tremendous success with them. They were—more or less seriously—revolutionaries and they were at loose ends. Here was a revolutionary gospel of unsurpassable force. Marx's glowing phrases and chiliastic prophecy were exactly what they needed in order to get out of the dreary desert of nihilism. Moreover, this compound of economic theory, philosophy and history suited the Russian taste to perfection. Never mind that the gospel was quite inapplicable to their case and really held out no promise to them. The believer always hears what he wants to hear, no matter what the prophet actually says. The further removed the actual situation was from the state of maturity which Marx visualized, the more ready were the Russian intellectuals —not only the professed socialists among them—to look to him for a solution of their problems.

Thus, a Marxist group emerged as early as 1883, to evolve into the Social Democratic party in 1898. Leadership and, at the beginning, membership were primarily intellectual of course, though sufficient success attended the underground organizing activity among the "masses" to enable sympathetic observers to speak of a fusion of labor groups under Marxist leadership. This accounts for the absence of many of the difficulties met by other Marxist groups in countries with strong labor unions. In any case at first, the workmen who entered the organization accepted the intellectuals' leadership with the utmost docility and hardly even pretended to decide anything for themselves. In consequence, developments in doctrine and in action were on strictly Marxian lines and on a high level. Naturally this drew the blessings of the German defenders of the faith who, beholding such disarming virtue, evidently felt that there must be some exceptions to the Marxian thesis that serious socialism can spring only from full-fledged capitalism. Plekhanov, however, the founder of the group of 1883 and the leading figure of the first two decades, whose able and learned contributions to Marxist doctrine commanded universal respect, really accepted this thesis and therefore cannot have hoped for the early realization of socialism. While valiantly fighting the good fight against reformism and all the other contemporaneous heresies that threatened the purity of the faith, and while upholding belief in the revolutionary goal and method, this true Marxist must have felt early misgivings at the rise, within the party, of a group that seemed bent on action in the immediate future, though he sympathized with it and with its leader, Lenin.

The inevitable conflict that split the party into Bolsheviks and Mensheviks (1903) meant something much more serious than a mere disagreement regarding tactics such as the names of the two groups suggest. At the time no observer, however experienced, could have realized fully the nature of the rift. By now the diagnosis should be obvious. The Marxist phraseology which both groups retained obscured the fact that one of them had irrevocably broken away from classical Marxism.

Lenin had evidently no illusions concerning the Russian situation. He saw that the tsarist regime could be successfully attacked only when temporarily weakened by military defeat and that in the ensuing disorganization a resolute and well-disciplined group could by ruthless terror overthrow whatever other regime might attempt to replace it. For this contingency, the likelihood of which he seems to have realized more clearly than did anyone else, he was resolved to prepare the appropriate instrument. He had little use for the semibourgeois ideology about the peasants—who of course in Russia constituted the relevant social problem—and still less for theories about the necessity of waiting for the workmen to rise of their own initiative in order to accomplish the grand revolution. What he needed was a well-trained bodyguard of revolutionist janissaries, deaf to any argument but his own, free from all inhibitions, impervious to the voices of reason or humanity. Under the circumstances and in the requisite quality such a troop could be recruited only from the intellectual stratum, and the best material available was to be found within the party. His attempt to gain control of the latter therefore amounted to an attempt to destroy its very soul. The majority and their leader, L. Martov, must have felt that. He did not criticize Marx or advocate any new departure. He resisted Lenin in the name of Marx and stood for the Marxist doctrine of a proletarian mass party. The novel note was struck by Lenin.

Since time immemorial, heretics have invariably claimed that they were not out to destroy whatever gospel they found in possession but, on the contrary, that they were trying to restore its pristine purity. Lenin, adopting the time-honored practice, exalted and out-Marxed Marx instead of renouncing allegiance. At the most, he gave the lead implied in the phrase that became so popular with Trotsky and Stalin, "Marxism in the epoch of imperialism." And the reader will readily see that, up to a certain crucial range, it was not difficult for Lenin to adopt both form and matter of unadulterated Marxism. Yet it is no less easy to see that from this stronghold he sallied forth to occupy an essentially un-Marxian position. Un-Marxian was not merely the idea of socialization by *pronunciamiento* in an obviously immature situation; much more so was the idea that "emancipation" was to be not, as the Marxist dogma has it, the work of the proletariat itself but of a band of intellectuals officering the rabble.[9] This meant more than a different view about agitatorial practice and compromises, more than a disagreement on secondary points of Marxist doctrine. This meant divorce from its innermost meaning.[10]

[9] As a matter of fact, contact with criminal elements was formed, though not by Lenin himself but by the lieutenants on the spot. This led to the activity of the "ex's" (shock groups engaged in practical "expropriations," i.e., holdups) both in Russia proper and in Poland. This was pure gangsterdom though western intellectuals swallowed an apologetic "theory" of it.

[10] For our purpose it is not necessary to comment further on the details of a well-known story. The following remarks will suffice. Lenin did not succeed in subjugating the Russian socialist party whose leaders on the contrary drew away from him as time went on; the difficulty of their situation, arising from their wish to keep up something like a united front without jettisoning their principles, is well illustrated by Plekhanov's vacillations. But Lenin did succeed in keeping his group together, in curbing it into obedience and in adjusting its course to the problems raised by the revolt of 1905 and its aftermath, including the presence of a Leninist element in the Duma. At the same time, he succeeded in keeping contact with, and standing in, the Second International (see below) of which he attended three congresses and in whose bureau he for a time represented the Russian party. This would hardly have been possible if his views and activities had been allowed to impress the representatives of the other nations as they impressed the majority of Russian socialists. As it was, that body, and western socialist opinion in general, looked upon him simply as the outstanding figure in the left wing of orthodoxy and bore with him and his unbending extremism, admiring him in some respects and not taking him too seriously in others. Thus in his sphere of politics he played a double role that was not without analogy with the double role of the tsarist regime whose international attitudes (as exemplified by its sponsoring international arbitration and security) also differed considerably from its attitudes at home.

Neither these achievements nor his contributions to socialist thought—most of them distinctly mediocre (as, by the way, were those of Trotsky)—would have secured him a place in the front rank of socialists. Greatness came after Russia's breakdown in the World War and was as much the result of a unique combina-

III. Socialist Groups in the United States

In the United States a totally different social pattern proved as unfavorable as was the Russian to the growth of a genuinely socialist mass movement. Thus the two cases present similarities that are no less interesting than the differences. If the agrarian world of Russia, in spite of the streak of communism inherent in the structure of the Russian village, was practically impervious to the influence of modern socialism, the agrarian world of the United States provided an anti-socialist force that stood ready to make short work of any activities on Marxist lines important enough to be noticed by it. If the industrial sector of Russia failed to produce a significant socialist mass party because capitalist evolution was so sluggish, the industrial sector of the United States failed to do so because capitalist evolution rushed on at such a vertiginous pace.[11]

The most important difference was between the respective intellectual groups: unlike Russia, the United States did not, until the end of the nineteenth century, produce an under-employed and frustrated set of intellectuals. The scheme of values that arose from the national task of developing the economic possibilities of the country drew nearly all the brains into business and impressed the businessman's attitudes upon the soul of the nation. Outside of New York, intellectuals in our sense were not numerous enough to count. Most of them moreover accepted this scheme of values. If they did not, Main Street refused to listen and instinctively frowned upon them, and this was much more effective in disciplining them than were the methods of the Russian political police. Middle-class hostility to railroads, utilities and big business in general absorbed almost all there was of "revolutionary" energy.

The average competent and respectable workman was, and felt himself to be, a businessman. He successfully applied himself to exploiting his own individual opportunities, to getting on or, in any case, to selling his labor as advantageously as possible. He understood and largely shared his employer's way of thinking. When he found it useful to ally himself with his peers within the same concern, he did so in the same spirit. Since roughly the middle of the nineteenth

---

tion of circumstances that made his weapons adequate as the result of his supreme ability in handling them. In this respect, though in no other, Professor Laski's proskynesis in the *Encyclopaedia of the Social Sciences* (article Ulyanov) is fully understandable, provided of course that intellectuals *must* prostrate themselves before the idols of their time.

[11] The presence of the "frontier" of course greatly reduced the possibilities of friction. The importance of this element, though great, is however likely to be over-estimated. That pace of industrial evolution incessantly created new industrial frontiers, and this fact was much more important than was the opportunity of packing one's bags and going west.

century this practice increasingly took the form of employees' committees, the forerunners of the postwar company unions that acquired their full economic and cultural significance in company towns.[12]

Beyond that, it was frequently good business for the workman to combine on a national scale with the other members of his craft in order further to improve his bargaining position as against employers directly and as against other crafts indirectly. This interest shaped many trade unions that are typically American, largely accounts for the adoption of the craft principle which is much more effective than any other principle can be in keeping away would-be entrants, and really produced workmen's cartels. Naturally enough, these cartels displayed that lack of radicalism which was and is so eloquently lamented by both domestic and foreign socialists and fellow travelers. Nothing but wage rates and hours mattered to them and they were quite prepared to study the wishes of the public or even of the employers in everything else, particularly in their phraseology. This is illustrated to perfection by the type and behavior of the leaders both of individual unions and of the American Federation of Labor which embodied that spirit, as well as by the attempts of the trade-union bureaucracy to enter, with trade-union funds, the sphere of industrial and financial enterprise that was quite congenial to them.[13]

To be sure, the fact that the creeds and slogans—the ideologies—were so unrevolutionary and so averse to class war is in itself of limited importance. American trade unionists were not much given to theorizing. If they had been they might have put a Marxist inter-

[12] The common sense of the arrangement and its particular suitability to American conditions are as obvious as is the fact that it was a thorn in the flesh of trade unions and also of the radical intellectuals of a later type. The slogans of our days—recently officialized—have thus stigmatized company unions as the product of a diabolical attempt by employers to thwart the efforts toward effective representation of the workmen's interests. While this view too is perfectly understandable from a standpoint from which militant organization of the proletariat is in the nature of a moral axiom—and from the standpoint of the corporative state that grows up before our eyes—it vitiates historical interpretation. The fact that employers provided facilities for this type of organization, often took the initiative and tried to influence it so as to be able to get along with it, does not exclude or disprove the other fact that company unions and their forerunners fulfilled a much-needed function and that, in the normal case, they served the interests of the men quite well.

[13] The figure of Warren Sanford Stone, of the Brotherhood of Locomotive Engineers, affords an excellent (though later) illustration of the last-mentioned aspect as well as of the others. Further examples from the time of Samuel Gompers will so readily occur to the reader that there is no need of mentioning them. But the above should not be interpreted to mean that the trade union with high entrance fees and long waiting lists which looks so strangely like a copper corner is or was the only kind of trade union in this country. On the contrary, immigrants imported every European variety, and, irrespective of this, forms similar to those found in Europe developed where conditions were favorable, that is, especially in the relatively old and consolidated locations and branches of industry.

pretation upon their practice. It remains true however that, bargaining aside, they did not consider themselves on the other side of the fence in all things and that cooperation—which those of us who do not like it will call collusion—with employers was in accord not only with their principles but also with the logic of their situation. Beyond a narrow range of questions, political action was not only unnecessary but even meaningless to them. And for the influence he was able to exert, the radical intellectual might just as well have tried to convert the board of the Pennsylvania Railroad.

But there was another world within the world of American labor. Along with elements of supernormal quality, immigration included from the first some substandard ones also which increased in relative as well as absolute numbers after the Civil War. These numbers were swelled by individuals who, though not subnormal as to physical fitness or intelligence or energy, yet gravitated into that group, owing to past misfortunes or to the persistence of the influence of the unfavorable environments from which they sprang or simply owing to restlessness, inadaptable temperament or criminal proclivities. All these types were an easy prey to exploitation which was facilitated by the absence of moral bonds, and some of them reacted by a blind and impulsive hatred that readily crystallized into crime. In many new and rapidly growing industrial communities where people of the most varied origins and propensities were thrown together and law and order had to be kept, if at all, by action that was itself outside of the law, rough people, made still rougher by the treatment they received, faced employers, or agents of employers, who had not yet developed a sense of responsibility and were often driven to brutal courses by a fear not only for their property but also for their lives.

There, so the socialist observer is inclined to say, was class war in the most literal sense—actual guns going off to illustrate the Marxist concept. As a matter of fact, it was nothing of the sort. It is hard to imagine any set of conditions less favorable to the development of political laborism or of serious socialism, and very little of either showed as long as those conditions lasted.

The history of the Knights of Labor, the one really important and nation-wide organization of all wageworkers regardless of skill or craft—and in fact of all who cared to join—covers about a decade of significant power and activity (1878-1889). In 1886 the Noble Order's membership was almost 700,000. The part of it which consisted of industrial—mainly unskilled—laborers energetically participated in or even initiated the strikes or boycotts that accompanied the depressions of that time. A scrutiny of programs and pronouncements reveals a somewhat incoherent medley of all sorts of socialist, cooperative and, occasionally, anarchist ideas that we can trace, if we wish, to a wide variety of sources—Owen, the English agrarian socialists, Marx, and 'the Fabians among them. The political point of view was much in evidence and so was the idea of general planning and of social reconstruction. But such definiteness of aims as we may discover is really due to our reading back from the standpoint of our own time. In reality there were no definite aims and it was precisely the comprehensive character of the ideology of the Good Life—Uriah S. Stephens, the founder, had been trained for the ministry—and of the American Constitution which appealed to so many people, farmers and professional men included. The Order thus was a sort of exchange for the plans of all kinds of reformers. In this respect it indeed filled a function which its leaders had in mind when they stressed the educational aspect of its activities. But an organization formed of such different clays was constitutionally incapable of action. When definitely socialist profession was insisted on, it broke. Similar movements (Populists, Henry George's and others) tell the same tale.

The obvious inference is that in the American environment of that time there was not and could not be either the requisite material or the requisite motive power for a socialist mass movement. This can be verified by following the thread that leads from the Knights to the Industrial Workers of the World. This thread is embodied in the career of a Marxist intellectual, Daniel De Leon, and hence should have, for the faithful, considerable specific weight.[14] It was under his command that, in 1893, socialists within the Order of the Knights rose against the old leader, Powderly, thereby, as it turned out, dealing a death blow to the organization. The idea was to create an instrument for political action on more or less Marxian lines. Class war, revolution, destruction of the capitalist state and the rest of it were to be sponsored by a proletarian party. But neither the Socialist Labor Party (1890) nor De Leon's Socialist Trade and Labor Alliance (1895) had any life in it. Not only was the working-class following small— this would not in itself have been decisive—but success even of the Russian kind, that is to say, conquest of a controlling nucleus of intellectuals, was not attained. The Socialist Labor party first split and then lost most of the remaining ground to the new Socialist party.

The latter came as near to being an orthodox success as any group did in this country. To begin with, its origin was orthodox. It arose from the labor struggles during 1892-1894, when strikes were broken by the use of force, the federal government and the judiciary lending resolute support to the employers.[15] This converted many a man who

---

[14] All the more so as Lenin himself went out of his way to pay homage, quite unusual for him, to De Leon's work and thought.

[15] It will be observed that this was done at a time when most European governments were rapidly adopting another attitude. However, this does not simply spell "backwardness" on this side of the Atlantic. It is true that the social and political prestige of the business interest was here much greater than anywhere else and that American democracy in consequence took a much narrower view of labor

had been previously a "conservative" craft unionist. At any rate, it converted Eugene V. Debs first to industrial unionism and then to the principle of political action. Secondly, the general attitude adopted by the Socialist party was orthodox. It tried to work with and to "bore from within" the trade unions. It gave itself a regular political organization. It was in principle revolutionary in the same sense as were the great socialist parties of Europe. Its doctrine was not quite orthodox. In fact it did not stress doctrinal aspects to any great extent —either under Debs or later—and it allowed considerable latitude to the teaching activities within its ranks. But though it never succeeded in absorbing the little local labor parties that kept on cropping up all over the country, it developed fairly well up to the postwar period when communist competition asserted itself. A majority of socialists would, I think, agree in calling it the one genuine socialist party of this country. Its voting strength, though swelled as that of most socialist parties is by non-socialist sympathizers, measures the scope there was for serious socialist effort.

De Leon however had another chance. It came from—and went with—the Western Federation of Miners whose radicalism, quite independent of any doctrinal background, was nothing but the product of rough people reacting to a rough environment. This union provided the corner stone for the structure of the I.W.W. (1905). De Leon and his associates added the wreckage of their own and other unsuccessful organizations as well as splinters mostly of dubious character—intellectual or proletarian or both—from everywhere and nowhere. But the leadership—and in consequence the phraseology—was strong. Besides De Leon himself, there were Haywood, Trautmann, Foster and others.

Shock tactics that knew no inhibitions and the spirit of uncompromising warfare account for a series of isolated successes, and the absence of anything else but phrases and shock tactics, for the ultimate failure that was hastened by quarrels with and defections to the communists as well as by incessant internal dissensions. But I need not retell a story that has been told so often from every conceivable standpoint. What matters to us is this. The organization has been called syndicalist—even anarchist—and later on the criminal syndicalism laws enacted in several states were applied to it. The principle of "direct" action on the spot and the doctrinal concession to

problems than did, say, the Junker government in Prussia. But one can recognize this and even judge it according to one's moral or humanitarian standard, and at the same time also recognize that partly owing to the undeveloped state of public administration, partly owing to the presence of elements with which no gentler method would have worked, and partly owing to the nation's determination to press forward on the road of economic development, problems did present themselves under a different aspect and would have done so even to a governmental agency completely free from bourgeois blinkers.

the Western Federation of Miners which assigned to industrial unions a basic role in the construction of socialist society—De Leon's contribution to or deviation from classical Marxism—no doubt suggest that it was. But it seems more correct to speak of the insertion of syndicalist elements into what substantially was and remained an offshoot of the Marxian stem than to base diagnosis entirely on those elements.

Thus that great sociologist, the man in the street, has been right once more. He said that socialism and socialists were un-American. If I catch his meaning, it amounts pretty much to what, less succinctly, I have been trying to convey. American development practically skipped the phase of socialism which saw the career of unadulterated Marxism and of the Second International. Their essential problems were hardly understood. The attitudes appropriate to them existed only as sporadic imports. American problems and attitudes occasionally borrowed these imported articles. But that was all. And the events of the next phase impinged on intellectuals and on a proletariat that had not gone through the Marxian school.

IV. THE FRENCH CASE; ANALYSIS OF SYNDICALISM

What syndicalism really is we shall see best in the French picture.[16] Before attempting to do so we shall briefly note a few things about French socialism in general.

First, its ideological history goes further back and is perhaps more distinguished than that of any other. But no single variety of it ever crystallized so completely and commanded allegiance so widely as did the socialism of, say, the Fabian type on the one hand and of the Marxian on the other. Fabian socialism requires English political society, and nothing like that developed in France—the great revolution and the subsequent failure of the aristocratic and the bourgeois elements to coalesce prevented it. Marxian socialism requires a broad and unified labor movement; or, as a rallying creed for intellectuals, it requires cultural traditions quite uncongenial to French *limpidité*. But all the other socialist creeds that have so far emerged appeal only to particular mentalities and social locations and are sectarian by nature.

Second, France was typically the country of the peasant, the artisan, the clerk and the small *rentier*. Capitalist evolution proceeded by measured steps and large-scale industry was confined to a few centers. Whatever the issues that divided these classes, they were economically conservative at first—nowhere else did conservatism rest on so broad

---

[16] Italian and Spanish syndicalism would do almost equally well. Only, in proportion to the number of illiterates, the anarchist element increases so much as to distort what I believe to be the true traits. This element has its place. But it should not be overemphasized.

a basis—and later on lent increasing support to groups that sponsored middle-class reform, among them the *radicaux-socialistes*, a party that can be best described by saying that it was neither radical nor socialist. Many workmen were of the same sociological type and of the same mind. Many professionals and intellectuals adapted themselves to it, which accounts for the fact that over-production and underemployment of intellectuals, though it existed, failed to assert itself as we should otherwise expect. Unrest there was. But among the malcontents, the Catholics, who disapproved of the anti-clerical tendencies that various circumstances brought to the fore in the Third Republic, were more important than the people who were displeased with the capitalist order of things. It was from the former and not from the latter that the real danger to the bourgeois republic arose at the time of the *affaire Dreyfus*.

Third, it follows that, though again for different reasons, there was not much more scope for serious socialism in France than there was in Russia or the United States. Hence she had a variety of socialisms and quasi-socialisms that were not serious. The Blanquist party whose hope was the action of "a few resolute men" may serve as an example: a small band of intellectuals with a bent for conspiracy and professional revolutionists together with the mob of Paris and two or three other big towns was all that ever came within the horizon of groups like that. Eventually however a Marxist *parti ouvrier* was founded by Guesde and Lafargue with a class-war program (1883) that had received the sanction of Marx himself. It developed on orthodox lines, fighting putschism of the Hervé type and anarchism on the one front and Jaurès' reformism on the other, much as its German counterpart did. But it never acquired similar importance and never meant nearly as much either to the masses or to the intellectuals, in spite of the merger of socialist groups in the *chambre* which was achieved in 1893 (48 seats as compared with the 300 occupied by governmental republicans) and eventually led to the formation of the Unified Socialist party (1905).

Fourth, I will simply state the fact, without attempting to go behind it, that the social pattern glanced at above precluded the emergence of great and disciplined parties of the English type. Instead, as everyone knows, parliamentary politics became a *cotillon* of small and unstable groups that combined and dissolved in response to momentary situations and individual interests and intrigues, setting up and pulling down cabinets according to the principles, as I put it before, of a parlor game. One of the consequences of this was governmental inefficiency. Another was that cabinet office came within the sight of socialist and quasi-socialist groups sooner than it did in countries whose socialist parties were much more powerful but whose politics were run according to somewhat more rational methods. Until the national emergency of 1914, Guesde and his group proved impervious to the temptation and consistently refused cooperation with bourgeois parties in the best orthodox style. But the reformist group which in any case shaded off into bourgeois radicalism and whose principles— reform without revolution—did not condemn such cooperation had really no reason to do likewise. Jaurès accordingly felt no compunction at the time of the Dreyfus crisis (1898) in lending support to a bourgeois government in order to defend the Republic. Thus an old problem of socialist principle and tactics, which was no problem at all in England or Sweden but a fundamental one everywhere else, suddenly burst upon the socialist world in a most practical form. It acquired its particular sting by an additional circumstance: supporting a bourgeois government was one thing, though bad enough from the standpoint of rigid orthodoxy, but sharing its responsibilities by actually entering it was quite another thing. M. Millerand did precisely this. In 1899 he entered the Waldeck-Rousseau cabinet— together with M. de Galliffet, a conservative general who was best known to the public for his vigorous participation in the suppression of the Paris Commune in 1871.

Two patriots sacrificing personal views in order to join forces in a national emergency—what of it? This, I suppose, will express the reaction of most of my readers. I need hardly assure them that personally I have no wish to hold that the two gentlemen disgraced themselves. Moreover, it may well be questioned whether even then M. Millerand should have been called a socialist at all.[17] Finally, the French working class has every reason to remember with gratitude what, legislatively and administratively, he did for it while in cabinet office.

At the same time, we must try to understand how "Millerandism" was bound to strike the Guesdists in France and orthodox socialists all over Europe. For them it spelled lapse and sin, betrayal of the goal, pollution of the faith. This was very natural and so was the anathema hurled at it by the international congress of Amsterdam (1904). But beyond and behind the doctrinal anathema there was a piece of simple common sense. If the proletariat was not to lend its back for ambitious politicians to use for climbing into power, every deviation from approved practice had to be most jealously watched.

[17] He had, it is true, risen to prominence among "left-wingers" by defending strike leaders and when he entered the Waldeck-Rousseau cabinet he was the chief figure among the sixty members of what was called the "socialist left." However he had done nothing that could not have been done equally well by a bourgeois radical. His later attitude as minister of public works (1909) and as minister of war (1912) hence spelled not quite so great a break as his enemies made out. His subsequent alliance with the *bloc national* and his conflict with the *cartel des gauches* during his tenure of the presidential office after 1920 were different matters yet they also admit of plausible justifications.

The trick of talking about national emergencies whenever it suits careerists to make a bid for power—after all, was there ever a situation that politicians did *not* consider an emergency?—was too well known and too discredited to impress anyone, particularly the French proletariat that had learned to rate political phrases at their true value. There was danger that the masses might turn away from political socialism in contempt.[18]

In fact, there was more than a mere danger. They were actually turning away from it. Beholding, as the whole nation did, the sorry spectacle of political inefficiency, incompetence and frivolity that was the product of the sociological pattern imperfectly sketched above, they placed no trust in the state, the political world, the scribblers, and had no respect for any of them or indeed for anything or anybody except the memory of some great figures of the past. Part of the industrial proletariat had conserved its Catholic faith. The rest was adrift. And to those who had overcome their bourgeois propensities, syndicalism was much more attractive than any of the available species of straight socialism the sponsors of which bade fair to reproduce, on a smaller scale, the games of the bourgeois parties. Revolutionary tradition of the French type of which syndicalism was the principal heir, of course greatly helped.

For syndicalism is not merely revolutionary trade unionism. This may mean many things which have little to do with it. Syndicalism is apolitical and anti-political in the sense that it despises action on or through the organs of traditional politics in general and parliaments in particular. It is anti-intellectual both in the sense that it despises constructive programs with theories behind them and in the sense that it despises the intellectual's leadership. It *really* appeals to the workman's instincts—and not, like Marxism, to the intellectual's idea of what the workman's instincts ought to be—by promising him what he can understand, viz., the conquest of the shop he works in, conquest by physical violence, ultimately by the general strike.

Now, unlike Marxism or Fabianism, syndicalism cannot be espoused by anyone afflicted by any trace of economic or sociological training. There is no rationale for it. Writers who, acting on the hypothesis that everything must be amenable to rationalization, try to construct a theory for it inevitably emasculate it. Some linked it to anarchism which, as a social philosophy, is completely alien to it in roots, aims and ideology—however similar the behavior of Bakunin's working-class following (1872-1876) may look to us. Others attempted to subsume it, as a special case characterized by a special tactical bent, under Marxism, which involves discarding all that is most essential to both. Still others have constructed a new socialist species to function as the

---

[18] The Italian socialists actually declined the invitation to join the cabinet that was three times extended to them by Giolitti (1903, 1906, 1911).

Platonic idea of it—guild socialism—but in doing so they had to commit the movement to a definite schema of ultimate values the absence of which is one of its salient features. The men who organized and led the *Confédération Générale du Travail* during its syndicalist stage (1895-1914) were mostly genuine proletarians or trade-union officers, or both. They were brimming over with resentment and with the will to fight. They did not bother about what they would do with the wreckage in case of success. Is that not enough? Why should we refuse to recognize the truth which life teaches us every day—that there is such a thing as pugnacity in the abstract that neither needs nor heeds any argument and cares for nothing except for victory as such?

But any intellectual can fill the void behind that brute violence in the way that suits his taste. And the violence itself, combined with the anti-intellectualism and the anti-democratic slant, acquires a significant connotation if viewed in the setting of a disintegrating civilization that so many people hate for all kinds of reasons. Those who at the time felt like that but hated not so much the economic arrangements of capitalist society as its democratic rationalism were not free to fall back on orthodox socialism which promises still more rationalism. To their intellectual anti-intellectualism—whether Nietzschean or Bergsonian—the syndicalist anti-intellectualism of the fist may well have appealed as the complement—in the world of the masses—of their own creed. Thus a very strange alliance actually came to pass, and syndicalism found its philosopher after all in Georges Sorel.

Of course all revolutionary movements and ideologies that coexist at any time always have a lot in common. They are the products of the same social process and must in many respects react in similar ways to similar necessities. Also, they cannot avoid borrowing from each other or splashing each other with their colors in their very squabbles. Finally, individuals as well as groups often do not know where, if anywhere, they belong and, sometimes from ignorance, at other times from a correct perception of advantage, they mix up contradictory principles into mongrel creeds of their own. All this confuses observers and accounts for the wide variety of current interpretations. It is particularly confusing in the case of syndicalism which flourished only so short a time and was soon to be deserted by its intellectual exponents. Nevertheless, however we may appraise what syndicalism meant to Sorel and what Sorel meant to syndicalism, his *Réfléxions sur la Violence* and his *Illusions du Progrès* do help us toward a diagnosis. That his economics and his sociology completely differed from those of Marx may in itself not mean much. But standing as it does right in the midst of the anti-intellectualist torrent, Sorel's social philosophy sheds a flood of light on the first practical manifestation of a social force that was and is revolutionary in a sense in which Marxism was not.

V. THE GERMAN PARTY AND REVISIONISM; THE AUSTRIAN SOCIALISTS

But why was it that the English methods and tactics did not prevail in Germany? Why that Marxist success which accentuated antagonisms and split the nation into two hostile camps? This would be easy to understand if there had been no extra-socialist groups to work for social reconstruction or if the ruling stratum had turned a deaf ear to their proposals. It becomes a riddle as soon as we realize that German public authority was not less but more alive to the social exigencies of the time than was English political society and that the work of the Fabians was being done not less but more effectively by a very similar group.

Germany did not lag behind but, until the passing of the security legislation primarily associated with the name of Lloyd George, led in matters of "social policy." Also, it was the government's initiative that placed those measures for social betterment on the statute book, and not pressure from below asserting itself by exasperating struggles. Bismarck initiated social insurance legislation. The men who developed it and added other lines of social improvement were conservative civil servants (von Berlepsch, Count Posadowsky) carrying out the directions of William II. The institutions created were truly admirable achievements and they were so considered all over the world. Simultaneously, trade-union activity was unfettered and a significant change occurred in the attitude of public authority toward strikes.

The monarchist garb in which all this appeared no doubt constitutes a difference as against the English procedure. But this difference made for more and not less success. The monarchy, after having for a time given in to economic liberalism ("Manchesterism" as its critics called it), simply returned to its old traditions by doing—*mutatis mutandis*—for the workmen what it had previously done for the peasants. The civil service, much more developed and much more powerful than in England, provided excellent administrative machinery as well as the ideas and the drafting skill for legislation. And this civil service was at least as amenable to proposals of social reform as was the English one. Largely consisting of impecunious Junkers—many of whom had no other means of subsistence than their truly Spartan salaries—entirely devoted to its duty, well educated and informed, highly critical of the capitalist bourgeoisie, it took to the task as a fish takes to water.

Ideas and proposals normally came to the bureaucracy from its teachers at the universities, the "socialists of the chair." Whatever we may think of the scientific achievements of the professors who organized themselves into the *Verein für Sozialpolitik*[19] and whose work often lacked scientific refinement, they were aglow with a genuine ardor for social reform and entirely successful in spreading it. They resolutely faced bourgeois displeasure not only in framing individual measures of practical reform but also in propagating the spirit of reform. Like the Fabians, they were primarily interested in the work at hand and they deprecated class war and revolution. But, also like the Fabians, they knew where they were going—they knew and did not mind that socialism loomed at the end of their way. Of course, the state socialism they envisaged was national and conservative. But it was neither a fake nor utopian.

The world at large never understood this social pattern and the nature of the constitutional monarchy it produced. At any rate, it has forgotten whatever it may have once known. But as soon as we get a glimpse of the truth, we find it still more difficult to understand how in that unplutocratic environment it was possible for the greatest of all socialist parties to grow up on a purely Marxist program and on a Marxist phraseology of unsurpassed virulence, pretending to fight ruthless exploitation and a state that was the slave of slave drivers. Surely this cannot be explained by the "logic of the objective social situation."

Well, I suppose we must recognize once more that in the short run —and forty years is short run in such matters—methods and mistakes, individual and group-wise *manque de savoir faire*, may count for much more than that logic. Everything else I could point to is obviously inadequate. There was, of course, the struggle for the extension of the franchise in the legislatures of the individual states. But much of what was most important to the industrial masses was within the competence of the imperial parliament (*Reichstag*) and for it Bismarck had introduced universal manhood suffrage from the first. More important was protection for agriculture—dear bread. No doubt this did much to poison the atmosphere, especially because its principal beneficiaries were the big and medium-sized estates in eastern Prussia and not the peasants. However, as to the real pressure exerted by it, the fact is conclusive that around 1900 emigration practically ceased. No—explanation cannot lie on that route.

But that *manque de savoir faire* plus German manners! We may make things clearer by the obvious analogy with Germany's behavior in matters of international relations. Before 1914, Germany's colonial and other foreign ambitions were—so it seems right to say at this

---

[19] I really wish I could induce the reader to peruse the short history of that unique organization that was so characteristic of what imperial Germany really was, though it has not been and probably never will be translated. Its author was for decades secretary of the *Verein*, and his story is only the more impressive for being so unpretentious. (Franz Boese, *Geschichte des Vereins für Sozialpolitik*, Berlin, 1939.)

distance of time—distinctly modest, especially if we compare them with the neat and effective moves by which England and France at that time increased their empires. Nothing that Germany actually did or indicated any intention of doing will bear comparison with, say, Tel-El-Kebir or with the Boer War or with the conquest of Tunisia or of French Indo-China. All the less modest and all the more aggressive, however, was the talking that Germans indulged in, and unbearably offensive was the swashbuckling manner in which even reasonable claims were presented. Worse than this, no line was ever adhered to; headlong forward rushes in ever-changing directions alternated with blustering retreats, undignified propitiations with uncalled-for rebuffs, until all the factors that make the world's opinion were thoroughly disgusted as well as disquieted.[20] Things were no different in domestic affairs.

The fatal mistake was really Bismarck's. It consisted in the attempt, explicable only on the hypothesis that he completely misconceived the nature of the problem, at suppressing socialist activities by coercion culminating in a special enactment (*Sozialistengesetz*) which he carried in 1878 and which remained in force until 1890 (when William II insisted on its repeal), that is to say, long enough to educate the party and to subject it for the rest of the prewar period to the leadership of men who had known prison and exile and had acquired much of the prisoner's and exile's mentality. Through an unfortunate combination of circumstances, it so happened that this vitiated the whole course of subsequent events. For the one thing those exile-shaped men could not stand was militarism and the ideology of military glory. And the one thing which the monarchy—otherwise in sympathy with a large part of what reasonable socialists considered as immediately practical aims—could not stand was sneers at the army and at the glories of 1870. More than anything else, this was for both what defined the enemy as distinguished from the mere opponent. Add Marxian phraseology—however obviously academic—at the party conventions on the one hand and the aforesaid blustering on the other, and you have the picture. No amount of fruitful social legislation and no amount of law-abiding behavior availed against that reciprocal *non possumus*, that cardboard barrier across which the two

[20] I want to make it quite clear that the above is not intended to attribute this policy, either wholly or primarily, to William II. He was no insignificant ruler. Moreover, he was fully entitled to the comment made upon him by Prince Bülow in the most unusual defense ever made for a monarch in a parliament: "Say what you will, he is no philistine." If he quarreled with the one man who could have taught him the technique of his craft, critics of his behavior to Bismarck should not forget that the quarrel was mainly about the persecution of socialists which the emperor wished to discontinue and about the inauguration of a great program of social legislation. If one disregards talk and simply tries to reconstruct intentions by following the emperor's acts from year to year, one cannot help arriving at the conclusion that he was often right in his views about the great questions of his time.

hosts reviled each other, made the most terrible faces at each other, devoured each other in principle—all without really meaning any serious harm.

From this state of things a situation developed that no doubt had its dangers—great power without responsibility is always dangerous—but was not anything like as uncomfortable as it might seem. The federal and state governments—or the old civil servants promoted to cabinet rank who formed those governments—cared primarily for honest and efficient administration, for beneficial and on the whole progressive legislation, and for the army and navy estimates. None of these objects was seriously jeopardized by the adverse votes of the socialists, the passing of the army and navy estimates in particular being assured most of the time by the support of a large majority of the population. The Social Democratic party in turn, well organized and brilliantly led by August Bebel, was absorbed in consolidating and expanding its vote which in fact increased by leaps and bounds. This was not seriously interfered with by the governments, the bureaucracy scrupulously observing the letter of the law which gave all the freedom of action really necessary for partisan activity.[21] And both the managing bureaucracy and the party had reason to be grateful to each other, especially during Bülow's tenure of power, for providing outlets for oratorical excess capacity of which both of them stood in need.

Thus the party not only developed satisfactorily but also settled down. A party bureaucracy, a party press, a staff of elder statesmen developed, all adequately financed, as a rule secure in their positions and, on the whole, highly respectable in every—and also in the bourgeois—sense of the word. A nucleus of working-class members grew up for whom membership was no longer a question of choice but a matter of course. More and more people were "born into the party" and educated to unquestioning acceptance of its leadership and catechism which then, for some of them, meant as much and no more than religious catechisms mean to the average man or woman of today.

All this was greatly facilitated by the inability of the non-socialist parties to compete effectively for the labor vote. There was an exception to this. The Centrist (Catholic) party, on the one hand, commanded all the talent required because it had the support of a priesthood of quite exceptionally high quality and, on the other hand, was prepared to make a bid for the labor vote by going as far in the direc-

---

[21] Administrative vexations were doubtless not absent, and socialists of course made the most of everything that could by any stretch be styled as vexatious. But this sort of thing did not go to great lengths as in fact the history of socialist activity from 1890 to the First World War in itself suffices to prove. Moreover, vexations of this kind are really in the nature of a service to the "persecuted" party.

tion of social reform as it felt itself able to do without affronting its right wing, and by taking its stand on the doctrines of the encyclicals *Immortale Dei* (1885) and *Rerum Novarum* (1891).[22] But all the other parties, though for different reasons and in different degrees, stood on a footing of mutual distrust, if not of hostility, with the industrial proletariat and never so much as attempted to sell themselves to any significant number of labor voters. These, unless they were active Catholics, accordingly had hardly any party to turn to other than the Social Democratic party. Unbelievable as such ineptitude seems in the light of English and American experience, it is yet a fact that the socialist army was allowed, amid all the clamor about the horrible dangers threatening from it, to march into politically unguarded territory.

We are now in a position to understand what, on the face of it, seems so incomprehensible, viz., why German socialists so tenaciously clung to the Marxian creed. For a powerful party that could afford a distinctive creed yet was completely excluded not only from political responsibility but from any immediate prospect of it, it was natural to conserve the purity of the Marxian faith once it had been embraced. That purely negative attitude toward non-socialist reform and all the doings of the bourgeois state—which as we have seen above was the tactical principle Marx recommended for all save exceptional cases—was really thrust upon it. The leaders were not irresponsible nor were they desperadoes. But they realized that in the given situation there was not much for the party to do except to criticize and to keep the banner flying. Any sacrifice of revolutionary principle would have been perfectly gratuitous. It would have only disorganized their following without giving to the proletariat much more than it got in any case, not on the initiative of the other parties but on that of the monarchist bureaucracy. Such small additional successes as might have been attained hardly warranted the party risk. Thus, serious, patriotic and law-abiding men continued to repeat the irresponsible slogans of revolution and treason—the sanguinary implications of which came so strangely from many a pacific and bespectacled countenance—blissfully conscious of the fact that there was little likelihood of their having to act upon them.

Before long however the suspicion began to dawn upon a few of them that some day or other the revolutionary talk might meet the

---

[22] Let us note in passing an interesting (almost American) phenomenon: here we have a political party that comprised within itself almost all shades of opinion on economic and social questions that it is possible to have, from the starkest conservatism to radical socialism, and yet was a most powerful political engine. Men of the most different types, origins and desires, extreme democrats and extreme authoritarians, cooperated with a smoothness that might have roused the envy of the Marxists, solely on the strength of their allegiance to the Catholic Church.

most deadly weapon of political controversy—smiles. Perhaps it was an apprehension of this kind or simply the perception of the almost ludicrous discrepancy between Marxian phraseology and the social reality of those times that eventually prompted no less a personage than old Engels to pronounce *ex cathedra*—that is to say, in a preface he wrote to a new edition of Marx's *Class Struggles in France*[23]— that street fighting presented certain inconveniences after all and that the faithful need not necessarily feel committed to it (1895).

This timely and modest adjustment roused the wrath of a small minority of thoroughgoing hotspurs, Mrs. Rosa Luxemburg in particular surpassing herself in fiery denunciations of the old man. But it was acquiesced in by the party—possibly with a sigh of relief—and further cautious steps in the same direction might perhaps have been tactfully made. When however Eduard Bernstein coolly proceeded to "revise" the whole structure of the party creed, there was a major row. After what I have said about the situation this should not be surprising.

Even the most worldly party is aware of the dangers involved in altering any of its more important planks. In the case of a party whose program and whose very existence were based on a creed every detail of which had been worked out with theological fervor, root-and-branch reform was bound to mean a terrific shock. That creed was the object of quasi-religious reverence. It had been upheld for a quarter of a century. Under its flag the party had marched to success. It was all the party had to show. And now the beloved revolution—that was to them what the Second Coming of the Lord was to the early Christians—was to be unceremoniously called off. No class war any more. No thrilling war cries. Cooperation with bourgeois parties instead. All this from a member of the old guard, a former exile, and, as it happened, one of the most lovable members of the party!

But Bernstein[24] went further still. He laid sacrilegious hands on the hallowed foundations of the doctrine. He attacked the Hegelian background. The labor theory of value and the exploitation theory came in for stricture. He doubted the inevitability of socialism and reduced it to tame "desirability." He looked askance at the economic interpretation of history. Crises would not kill the capitalist dragon; on the contrary, with time capitalism would gain in stability. Growing misery was nonsense of course. Bourgeois liberalism had produced

---

[23] It has been shown by Ryazanov that the editor of this book took liberties with Engels' text. But the above argument is not affected by even the highest possible estimate of the ravages of his pencil. See Ryazanov, *Karl Marx and Friedrich Engels* (translated by Kunitz, 1927).

[24] The two books of his that are most relevant for our purpose are *Die Voraussetzungen des Sozialismus und die Aufgaben der Sozialdemokratie* (1899), translation by E. C. Harvey, 1909, and *Zur Geschichte und Theorie des Sozialismus* (1901).

lasting values which it was worth while trying to conserve. He even said that the proletariat was not everything. Think of that!

This of course was more than the party could stand. It would have been unbearable even if Bernstein had been incontestably right on every point, for creeds embodied in an organization cannot be reformed by means of holocausts. But he was not. He was an excellent man but he was not Marx's intellectual peer. We have seen in Part I that he went too far in the matter of the economic interpretation of history which he can hardly have fully understood. He also went too far in his assertion that developments in the agrarian sector refute Marx's theory of the concentration of economic control. And there were other points inviting effective reply so that the champion of orthodoxy, Karl Kautsky,[25] found it not too difficult to hold his ground—or some of it. Nor is it so clear that it would have been to the advantage of the party had Bernstein's tactical recommendations prevailed. A wing would certainly have broken away. The prestige of the party would have suffered greatly. And, as has been stated before, no immediate gain would have accrued. There was hence a lot to be said for the "conservative" view.

Under the circumstances, the course which Bebel took was neither so obviously unwise nor so obviously tyrannical as fellow travelers and other critics made out at the time. He denounced Revisionism vigorously, so vigorously as to keep his hold on his leftists. He had it anathematized at the conventions in Hanover (1899) and Dresden (1903). But he saw to it that the resolutions reaffirming class war and other articles of faith were so framed as to make it possible for "revisionists" to submit. They did, and no further measures were taken against them though there was, I believe, some cracking of the whip. Bernstein himself was allowed to enter the Reichstag with the support of the party. Von Vollmar remained in the fold.

Trade-union leaders shrugged their shoulders and murmured about the chewing of doctrinal cud. They had been revisionists all along. But so long as the party did not interfere in their immediate concerns and so long as it did not call upon them to do anything they really disliked, they did not much care. They extended protection to some revisionists and also to some of their literary organs. They made it quite clear that, whatever the party's philosophy, business was business. But that was all.

The intellectual revisionists for whom doctrine was not a matter of

[25] From that time on, Kautsky, the founder and editor of the *Neue Zeit* and author of several treatises on Marxist theory, held a position that can be described only in ecclesiastical terms, upholding the "revolutionary" doctrine against revisionism as he was later on to uphold orthodoxy against the bolshevik heretics. He was the most professorial of men and much less lovable than Bernstein. On the whole, however, both sections of the party must be congratulated on the moral as well as on the intellectual level of their champions.

indifference, and the non-socialist sympathizers some of whom would have liked to join a socialist party that did not stress class war and revolution, thought differently of course. It was they who talked about a party crisis and shook their heads about the future of the party. They had every reason to do so. For *their* future in and around the party was indeed jeopardized. In fact Bebel, himself no intellectual and no friend to parlor pinks, lost no time in warning them off the premises. The rank and file of the party however were but little disturbed about all this. They followed their leaders and repeated their slogans until, without any compunction about what Marx or, for that matter, Bebel would have said, they rushed to arms in order to defend their country.

Some interesting light is shed on the development we have just been surveying by the parallel yet different development in Austria.[26] As we should expect from the much slower pace of capitalist development, it took twenty years longer to become a political factor of importance. Rising slowly from small and not very creditable beginnings, it eventually established itself in 1888 (convention of Hainfeld) under Victor Adler, who had succeeded in the almost desperate task of welding together the socialists of all the nations who inhabited that country and who was to lead them, with consummate ability, for another thirty years.

Now this party was also officially Marxist. The little circle of brilliant Jews that formed its intellectual nucleus,[27] the Neo-Marxists, even contributed substantially to the development of Marxian doctrine as we have seen in Part I—going on along orthodox lines, altering them no doubt in the process but fighting, bitterly and ably, anyone else who tried to do so, and always keeping to the revolutionary ideology in its most uncompromising form. The relations with the German party were close and cordial. At the same time, everyone knew that Adler would stand no nonsense. Having, for cultural and racial reasons, much more authority over his intellectual extremists than Bebel ever had over his, he was able to allow them all the Marxism they wanted in their cafés and to use them whenever he saw fit without letting them interfere with what really mattered to him, the organization and the party press, universal suffrage, progressive legislation and, yes, the proper working of the state. This combina-

---

[26] By Austria I here mean the western half of the Austro-Hungarian monarchy which since 1866 had a parliament and a government (lacking however the departments of foreign affairs and of war) of its own that were coordinated on a footing of equality with the parliament and government of the eastern half—Hungary or, to use official language, "the countries of the Holy Crown of St. Stephen." The Hungarian Social Democratic party took its pattern from the Austrian, but never attained quantitative significance.

[27] Trotsky, as yet under the name of Bronstein, occasionally showed up among them and seems to have experienced their influence.

tion of Marxist doctrine and reformist practice answered admirably. The Austrian governments soon discovered that here was a factor, no less important than the church or the army, that from its own interest was bound to support the central authority in its perennial struggle with filibustering nationalist oppositions, particularly the German and the Czech. These governments—mostly civil servants' cabinets as in Germany although attempts were made incessantly by the crown to insert politicians, at least as ministers without portfolio—thereupon proceeded to extend favors to the party, which reciprocated in full.[28] And when a government (a civil servants' cabinet headed by Baron Gautsch) took up the cause of universal suffrage, Adler, without encountering any opposition among his followers, was able to declare publicly that, for the time being, the socialists were a "governmental party" (*Regierungspartei*), although cabinet office was neither offered nor would have been acceptable to them.[29]

VI. The Second International

The internationalist plank in the program of the Marxist parties called for an international organization like the defunct First International. The other socialist and laborite groups were not internationalist in the sense of the Marxian creed. But, partly from the inheritance of bourgeois radicalism and partly from aversion to the upper-class governments of their respective nations, they had all of them acquired, though in varying degrees, internationalist and pacifist views and sympathies so that international cooperation occurred readily to them. The foundation of the Second International (1889) thus embodied a compromise that really attempted to reconcile the irreconcilable but worked until 1914. A few remarks will suffice on this subject.

There was the international bureau. And there were the congresses with their full-dress debates on questions of tactics and of principle. Measured by tangible achievements, the importance of the Second International might well be equated to zero. And at zero it has indeed been evaluated both by revolutionary activists and by laborites. As a matter of fact, however, it was not meant for immediate action of any

[28] A device which the socialists repeatedly used in order to help the government was this. When nationalist filibusters paralyzed parliament and all business was at a standstill, they would move "urgency" for the budget. The urgency motion when duly passed practically meant that the measure thus declared urgent went through if there was a majority for it (which was always available in the case of the budget) irrespective of those formal rules of parliamentary procedure which the filibuster made it impossible to observe.

[29] The chief difficulty was, I suppose, in the strong stand that the German party had taken in the matter. Scruples of the Austrian socialists themselves were second in importance. Aversion of the Austrian bureaucracy or of the old Emperor, if any, was a bad third among the factors which prevented that consummation.

sort; action, whether revolutionary or reformist, could at that time have been only national. It was to organize contacts between the affiliated parties and groups, to standardize views, to coordinate lines of advance, to restrain the irresponsible, and to urge on the laggard, to create, as far as possible, an international socialist opinion. All of this was, from the socialist standpoint, extremely desirable and important though in the nature of things positive results would have taken many decades to mature.

Accordingly, the chief and the members of the bureau were anything but a directing board of international socialism. There was no policy for them to shape and no program to impose such as there had been in the case of the First International. The national parties and labor groups were left perfectly autonomous and free to join other international organizations that might suit their particular aims. Trade unions—also cooperatives and educational bodies—were welcomed and even courted but they did not play the leading role. The national parties were nevertheless kept on a common ground that was sufficiently broad for Stauning and Branting on the one hand and Lenin and Guesde on the other to move on. Some of the members of that international institute no doubt sneered at the chicken-hearted reserve of others and the latter objected to the hotheaded radicalism of the former. And sometimes things came perilously near a showdown. On the whole however they all took a course in socialist diplomacy at the hands of one another. Since this *modus vivendi*—with plenty of freedom for agreeing to differ—was the only possible one, this was in itself a great achievement.

Strange as it may sound, it was the Germans who were—with Russian and Guesdist support—primarily responsible for it. They were the one great Marxist party and they gave the common ground a coating of Marxism. But they realized quite clearly that the majority of the men who represented the socialist forces outside of Germany were not Marxists. For most of these men it was a case of signing the thirty-nine articles while reserving an unlimited freedom of interpretation. Naturally enough, the more ardent believers were shocked at this and talked about the faith being degraded to a matter of form that had no substance in it. The German leaders however put up with it. They even tolerated straight heresy which they would have attacked furiously at home. Bebel knew how far he could go and that his forbearance, immediately met as it was by English forbearance, would pay in the end as, without the war, it assuredly would have done. Thus he maneuvered to cement the proletarian front with a view to vitalizing it in time, and in doing so he showed an ability that, if Germany's diplomacy had had it, might have prevented the First World War.

Some results did mature. The somewhat indefinite discussions of the first decade or so were eventually focused on foreign policy and something like a common view began eventually to emerge. It was a race against time. This race was lost. Every journalist who now refers to that epoch feels entitled to condemn the International for what he styles the failure of international socialism at the outbreak of the catastrophe. But this is a most superficial view to take. The extraordinary congress at Basle (1912) and its appeal to the workers of all nations to exert themselves for peace was surely all that it was possible to do under those circumstances. A call for a general strike issued to an international proletariat that exists nowhere except in the imagination of a few intellectuals would not have been more effective, it would have been less so. To achieve the possible is not failure but success, however inadequate the success may prove in the end. If failure there was, it occurred at the domestic fronts of the individual national parties.

CHAPTER XXVII

FROM THE FIRST TO THE SECOND
WORLD WAR

I. THE "GRAN RIFIUTO"

As MEMBERS of their international organization, the socialist parties had done all they could to avert the war. But when nevertheless it broke out, they rallied to their national causes with a readiness that was truly astounding. The German Marxists hesitated even less than the English laborites.[1] Of course it must be borne in mind that every belligerent nation was fully convinced that it was waging a purely defensive war—every war is defensive or at least "preventive" in the eyes of the nations that wage it.[2] Still, if we reflect that the socialist parties had an indubitable constitutional right to vote against war budgets and that within the general moral schema of bourgeois democracy there is no obligation to identify oneself with national policy—men far removed from socialist anti-militarism in fact disapproved of the war in all the belligerent countries—we seem to face a problem that is not solved by doubtful references to Marx or to previous declarations by Bebel and von Vollmar that they would defend their country if attacked. There should have been no difficulty in recalling Marx's true teaching on the subject. Moreover, defending one's country means only doing one's duty with the army; it does not imply voting with the government and entering into *unions sacrées*.[3] Guesde and Sembat in France and Vandervelde in Belgium who took office in war cabinets, and the German socialists who voted the war budgets, thus did more than loyalty to their nations required, as then commonly understood.[4]

There is but one solution to the puzzle. Whether or not the majority of socialist politicians believed in Marxian internationalism —perhaps this belief had by that time shared the fate of the cognate

[1] The English Labour party was in fact alone in making a serious stand for peace in 1914, though it joined the war coalition later on.

[2] This is why the attempt made by the victors to decide the moral issue by means of a clause in an imposed peace treaty was not only so unfair but also so foolish.

[3] Nor is it true that failure to do so would have weakened the national cause. Lord Morley's resignation clearly did not injure England.

[4] Many of us will think differently at present. But this merely shows how far we have traveled from the old moorings of liberal democracy. To exalt national unity into a moral precept spells acceptance of one of the most important principles of fascism.

belief in a spectacular revolution—they certainly realized that any stand taken upon the gospel would have cost them their following. The masses would have first stared at them and then they would have renounced allegiance, thereby refuting *via facti* the Marxian doctrine that the proletarian has no country and that class war is the only war that concerns him. In this sense, and with a proviso to the effect that things might have been different if the war had impinged after a longer spell of evolution within the bourgeois framework, a vital pillar of the Marxian structure broke in August 1914.[5]

This was in fact widely felt. It was felt in the conservative camp: German conservatives suddenly began to refer to the socialist party in language that was the pink of courtesy. It was felt in that part of the socialist camp in which the faith still retained its old ardor. Even in England MacDonald lost the leadership of the labor party and eventually his seat rather than join the war coalition. In Germany, Kautsky and Haase left the majority (March 1916) and in 1917 organized the Independent Social Democratic party, though most of its important members returned to the fold in 1919.[6] Lenin declared that the Second International was dead and that the cause of socialism had been betrayed.

There was an element of truth in this. So far as the majorities of the Marxist parties were concerned, socialism at the crossroads had in fact not stood the test. It had not chosen the Marxist route. The creeds, the slogans, the ultimate goals, the organizations, the bureaucracies, the leaders had not changed. They remained on the morrow of the *gran rifiuto* what they had been on its eve. But what they meant and stood for had changed all the more. After that *experimentum crucis* neither socialists nor anti-socialists could any longer look at those parties in the same light as before. Nor could those parties themselves go on with their old antics. For better and for worse they had stepped out of their ivory tower. They had testified to the fact that the fate of their countries meant more to them than did the socialist goal.

The case *was* different however with those of them who, like the Social Democratic parties of the Scandinavian countries, never had

[5] To some extent this must also be attributed to the success of non-socialist reforms.

[6] It is worth noting that the Independents recruited themselves by no means exclusively from the uncompromising Marxists. Kautsky and Haase belonged to that sector, but many who joined with them did not. Bernstein, for instance, joined and so did several other revisionists whose motive cannot have been respect for the Marxian faith. But there is nothing to wonder at in this. Orthodox Marxism was of course not the only reason a socialist might have had for disapproving the course taken by the majority. These revisionists simply shared Ramsay MacDonald's persuasion.

been in any ivory tower. And even with the others the case will *look* different to observers who never took those revolutionary antics seriously. As regards the German party in particular, it may well be nearer the truth to say that the "social traitors"—as they were dubbed—simply came down from unrealistic clouds and that the national emergency taught them to stand on their feet instead of on their heads—which, so some of us will add, was all to their credit and no *rifiuto* at all. But whichever view we take, there cannot be any doubt that the new attitude of responsibility drastically short-ened the long stretch that before 1914 seemed to lie between them and the natural goal of every party—office. I am far indeed from attributing to German Social Democrats any calculations of this kind or from doubting the sincerity of their decision not to take office in bourgeois society. But it is obvious that, as a result of the stand they took at the beginning of the war, they were—if I may say so— "sitting pretty" at the end of it. Unlike the other parties, they had not compromised themselves by running along in full cry. But neither had they deserted their nation in the hour of danger.

II. THE EFFECTS OF THE FIRST WORLD WAR ON THE CHANCES OF THE SOCIALIST PARTIES OF EUROPE

1. Any major war that ends in defeat will shake the social fabric and threaten the position of the ruling group; the loss of prestige resulting from military defeat is one of the hardest things for a regime to survive. I do not know of any exception to this rule. But the converse proposition is not so certain. Unless success be quick or, at all events, striking and clearly associated with the performance of the ruling stratum—as was, for instance, Germany's success in 1870—exhaustion, economic, physical and psychological may well produce, even in the case of victory, effects on the relative position of classes, groups and parties that do not differ essentially from those of defeat.

The First World War illustrates this. In the United States the effort had not been sufficiently prolonged and exhausting to show it. Even here the administration responsible for the war suffered a crushing defeat at the polls. But in all other victorious countries the prestige of the ruling strata and their hold on their people were impaired and not enhanced. For the fortunes of the German and English socialist parties, this meant the advent of power or, at all events, office. In Germany control of the central organs of society was thrust upon the party: though in order to save doctrinal face some of them as well as some anti-socialists insisted on speaking of a revolution, the fact was that they undertook government by request —and a humble request it was. In England the labor vote that had been at little over half a million in January 1910 and not quite two millions and a quarter in 1918,[7] went to 4,236,733 in 1922 and to 5,487,620 in 1924 (8,362,594 in 1929). MacDonald reconquered the leadership and in 1924 the party came into office if not really into power. In France the structure of the political world prevented any such clear-cut consummation, but the general contours were the same: there was a syndicalist revival immediately after the war, but the Confédération Générale du Travail, leaving the newly founded Confédération Générale du Travail Syndicaliste and the communist Confédération Générale du Travail Unitaire to absorb inadaptable elements, discouraged revolutionary courses and slowly prepared itself for a dominant political role.

Moreover, the socialist or quasi-socialist parties who then shouldered the responsibility that came to them may well have felt that they had almost a monopoly of many of the qualifications required in order to make a success of their venture. Better than any other group they were able to handle the masses that seethed with discontent. As the German example shows, they even were in a better position than anyone else was for the time being to deal firmly with revolutionary outbreaks—if need be, by force. At any rate, they were the very people to administer the right dose of social reform, to carry it on the one hand, and to make the masses accept it on the other. Most important of all, they were, from their standpoint, quite justified in believing that they were also the people to heal the wounds the "imperialist war" had inflicted, to restore international relations and to clear up the mess which, without any fault of theirs, purely bourgeois governments had made of the peace. In this they committed the same kind of error which from a different standpoint was committed by their bourgeois competitors who believed in collective security, the League of Nations, the reconstruction of gold currencies and the removal of trade barriers. But once we grant the erroneous premise we must also grant that the socialists were right in hoping for success, particularly in the field of foreign policy.

2. The achievements of the two MacDonald governments—MacDonald's and Henderson's work at the foreign office—are sufficient to illustrate this. But the German case is still more significant. First of all, only the Social Democrats were in a moral position to accept the peace treaty and to support a policy that aimed at fulfilling its provisions. They lamented the national catastrophe, of course, and the burdens it imposed. But feeling as they did about military glory, neither the defeat itself nor the peace spelled unbearable humiliation for them. Some of them almost subscribed to the Anglo-French theory of the war. Most of them cared little for rearmament. While other Germans looked on in sullen disgust, they worked for peaceful

[7] The increase from 1910 to 1918 is wholly accounted for by the enfranchisement of women and the simplification of the electoral qualification.

understanding with the victors in a spirit that was perfectly free, **if** not from resentment, yet from passionate hatred. In the matter of what to others was an imposed democracy, they even saw eye to eye with the western nations: having disposed of the communist revolts in 1918-1919 and having by judicious compromise acquired a dominant role in domestic politics, they were in their most democratic mood.

Second, their hold on the masses was strong enough to make this attitude politically effective. For the moment, a great part of the population saw things in the same light. Their views of the situation and the right way of dealing with it temporarily became the official view whatever the politics of the government that happened to be in office. They provided the political support for the coalitions which negotiated the Dawes plan and the Locarno pact and which could never have been formed or, if formed, could never have taken that line without them. Stresemann was no socialist. Yet the policy associated with his name was the policy of the Social Democratic party—the policy for which they were to get all the credit during one decade and all the punishment in another.

Third, they were at an advantage in their relations to political opinion abroad. The world knew little about Germany. But it understood two things: on the one hand, it realized that there was a party that was ready to accept for good many of the postwar arrangements and in fact quite approved of some of them, a party that was the enemy of what France and England had convinced themselves was *their* enemy; on the other hand, it realized that German Social Democracy need not be feared on other counts—however conservative a government might be, there was no need for it to object to German as it did object to Russian socialism. In the long run this was a weakness. It had much to do with the dilatory treatment dealt out to German grievances, for it induced the foreign offices of England and France to believe that Germany would remain indefinitely the meek petitioner who could be made happy by assurances that some day he might be promoted to a position of equality with the superior nations. In the short run, however, and especially during the dark days of the Ruhr invasion, it was an asset: the party—or rather governments known to depend on the support of the party—had an entrée that would have been denied to others.

Fourth, there were the old contacts of the Social Democratic party with the corresponding parties in other countries which dated from the Second International. These contacts had not been completely severed by the war. After all, the Second International had never been officially dissolved, and many individuals and groups within it —especially, but by no means exclusively, those of the neutral countries—had kept their internationalist beliefs intact. The secretary (C.

Huysmans) had continued to act, and in 1917, on the suggestion of the Scandinavian socialists, he had even made an attempt to convene a congress which failed only because the Allied powers, by that time determined to crush their adversary, refused to grant passports.[8] Thus it was but natural that many socialists should have thought of reviving it as a matter of course.

3. It was revived but not without difficulties. The first conferences that were held for this purpose in 1919 and 1920 were only moderately successful. The Communist (Third) International that had emerged meanwhile (see below) exerted an attraction that proved a serious obstacle to unity among the laborite and socialist parties of the world. And several important groups that were in no mind to throw in their lot with the communists still wanted something more up to date than the Second International. This situation was met successfully by a clever tactical device. On the initiative of the Austrian Socialists who were joined by the German Independents and the English Independent Labor Party, a new organization, the Workers' International Union of Socialist Parties (the so-called Vienna International), was formed in order to radicalize the groups in the revived Second International, to restrain the groups that leaned too much toward communism and to bring them both into line by judicious formulations of aims.[9]

The meaning of the venture is exactly rendered by the sobriquet the communists immediately found for it, the "International number two and one-half." That is precisely why it was able to serve the needs of the time. At the Congress of Hamburg (1923) the Second and the Vienna Internationals were united in order to form the Labor and Socialist International, to stigmatize the peace as "imperialist" and to call for a united front against international reaction—which at any rate sounded well—for the eight-hour day and for international social legislation. The reduction of Germany's indemnity to a definite and reasonable figure, the abolishment of interallied debts and the evacuation of German territory had been declared necessary a year before (Frankfort Resolutions, 1922). In the light of subsequent events we cannot fail to realize how great an achievement—and service—that was.

[8] Before that there had actually been two conventions in Switzerland—at Zimmerwald (1915) and at Kienthal (1916)—which acquired, contrary to the original intention I believe, a different color owing to the fact that the attendance was not representative of the official parties. I shall return briefly to them later on.

[9] Some of those formulations would have done credit to any eighteenth-century diplomatist. The great stumbling block was class war. The continental groups could not live without it, the English could not live with it. So, when the merger was consummated at the Congress of Hamburg, the *Klassenkampf* and the *lutte des classes* were retained in the German and French texts but in the English text they were replaced by an unrecognizable circumlocution.

III. Communism and the Russian Element

1. Meanwhile, communist parties were rapidly developing. In itself this is only what we should have expected. Nor was it dangerous. Any party that experiences the sobering influence of responsibility will unavoidably have to leave room for groups further to the left (or right) to develop in, and such room is not likely to remain unoccupied for long. Provided defection can be kept within bounds, this need not be more than a nuisance—it may even be preferable to keeping unruly elements in the fold. Socialist parties had always had trouble with hyper-radical wings.[10] That such "leftist" groups should gain ground in the troubled days that followed upon the war and that they should seize the opportunity to acquire the status of distinct parties is no more surprising than that they should follow classical usage and call themselves "communist" or that they should display a much stronger internationalist slant than the official parties did at the time.

Bear in mind that all this is completely independent of the Russian aspect of the case. There would be communist parties and there would be a Communist International if the tsars still reigned over Russia. But since the Russian element became a factor in shaping the fortunes of both socialism and communism all over the world—in fact, in shaping the social and political history of our time—it is essential to restate how it developed and to appraise its nature and importance. For this purpose we shall divide its development into three stages.

2. At first—that is to say, until the bolsheviks seized power in 1917 —there was nothing particularly Russian about the development of the communist groups except that the strongest man happened to be a Russian and that a streak of Mongol despotism was present in his scheme of thought. When at the outbreak of the war the Second International suspended itself *via facti*, and when Lenin declared that it was dead and that the hour had struck for more effective methods, it was natural for those who felt as he did to get together. Opportunity presented itself at the two conventions that were held in Switzerland, at Zimmerwald (1915) and at Kienthal (1916). Since practically all of those who had espoused the causes of their nations

[10] The splits that occurred in England and Germany over the war issue were of course a different matter and of only temporary importance. Even the German Spartacus League, founded in 1916 by Karl Liebknecht and Rosa Luxemburg, though it went much further in its opposition to war than the Independents approved, took time to develop a definitely hostile attitude and even then did not go, officially at least, beyond insisting on the letter of the old Erfurt program. So far as I know, neither Liebknecht nor Mrs. Luxemburg ever completely severed contact with the party. The latter was one of the most relentless critics of bolshevist practice.

stayed away, the attending militants found little difficulty in—more or less—rallying to Lenin's program of converting the imperialist war into an international revolution. There was more in this than a mere profession of faith in pristine Marxism and its Messianic promise. There was, with some of them, also the clear perception of the truth, to which the bourgeois of all countries were so completely blind, that the fabric of bourgeois society is unequal to the strains and stresses of prolonged "total" warfare and that breakdowns would occur at least in some countries. Beyond that however Lenin's leadership was not accepted. Most of those who were present thought of convincing, bullying and using existing socialist parties rather than of destroying them. Moreover—and in this Lenin agreed—the international revolution was to be brought about by the individual actions of the national proletariats, and in the "advanced" countries first.

The second stage I date from 1917 to 1927, that is to say, from the rise of the bolsheviks to power in Russia to Trotsky's expulsion from the Central Committee of the Bolshevik party (October 1927). That decade witnessed the emergence of communist parties and of a Communist (the "Third") International. It also witnessed the (for the time being) definitive break with the socialist and laborite parties which, in the case of Germany, was embittered beyond remedy by the severely repressive measures adopted by the Social Democrats in power during the winter of 1918 to 1919. And finally it witnessed the forging of the Russian chain.

But during the whole of that decade, the chain neither galled nor distorted. It must be remembered that the bolshevik conquest of the rule over the most backward of all the great nations was nothing but a fluke.[11] To a certain extent Lenin himself recognized this. He repeated over and over again that final victory would be won only by the action of the revolutionary forces in more advanced countries and that this action was the really important thing. Of course he dictated to communists as he had done before, and he insisted on a strictly centralist organization of the Communist International —whose bureau took power to prescribe every move of the individual parties—but he did so in his role of communist leader and not in his role of Russian despot. That made all the difference. The headquarters of the International were in Moscow, the actual leader was Russian, but policy was directed in a thoroughly internationalist spirit, without any particular reference to Russian national interests and on principles with which the communists of all countries

[11] For this fluke, bolshevism was possibly indebted to the German general staff, by whose orders Lenin was transported to Russia. If this should be thought an exaggeration of his personal share in the events of 1917, there were enough other chance factors in the situation to teach us the freakishness of this piece of history.

substantially agreed. Though the personal relation between the Bureau of the International and the Political Bureau of the Soviet power[12] was then much closer than it was later on, the two were nevertheless much more nearly distinct agencies. Thus the International itself and the individual parties did not behave differently than they would have behaved in the absence of the link with Russia.

During that decade, therefore, the importance of the Russian connection, though great, did not amount to more than this. First of all, there was the weighty fact that however insignificant in quality and quantity of membership a communist group might be and however little claim to being taken seriously it might have, it could bask in the glory reflected by that other group which had conquered an empire, and it could derive encouragement from such a backing. Second, bolshevist reality notwithstanding—the terror, the misery, the confession of failure implied in the adoption of the New Economic Policy after the Kronstadt revolt—it was henceforth possible to point to a socialist system that "worked." The bolsheviks proved themselves masters in the art of exploiting the fact that public opinion in England and the United States will swallow anything provided it is served up in the garb of familiar slogans. This of course also redounded to the advantage of the other communist parties. Third, so long as communists of all countries (Lenin himself included) believed in the imminence of a world revolution, the Russian army meant as much to them as the army of Tsar Nicholas I had meant to the reactionary groups during the second quarter of the nineteenth century.[13] In 1919 such hopes were less unreasonable and nearer to fulfillment than people are now prepared to believe. It is true that communist republics were actually established only in Bavaria and in Hungary.[14] But in Germany, Austria and Italy

[12] In Lenin's time, administrative authority was wielded by the Political Bureau, run by Lenin himself, by the Military Council, Trotsky's domain, and by the Cheka, then managed by Dzerzhinsky. All three bodies were unknown to the constitution of the Soviet state, which vested that authority in the "Soviet of the People's Commissars." Perhaps they should theoretically be called organs of the party. But the party was the state.

[13] It should be noticed that communists had dropped anti-militarism and non-interventionism as easily as they had dropped democracy.

[14] The Hungarian case (the government of Béla Kun) is highly instructive. The paralysis of the upper classes and the indifference of the peasantry made it possible for a small group of intellectuals to seize power without meeting significant resistance. They were a strange crowd—some of them displaying (the same was true in Bavaria) unmistakably pathological symptoms—and utterly unequal to this or any other serious task. But they had unbounded confidence in themselves and their creed and no objection whatever to terrorist methods. And that proved quite sufficient. They were allowed to stage their opera and might have gone on for an indefinite time if the Allies had not permitted (or ordered) the Rumanian army to eject them.

the social structure was perilously near toppling and there is no saying what would have happened in those countries and possibly farther west if Trotsky's war machine had been in working order at that time and not engaged in the civil and the Polish wars.[15] It should not be forgotten that the Communist International was founded in that atmosphere of impending life and death struggle. Many things which acquired a different meaning afterwards—such as the centralized management that has unlimited power over the individual parties and deprives them of all freedom of action—may then have seemed quite reasonable from that aspect.

The third stage I have dated from the expulsion of Trotsky (1927) because this is a convenient landmark in the rise of Stalin to absolute power. After that every actual decision in matters of policy seems to have been his, though he still met some opposition in the Political Bureau and elsewhere until the "trial" of Kamenew and Zinoviev (1936) or even until Yezhov's reign of terror (1937). For our purpose this means that every decision was thenceforth the decision of a Russian statesman acting on behalf of national Russian interests as seen from the standpoint of a streamlined despotism. And this in turn, if correct, defines what his attitude to the "Comintern" (the Communist International) and to foreign communist parties must have been. They became tools of Russian policy, taking rank within the huge arsenal of such tools and being realistically evaluated relative to others according to circumstances. Up to the present war which may revive it, the world revolution was a frozen asset. The surviving veterans as well as the neophytes of internationalist communism may have been contemptible. But they were still of some use. They could preach the glories of the Russian regime. They could serve as pins with which to prick hostile governments. They increased the bargaining power of Russia. So it was worth while to go to some trouble and expense in order to keep them in subjection, to supervise them by agents of the secret police, and to man the Comintern's bureau with absolutely obsequious serfs who would obey in fear and trembling.

3. In all this (and in lying about it) Stalin followed the established practice of the ages. Most national governments have acted as he did and it is pure hypocrisy to profess specific indignation in his case.

[15] Therefore it is doubtful whether it is correct to say that the western powers acted foolishly and inefficiently in supporting in a half-hearted way the various counterrevolutions that were attempted in Russia, particularly the Denikin and Wrangel ventures. It seems to me that, whether by a shrewd appraisal of the situation or by luck, they attained exactly what they could have wished: they neutralized the Soviet power at a crucial moment and thus stopped the advance of bolshevism. Less than this would have endangered their own social systems; more than this would have involved prolonged, costly and perhaps unprofitable efforts that might easily have defeated their aims.

The most obvious examples are afforded by the practice of governments who espoused a religious creed. As long as the respective creeds were sufficiently vital to motivate action, these governments often used foreign groups of the same creed for their purposes. But, as the history of the years from 1793 to 1815 is sufficient to prove, the practice is much more general than these examples suggest. No less standardized is the reaction—phraseological and other—by the governments which are affected by it: politicians of all types and classes are happy to seize the opportunity of calling an opponent a traitor.

But for the communist parties outside of Russia it was a serious matter to receive orders from a *caput mortuum* in the hands of a modernized tsar. Their abject servility raises two questions, one as to its causes and another as to its possible bearing on the future character and fate of revolutionary socialism.

The first question is perhaps less difficult to answer than it seems. All we have to do is to put ourselves in the communist's chair and, taking account of his type, look at his situation in a practical spirit. He would not object to the Stalin regime on humanitarian considerations. He may even glory in the slaughter—some neurasthenic degenerates do, and others, the communists from failure and resentment, experience satisfaction at the sufferings of a certain class of victims. Moreover, why should he resent cruelties that do not prevent thoroughly bourgeois people from idolizing the regime? Why should he, on that ground, condemn bolshevism when the Dean of Canterbury does not?[16] Why indeed?

Again, there was hardly any reason for communists to object on the ground of Thermidorism. This phrase was first used by the opponents of the New Economic Policy but Trotsky adopted it later in order to stigmatize Stalin's regime as "reactionary" in the sense in which the action of the men who overthrew Robespierre in 1794 was "reactionary." But it is completely meaningless. After all, it was Stalin who collectivized agriculture, "liquidated" the Kulaks, reversed the New Economic Policy. In fact, like a good tactician, he suppressed opposition and substantially carried out the opposition's program.

Finally, what the protecting power does at home is not of primary importance to the communist in another country as long as that power plays fair with him. And even if it does not play fair with him, what is he to do? The chain tightened and galled. But it also

[16] The sentiments expressed in the book by that ecclesiastic cannot be defended on the ground that the principles of the "Russian experiment" are one thing and the mode of its execution is another thing. For the really terrible point about the Stalin regime is not what it did to millions of victims but the fact *that it had to do it if it wished to survive.* In other words, those principles and that practice are inseparable.

supported. The socialist parties would not have accepted him. The normal healthy-minded workman turned from him with a groan. He would have been at loose ends like Trotsky. He was in no position to do without the chain,[17] and in accepting his slavery he may have hoped—he may still hope—that junctures will arise in which he may be able to pull it his way . . . after the present World War perhaps . . .

The last point goes some way toward answering the second question. Certainly there is a possibility that Russian despotism will spread over the ruins of European civilization—or even beyond them —and that in this case the communist parties all over the world will be turned into Russian garrisons. But there are many other possibilities. And one of them is that the Russian regime will founder in the process or that in spreading over other countries it will acquire traits more congenial to the individual national soils. A special case of this kind would be that in the end the Russian element will have changed *nothing* in the future character of revolutionary socialism. To bank on this is no doubt risky. But it is not as foolish as it is to hope that our civilization will emerge unscathed from the present conflagration—unless of course this conflagration subsides more quickly than we have a right to expect.

IV. ADMINISTERING CAPITALISM?

1. So far, then, we have not seen any convincing reason why the experiments in political responsibility that socialist parties made after 1918 should not have been perfectly successful. To repeat: in some countries—in Sweden for instance—socialists merely continued to consolidate a power they had acquired before; in others, power had come naturally to them without having to be conquered by revolutionary action; in all countries, they seemed to be much more in a position to grapple with the great problems of the time than was any other party. As I have put it before, they almost seemed to monopolize the essential conditions for success. Moreover, though most of them had not had any previous experience in office, they had acquired plenty of experience of a most useful sort in organizing,

[17] This of course particularly applies to the communist group or groups in the United States. The conditions of American politics are not favorable to the growth of an official communist party—a few county treasurerships do not go far from the recruiting standpoint. But the importance of the communist element must not be measured by the membership of the official party. Those intellectuals who are either straight communists or fellow travelers have really no motive to join it. They have every motive to stay out of it, for they are much better able to serve if, without carrying the badge, they conquer positions on opinion-producing committees or in administrative bodies and so on, remaining free to deny, with perfect truth, that they are communists in a party sense. Such invisible groups are incapable of concerted action except for the lead from Moscow.

negotiating and in administration. In fact, it should be stated at once that they hardly ever did a downright foolish thing. Finally, neither the inevitable emergence of a new party to the left of the socialists nor the connection of that party with Moscow was as serious for them as their opponents tried to make out.

But in spite of all this, their situation was everywhere precarious. To the true believer it might well have seemed an impossible one. For all those tactical advantages hid a fundamental difficulty which they were powerless to remove. The war and the upheaval caused by the war had brought the socialists into office; but below the tatters of the old garb, the social organism, and in particular the economic process, were still what they had been before. That is to say, socialists had to govern in an essentially capitalist world.

Marx had visualized the conquest of political power as the prerequisite of socialization which was to be taken in hand immediately. This implied, however, as in fact Marx's argument implied throughout, that the opportunity for that conquest would occur when capitalism had run its course or, to use our own phrase again, when things and souls were ripe. The breakdown he thought of was to be a breakdown of the economic engine of capitalism from internal causes.[18] Political breakdown of the bourgeois world was to be a mere incident to this. But now the political breakdown— or something akin to it—had happened, and the political opportunity had occurred, while the economic process was nowhere near maturity as yet. The "superstructure" had moved more quickly than the propelling mechanism. It was a most un-Marxian situation.

The student in his closet may speculate about what the course of things would have been if the socialist parties, recognizing the state of things, had refused the Trojan horse of office, remained in the opposition and allowed the bourgeoisie to deal with the wreckage left by the war and by the peace. Perhaps it would have been better for them, for socialism, for the world—who knows? But for men who by that time had learned to identify themselves with their nations and to take the point of view of responsibility there was no choice. They resolutely faced what fundamentally was an insoluble problem.

There was a social and economic system that would not function except on capitalist lines. The socialists might control it, regulate it in the interest of labor, squeeze it to the point of impairing its efficiency—but they were unable to do anything specifically socialist. If they were to run it, they would have to run it according to its logic. They would have to "administer capitalism." And this they

---

[18] This in part explains the favor enjoyed in the United States by theories which aim at showing that capitalism is as a matter of fact breaking down from internal causes. See ch. x.

did. Something was done to dress up their measures in socialist phrases, and the magnifying glass was applied, with some success, to every difference between their policy and what the bourgeois alternative was in each case supposed to be. In substance however they had to do what liberals or conservatives would also have done under the same circumstances. But, though the only possible course,[19] this was, for the socialist parties, a most dangerous one to pursue.

Not that it was entirely hopeless or, from the standpoint of the socialist faith, entirely incapable of defense. At the beginning of the twenties, socialists in Europe may well have hoped that, with luck and cautious steering, they would establish themselves in or near the centers of political power so as to be able to avert any danger of "reaction" and to buttress the position of the proletariat until the day when it would be possible to socialize society without any violent break; they would preside over the euthanasia of bourgeois society and at the same time make sure that the process of dying went on all right and that the victim would not experience a comeback. But for the presence of other factors than those which enter the socialist's or the labor man's picture of society, this hope might have come true.

Defense from the standpoint of the Faith might have been based on the proposition stated above, viz., that the situation was a novel one and had not been foreseen by Marx. The bourgeois victim turning to the socialists for shelter—such a case was evidently not provided for in his schema. It might have been argued that under the circumstances even mere "administering capitalism" was a great step in advance. Nor was it a question of administering capitalism in the capitalist interest but of doing honest work in the field of social reform, and of building a state that would pivot on the workman's interests. In any case that was the only thing to do if the democratic road was to be chosen, for the immaturity of the situation asserted itself precisely by the fact that there were no majorities to be had for the socialist alternative. No wonder that the socialist parties which had resolved to accept office under such circumstances loudly proclaimed their allegiance to democracy!

Thus, the political hack's craving for office was capable of justification on the highest grounds of doctrine and proletarian interest. The reader will have no difficulty in visualizing how such comfortable concordance must have impressed radical critics. But since later events have induced so many people to speak of the failure of that policy and to lecture the leaders of that time on what they ought to have done, I do wish to emphasize both the rationale of their

[19] I do not propose to discuss, as another possibility, an attempt at fundamental reconstruction on Russian lines. For it seems to me too obvious that any such attempt would have speedily ended in chaos and counterrevolution.

views and the compelling nature of the pattern within which they had to act. If failure there was, its causes must be looked for elsewhere than in stupidity or treason. In order to convince ourselves of this we need only glance at the English and German cases.

2. As soon as the orgy of nationalist sentiment that accompanied the close of the war subsided, a genuinely revolutionary situation developed in England, the temper of the masses asserting itself, for instance, by political strikes. Responsible socialists and responsible laborites were so completely driven together by these events—and by the danger of the nation's being goaded into a truly reactionary mood —that they henceforth accepted a common leadership, at least as far as parliamentary maneuvering was concerned. The lion's share of the combined weight went to the labor interest and, within the labor interest, to the bureaucracy of a few big unions so that an opposition of disgruntled intellectuals developed almost at once. These intellectuals objected to the laborite character of the alliance and professed themselves unable to see anything socialist about it. The ideological opportunism of the laborites lends some color to this view but, stressing the facts of the situation rather than slogans, we shall nevertheless equate the whole of the political labor forces, as far as they then accepted MacDonald's leadership, with the Social Democratic party of Germany.

Having successfully emerged from that revolutionary situation the party steadily improved its position until MacDonald came into office in 1924. He and his men made so creditable a showing that even malcontent intellectuals were temporarily subdued. In matters of foreign and colonial policy, this government was able to strike a note of its own—particularly with respect to Russia. In domestic affairs, this was less easy to do, mainly because fiscal radicalism had been (and continued to be) carried, quite as far as was possible under the circumstances, by conservative governments dependent upon a share in the labor vote. But while in legislation the labor government did not go beyond comparative details, it proved itself qualified to administer the nation's affairs. Snowden's excellent performance in the office of chancellor of the exchequer would have sufficed to show to the nation and to the world that labor was fit to govern. And this was in itself a service to the cause of socialism.[20]

Of course *that* success was greatly facilitated and any other kind of success was rendered more difficult or even impossible by the fact that the labor government was in a minority and had to rely not only on the cooperation of the liberals—with whom they had much in common, for instance their free-trade views—but also, to some extent, on the tolerance of the conservatives. They were in much the

[20] Moreover, from the standpoint of party tactics, it made things much more difficult for the conservatives than headstrong radicalism would have done.

same situation as the conservatives were during their short spells of office in the 1850's and 1860's. It would not have been so easy for them to take a responsible attitude if they had had a majority. But, as stated above, the very fact that they had not should have proved even to a Marxist tribunal that the time had not yet come for a stronger course of action—at all events, on any plan that would answer democratic requirements.

The rank and file however did not appreciate all this. Still less did the masses realize that they owed to the labor party not only what that party itself accomplished but also part of what was being done for them by its conservative competitor for the labor vote. They missed spectacular proposals of reconstruction and promises of immediate benefits, and did not know how unfair they were when they naïvely asked: "Why don't the socialists do something for us now they are in power?" The intellectuals who did not relish being sidetracked naturally availed themselves of the opportunity afforded by this mood in order to attack the sway of the laborites over the true socialists and to work up current grievances into horrible wrongs callously neglected by tyrannical trade-union bureaucrats. Under their influence the Independent Labor party grew increasingly restive during the subsequent years of opposition especially when MacDonald proved impervious to their arguments for a more radical program.[21] Thus, to many people, success looked much like failure, and responsibility much like cowardice.

This was unavoidable however. The difficulties and dangers that are inherent in a policy of socialist parties which involves accepting office under conditions of "immaturity" are still better illustrated by the history of MacDonald's second ministry.[22] Historians have learned

[21] That program primarily ran in terms of the socialization of banking and of certain key industries and hence was not really on the lines of orthodox socialism. But under the circumstances it was advertised as the genuine thing whereas MacDonald's was styled "reformist"—a term which according to classical usage applies equally well to the I.L.P. program.

[22] Readers may miss a comment on the general strike of 1926. Though it was to the interest of both parties to the contest to minimize its symptomatic importance and though the official theories of it have been shaped accordingly, it was much more than a series of tactical errors issuing in a situation in which the trade-union congress had to "bluff" and the conservative government had to "call the bluff." We need only ask ourselves what the consequences of a success would have been, for the authority of government and for democracy, in order to realize that the strike was an historical event of the first order of importance. If that weapon had proved effective, the trade unions would have become absolute masters of England and no other political, judicial or economic power could have continued to exist beside them except on sufferance. And in this position they could not have remained what they were. However reluctantly, the leaders would have had to use the absolute power thrust upon them.

For our purpose, only two points need be noticed. First, the situation described above, in particular the discontent that spread among the rank and file and was

to do justice to the statesmanship of Sir Robert Peel.[23] I trust that they will learn to do justice to the statesmanship of MacDonald. He had the singular misfortune of coming in at the very beginning of the world depression which, moreover, was the immediate cause of the breakdown of the international system embodied in the League of Nations.

Lesser men might have thought—lesser men did think, as a matter of fact—that an opportunity had come for fundamental reconstruction. This would have rent the nation in two and there cannot be any doubt about what the result would have been. Short of fundamental reconstruction, however, a policy of monetary expansion combined with less-than-fundamental social reform—individual measures of nationalization for instance and additional security legislation—and resort to mercantilist policies in the field of international relations was being widely recommended. But part of this program would undoubtedly have intensified the depression, and the rest of it—abandonment of the gold parity of the pound and mercantilism—meant so radical a break with the national tradition and with the tradition of the labor party itself that the socialists would hardly have been able to carry it, still less to make a success of it; to carry it safely and effectively it had to be carried by consent, that is to say, by a coalition.

So long as coalition was not possible, therefore, MacDonald and his men applied themselves to the task of working the system as they found it. This, under such conditions, was the most difficult of all the tasks they could have undertaken. While everybody was clamoring that "something" must be done at once, while irresponsibles of all types had the floor to themselves, while the masses were grumbling, businessmen despairing, intellectuals ranting, they steadily fought every inch of their ground. At home they kept order in the finances, they supported the pound and they refrained from speeding up the legislative machine. Abroad they strove with desperate energy —and considerable success—to make the Geneva system work and to reduce dangers and tensions all around. When the time had come and the national interest seemed to warrant the party risk, they took the plunge and helped the National Government into existence.

It is a melancholy reflection that, in many and important cases, a

---

sedulously fostered by many irresponsible elements, had much to do with the causation of the strike. Second, the strike did not impair the power of the party as it might have done. On the contrary, defeat seems to have produced a radicalization of the masses which partly accounts for the party's success in 1929.

[23] The analogy extends from certain features of the political and economic situations that confronted both men (although Peel had the advantage of entering upon office *after* the crisis of 1836-1839) to matters of political detail. In both cases there was a party split, boldly risked and eventually boldly accepted; in both cases the leaders were felt to be "traitors."

policy is bound to be the more unpopular with the public and with the intellectual critic the wiser it is. This is a case in point. To the radical critic who failed to link up that policy with the comparative mildness of the depression in England and with the steadiness of the subsequent recovery, there was nothing in it except weakness, incompetence, hidebound traditionalism, if not traitorous abandonment of the socialist cause. What probably was one of the best performances in the history of democratic politics and one of the best examples of action responsibly decided on from a correct perception of an economic and social situation, the critic looked upon with "shame and disgust." At best he considered MacDonald simply as a bad jockey who had brought the horse to its knees. But the hypothesis that appealed to him most was that the MacDonald government yielded to the diabolical whisperings (or worse) of English bankers or to the pressure of their American backers.

Unfortunately, such nonsense is a factor of real importance and must be taken account of in any attempt at prognosis. It may seriously interfere with the ability of socialist parties to serve the cause of civilization during the transitional age in which we live. But if we discard this element and also the truism that any party which makes a sacrifice in the national interest will suffer for it in the short run, we shall have little difficulty in recognizing that in the long run the labor influence may well turn out to have been strengthened by MacDonald's second tenure of office. Again the analogy with Sir Robert Peel's second ministry will help to illustrate this. Peel's conservative majority split on the issue of the repeal of the corn laws. The Peelite wing, though much more numerous and important than MacDonald's personal following, soon disintegrated. The conservative party was maimed and proved unable to get into power—though it got three times into office—until Disraeli's great victory in 1873. But after that and until Sir Henry Campbell-Bannerman's victory in 1905, it held power for about two-thirds of the time. More important than this, the English aristocracy and gentry, politically speaking, held their own *all* the time much better than they would have done if the stigma of dear bread had not been removed.

As a matter of fact, the labor party quickly recovered and consolidated its position in the country during the years that followed upon the split. It is safe to say that even in the normal course of things—irrespective of the war, that is—the socialists would have again come into office before long, with increased power and better chances of success, and that they would have been able to take a stronger line than they had taken previously. But it is equally safe to say that both as to their program and as to their ability to give effect to it, their policy would have differed only in degree from the

MacDonald policy—principally by some individual measures of socialization.

3. The postwar career of the German Social Democratic party of course differs from that of the English labor party in many particulars. But as soon as the German socialists who stayed in the Social Democratic party had accepted office and made up their minds to fight communism they were just as much committed to "administer capitalism" as were their English colleagues. If we grant these premises and take account of the fact that they did not have, and could not expect to have in the calculable future, a majority either in the federal parliament or in the Prussian diet or in the population, everything else follows with inexorable logic. In 1925 the total population was about 62 millions. The proletariat (laborers and their families; I include the domestic servants) numbered not quite 28 millions and part of the vote of this class went to other parties. The "independent" population was not much smaller—about 24 millions —and largely impervious to the socialist persuasion. Even if we exclude an upper stratum—say one million—and confine ourselves to the groups that count at the polls—the peasants, artisans, retailers— there was not much to be conquered there, not only for the moment but even for the near future. Between these two groups there were the white-collar employees, no less than 10 millions of them including their families. The Social Democratic party of course realized that this class held the key position, and made great efforts to conquer it. But in spite of considerable success, these efforts only served to show that the white collar is a much more serious barrier than it should be according to the Marxian theory of social classes.[24]

Thus, even if the communists had been the allies of the Social Democrats instead of being their bitterest enemies, the party would still have been in the minority. It is true that the non-socialist majority was not actively hostile in all its sections: the left-wing liberals (the Democratic People's party), stronger in talent than in numbers, were always ready for cooperation (up to a point). It is also true that this majority was split up into many groups which were quite incapable of acting in unison and whose members and supporters were not anything like as disciplined as were the Social Democrats them-

[24] When confronted with this fact socialists usually derive comfort from the arguments that non-socialist employees are just erring sheep who have not yet found their true political location but who are sure to find it eventually, or that they are prevented from joining the party by the ruthless pressure exerted by their employers. The first argument will not carry conviction to anyone beyond the Marxian fold—we have seen that the theory of social classes is one of the weakest links in the Marxian chain. The second argument is false as a matter of plain fact. Whatever truth it may have contained at other times, the German employers of the twenties were, save exceptions without quantitative importance, in no position to influence the vote of their employees.

selves. But sensible people who were neither able nor willing to embark upon hazardous courses would nevertheless feel that there was for them but one line to take—the line of democracy—and that this line spelled coalition.

The party that best qualified for the role of an ally was the Catholic party (the Center). It was powerful. Before the advent of Hitler it seemed that nothing could shake the loyalty of its supporters. Its organization was excellent. Provided the interests of the church were safeguarded, it was prepared to go nearly as far in social reform of the immediately practical kind as were the socialists themselves, in some respects even further. Not harboring any particularly fervent feelings for the displaced dynasties, it stood squarely behind the Weimar constitution. Last but not least, it welcomed spoils-sharing arrangements that would guarantee its preserves. Thus understanding came about with what to the foreign observer might seem surprising ease. The socialists treated the Catholic Church with the utmost deference and tact. They made no difficulties about a concordat with the pope that gave the clergy more than it ever had had under the heretic Hohenzollerns. As to policies, there were hardly any dissensions at all.

But although this alliance was fundamental, no party that professed allegiance to the Weimar constitution was excluded from office. Democrats, National Liberals, Nationals (= Conservatives) were all of them admitted, even to positions of high command. Coalition as a universal principle meant compromise as a universal principle. The necessary concessions as to measures were in fact readily made. The army was left alone, practically under management of its own choosing, and adequately provided with means. Eastern Prussia was subsidized and agriculture in general was the object of solicitous care. Some implications of this which might not quite tally with socialist professions were made more palatable to the proletariat that paid the bill by calling this sort of thing Planning—perhaps the reader feels that there is nothing new under the sun.

In its attitude toward the industrial masses and toward its own program the Social Democratic party laborized itself. At the beginning a token payment was made by the passing of a very moderate bill of which the most radical feature consisted in the word Socialization that was inserted in its title (1919). But the socialists soon shelved all this in order to apply themselves to labor legislation of the kind made familiar to Americans by the New Deal. This satisfied the trade unions whose bureaucracy was increasingly allowed to form the operative section of the party's policy-making machine.

This, so one might think, should have been difficult for a party with a Marxian tradition that continued to prevail in the party schools. But it was not. Except for a certain amount of communist defection, the intellectuals from whom opposition within the party could have been expected to arise were kept well in hand. Unlike the English party, the German one had settled down in the administrative apparatus of the Reich, the states and the municipalities. Moreover, it had, in its press and elsewhere, many jobs of its own to offer. This patronage was energetically used. Obedience spelled preferment in the civil service, in the academic career, in the numerous public enterprises and so on. These means were effective in bringing radicals to heel.

The firm hold the Social Democrats acquired on all the parts of the machinery of public administration not only made for stricter discipline but also helped to increase membership and, beyond membership, the vote on which the party was able to count. Of course it also increased its power in other ways. For instance, the socialists secured dominant power in the Prussian Free State. This gave them control of the police force and they were careful to choose party members or reliable careerists for police presidents (chiefs of police) in the big towns. Thus they buttressed their camp until their position seemed impregnable according to all ordinary standards. And, again according to all ordinary rules of political analysis, even an orthodox Marxist could have comforted himself by arguing that in those trenches they could quite comfortably dwell till things in their secular course would of themselves change minority into majority and draw the curtains that veiled the Ultimate Goal for the time being. Quotation from the Communist Manifesto . . .

Irrespective of the mechanics of the party's power plant, the political setup as well as the general social situation looked eminently stable. Moreover, whatever might be urged against many individual measures, legislative and administrative, on the whole the coalition's policies made for and not against stability. Much that was done must command our sincere respect. Nothing that was done qualifies for explanation of anything worse than the ordinary measure of discontent that every regime elicits which lacks authority and glamour. The only possible exception to this lies in the financial sphere. Part of the cultural and political achievements of this governmental system was associated with large and rapidly increasing public expenditure. Furthermore, this expenditure was financed by methods—though a highly successful sales tax was among them—which drained the sources of accumulation. So long as the inflow of foreign capital continued, all went comparatively well, although budgetary and even cash difficulties began to appear more than a year before it ceased. When it did cease, that well-known situation emerged which would have undermined the position of the most magnetic of leaders. All in all, however, the socialist critics of the party and its conduct during this spell of power will be entitled to boast of no mean achievement if, in case they were ever installed in office, they should do equally well.

V. The Present War and the Future of Socialist Parties

How the present war will affect the fortunes of existing socialist groups of course depends on its duration and outcome. For our purpose, I do not see any point in speculating about this. Let us however, by way of example, consider two cases out of a great many possible ones.

Even now (July 1942) many observers seem to expect that Russia will emerge from the war with a great access of power and prestige, in fact that Stalin will emerge as the true victor. If this should be so, it does not necessarily follow that a communist world revolution will be the consequence or even that there will be "Russification" of continental Europe accompanied by an extermination of the upper strata and a settlement of accounts with non-communist socialist (and Trotskyite) groups. For even barring a possible Anglo-American resistance to the expansion of Russian power, it is not certain that the self-interest of Russian autocracy will lie in that direction. But it is certain that the chances for such a consummation—realization of the full Lenin program—would be immeasurably increased. However this world revolution might differ from the Marxian idea, it would for those who are willing to accept it as a substitute doubtless cease to be a daydream. And not only as regards Europe.

In that case the fate of orthodox socialism and all it stands for would be sealed. And so it would be, on the continent of Europe, in case the fascist powers hold their own. If however we again assume complete victory of the Anglo-American-Russian alliance—that is to say, a victory that enforces unconditional surrender but with all the honors held by England and the United States—then we see readily that orthodox socialism of the German Social Democratic or of a still more laborite type stands a much better chance to survive on the continent of Europe, at all events for some time. One reason for believing this is that people, if they find both the bolshevist and the fascist routes barred, may well turn to the Social Democratic republic as the most obvious of the remaining choices. But there is a much more important reason: laborite socialism will enjoy the favor of the victors. For the consequence of so complete a victory as we now envisage will be Anglo-American management of the affairs of the world—a kind of Anglo-American rule which, from the ideas we see taking shape under our eyes, may be termed Ethical Imperialism. A world order of this kind in which the interests and ambitions of other nations would count only as far as understood and approved by England and the United States can be established only by military force and upheld only by permanent readiness to use military force. It is perhaps unnecessary to explain why, in the political and economic conditions of our time, this would mean for these two countries a social organization that is best described as Militarist Socialism. But it is clear that the task of controlling and policing the world would be much facilitated, on the one hand, by the re-creation and new creation of small and inefficient states in Europe and, on the other hand, by installing governments of the laborite or Social Democratic types. Especially in Germany and Italy, the debris of the Social Democratic parties would constitute the only political material from which to construct governments which could possibly accept this world order for longer than a period of prostration and cooperate with the agents of the world protectorate without mental reservations. Whatever it may be worth, this is the chance of Liberal Socialism.

From the standpoint of the subject of this book however (though from no other) all this is of secondary importance. Whatever the fate of particular socialist *groups,* there cannot be any doubt that the present conflagration will—inevitably, everywhere, and independently of the outcome of the war—mean another great stride toward the socialist *order.* An appeal to our experience of the effects of the First World War on the social fabric of Europe suffices to establish this prognosis. This time however the stride will be taken also in the United States.

But that experience, though a valuable guide, is an inadequate one. A quarter of a century has elapsed. This is no negligible span even as regards the secular forces that make for socialism in the sense explained in Part II. Independently of everything else we shall be confronted at the end of this war with an economic situation, a social atmosphere, a distribution of political power substantially different from those of 1918. Much however has happened during these twenty-five years that could not have been predicted from secular tendencies alone. Among other things there was the great depression which, impinging upon a delicate situation, shook social structures to their foundations, nowhere more than in this country. Still more effective in undermining these structures were the policies by which that depression was handled. And this must be attributed largely to political configurations that were in part accidental. The consequences are obvious. In particular, huge bureaucracies have developed that by now are powerful enough to hold their ground and to implement policies of fundamental reconstruction.

In no country will war taxation of business and of the business class be reduced in the proportion in which it was reduced after 1919. This may in itself suffice to paralyze the motors of capitalism for good and thus provide another argument for government management. Inflation, even if it should go no further than is, for instance in this country, unavoidable in the present political pattern, may well do the rest, both directly and, through the radicalization of the expropriated holders of bonds and insurance policies, indirectly. Moreover, nowhere will war controls be liquidated to the extent the experience of the years after 1918 might lead us to believe. They will be put to other uses. In this country steps are already being taken to prepare public opinion for governmental management of postwar adjustments and to put the bourgeois alternative out of court. Finally, there is no reason to believe that governments will ever relax the hold they have gained on the capital market and the investment process. To be sure, this does not sum up to socialism. But socialism may, under such conditions, impose itself as the only practicable alternative to deadlocks and incessant friction.

Details and phrases will of course differ in different countries. So will political tactics and economic results. English developments are comparatively easy to foresee. The labor men entered the Churchill government in response to the call of emergency. But, as has been pointed out before, they were then well advanced on the road to office *and* power irrespective of any emergency. Therefore they will quite naturally be in a position to manage postwar reconstruction alone or—which may prove to be the most effective method—in a coalition they would control. The war economy will have realized some of their immediate aims. To a considerable extent they will only have to keep what they have got already. Further advance toward the socialist goal can be expected to be relatively easy in conditions in which there is not much left for capitalists to fight for. And it may prove possible to be quite frank about it and to carry out socialization soberly, in an orderly way, and largely by consent. For many reasons, but principally because of the weakness of the official socialist party, prognosis is less easy in the case of this country. But ultimate results are not likely to be different, though slogans are almost sure to be—and costs in terms of both welfare and cultural values.

Once more: it is only socialism in the sense defined in this book that is so predictable. Nothing else is. In particular there is little reason to believe that this socialism will mean the advent of the civilization of which orthodox socialists dream. It is much more likely to present fascist features. That would be a strange answer to Marx's prayer. But history sometimes indulges in jokes of questionable taste.

CHAPTER XXVIII

THE CONSEQUENCES OF THE SECOND
WORLD WAR

Mundus regitur parva sapientia

A LITTLE more can now (July, 1946) be added to what was said in the last section about the effects of the war on the social structure of our epoch and on the position and prospects of orthodox (i.e. non-Communist) socialist groups. It was obvious in July, 1942, that, whatever the fate of particular socialist *groups*, there would be another great stride toward the socialist *order*, and that this time the stride would be taken also in the United States. It was also clear that the fortunes of existing socialist groups would depend on the duration and outcome of the war. It was finally suggested that, in the event of a complete victory (implying unconditional surrender for the enemy) of the Anglo-American-Russian alliance, the results for orthodox socialism would differ according to whether Stalin emerged as the true victor or whether all the honors were held by England and the United States. In the latter eventuality orthodox socialism of the German Social Democratic type or laborism of the English type would stand a good chance to improve their position on the continent of Europe.

Stalin has emerged master of eastern Europe. England and the United States are struggling to maintain some influence in central and western Europe. The fortunes of socialist and communist parties reflect these conditions. But there is another element that may substantially affect the social situation all over the world, namely, economic developments in the United States which may possibly tell in favor of the capitalist order. This chapter will therefore deal, first, with the position of orthodox socialism and laborism and in particular with the English situation; second, with the possible effects of conspicuous industrial success in the United States; third, with the possible effects of Russia's political success. Our argument thus divides up naturally into three parts, namely

I England and Orthodox Socialism
II Economic Possibilities in the United States
III Russian Imperialism and Communism

I

England and Orthodox Socialism

Many facts go to show that, irrespective of the Russian element in the case, the effects of the Second World War on the social situation in Europe would have been similar to those of the First World War, only stronger. That is to say, we should have witnessed acceleration of the existing trend toward a socialist organization of production *in the sense defined in this book.*

The most important of those facts is the success of the English Labour party. As has been pointed out in the last chapter, this success was to be expected and should not have surprised anybody. Nor was it more complete than we should have expected. Owing to the English electoral system, the actual redistribution of seats is apt to give an exaggerated picture. There were about twelve million labor votes against about ten million conservative votes. The days of liberalism are over, of course, but even the surviving dozen of liberal members represent more votes than do seventy-two Labour members taken at random. In other words, under a system of proportional representation, the Labour party would not have gained a parliamentary majority over Conservatives and Liberals combined though a Labour-Liberal coalition would have enjoyed a comfortable margin. The very rationale of the English electoral system is to produce strong governments and to avoid dead-locks. This is what it has done in this case. But the national situation as distinguished from the parliamentary one is, nevertheless, not a matter of indifference for an estimate of what is. and what is not, politically possible. The obvious inference is strengthened by the fact that the groups to the left of the official Labour party failed con-spicuously to improve their parliamentary position: the Independent Labour party just retained its three seats and the Commonwealth plus the Communist parties lost one of the four they previously held. In view of the many reasons there were to expect "radicalization," this is truly remarkable and a striking proof of England's political maturity.

This situation is bound to assert itself. In fact it has done so already, both in the complexion of the Cabinet and in the measures taken or foreshadowed. The reader is asked to read again what has been written in this book under the heading of Socialist Policy before the Act (Chapter XIX, section IV). He will observe, first, that all the Labor government does, or is proposing to do, is in the spirit and on the principles of the program there outlined; and, second, that actual practice does not go nearly as far. The nationalization of the Bank of England, in particular, is a highly significant symbol and may there-fore stand out as a historical landmark. But its practical importance may well be equated to zero: the bank has been practically a department of the Treasury ever since 1914 and under modern conditions no central bank can be anything else. And such things as the coal measure or full-employment legislation are hardly controversial any more—in England. The way in which the Labor government deals or is likely to deal with them will presumably command all but universal consent. Tournaments on questions of fundamental principle will no doubt enliven the serious work; but not because these questions or the differences about them are so very important but because governments and parliaments cannot live without them. All this is as it should be. No doubt it is once more a case of administering capitalism but, both because of the war and the lapse of time, this will be done with clearer purpose and a firmer hand than before and with ultimate liquidation of private enterprise more clearly in view. Three points deserve, however, particular attention.

First, it is precisely this almost ideal conformity of political action to the data of the social and economic situation which is so important and, from the standpoint of private-property society, so dangerous. Whatever intellectual extremists might say—and, of course, the attitude of the Labour government makes business for them—the stride toward a socialist England will be the more substantial because there is so little nonsense about it. Steps so responsibly taken will not have to be retraced. Barring upsets from outside, social, political and economic disaster may be successfully avoided. If the government succeeds in keeping to its line, it will fulfill exactly the task that lies between the tasks of laborite governments without power (such as McDonald's were, see above Chapter XXVII, section IV) and the tasks of laborite governments of the future whose parliamentary majority will be paralleled by a majority of the electorate. This is the only hope for democratic socialism. Such hope as there is for it on the continent of Europe is, of course, somewhat strengthened by the English paradigma.

Second, we have noticed in the preceding chapter that the earlier socialist thinkers never foresaw, and could not have been expected to foresee, a situation in which political power would be thrust upon labor and in which the bourgeois victim would turn to it for protection. We have also noticed another thing they did not and could not foresee, namely, the extent to which it would prove possible to expropriate the bourgeois structure, without *formally* destroying the legal framework of the capitalist order and by such unrevolutionary methods as taxation and wage policies. War taxation and war controls certainly cannot be fully maintained. But retreat from them may be brought to a halt at a line at which some of the most popular items of the socialist program are automatically fulfilled. Equalization of incomes after taxes is already carried so far as to impair the efficiency, to use the Russian phrase, of "specialists" such as physicians or engineers. This is indeed done by means of a clumsy and costly apparatus and it may before long occur to people that it might be better to limit incomes paid out to what direct taxes leave of them instead of paying out what has to be recovered again. In any case, however, the orange to be squeezed, and with it much radical rhetoric, is apt to run dry.

Third, suppose that in the next election labor improves upon its present position and gains the support of a substantial majority of the electorate, what is the government to do? They may go a little further in the direction of equalizing incomes; they may improve social services, on Beveridge-Plan and other lines, a little beyond what any government would do; they may go considerably further in socializing industries. But none of this will be easy going. We have seen that, in the conditions of modern England, there is little purely economic objection to a large measure of socialization. Nor is bourgeois resistance likely to prove a serious obstacle; England depends on her industrialists' work much more than did Russia in 1917, but unless they are unnecessarily antagonized their co-operation may be secured. Nor, finally, need we attach much importance to the argument that appeals so much to more ardent votaries of socialization, viz., that the cabinet system is not adequate to the task of carrying socialization: intellectuals who delight in the vision of dictatorial methods may indeed doubt its efficiency; but it is the only system that is available for carrying socialization democratically—the actual administration of the socialized industries will of course require semi-autonomous organs with which cabinets would have to co-operate as they do, say, with the general staff, of their armies. But the real problem is labor. Unless socialization is to spell economic breakdown, a socializing government cannot possibly tolerate present trade-union practice. The most irresponsible of politicians would, in the case envisaged, have to face the basic problem of modern society that only Russia has solved, the problem of industrial discipline. A government that means to socialize to any great extent, will have to socialize trade unions. And, as things actually are, labor is of all things the most difficult to socialize. Not that the problem is insoluble. In England, the chances for successful solution by the political method of democracy are greater than they are anywhere else. But the road to solution may be tortuous and long.

Except for the Russian element, the political situation on the continent of Europe is essentially similar. Where there is a free choice, we observe a strong tendency for the masses to keep or revert to their allegiance to either social-democratic or else to Catholic parties. The most obvious instances are the Scandinavian countries. But a similar trend may be discerned even in Germany, and it is safe to assert that if she were free and uninfluenced, something very like the Weimar Republic would emerge from all the present misery. Though the evidence to this effect is in part invalidated by the favor shown to the Social Democrats by the English and American authorities, it is strengthened by the fact that the Russian authority also permitted reconstruction of a Social Democratic organization in its zone. Impossible political and economic conditions, irrationally imposed upon the German people, will of course discredit the laborite governments and annihilate their chances, such as they are, of establishing themselves. But still, if for the sake of a mental experiment we choose to neglect the Russian element of the case and if we further choose to postulate that the United States and England act toward Germany in the manner dictated alike by common decency and common sense, this would be the general diagnosis and prognosis to adopt. A similar prognosis suggests itself for other countries though with various qualifications: laborite régimes—in Catholic countries more often than not in coalition with Catholic parties—with home-grown and not too important communist groups to the left of them and a policy more advanced than was that of the twenty's but still on the same lines, with all this implies, economically, politically and culturally. The little example of Austria is instructive. The Christian Socialists (Catholic party, comprising the conservative elements) came off well, the Communists did badly, the Social Democrats just about regained their old position, with most of their surviving old leaders well entrenched in the party's high command. Even programs have not greatly changed so far as general principles are concerned. The recent move toward socialization has not been made from choice. The cases of the other small countries so far as independent of Russia come within the same type and so does that of Italy. The French case differs from this type owing to the strength of the Communists (see below, section III). And only our inability to understand any pattern except our own prevents us from realizing that the Spanish case is really the most unproblematical of all.[1]

II

Economic Possibilities in the United States

1. Redistribution of Income through Taxation
2. The Great Possibility
3. Conditions for Its Realization
4. Transitional Problems
5. The Stagnationist Thesis
6. Conclusion

[1] The Franco régime simply reproduces an institutional pattern that, from necessities that should be easy to understand, became well established in nineteenth-century Spain. Franco did and does what had been done before him by Narvaez, O'Donnell, Espartero, Serrano. The fact that unfortunate Spain has become at present the football in the game of international power politics in which she has no stake herself, is responsible for a propaganda that obscures a very simple state of things.

1. When discussing the English case, we have noticed that under modern conditions—to an extent undreamed of by nineteenth-century socialists—it is possible to extract from the bourgeois stratum, by taxation and wage policies, the bulk of what in Marxist terminology is called Surplus Value.[2] The same observation applies to the United States. To an extent which is not generally appreciated, the New Deal was able to expropriate the upper income brackets even before the war. One indication will have to suffice, one that shows no more than the effects of the increase in the (personal) Income and Surtax and these only *up to 1936*: in 1929, when Total Income Paid Out was estimated at 80.6 billion dollars, the brackets above $50,000 (taxable income) retained 5.2 billions after income and surtax; in 1936, when the total of income paid out was estimated at 64.2 billion dollars, not quite 1.2 billions.[3] Taxable income above $100,000 was *even then* wholly absorbed if account be taken of estate taxes. From the standpoint of naïve radicalism, the only trouble with these and subsequent measures of confiscation is that they did not go far enough. But this does not alter the fact with which we are concerned for the moment, viz., that irrespective of the war, a tremendous transfer of wealth has actually been effected, a transfer that quantitatively is comparable with that effected by Lenin. The present distribution of disposable incomes compares well with the one actually prevailing in Russia, particularly in view of the further fact that owing to the greater importance in the upper-bracket budgets of personal services and of commodities that contain relatively much labor, the purchasing power of the upper-bracket dollar has in the United States fallen much more than has that of the lower-bracket dollar.[4] Moreover, we may also repeat an-

[2] The reader will, of course, observe that the proposition asserts nothing about the effects of such a policy upon the size—and long-run rate of increase—of the national income. In particular, it does not exclude the possibility that labor might receive less real income, in total amount and in the long run, if incomes were completely equalized than it would receive if the whole of the Marxist surplus value accrued to the "capitalist" stratum.

[3] See the highly instructive article by I. de Vegh on *Savings, Investment, and Consumption*, American Economic Review (Papers and Proceedings of the 53d Annual Meeting, February, 1941, pp. 237 et seq.). As there explained, the data from which the sums retained were calculated exclude income from wholly tax-exempt government securities and include capital gains. Moreover, these sums are, of course, not strictly comparable with the figures of total income paid out (Commerce estimates), which may, however, be considered as indices of the comparable figures. The reason why I have not simply taken the latter (from *Statistics of Income*) is obvious, but the choice of the years of comparison needs explanation: 1929 was the year for which incomes above $50,000 after income and surtax were at an absolute maximum; 1936 has been chosen because it was the last year that was, first, unaffected by the recession of 1937-1938 and, second, completely free from war influences that asserted themselves from 1939 on.

[4] Comparison between different countries is of course difficult and perhaps never quite convincing. But the Russian act of April 4, 1940, concerning the income tax, reveals that incomes as low as 1,812 rubles per year were subject to it. It also reveals the existence of incomes of over 300,000 rubles which were then taxed at

other observation made earlier concerning England. The pressure on the upper brackets is, of course, not confined to "$50,000 and above." To a diminishing degree it extends down to the incomes of $5,000. And there cannot be any doubt, especially in the case of doctors in the middle ranges of professional success, that this sometimes results in loss of much-needed efficiency.

So far, then, the effect upon the social structure of the war plus the labor troubles that were its natural consequence would seem to be much the same as in England. The fact that in the United States there is no well-organized national labor party might set us speculating about the possibility of a development on the lines of guild socialism instead of one toward centralist socialism. Otherwise this fact only strengthens the case for the prognosis that has been elaborated in this book, for pressure groups are just as powerful as parties and much less responsible, hence more effective battering rams.

2. But there is another fact about the social situation in the United States that has no analogue anywhere else in the world and may conceivably affect our diagnosis concerning the chances of the private-enterprise system, at least for a short run of fifty years or so, namely, the colossal industrial success we are witnessing. Some observers seem to think that this success which has won the war and, in addition, has protected American labor from privation, will dominate the postwar situation also, to an extent that may annihilate the whole case for socialism so far as it is of a purely economic nature. Let us put this argument into its most optimistic form.

Neglecting for the moment the complex of transitional problems

---

the rate of 50 per cent. Now, let us neglect the tax on the lowest incomes entirely and put the modal income in the 1,812-2,400 ruble group at 2,000 rubles; further, let us put the modal *retained* income in the highest group at no higher than 150,000 rubles (though those 300,000 rubles before tax were a lower limit). Then we discover that the higher of these modes was 75 times the lower one. Even if we put, for 1940, the American equivalent (not of course in purchasing power, but in the sense of equivalent position in the income scale) of the lower mode at as low as $1,000, we shall evidently not find much in the United States income distribution of *retained* incomes (even apart from the reductions specifically motivated by the requirements of war finance) to support, in the light of the Russian paradigma, the current phrases about atrocious inequalities, "concentration of power" as measured by concentration of income, and the like. The evidence presented in the well-known book by Bienstock, Schwarz and Yugov on *Industrial Management* in Russia tends to support this view. Many other details point in the same direction, for instance, the fact that those ranges of the professions who could formerly but cannot now afford domestic servants in the United States, do enjoy this privilege—worth a ton of electrical household gadgets—in Russia. All this still fails to take account of advantages that do not pass through income accounts. The power and social position—which is one of the main reasons for valuing a high income—of the industrial manager, especially if leader of the local unit of the Bolshevik party, is far and away above that of an American industrialist.

Interesting phenomenon—this Lag of Ideas! Many well-meaning people in this country *now* profess horror or indignation at social inequalities which did exist fifty years ago, but no longer do. Things change, slogans remain.

and fixing upon 1950 as the first "normal" year—a practice quite common with forecasters—we will put the Gross National Product—value of all goods and services produced before allowance for depreciation and depletion—evaluated by means of the B. L. S. price-level index for 1928, hypothetically at two hundred billions. This is, of course, not a prediction of the actual volume of production to be expected in that year. It is not even an estimate of what potential production at high if not "full" employment will be. It is an estimate of what this potential production might be provided certain conditions are fulfilled which will be stated presently. As such, it is high but neither unusual—higher figures have been mentioned—nor unreasonable. It conforms to past experience of the long-run average performance of the system: if we apply our "normal rate of growth of 3.7 per cent per year" (see above Chapter V) to the 1928 gross national product figure, which was about ninety billions, we get a little under two hundred billions for 1950. No undue importance should be attached to this. But I will nevertheless repeat that an objection to the effect that this extrapolation is meaningless *because* output failed to increase at that rate in the thirties would miss the point and only prove the objector's inability to grasp it. However, so far as potential production is concerned, the indications afforded by the system's actual performance during the war are certainly more convincing: if war statistics are anything to go by, the gross national product, reduced to the 1928 price level, was in 1943 pretty much what it should have been in order to reach the two hundred billion goal by 1950.

Now *suppose* that this possibility be actually realized.[5] And let us,

[5] It is assumed that realization of this possibility involves a forty-hour week plus overtime at bottlenecks. But full employment is not assumed. Definitions of full employment and estimates of the amount of employment that satisfies any given definition vary widely and involve not only statistical but also some rather delicate theoretical issues. I must rest content to state that, in the conditions of the United States labor market and assuming that the total labor force will be something like sixty one millions in 1950 (counting in two or three millions in the armed forces), I do not see that the number of *statistically* unemployed women and men can possibly be, in that year, below five or six millions, a figure which includes, besides genuinely involuntary unemployment (i.e., involuntary unemployment that would be involuntary unemployment according to *any* definition), a large allowance for semi-involuntary unemployment and merely statistical unemployment. The figure does not include "hidden" unemployment. I believe it to be compatible with the two hundred billion goal for that year. It has little to do with vices specific to the capitalist system, but much with the freedom capitalist society grants to labor. Even in Sir William Beveridge's book on full employment there are chastely veiled hints at direction and compulsion. It should be added, however, that I visualize 1950 as a year of cyclical prosperity. If it is not, then our discussion should be understood to refer to the prosperous year next to it. On an average of good and bad years (statistical) unemployment should be higher than five or six millions—seven to eight perhaps. This is nothing to be horrified about because, as will be explained, adequate provision can be made for the unemployed. But the cyclical fluctuations of capitalist economy arè mainly responsible for any excess above "normal" unemployment.

for replacement and new "investment" (including houses), make the ample deduction of forty billions (20 per cent, equal to Professor Kuznets' average by decades, for 1879-1929).[6] The significance of the remaining one hundred and sixty billions for our subject rests upon two facts. First, short of atrocious mismanagement, the huge mass of available commodities and services that this figure (which still does not include new houses) represents, promises a level of satisfaction of economic needs even of the poorest members of society including the aged, unemployed and sick, that would (with a forty hour week) eliminate anything that could possibly be described as suffering or want. It has been emphasized in this book that the case for socialism is by no means wholly economic and also that increasing real income has so far entirely failed to conciliate either the masses or their intellectual allies. But in this instance, the promise is not only spectacular but immediate: not much more is involved in its fulfillment than that the abilities and resources that have proved their power during the war, turn from production for war purposes, including the exports of consumers' goods to Allied countries, to production for the purposes of domestic consumption; after 1950 the argument would apply *a fortiori*. Second—again short of atrocious mismanagement—all this can be accomplished without violating the organic conditions of a capitalist economy, including high premia on industrial success and all the other inequalities of income that may be required in order to make the capitalist engine work according to design. *In the United States alone there need not lurk, behind modern programs of social betterment, that fundamental dilemma that everywhere else paralyzes the will of every responsible man, the dilemma between economic progress and immediate increase of the real income of the masses.*

Moreover, with gross national product at 200 billions, there is no difficulty in collecting public revenue in the amount of 40 billions without injury to the economic engine. A sum of 30 billions is sufficient, at 1928 prices, to finance all the functions actually fulfilled by the federal, state and local governments in 1939 plus a greatly enlarged military establishment plus the service of the debt and other permanent obligations that have been incurred since.[7] This will leave roughly 10 billions—at 1928 prices or a correspondingly higher amount at any

[6] A depreciation allowance of about ten to 12 per cent is not unduly high for a system running at as high a level of production. Eight to ten per cent for "new" investment is certainly ample and, according to most forecasters, too much. See below, *sub* 5.

[7] For the purpose in hand, it is not necessary to distinguish between public expenditure on goods and services and "transfers." But it is assumed that, roughly, the thirty billions would divide up into twenty-five billions for the former and five billions of the latter. It should be observed that this takes no account (for 1950) of veterans' pensions and other benefits, a problem that should be treated apart.

higher price level that may prevail[8]—in 1950 and much more than this in another decade, for the financing of new social services or of improvements in the existing ones.

3. But it is here, namely, in the sphere of public finance and administration, that the meaning of our proviso—"short of atrocious mismanagement"—is most vividly brought home to us. For in this sphere we actually have mismanagement of national resources that is truly atrocious. With present principles and present practice, it is *not* true that 40 billions can be collected, at a 200-billion level of gross national product, without injury to the economic engine. And it is *not* true that the 30 billions—or whatever may correspond to them at price levels other than that of 1928—meet the requirements mentioned. This is only true if the whole of the public administration be rationalized with a view to eliminating double and triple-track activities—such as we have in the case of the income taxes, to mention but one example —overlapping both of federal agencies and of federal and state and local agencies—lack of effective co-ordination and well-defined individual responsibility—which, in the federal case, is mainly due to the nonexistence of well-knit "ministries" and to the existence of a large number of semi-independent "authorities" or "boards"—and many other things that are sources of waste and obstacles to efficiency, but above all, that spirit of waste that delights in spending a billion where 100 million would do. The present state of things portends nothing but evil for public management of finance and industry and, in fact, is in itself good and sufficient reason to oppose it for many who are anything but "economic royalists."

Nor is this all. *Economy*—how unpopular this word has become!— may in a sense be less necessary in a wealthy country than it is in a poor one, namely in the sense that waste threatens want in the latter and not in the former. But in another sense, economy—that is, real economy and not the sham economy of the bureaucracy and of Congress who are ready enough to save pennies while squandering billions —is just as necessary in a rich country in order to make efficient use of its wealth as it is in a poor country in order to secure bare subsistence.[9] And this applies not only to the cost of public administration but also to the use of funds that are to be paid out in various benefits. The classic example is, of course, provision for unemployment so far as it consists in payments to individuals. Unless the behavior of workmen, in employment and out of it, be as strictly under public control as it is in Russia, economical use of the funds available for the support of the unemployed inevitably means that the benefit must be substan-

---

[8] Revenue cannot, in general, be assumed to change in proportion to price level. For our purpose, however, which is merely to gain a rough idea, we may adopt this simplifying hypothesis.

[9] The theory that holds the exact opposite of this will be discussed below, *sub* 5.

tially below the wages the unemployed can hope to earn. As United States statistics of labor turnover suggest, there is normally in the country a large fringe of half voluntary and half involuntary unemployment, the burden of which is bound to be increased, by loose administration of unemployment benefits or by rates that are high relatively to wages, so as to destroy the possibility of attaining the two hundred billion goal.

There is still another condition that would have to be fulfilled in order to justify this possibility: "Politics" and bureaucracy must not prevent our reaching it. Nothing should be more obvious than that the business organism cannot function according to design when its most important "parameters of action"—wages, prices, interest—are transferred to the political sphere and there dealt with according to the requirements of the political game or, which sometimes is more serious still, according to the ideas of some planners. Three examples must suffice to illustrate this. First, the actual labor situation, if it persist, is in itself sufficient to obstruct progress toward that goal of a two hundred billion gross national product and, still more, progress beyond it. The resulting wage rates are only one reason for this; dislocation of entrepreneurial planning and disorganization of workers even when employed are equally important. Besides preventing an otherwise possible expansion of output, these conditions also reduce employment below its otherwise possible level by putting an abnormal premium on everybody's employing as little labor as possible—they induce a sort of "flight from labor.[10]

[10] It will be observed that increase in output and increase in employment are not treated as synonymous. It is, in fact, possible, within certain limits, to decrease employment without decreasing output or to increase the latter without increasing the former. The reason why in current literature output and employment are often made to vary proportionately is to be found in one of the fundamental features of the Keynesian system. This system is restricted to dealing with quite short-run chains of causation by the assumption that quantity and quality of industrial equipment remain constant so that the combination of factors of production cannot change significantly. If this were so (and in the shortest run it is approximately so), then of course they vary together though, in general, not proportionately.

It will also be observed that our argument implies that changes in money wage rates may cause changes in employment of opposite sign. I believe, in fact, that the high level of American money wage rates has always, but especially in the thirties, been a major cause of American unemployment, and that similar consequences are to be expected in the future if high-wage policies be continued. This proposition contradicts the teaching of Keynesian orthodoxy as well as that of some other economists and cannot be established here. It is therefore fortunate that, for our present purpose, and so far as 1950 is concerned and not any later development, a weaker proposition will do which would have commanded the assent of the late Lord Keynes: under the conditions that are likely to prevail in this country during the next four years, and unless compensated by additional increases in prices, higher wage rates will adversely affect both output and employment and the latter more than the former.

Second, whatever the reader may believe to be its virtues, price control as practiced hitherto is another obstacle to the expansion of output. I have heard that the Stalinist régime encourages criticism of its bureaucracy. Evidently, this is not so with us. I will defer to prevailing etiquette by granting outright that many able men have done excellent service in the O. P. A.; that many others, not so able, have still done their best; and I will suppress any doubts that may exist in my mind concerning its achievements up to the present moment, especially because its most conspicuous failures link up with circumstances over which it had no control. But it should really be admitted, at least for the present and future, that the policy of encouraging increases in wage rates combined with price control, unless *intended* to enforce surrender of private enterprise, is irrational and inimical to prompt expansion of output; that the disturbance of the system of relative prices resulting from the fact that the regulating agency can "keep the lid on" some prices—the prices of producers with little political pull—very much more effectively than on others—the prices of producers with plenty of political pull—reduces the degree of economic efficiency of the system; that price fixing *per se* does not define the whole extent of the damage done: equally important is the premium that the practice of "subsidizing" high-cost and "squeezing" low-cost producers puts upon inefficiency.[11]

The bureaucracy's persistent hostility, strongly supported as it is by public opinion, to industrial self-government—self-organization, self-regulation, co-operation—is a third obstacle to orderly progress and, incidentally, to a development that might solve many problems of business-cycle policy and eventually also the problem of transition to a socialist régime. Spokesmen of the bureaucracy invariably deny that there is any foundation for this view because joint action of businessmen becomes illegal and open to prosecution only if it implies "collusive restraint." But, even if this legalistic interpretation of prevailing practice could be accepted—and if the official theories of what constitutes collusive restraint or, in general, anti-social practice could also

[11] I do not pretend to know what will eventually come of the muddle occasioned by the presidential veto of the first Price Control Act and the passage of one a month later providing for rapid decontrol. Since, however, I am prepared to argue that the O. P. A., as it actually functioned, was bound to bar the way toward an efficient peace economy and since the possible consequences of that muddle are sure to be represented as proof positive of the necessity of retaining price control, I must ask the reader to consider two things. First, an argument for the repeal of price control is not an argument for letting it lapse, without preparation or transitional substitute, when nobody expected it or seems to have been prepared for it. Second, if in response to its defeat, the Administration hits out vindictively at targets chosen for their unpopularity rather than for any defensible reason, consequences may ensue that are entirely unconnected with the lapse of price control *per se*. As to the problem of inflation, see below *sub* 4.

be accepted[12]—it would still remain true (a) that the concept of "restraint" includes the bulk of attempts at industrial co-operation with regard to price and output policy even where such co-operation does fill a much-needed function; (b) that borderline cases and cases in which the element of restraint enters without constituting the main point of an agreement are not sure to be considered with impartiality by a personnel that contains many men inadequately familiar with the nature of business problems and some who are violently opposed to the system they are to regulate or at least to the "big-business" sector of it; and (c) that the ever-present threat of prosecution for offenses which it is not always easy to distinguish from unoffending business practice may have effects on the conduct of business nobody intends it to have.

The last point illustrates an aspect of labor troubles, O. P. A. troubles, and "antitrust" troubles that never receives the attention it merits, namely, the consequent drain on entrepreneurial and managerial energy. The businessman who is incessantly thrown out of his stride not only by having to face ever new institutional data but also by having to be "up before" this or that board, has no steam left for dealing with his technological and commercial problems. It is highly revelatory of the mechanistic attitude of economists and of their remoteness from "real life" that not one in ten will recognize this particular "human element" of what is after all a human organism —though no sensible man can possibly fail, for example, to link up the relatively poor showing made by the physical-volume index of industrial production in 1945 with this element as *one* of its many causes. Nor is this all. Success in conducting a business enterprise depends under present conditions much more on the ability to deal with labor leaders, politicians and public officials than it does on business ability in the proper sense of the term. Hence, except in the biggest concerns that can afford to employ specialists of all kinds, leading positions tend to be filled by "fixers" and "trouble shooters" rather than by "production men."

---

[12] As a matter of fact, however, these theories cannot be accepted. They cover indeed a range of practices which everyone will agree must be outlawed by any legal system. But beyond these there is another range of practices with regard to which the legal mind simply adopts the attitude dictated by popular prejudices. An important source of examples is discrimination. Even the most competent economist will experience considerable difficulties in analyzing *all* the long-run effects of a given case. If justice is administered on nothing but general legal or popular slogans and by demonstration "drives," the element of sound sense contained in the anti-discrimination attitude may completely disappear. And the well-meant method of selective prosecution which is intended to allow for cases where formally illegal discrimination benefits *all* parties concerned—everyone who ever had an elementary course in economics knows, or should know, such cases—may then only avail to add a most irritating arbitrariness. It is only in a passing remark that we can indicate methods of remedying this state of things.

It may seem to the reader that policy on the lines indicated by all this is out of the question—that it is bound to break down in a storm of righteous indignation or founder on the rocks of sabotage and other forms of resistance and that, therefore, the two hundred billion goal itself is little better than a daydream. But this does not quite follow. On the one hand, the economic engine of this country is strong enough to stand *some* waste and irrationality—including, as we know, some avoidable unemployment, the price of individual freedom. On the other hand, politicians and the public have of late displayed some signs of "coming round." And we must not forget that malleability of human nature which has been so much emphasized in this book (see especially Chapter XVIII, section II). The experiment of the New Deal and war periods may be inconclusive because the industrial bourgeoisie never expected those conditions to last. But some "education" has probably been effected. Thus relatively small adjustments of existing taxation may be all that is required, if not for maximum efficiency, yet for an adequate degree of it.[13] In another direction, a

[13] For instance—this is not intended to be more than an example from a set of possible methods—the following measures might be substantially sufficient. (a) Elimination of the double taxation of that part of the returns to corporate industry which is paid out in dividends; in view of the British practice, this would hardly justify a "storm of righteous indignation": our practice is the German one and the purely formal argument for it is due to the German economist, Adolf Wagner (1835-1917). (b) Permission to deduct from taxable income that part of individual income which is invested. Personally, I agree with Professor Irving Fisher's opinion that the part *saved* should be deducted (particularly in view of the danger of inflation). But in order to spare Keynesian susceptibilities I limit myself to the part invested. Technical difficulties are not serious, at least not insuperable. (c) Adoption of one of several methods that are available in order to allow full deduction of losses over time. (d) Nationalization, systematization, and development of sales or turnover taxes. This should appeal to admirers of Russia instead of sending them into paroxysms of rage. As a matter of fact, at rates like the Russian ones (e.g., thirty-one cents per pound on the best quality of wheat flour [in Moscow and for 1940] or, since translation of ruble amounts into dollar amounts is a doubtful matter, sixty-two per cent of the retail price of potatoes, seventy-three per cent of that of sugar, eighty per cent of that of salt; see P. Haensel, "Soviet Finances" in *Openbare Financiën*, No. 1, 1946) and in a population so desperately poor as the Russian one, the sales tax may indeed be a terrible scourge; but at moderate rates and in a country as rich as the United States it is an excellent and perfectly harmless tool of public finance, especially useful in financing purposes that benefit exclusively the low-income groups. Five or six billions could be raised by it without anyone's feeling the burden. But since state and local governments would have to be compensated for the loss of revenue incident to the nationalization of the tax—it is not strictly correct, of course, to speak of "introduction"—and since, moreover, certain adjustments of existing excises would be necessary, the net gain to the Federal Treasury cannot be estimated at more than about two to three billion dollars, so that sales tax plus specific excises might yield something like nine to ten billions in all. (e) Nationalization and drastic downward revision, in favor of wives and children, of the estate taxes, the reason for this being that existing legislation eliminates, by confiscation above very moderate figures, one of the essential elements of the capitalist scheme of things. Whoever approves of this confiscation for extra-economic reasons

relatively small increment of legal protection—to be granted, perhaps, by means of a proper codification of industrial law—might take the sting or threat of arbitrary vexation out of the businessman's working day and increasing experience of the regulating bodies and better training of their staffs might do the rest.[14] Moreover, the country has given proof, not long ago, of its willingness to accept legislation like the N. R. A. And as regards the labor situation, some comfort may perhaps be derived from the fact that policy on the lines contemplated not only need not renounce a single item of what most people will consider the main achievements in social reform of the New Deal but also would provide the economic basis for further advance. It should be noticed in particular that the Annual Wage is a threat to the chance of attaining our goal only if it be introduced, administered, and financed in such ways as to do the maximum of harm. In itself, it is a perfectly possible proposition.[15]

Even so, it takes a lot of optimism to expect that these necessary adjustments will be effected—or even that the conditions of the country's politics can produce the will to undertake such serious and self-denying work, unglorified by slogans, bristling with difficulties of detail, and eminently thankless. The mass of the people would like

---

is, from his standpoint, quite right in advocating a constitutional amendment to that effect; whoever approves of this confiscation on the economic argument to be found on p. 373 of the late Lord Keynes's *General Theory of Employment, Interest and Money*—or a derivative of this—is quite wrong.

We are not concerned with the question what would satisfy the interests affected *politically*. As a matter of fact, however, most proposals of tax reform that have so far come from businessmen's organizations are distinctly modest which, if not otherwise relevant for our argument, seems to show how effectively the business class has been "educated."

[14] I am adverting here to a point that is important for many more topics than the one in hand. A good bureaucracy is a slow growth and cannot be created at will. The bureaucratic organs of the United States display the ailments of rapid growth to an extent which makes a temporary policy of taking in sails a matter not only of the public interest but of their own. Among other things, the Washington bureaucracy has not yet discovered its place. It happens again and again that individual members of it pursue programs of their own, feel themselves to be reformers and negotiate with Congressmen, Senators, and members of other agencies over the heads of their chiefs. Some idea may suddenly acquire compelling force of which nobody knows the origin. That way lies chaos and failure.

[15] To illustrate this point, let us recall a bit of recent history. New Dealers in the early thirties, adopted the practice of sneering at the slogan Reform vs. Recovery. The sneer proves that they were perfectly aware of the element of truth in it. In fact, as political slogans go, this one was perfectly fair. But it should be understood to refer to the bungling and irresponsible manner in which "reform" was carried out, not to any of its professed aims. We are in a similar position now and the misfortune is that injury to the economic process of capitalism is for some people precisely the feature of reform they like best. Reform without such injury would be all but unattractive to them. And reform paralleled by a policy that insures capitalist success would be the worst that could befall them.

the America that might emerge from the job but they would hate the man who takes it in hand.

4. We have not yet mentioned Transitional Problems. They are in fact not relevant to our subject except in this respect: transitional difficulties may produce situations and induce measures that are likely to impede the expansion of output quasi-permanently and to invalidate our "estimate of possibilities" completely. The most obvious as well as most serious instance is the danger of inflation. The wholesale price index for 1920 was about 2.3 times the one of 1914. This happened in consequence of a war effort that was not only much smaller and shorter than the recent one in terms of goods and services but also more responsibly financed per unit of goods and services. There was nothing like the present backlog of demand. And tax privileges had provided an adequate motive for investors to keep large blocks of war bonds for good. As it is, Total Deposits Adjusted (time and demand, other than interbank and United States Government deposits, less items in process of collection) and Currency Outside of Banks amounted, in April of the current year to 174 billions (55.17 in June 1929, and 60.9 in June 1939), and there is no saying what part of the public's holdings of government bonds will be turned into cash *for purposes other than repayment of debt.* Any sensible person should be able to form an opinion about what this means under the given circumstances, especially in view of the government's encouragement of, or connivance at, the reckless but universal demand for higher money wage rates—for inflation comes through the payroll.[16] The same sensible person should not find it difficult to make up his mind regarding writers who preach that there is "no" danger of inflation[17] as well as regarding writers who see wild inflation round the corner. In order to make the one point that is relevant to our argument and in the face of the impossibility of treating the problem satisfactorily here, let me proffer my personal opinion merely for the sake of definiteness: It seems to me to be possible—*possible*—to aim, for 1950, at a price level about 50 per cent above the 1928 figure (with bursts beyond that in the interval); it seems to me to be *rational* to use, to this extent, price-level movements as an instrument of adaptation; and it seems to me that the terrors of such an increase in general prices as well as the terrors of a descent from it in later years are greatly exaggerated.

[16] The reader will please observe that this particular statement is good Keynesianism and should therefore command assent from Washington economists.

[17] Among these we must include some of those forecasters of postwar demand who predicted that, immediately upon the cessation of a great part of the government's war demand, a slump and widespread unemployment, calling for further deficit spending was sure to follow. On these (short-run) predictions, see E. Schiff's article in a forthcoming number of the *Review of Economic Statistics.* Corresponding long-run predictions will be discussed below, *sub 5.*

But in order to keep the inevitable increase in prices within that limit, a number of measures are necessary, all of which are highly unpopular, all of which require, in order to produce their result, experience and ability that I do not see, and some of which will, to some extent, reduce the speed of the expansion of output; nobody can counteract threatening inflation without also interfering with production. Now, if, instead, nothing is done except setting up another O. P. A. and taxing heavily precisely those incomes from which—even according to the doctrine held by our radicals—inflation does *not* threaten and if in addition wage rates are being pushed up regardless of consequences, a situation may well arise in which, in desperation, Washington may resort to clumsy and brutal measures such as devaluation, "freezing" deposits, assuming "direct control," punishing "profiteers" and "monopolists," or some other scapegoats, keeping carefully clear of the farmers. And this may upset apple carts to such an extent as to bring us into the immediate vicinity not of the two hundred billion goal but of some half-baked socialism. *May*. There are, of course, other possibilities.

5. It remains to notice what to many economists is *the* postwar problem *par excellence*: how to secure adequate consumption. So far we have indeed seen many reasons for doubting whether the goal envisaged—a gross national product of two hundred billions in 1928 dollars—will actually be reached by 1950. But all of them were founded upon the possibility or likelihood that obstacles *external* to the business process might bar the way. The power of the business process itself to produce that result has, however, been called in question by many economists most, but not all of whom are identified with certain articles of political as well as scientific faith. We will refer to them by a term that has gained some currency, Stagnationists.[18]

The relevant type of stagnationist theory has been developed by the late Lord Keynes. With its application to the case in hand the reader can best familiarize himself by studying one or more of those estimates of postwar demand that have been produced during the last few years.[19] Their authors agree with us in estimating *potential* production for 1950 at figures that are of the same order of magnitude as is our own so that we may, for the sake of simplicity, continue to speak of a gross national product of two hundred billions. They are even more optimistic than we in that they do not insist on the necessity of environmental conditions favorable to

[18] On some general aspects of the stagnationist thesis, see above, Chapter X.

[19] The most important of them have been critically analyzed by Mr. A. G. Hart in his article, "Model Building and Fiscal Policy," *American Economic Review*, September, 1945. Further references are therefore unnecessary.

capitalist achievement,[20] but reason on the tacit assumption that present political, administrative, and labor practices persist. Moreover, I shall waive any objections I may have against their estimates of the inevitable minimum of unemployment, or the validity of their statistical methods, and I shall also accept the various hypotheses by means of which they arrive at the figures of Net National Income and of Disposable Income (the sum total of individual incomes after tax and compulsory nontax payments). For definiteness, let us suppose that this disposable income figures out at about 150 billions and that corporate undivided profits are about 6 billions.[21]

Postwar demand, that is to say, the sum total which it is expected private households will spend on consumers' goods (except new homes), is then derived by calculating, from the data for the period preceding the war, say, 1923-1940, the average relation between per capita expenditure on these consumers' goods and per capita disposable income, both deflated by the cost-of-living index, and by applying this relation to a disposable income of 150 billions.[22] If this procedure yields, for example, the sum of 130 billions, we are left with a residual in the amount of 20 billions for savings or, if we add the corporate undivided profits, with 26 billions. The argument usually goes on to survey the available outlets for this sum, the investment opportunities (new housing, additions to inventories, plant and equipment, foreign investment) and to conclude or to suggest that these cannot possibly absorb anything like as much as people will want to save at the 1950 full-employment level of national income, at least not without the help of government. Hence, the necessity of government expenditure at home or government action forcing "foreign investment." Of late, however, another recommendation has come into favor. Since, under present conditions, anyone who advocates government deficit financing is in obvious danger of making

[20] I confess that I have wondered occasionally whether they are aware of the tremendous compliment to private enterprise which this implies.

[21] These figures approximate those of one of the postwar-demand estimators. They are not mine. Nor are they compatible with the experimental figures on which we reasoned in section II. For the procedure as applied to past periods—where hypotheses are of course replaced by facts—see e.g., Federal Reserve Bulletin, April, 1946, p. 436. It should, however, be observed, first, that these figures are in current dollars and, second, that the huge amount of "net savings of individuals" proves nothing for the saving percentages of "normal" times and that even the figures for 1937, 1938, 1939 and 1940 should not be accepted uncritically and especially not without reference to the definition of saving adopted by the Department of Commerce.

[22] Actually, the procedure is somewhat more complicated than that. The regression equations used also contain a trend factor that is to take account of possible changes of the relation over time. Moreover, some account is also taken of the effects of deferred demand and of the accumulation of liquid means. But, in order to concentrate on the salient point, we do not go into all this.

himself ridiculous, Washington economists have veered round to recommend balanced budgets, but budgets balanced at a very high level of taxation, the taxes to be highly progressive so as to eliminate the high incomes from which the menace of saving primarily proceeds. This accords with the slogan that (owing to the saving done by the receivers of high incomes) "in modern societies, the ultimate cause of unemployment is the inequality of incomes."

Thus the high level of national income to which we have looked for the solution of a good many economic and social problems is itself made out to be the most serious problem of all. Since high income means high savings and since these savings will not be entirely offset by investment expenditure, it will not be possible for the economy to keep on that high level of income and employment—unless fiscal policy keeps it there—if indeed this high level can be reached at all. It should be observed that, at least in part, this theory commands the support of public opinion and in particular of business opinions. Nothing is more common than the view that everything will be all right if only we can induce people "to use their incomes fully" or if only we can "get enough consumers' demand." It is a question of some interest why intelligent men who certainly have no stake in any political program involving government expenditure or equalization of income, should nevertheless feel concern on this score. The salesman mentality of the country coupled with the experience of the twenty years preceding the war is all the explanation I can offer for the astounding fact that the theory in question is not simply laughed out of court.

Those opponents of this theory miss the point who try to argue that gross national product, hence income, will be smaller and that investment opportunities will turn out to be greater than estimators assume who are so optimistic when it comes to estimating the former and so pessimistic when it comes to estimating the latter. There may be much truth in arguments on these and similar lines. In particular, it may be emphasized that in 1830 nobody foresaw or could have foreseen the capital requirements of the railroad age or, fifty years later, the capital requirements of the age of electricity. But the decisive argument is much simpler than all that. The theory rests upon the postulate that individuals save, according to a stable psychological law,[23] irrespective of the presence or absence of investment oppor-

[23] This psychological law says that a *community's* expenditure upon consumption, C (hence also the amount it desires to save S) depends upon national income, Y, in such a manner that, when Y increases by ΔY, C increases by $\Delta C < \Delta Y$ or $\dfrac{\Delta C}{\Delta Y} < 1$. This is the genuine Keynesian hypothesis about what is known as the Consumption Function. But Keynes himself used occasionally, and his followers use often, the stronger assumption that, as income increases, the saving *percentage* increases. We are concerned only with the genuine hypothesis. It should, however,

tunity. Evidently this is not the normal case. Normally people save with a view to some return, in money or in services of some "investment good." It is not only that the bulk of individual savings—and, of course, practically all business savings which, in turn, constitute the greater part of total saving—is done with a specific investment purpose in view. The decision to invest precedes as a rule, and the act of investing precedes very often, the decision to save. Even in those cases in which a man saves without specific investment purpose, any delay in coming to an investment decision is punished by the loss of return for the interval. It seems to follow, first, that unless people see investment opportunities, they will not normally save and that a situation of vanishing investment opportunity is likely to be also one of vanishing saving; and, second, that whenever we observe that people display "liquidity preference," that is to say, a desire to save unaccompanied by a desire to invest—a desire to hoard—this must be explained by special reasons and not by appeal to any psychological law postulated *ad hoc*.

Such reasons do exist, however, and there is one among them that is of considerable importance in the depth of cyclical depressions—on a broad average, in one year out of ten. When things look black and people expect nothing but losses from any commitment they might contemplate, then of course they will refuse to invest their current savings (and even to reinvest sums that currently return to them owing to the termination of previous commitments), or they will defer investment in order to profit by further reductions in prices. At the same time, savings will be not only not reduced but increased by all those who expect impending losses of income, in their business or through unemployment. This is an important element in the mechanism of depressions and public deficit spending is indeed one of the most obvious means for breaking such "vicious spirals." However, no defense of any "oversaving" theory can be based upon it because it occurs only as a consequence of a depression that hence cannot itself be explained by it. But it yields a psychological explanation of the Keynesian psychological law. The great depression of 1929-1932 and the slow recovery from it are still in everybody's mind. And the psychological law and the theory of hoarding that is based upon it are simply generalizations from that experience.[24]

---

be observed that it is a misuse of terms to call it a psychological law. Psychological laws in economics are doubtful customers at best. But the proposition in question has not even so much title to being dignified by this term as has, e.g., the proposition that our wish for one more slice of bread decreases in intensity as we go on eating more and more slices.

[24] Adaptation of the above argument together with certain wartime factors will, it is hoped, explain wartime accumulations of liquid means without recourse to the hypothesis of an insatiable hunger for hoards inherent in human nature.

Depression-hoarding is therefore not a genuine exception to our general proposition, viz., that decisions to save depend upon and presuppose decisions to invest, though the converse is not true, because it is obviously possible to finance an investment by a bank loan in which case there is no point whatever in speaking of anyone's saving.[25] There are genuine exceptions, besides apparent ones. But neither are of any importance. Instances of genuine exceptions are hoarding with the intention of accumulating a treasure which as everybody knows has been done extensively in India, China, and Egypt; and, temporarily, saving from a habit which once formed may outlive its rationale as may any other habit.[26] Instances of apparent exceptions, similar to our case of depression-hoarding, are accumulations for the purpose of financing a very heavy piece of investment, a possible but evidently unimportant case; or "saving" that is undertaken for the purpose of providing for contingencies, old age and so on and would be undertaken even if there were no opportunities for acquiring any "return" other than a feeling of security.[27]

[25] Our proposition is, however, not so simple as it may seem to readers unfamiliar with the discussion that has been carried on ever since the publication of Lord Keynes's *General Theory* (1936). It resembles rather than repeats an old theorem of the "classical theory" (Turgot, A. Smith, J. S. Mill) and cannot be sustained by the reasoning that satisfied the classics. A long and tedious argument would be necessary in order to establish it fully, an argument which it is so discouraging to have to work out because it yields but few new and interesting results and beyond this merely destroys what has been built up with so much trouble during the thirties. Lack of space prevents us, however, from going into it. But one point must be mentioned in order to avoid a misunderstanding that would be as regrettable as it would be natural. Though our proposition shows that the stagnation thesis cannot be based upon the element of saving and though this may be expressed by saying that there is no problem of saving *in this sense*, it does not amount to saying that there are no problems of saving *in other senses*. There are. Most of them center around the case in which individual savings, by way of purchase of securities, are applied to the repayment of bank debts incurred by firms in the course of expanding their plant and equipment. But this is another matter.

[26] The persistence of saving habits that are deeply rooted in the bourgeois scheme of life, especially in the puritan variant of it, may not seem to be unimportant. But the vanishing of investment opportunities that would render those habits irrational would, in the absence of external factors, be a slow process during which adaptation could and would have time to do its work. Washington economists who wish to assert, nevertheless, that the persistence of saving habits that have become irrational is a factor in the economic situation are therefore faced by an unenviable alternative: they would have to admit *either* that the situation of the thirties was one of depression hoarding—which spells surrender of the secular-stagnation thesis —*or* that attractiveness of investment was with comparative suddenness reduced by an external factor which could be no other than the policies they themselves supported. If they adopt the latter view, it is certainly not for me to object.

[27] The unimportance of this follows mainly from two facts: first, that these accumulations are currently depleted (though, with changing national income and age distribution of the population increments and decrements will not, in general, exactly balance); and, second, that so long as there is any saving at all that is

Thus, if the sorrows of stagnationists were the only ones to trouble us, we should entertain no misgivings about reaching the two hundred billion gross national product. And if twenty billions proved more than can be newly invested, at a rate of return satisfactory to the marginal saver, why, people would be only too happy to consume the excess. We should worry neither about measures to make them "fully use their incomes" nor about outlets for corporate and individual savings. In particular, we should not think it necessary to force foreign investment, advocacy of which under present conditions is nothing but an attempt to make palatable to the country what really amounts to imposing a war indemnity upon it.[28]

On the other hand, we should agree with the advocates of government deficit spending so far as this: Whenever there is danger, either from causes inherent to the business-cycle mechanism or from any other, of a "downward cumulative process," that is to say, whenever a situation threatens to emerge in which A's restriction of production induces B to restrict and so on throughout the economy, in which prices fall because they have fallen, in which unemployment feeds upon itself, government deficit spending will stop this "vicious spiral" and therefore, if we choose to neglect all other considerations, may be justly called an efficient remedy.[29] The true objection is not against

---

motivated by monetary returns, the presence in the total "supply" of an element that is not so motivated does not prove any tendency toward excess saving. This case needs no strengthening. But actually it may be reinforced by observing that under modern conditions insurance greatly reduces the amounts necessary to attain the objects of contingency saving: of old, provision e.g. for old age and for the needs of wives and children normally meant the accumulation of a "fortune" (though of course this was not left uninvested); now such provision is effected by "with-holdings from consumption" to the amount of insurance premia. The increase in insurance during the last twenty-five years, therefore, indicates the exact opposite of what it is made to indicate in stagnationist writings.

[28] Far be it for me to say or to imply that, on moral or political grounds, a case cannot be made for large sacrifices on the part of the American people. But the case ought to be put frankly upon the moral and political grounds and not upon a denial of the reality of these sacrifices, based on questionable economics. The suggestion that part of the excessive savings might usefully be directed into channels where evidently there is no hope for repayment, let alone returns, is the more insidious because the class whose task it might be to oppose such a policy will accept it with alacrity: for under a system of government guarantees the individual businessman risks little or nothing. And he attaches little if any weight to the national loss—especially if told that this loss, owing to the employment it secures, is really a national gain.

[29] This is why the Murray bill in its original form (not only in the form in which it has been enacted) was unexceptionable *so far as purely economic considerations are concerned*. The wholesale condemnation of income-generating government expenditure under *any* circumstances is understandable and may be justifiable in people who think that, once the use of this tool be granted, the door will be wide open for all kinds of legislative and administrative irresponsibilities. But it cannot be upheld on purely economic grounds.

income-generating government expenditure in emergencies once they have arisen but to policies that create the emergencies in which such expenditure imposes itself.

6. Unfortunately, however, if it were a question of predicting what will actually happen, our result would not differ so much from that of the stagnationists as the reader might expect. Though there is nothing to fear from people's propensity to save, there is plenty to fear from other factors. Labor unrest, price regulation, vexatious administration and irrational taxation are quite adequate to produce results for income and employment that will look exactly like a verification of the stagnationist theory and may indeed produce situations in which public deficit spending imposes itself. We may even witness what will look like oversaving, namely, conditions in which people will be reluctant to carry out their investment decisions. We have been discussing a possibility. We have found that there are no causes inherent in the business process itself to prevent it from being realized. We have also seen that there are causes external to the business process that may do so. Beyond this I do not pretend to know what the actual outcome will be. Whatever it is, it will be a dominant factor in the social situation not only in the United States but also in the world. But only for the next half century or so. The long-run diagnosis elaborated in this book will not be affected.

III

Russian Imperialism and Communism

The other factor that is relevant to our diagnosis is Russia's victory over her allies. Unlike the economic success of the United States, this victory is not a possibility only, but, for the time being, an accomplished fact. Starting from a position that was none too strong—a position in which Russia according to all ordinary rules of the political game might have had to accept whatever her allies thought fit to impose and to take a back seat in the new international order—she raised herself to a position of power far beyond any she ever held under the tsars, in spite of everything that England and the United States can possibly be assumed to have wished or to have fought for. And—supreme achievement!—methods peculiar to her system of government have enabled her to extend her actual power beyond her official conquests and at the same time to make it appear much smaller than it is—so that those sham concessions at danger points that satisfy escapists and appeasers never involve any real sacrifice even if they do not, as is sometimes the case, spell actual gain.[30] If the reader recalls

[30] For instance, the granting of sham independence to countries under complete control, such as Poland, which we persist in treating as independent agents, adds

the aims by which the United States Government motivated its policy since 1939—democracy, freedom from fear and want, small nations, etc.—he will have to realize that what has occurred amounts to a surrender not much less complete than might have been expected from a military victory of Russia over her two chief allies.

This result first of all calls for explanation. I am afraid that those analysts of history who recognize nothing but impersonal factors —plus, perhaps, an element of chance—will not do very well at this task. The impersonal or objective factors were all against Russia. Even her huge army was not simply the product of a numerous population and a rich economy, but the work of one man who was strong enough to keep that population in abject poverty and submission and to concentrate all the forces of an undeveloped and defective industrial apparatus on the one military purpose. But this would not have been enough. Those who never understand how luck and genius intertwine, will of course point to lucky chances in that long series of events that culminated in that stupendous success. But this series of events contains as many or more desperate situations in which the bolshevist régime had every chance to perish. Political genius consists precisely in the ability to exploit favorable possibilities and to neutralize unfavorable ones so completely that, after the fact, the superficial observer sees nothing but the former. Following events from that first master stroke—the "understanding" with Germany—we behold a master's handiwork. It is true that Stalin never encountered a man of comparable ability. But this only reinforces the case for a philosophy of history that leaves adequate room for the quality of leading personnel and for the special case of this—the quality of the leading individual. The only concession that realistic analysis can make to the "impersonal theory" is this: An autocrat is, in matters of foreign policy, unhampered by all those considerations that distract the attention of a democratic leader.[31]

---

to the votes that are at the disposal of Russia in international bodies, and also to the subsidies and loans that the Russian government may receive; Russia would be weaker than she is if she had annexed the whole of Poland outright.

[31] Some readers will observe that we are at this point brushing against an old controversy between sociologists of history and also between historians. It is therefore necessary to state that I am not preaching hero-worship or adopting the slogan: "history is made by [individual] men." The methodology involved in the argument of our text comes to not more than this. In explaining a historical course of events, we make use of a large array of data. Among these data are climate, fertility, size, and so on of countries, but also the qualities, invariant in the short run, of their populations. And since quality of population does not determine uniquely the quality of the political personnel and this in turn does not determine uniquely the quality of leadership, these two must be listed separately. To put it differently: in a given situation, brain and nerves of the man at the helm are just as objective facts as are iron content of the country's ore and presence or absence of molybdenum or vanadium.

But, second, though we may understand, by attending to developments in detail, how this unbelievable situation has arisen, this does not help us to understand how it is that the world puts up with it now that it is before everyone's eyes. The problem reduces to the attitude of the United States. For the countries of continental Europe, exhausted, starving, and exposed to Russian retaliation as they are, can certainly not be counted on for significant resistance. The only continental country really independent of Russia is Spain—a fact that Russia's policy toward her has recently brought home to most of us. France that might be almost equally independent has the strongest Russian garrison of all, in the shape of her Communist party.[32] As regards England, there are plenty of symptoms to show that had she had her way the whole course of events since 1941 would have been quite different and that all England that counts politically views the present situation with disgust and apprehension. If, nevertheless, she does not take a strong line, this can only be due to the fact that if she did she would be taking a terrible risk, the risk of having to fight a war with Russia singlehanded. For though it is very likely that the United States would join her, *it is not certain*. Why?

To an observer from another planet nothing could be more obvious than that from every consideration of honor and interest this country cannot tolerate a situation in which a great part of humanity is deprived of what we consider to be elementary human rights, in which there is more cruelty and lawlessness than the war was under-

---

[32] This fact is extremely interesting. Probably there were some Americans who believed that the French people would hail their liberation in transports of joy and gratitude and that they would settle down at once to the task of rebuilding a democratic France. As a matter of fact, we find what Léon Blum euphemistically described as *convalescence fatiguée* or, in plain English, a universal reluctance to working the democratic method. There are the three parties of about equal numerical strength and equally incapable of producing effective government on democratic lines: the M. R. P. (*mouvement républicain populaire*, the Catholic and Gaullist party), the regular Socialists, and the Communists. For us three points only are relevant: first, the practically complete absence of "liberal" groups; second, the absence of any group with which the United States politician could wholeheartedly co-operate; third and most important, the strength of the Communists. Manifestly, this strength cannot be explained by a conversion to Communist principles of so large a number of Frenchmen. Many of them cannot be Communists at all in the doctrinal sense. Those who are not, are Communists *ad hoc*, that is to say, Communists by virtue of their conception of the national situation. But this means that they are simply pro-Russian. They look upon Russia as "the great fact of our day," the power that (reconstruction dollars apart) really matters, the power to which *il faut s'accrocher* and with which, in order to be reborn, France must side, against England and the United States, in any future struggle—which, precisely thereby, is to be turned into something styled world revolution. Fascinating bunch of problems that open up at this point! But my regret at the impossibility of going into them is somewhat mitigated by the conviction that my readers would refuse to follow the argument.

taken to curb, in which tremendous power and prestige is concentrated in the hands of a government that embodies the negation of principles that mean something to the large majority of the people of the United States. Surely it was not worth while for this people to undergo sacrifices to carry on a conflict in which untold horrors were inflicted upon millions of innocent women and children if the chief result is to free the most powerful of all dictators from the two armies that hemmed him in. Surely this is a case where a job half done is worse than nothing. Moreover, the other half would have been not only possible but relatively easy because after Japan's surrender this country's military forces and techniques, not to speak of her economic power to give or withhold, assured her unchallengeable superiority.

But if that observer from another planet argued on these lines, we should have to reply that he does not understand political sociology. In Stalinist Russia, foreign policy is foreign policy as it was under the tsars. In the United States, foreign policy is domestic politics. There is indeed a tradition flowing from Washington's advice. But it is essentially isolationist. There is no tradition and there are no organs for playing the complex game of any other foreign policy. When violently excited by propaganda the country may enter upon or accept an activist course of interference beyond the seas. But it soon tires of it, and tired it is now—tired of the horrors of modern warfare, of sacrifices, taxes, military service, of bureaucratic regulations, of war slogans, of world-government ideals—and very anxious to return to its habitual ways of life. Urging it on to further strenuous exertion —in the absence of any immediate danger of attack—would be bad political business for any party or pressure group that might wish to undertake it. But no such wish seems to be entertained by any party or group. Those who are actuated by a passionate hatred of Germany or of the national-socialist régime are content. With the same arguments which they used to stigmatize as escapist, they now support the policy toward Russia which they used to stigmatize as appeasement in the case of Hitlerite Germany. And if we go through the list of the interests that form the pattern of American politics, we find that they all agree, though for different reasons, in favoring appeasement. Farmers do not care much. Organized labor may or may not be significantly influenced by a genuinely pro-Russian wing and it may or may not be true that unions, or some of them, would actively obstruct any war against Russia. We need not go into this question —usually dealt with by reckless denials or reckless assertions—because all that matters for the situation as it presents itself at the moment to the politician is the fact that nobody doubts, viz., that labor which was not pro-war in 1940 is definitely anti-war now. The most interesting observation to make, however, is that the same holds for the business class and that its attitude, though of course not pro-Russian in feeling or intention, actually is pro-Russian in effect. Radical intellectuals love to attribute to the bourgeoisie an intention to jump at the throat of the Soviet Republic. They certainly would describe a war with Russia as a war waged upon socialism by big business. Nothing can be more unrealistic. The business class, too, is tired of war slogans, of taxes, of regulations. War with Russia would stem a tide that for the moment is running in favor of business interests, and would mean still more taxation and still more regulation. It would put labor in a still stronger position. It would, moreover, not only disturb domestic business but cut off prospective business of a very alluring kind. Soviet Russia may become a very big customer. She has never yet failed to pay promptly. And many a good bourgeois' anti-socialist convictions are being undermined by this fact. This is the way the bourgeois mind works—always will work even in sight of the hangman's rope. But it is not difficult to rationalize away this unpleasant sight. Let Russia swallow one or two more countries, what of it? Let her be well supplied with everything she needs and she will cease to frown. After twenty years Russians will be just as democratic and pacific as are we—and think and feel just as do we. Besides, Stalin will be dead by then.[33]

Once more: the purpose of this book is not to guide readers toward definite practical conclusions but to present pieces of analysis that may be useful to them in drawing their own practical conclusions. Moreover, in matters so subject to chance and to the intrusion of new and unexpected factors, prediction can be no more than prophecy and

[33] The last sentences are all quotations. They are so revealing and valuable precisely because they are not answers to interview questions that the person interviewed recognizes as such. They were spontaneous utterances made without awareness of the fact that the speaker was revealing mental processes of his or, more precisely, an alogical and semiconscious attitude of his that he was trying to rationalize *for himself*. Excepting the third which stood alone in its naïveté, the statements, or closely similar ones, have been heard more than once. In almost every case the irrationality of the speaker's attitude (including its inconsistency with the attitudes of 1939-1941) has been pointed out to him. In no case was there any logically presentable reply or any reaction except (a) display of a sort of good-natured annoyance or (b) a gesture of hopelessness that seemed to admit the criticism but with some such proviso as "what's the good?"

In view of a point that has been made earlier in this section, I must, however, add that there is in fact something in the fourth escape from reality. If it be true, as I myself have held, that abilities such as those of Russia's leader occur extremely rarely in any population, it seems in fact that the action of nature will solve many a problem in due course. Only, if it be admitted that there is *something* in the argument, it should also be stated that too much may be made of it. In some respects, an enemy of supreme ability is easier to deal with than is a less capable one—which is not really a paradox. Moreover, though it does require genius of the first order to build up, e.g., the Standard Oil concern, it does not require genius to run it once it has been built up. The Russian century once started may run its course almost of itself.

hence can have no scientific standing. Trusting that this is thoroughly understood, I now will nevertheless, by way of summing up this part of our argument, adopt what seems to be a reasonable inference, but for no other purpose than *pour fixer les idées.* To put it differently: What we are about to do is exactly what we have been doing in this book all along with reference to the great subject of socialism in general: we are extrapolating observable tendencies.

The facts we have glanced at suggest that, unless Stalin makes the first mistake of his life, there will be no war in the next years and Russia will be left undisturbed to develop her resources, to rebuild her economy, and to construct by far the greatest war machine, absolutely and relatively, the world has ever seen. The proviso inserted which restricts but does not, I think, annihilate the practical value of this inference, means this: A *spectacular* act of aggression—an act of aggression so spectacular that even fellow travelers would have difficulty in explaining it as perfectly justified "defense"—may no doubt precipitate war at any moment. But against this possibility must be set the facts, first, that nothing in the foreign policy of the Stalinist régime is more striking than is its cautious patience; second, that this régime has everything to gain by being patient; third, that, acting from a pinnacle of imperialist success, it can afford to be patient and to surrender outposts whenever there is a sign of real danger or whenever it faces "a firmer tone" as it had to of late.[34] The outlook will, however, materially change after a reconstruction period of, say, ten years. The war machine will be ready for use and it will become increasingly difficult not to use it. Moreover, unless England embraces bolshevism and *in addition* renounces all of her traditional position, the mere existence of that independent isle may prove as unbearable to Russian autocracy as it proved to be to Napoleonic autocracy—and vice versa. Perception of this fact is, of course, the essence of Churchillian warnings and the rationale of the armament race that has already started.

But in order to appreciate all this, another thing must be borne in mind. In peace and in a possible future war, still more in these intermediate situations that are not war but dominated by the threat

[34] It should be observed, in order to illustrate the force of the argument, that none of these three facts were present in the German case such as it stood in 1939. Some readers will deny this with respect to the third fact, at least for the situation that prevailed after Munich. But this is only because our attitude toward German ambitions is quite different from that which we take at present toward Russian ambitions. The decisive point, viewed from a political angle, is that Germany had not then fully recovered her national territory, whereas the Stalinist régime has only to compromise, if at all, about positions in nationally foreign territories, which is a much easier thing to do. Moreover, "the firmer tone" mentioned in the text has so far been resorted to only in order to ward off additional encroachments.

of war, the Communist groups and parties all over the world are naturally of the greatest importance for Russian foreign policy.[35] In consequence, there is nothing surprising in the fact that official Stalinism has of late returned to the practice of advertising an approaching struggle between capitalism and socialism—the impending world revolution—the impossibility of permanent peace so long as capitalism survives anywhere, and so on. All the more essential is it to realize that such slogans, useful or necessary though they are from the Russian standpoint, distort the real issue which is Russian imperialism [36] and has, apart from fifth-column considerations, nothing to do with socialism. The trouble with Russia is not that she is socialist but that she is Russia. As a matter of fact, the Stalinist régime is essentially a militarist autocracy which, because it rules by means of a single and strictly disciplined party and does not admit freedom of the press, partakes of one of the defining characteristics of Fascism [37] and exploits the masses in the Marxist sense. We may understand, and condole with, the American intellectual who is so circumstanced as to have to call this democratic socialism—at least in prospect—though

[35] For the purpose of the argument that is to follow it is fortunately not necessary to go into the question of how strong the Communist fifth column actually is in this country. It is, at any rate, much stronger than appears from any statistics or from any official declarations of spokesmen for labor groups, and certainly not negligible. Discussion on this point and on the possible consequences of pro-Russian attitudes on the efficiency of a possible war effort are, I think, rendered next to valueless not only by the prevalence of interested over- or under-statement, but also by the failure of participants to define the issue clearly. One's attitude may be pro-Russian in effect, as we have seen, without being pro-Russian in feeling or intent. And it may be Communist without being effectively pro-Russian. All these variants—some of which are not relevant to a man's behavior if war be actually declared—must be carefully distinguished.

[36] The phrase imperialism being among the most misused ones in the whole stock of popular political theory, it is necessary to define the meaning which it is intended to carry here. For our limited purpose, however, it is not necessary to analyze the phenomenon as I attempted to do in a monograph published about thirty years ago and to adopt the definition appropriate to an elaborate analysis. Instead, the following definition will suffice though I consider it utterly inadequate (it is, however, compatible with the use we made of the term in Chapters IV and XI of this book): imperialist is a policy that aims at extending a government's control over groups other than co-national ones against their will. This is what Russia did, before the war, in the cases of Outer Mongolia and Finland and, during and after the war, in all cases. The point is that this policy knows no inherent limit. Motivating phrases are irrelevant.

[37] This is another phrase that through misuse has lost all definite meaning. Its use in United States common parlance in fact suggests the definition: Fascist is any policy, group, or country which the speaker or writer who uses the phrase does not like. In our text, however, it means, in accordance with the political theory presented in this book (Chapter XXII), the political method of monopolistic vs. competitive leadership. It will be observed that this does not amount to saying that in any or every other respect Stalinism is "the same thing" as Hitlerism or Italian Fascism.

we may resent the insult to our intelligence that is implied in his expectation of being believed. But the visible tendency of such a régime to extend its sway over the whole of Europe and Asia evidently cannot be simply identified with any tendency of socialism to spread. It does not even follow that the expansion of Russian rule will make for socialism in any of the more usual senses of the word. Whether it will or not depends entirely on the real and putative interests of the Russian autocracy (see last section of preceding chapter). This may be illustrated by the analogous case of the religious policy of Stalinism: so long as it suited the autocrat, religion was the opium of the people; as soon as he realized that the Orthodox Church might prove a more useful tool of foreign policy in some parts of the world than either Communism or the World Federation of Trade Unions (1945), Russia was declared to be a "Christ-loving nation" and in the place of the tsarist "chief procurator of the Holy Synod," emerged, along with a new Patriarch—who immediately proved himself a zealous tourist in Eastern countries—a Communist chairman of the "council for the affairs of the Orthodox Church." It is true that there is a strong reason for expecting nationalization of industry in all countries in which Russia is free to act without feeling hampered by tactical considerations of foreign policy: a nationalized industry is easier to manage and to exploit for a conqueror and cannot become a center of opposition. But there is no other reason. And it is impossible to say whether or not this motive will prevail over other possible ones.[38] It is even conceivable that further advance of the Russian power may eventually prove an impediment to developments in the direction of what most people think of and feel about when they utter the word Socialism.

To confuse the Russian with the socialist issue—unless it is a trick perpetrated in the service of Russia—is therefore to misconceive the social situation of the world. The Russian issue bears upon the socialist issue in two ways only. First, by virtue of the logic of their situation, the presence of Communist groups and of pro-Communist wings in non-Communist groups will tend to radicalize labor politics. This is not always so—the French Communists, e.g., voted against two important measures of socialization. But upon the whole, and if for no

[38] The reader will please notice that all the statements of fact, made or implied in the above argument, are verifiable, if need be, from official Russian sources. In fact, all that is material to our argument, especially to our diagnosis of the nature of the Russian régime, can be established without recourse to any statement of fact that could possibly be challenged. I have purposely refrained from mentioning anything, however valuable it might have seemed for further illustration of the nature of the régime, that might raise questions of fact, such as murder in the conquered or controlled countries, chain gangs in Georgia, concentration camps. Our argument would not be affected in the least if anything that could be called an atrocity were entirely absent.

other purpose than for the purpose of disorganizing capitalist countries, that logic of the situation will be allowed to assert itself. Second, in the case of a war we shall have the social and political consequences that any war has under modern conditions—the fact that it is a war between a supposedly socialist and a supposedly capitalist country will make little difference.

Comments on Further Postwar
Developments

PREFACE TO THE THIRD
ENGLISH EDITION, 1949

THIS new edition gives me the opportunity to comment, from the standpoint of this book, upon the English developments of the last two years—to insert them, as it were, into the general framework of the analysis that I have endeavoured to construct. In the time and space at my disposal, it is but *membra disjecta* that I have to offer. But there is also another point that I wish to be clearly understood from the outset. Nothing is farther from my mind than any intention to criticize another country's policy or to offer "advice." I should consider this to be nothing short of impertinent. If certain turns of phrase nevertheless read as if I harbored such an intention, readers will please realize that this is merely one of the many undesirable consequences of extreme brevity.

Before reading what follows, readers should peruse Section IV of Chapter XIX and Section I of Chapter XXVIII, which I have left unchanged, as I have the rest of the book.

1. Viewed from our standpoint as well as from any other, the English picture is complicated, and its main features are blurred by the fact that a process of social transition interferes with, and is in turn interfered with by, another process of transition which—since it is hardly possible, international relations being what they are, to speak of a transition from a war economy to a peace economy—had better be called a process of readjustment under conditions of suppressed inflation. Although distinct in logic, these two processes are too closely interwoven to admit of separate treatment. But we shall cut the Gordian knot and separate them all the same. We can do so with a relatively easy conscience because a modern conservative government, should the next elections produce one, will also have to manage readjustment in the given situation and in a society in which the labor interest dominates and the free-enterprise "beacon light is quenched in smoke." In other words: if the labor government should be replaced by a conservative one—a question which I cannot claim any competence to answer—this would presumably make much less difference than ardent partisans profess to believe except of course that nationalization would not be carried further.

2. Let us then glance for a moment at that component of England's economic policy of the last two years which will bear interpretation as "socialist policy before the act" in the sense assigned to this phrase

in Section IV of Chapter XIX. The reader will observe that so far the labor government has kept well within the program of nationalization there outlined and that, as regards the most controversial point of this program—namely point 6: socialization of the steel industry—it has with remarkable moderation deferred definitive action until after the next elections. I readily admit that there is room for honest difference of opinion as to whether or not this socialization or nationalization program should be called socialist at all. But I am positive that nothing else that has been actually done can be so called. For most of the "planning" that has been actually done or suggested has nothing specifically socialist about it unless we adopt a definition of socialism that is much too wide to be of any analytic use. Some of the planning schemes and especially some of the research work done in order to implement them do, of course, point in the socialist direction, but a long time will elapse before income accounting and input and output analysis—both of which are farther advanced in the United States than they are in England—can be expected to bear consumable socialist fruits.

More important, however, is another aspect of the situation. Of all the things that have happened in England during the last two years nothing has struck me more vividly than has the weakness of the resistance that has been offered to advance along the socialist line. The conservative opposition in Parliament has kept strictly within the bounds of ordinary parliamentary routine and less heat has been generated by the issue of social reconstruction than by several relatively secondary issues of the past such as free trade, Ireland, and the people's budget. Both in Parliament and in the country the important sector of the conservative party which envisages questions of social reconstruction with perfect equanimity has gained ground. The conservative press has, of course, proffered its criticisms; it has argued, expostulated, ridiculed as it had done many times before, but not more so. A critical literature of books and pamphlets has poured forth as on previous occasions when major issues were under discussion, but if it occurred to a statistically-minded observer to measure the importance of issues by the number of volumes or pages produced by the "No's," he could not possibly rate the importance of the socialist issue very highly. This is not the manner in which a strong nation reacts to attack upon principles to which it is firmly attached. I infer that the principle of free enterprise is no longer among them. Socialism has ceased to be resisted with moral passion. It has become a matter to be discussed in terms of utilitarian arguments. There are individualist diehards, of course, but they do not seem to evoke sufficient support to count politically. And *this* is the writing on the wall —proof that the ethos of capitalism is gone.

3. This situation seems to me to bear out my diagnosis of 1942

and to verify, so far as verification is possible in such matters, the arguments by which it was arrived at. I have read the brilliant book by my eminent colleague, Professor Jewkes, with respect and admiration,[1] but I have to confess that my sincere wish to be converted has not been fulfilled. Professor Jewkes's very approach to the problem —an approach that bears much more closely upon the vexations incident to the policy of readjustment than it does upon the issues of socialism—might even be added to the accumulating evidence in favour of the thesis of this book.

The possibility of settling the question whether to socialize or not by means of the apparatus of parliamentary democracy has been established, and so has been the particular method congenial to this political system, viz., the method of piecemeal socialization. The beginnings made may not amount to more than this and may be indicative of nothing but a long-time trend. Nevertheless they seem to show clearly what we are to understand not only by democratic socialization, but also by democratic socialism. They show that socialism and democracy may be compatible *provided the latter be defined as it has been in Chapter XXII of this book.* In Chapter XXIII it has been pointed out that the principle of political democracy—the principle that governments should emerge from competitive struggles for votes— does, to some extent, guarantee freedom of speech and freedom of the Press, but that, for the rest, democracy has nothing to do with "freedoms." In particular, as regards the "freedoms" with which the economist is concerned, the freedom of investment, the freedom of consumers' choice, and the freedom of occupational choice, we have now interesting experimental material before us that goes to show that these "freedoms" may be restricted quite as much as, and in some respects more than, socialist governments are likely to require under normal conditions. The freedom of private investment, under the conditions of modern taxation, has lost the better part of its meaning in any case; but we also see how investments may be transferred—whatever we, as individuals, may think of the results—from the private to the public sphere. The freedom of consumers' choice, in a socialist community working under normal conditions, could be much greater than it is now; but in addition we see that the malleability of tastes is greater than observers used to believe, for people do not resent restrictions to the point of active resistance even though the necessity of

[1] John Jewkes, *Ordeal by Planning*, 1948. With due gratitude for his courteous criticisms of my argument, I must confess that I do not in all points recognize my own views in the views criticized. For instance, I should much prefer to say that the entrepreneurial function, owing to the steady expansion of the range of the calculable, is bound to become obsolescent rather than that it is actually obsolete anywhere by now. Nor did I intend to deny that there is still room for military leadership. Only this leadership does not mean quite what it did mean when Napoleon, bullets whistling around him, stood at the bridge at Arcole.

actual restrictions is not evident to everyone. Similarly, restrictions upon occupational choices will normally not have to amount to "compulsion" except in a relatively small minority of cases, especially if the list of admissible choices be rationally coupled with a list of differential rewards; and we see that people properly conditioned to accept governmental "directions," do not mind them greatly.

Let me repeat once more, though it should not be necessary to do so: these are inferences from facts that could be fully established but in no sense expressions of my personal preferences. Personally, I prefer other cultural patterns.

4. As already indicated, criticism of the economic policy of the labor government is being directed primarily against its management of the "process of readjustment under conditions of suppressed inflation." The government and the bureaucracy have indeed supplied plenty of ammunition for use against themselves by a torrent of detailed regulations about the admissible circumference of green onions and similar matters, by ill-considered administrative decisions, and by official pronouncements that are easy to ridicule. They have suppressed many activities, entrepreneurial and other, that might have improved the country's economic situation. But they have also avoided postwar readjustment by catastrophe and carried labor through critical years, without unemployment, on a rising level of real income. And, if this be the only recognized aim of economic policy as it seems to be with many economists, it is as possible to speak of success as it is, from several other standpoints, to speak of failure. It should be added that this has not been accomplished, as it might have been, by means of complete diregard of the future: the large amount of public investment that has been carried out, may be open to criticism as regards the individual items; but the fact remains that the necessity of rejuvenating the nation's economic apparatus has not been neglected in spite of all the protests against excessive investment that have been voiced by many people, some eminent economists among them. However, we are concerned with one question only. It is this: how will the gradual elimination, within the period of the Marshall aid, of the untenable features of the situation affect the prognosis for our issue, socialism *vs.* capitalism? Or in other words: since the solution that straight socialism might have to offer is obviously not practical politics, and since in consequence the solution has to be looked for in the opposite direction, will socialism, in England and elsewhere, suffer a setback and will the system of private enterprise take on another lease of life?

I do not think that this question is very difficult to answer. Short of another world war there will be a setback but not a serious or prolonged one. Private enterprise will regain some of the ground that it has lost but not very much. Fundamentally, the social situation will remain what it is and there is little likelihood that the shackles upon private enterprise will be removed sufficiently to allow it to work according to design. The argument that leads to this conclusion will be outlined in the two remaining sections of this Preface. It applies to England only. As should be obvious, diagnosis and prognosis are different for the United States. The pious wish that some European economists seem to harbor, viz., that there will be a spectacular breakdown in the latter country—other than a readjustment crisis—and that this breakdown will mean the *coup de grâce* to capitalism is not likely to be fulfilled, whatever American politics may do to the vast possibilities that unmistakably loom in the immediate future.

5. Among the untenable features of the English situation I do not include rationing and the detailed regulations of both consumers' and producers' behavior. These are but a method for suppressing the effects of inflation and will disappear when they have served their purpose: in spots they are disappearing already. But the state of suppressed inflation is itself a consequence of more fundamentaal difficulties and, but for these, could have been readily dealt with by well-known traditional remedies such as a budget surplus, reinforced by special taxation in order to reduce the volume of redundant purchasing power, and the appropriate credit policy. These means are actually being used now— not without success—although, in the given circumstances, they cannot be used to full effect because no great surplus is possible so long as the food subsidies remain what they are, because the possibilities of taxation, so far as the higher income brackets are concerned, are exhausted —in England there are no longer any people who are "rich after taxes" —and because a higher interest rate meets with apparently invincible resistance. But the basic difficulty is excess consumption, that is, a real wage bill plus the real cost of social services which are, on the one hand, incompatible with the other conditions of the English economy at its present level of productivity and, on the other hand, the obstacles that prevent it from rising to a higher level. Usually, the problem is formulated in another and less unpalatable manner. It is England's international balance of payment which is being made the one untenable feature in the picture of her economic situation so that the goal to be attained within the period of the Marshall aid appears to be an export surplus that will reinsert her into the world's economy and assure effective interchangeability between the pound and the dollar. This way of putting the problem is not erroneous. The error consists in believing that it spells out a diagnosis that differs from ours. For in order to reach that goal and to stay there without either foreign help or internal pressure it is necessary to normalize England's domestic situation, as a little reflection and quite elementary economics suffice to show. Something may indeed be gained by more or less mercantilist exploitation of the strong points in England's international position and by regulative import and export policies. Even-

tually, when the goal comes in sight, devaluation of the pound may help over the last steps towards it. But the fundamental condition for durable success is adjustment of her economic process in such a way as to make it once more produce, along with the goods for her domestic consumption and the goods and services that are to pay for her imports, a genuine net surplus for investment at home and abroad. This cannot be accomplished without a temporary decrease of consumption and a permanent increase of production; and these in turn cannot be brought about without an unpopular reduction in public expenditure and a still more unpopular shift of the burden of taxation.

6. On weighing the implications of this, the reader will have no difficulty in realizing the magnitude of the political problem involved. Whatever is to be achieved will have to be achieved by difficult manœuvering at an indefinite number of points. It seems reasonable to expect that nowhere will success go beyond the absolute minimum because things being what they are every move will bear interpretation as an uncompensated sacrifice of some vested interest of labor. And absolute minima are not enough in order to reconstruct free-enterprise society and to allow it to show what it can do. If proof of this were needed, the experience of the 1920's would suffice to provide it. Therefore, we cannot expect a break in social trends. A breathing spell for private enterprise is not unlikely to occur, not only under a conservative but also under a labor government. But if it occur at all this will be much more because of the illogical association of socialist policies with postwar vicissitudes than because of aversion, whether logically defensible or not, from these socialist policies themselves.

Cambridge, Mass.
  April 1949

THE MARCH INTO SOCIALISM[1]

IN ORDER to minimize the danger of misunderstandings that is ever present in discussions on topics such as the one of this session, I want first of all to settle a few preliminary points before taking up my subject *which is the relevance, for the economic future of this country, of the present state of inflationary pressure.*

1. For the purposes of this paper, I define (centralist) socialism as that organization of society in which the means of production are controlled, and the decisions on how and what to produce and on who is to get what, are made by public authority instead of by privately-owned and privately-managed firms. All that we mean by the March into Socialism is, therefore, the migration of people's economic affairs from the private into the public sphere. Observe that, though both socialists and antisocialists have of course ideas of their own on the subject, it is hardly possible to visualize a socialist society in this sense without a huge bureaucratic apparatus that manages the productive and distributive process and in turn may or may not be controlled by organs of political democracy such as we have today—a parliament or congress and a set of political officers who depend for their position upon the results of a competitive struggle for votes. Therefore we may equate the march into socialism to a conquest of private industry and trade by the state. The apparent paradox that this very same process is described by classic socialist doctrine as the "withering away of the state" is easily resolved if we take account of the Marxist theory of government. Observe further that socialism does not exclude decentralized decision-making in the administrative sense—just as the central management of an army does not deny all initiative to commanders of subgroups. And observe, finally, that socialism in our sense does not

[1] Joseph Schumpeter delivered his address, "The March into Socialism," before the American Economic Association in New York on December 30, 1949, from notes and not from a prepared manuscript. He was writing up these notes for the *Proceedings* and had all but finished his paper the evening before his death. He expected to complete it the next day (January 8, 1950) before leaving for Chicago to deliver the Walgreen Foundation Lectures. This paper is a first draft but carefully written in his own hand as were all his writings; there was no opportunity for him to make minor corrections or to write the concluding paragraphs. The corrections which consist largely in supplying punctuation or an occasional missing word have been kept to a minimum. The brief concluding paragraphs have been supplied by his wife from notes and memory.

necessarily—that is, by logical necessity—exclude the use of competitive mechanisms as we see, e.g., from the Lange-Lerner model. Freedom of consumers' choice and of choice of occupation may, but need not necessarily, be restricted in socialist societies.

2. I do not advocate socialism. Nor have I any intention of discussing its desirability or undesirability, whatever this may mean. More important is it, however, to make it quite clear that I do not "prophesy" or predict it. Any prediction is extrascientific prophecy that attempts to do more than to diagnose observable tendencies and to state what results would be, if these tendencies should work themselves out according to their logic. In itself, this does not amount to prognosis or prediction because factors external to the chosen range of observation may intervene to prevent that consummation; because, with phenomena so far removed as social phenomena are from the comfortable situation that astronomers have the good fortune of facing, observable tendencies, even if allowed to work themselves out, may be compatible with more than one outcome; and because existing tendencies, battling with resistances, may fail to work themselves out completely and may eventually "stick" at some halfway house. Let us illustrate this point by point.

First, no competent—and, of course, sufficiently detached—observer of Russia in the Stolypin era could have diagnosed the presence of any tendency toward anything at all like the Lenin system or, in fact, anything but rapid economic evolution and a lagged adaptation of institutions to the results of that evolution. It was a war and the consequent military and administrative breakdown which produced the Bolshevist regime and no amount of unscientific determinism avails against this fact. Second, for the sake of brevity, I speak of centralist socialism only because it holds a place of honor in the discussion. But other possibilities should not be neglected. Familiar facts of our own trade-union practice suggest that a development towards some form of guild socialism is not entirely off the cards. And other familiar facts suggest that observable tendencies, or some of them, may be compatible with forms of social reorganization that are not socialist at all, at least not in the sense which has been adopted for this paper. For instance, a reorganization of society on the lines of the encyclical *Quadragesimo anno,* though presumably possible only in Catholic societies or in societies where the position of the Catholic Church is sufficiently strong, no doubt provides an alternative to socialism that would avoid the "omnipotent state." Third, most observable tendencies of any kind stop short of complete achievement. Thus, a socialist regime in this country would have to be bold indeed if it ever thought of touching the subsidized independence of the farmer. Even the position of the "small businessman" might prove too strong for bureaucracy to conquer, and a large fringe may therefore be covered indefinitely by compromise arrangements.

Still more important is something else, however. As economic cares migrate from the private to the public sphere, many urges that favor this migration become satisfied, wholly or partly, so that the tendency may lose momentum. Some economists will add that any gradual movement towards a centrally-planned economy offers opportunity for unfavorable developments to be experienced which may act as brakes. I have no time to explain the reasons why I do not rate either possibility very highly and why, in particular, results that are felt to be unfavorable by sufficiently important groups are more likely to exert a propelling, than they are to exert a restraining, influence—that is, that the remedy for unsuccessful socialization which will suggest itself, will be not less but more socialization. But for our purpose it is essential to notice that most of the arguments that are framed in order to arrive at a result favorable to the survival of the private-enterprise economy do not really deny the existence of a tendency toward socialism in our sense, but only deny that it will work itself out completely. Since nobody can dispute this possibility, there is danger that the controversy will resolve itself into a battle of words, especially in the United States where mere words count for so much, where the term Socialism is not popular except with some relatively small minority groups, and where many people who like the thing at the same time dislike the word and prefer to substitute another, e.g., Liberalism.[2] Hence brief attempt at classification seems to be indicated.

3. The reasons for believing that the capitalist order tends to destroy itself and that centralist socialism is—with the qualifications mentioned above—a likely heir apparent I have explained elsewhere. Briefly and superficially, these reasons may be summed up under four heads. First, the very success of the business class in developing the productive powers of this country and the very fact that this success has created a new standard of life for all classes has paradoxically undermined the social and political position of the same business class whose economic function, though not obsolete, tends to become obsolescent and amenable to bureaucratization. Second, capitalist activity, being essentially "rational," tends to spread rational habits of mind and to destroy those loyalties and those habits of super- and subordination that are nevertheless essential for the efficient working of the institutionalized leadership of the producing plant: no social system can work which is based exclusively upon a network of free contracts between (legally) equal contracting parties and in which everyone is supposed to be guided by nothing except his own (short-run) utilitarian

[2] For obvious reasons, this is still more the case with the term Communism which, barring the Russian angle, should be used synonymously with Socialism.

ends. Third, the concentration of the business class on the tasks of the factory and the office was instrumental in creating a political system and an intellectual class, the structure and interests of which developed an attitude of independence from, and eventually of hostility to, the interests of large-scale business. The latter is becoming increasingly incapable of defending itself against raids that are, in the short run, highly profitable to other classes. Fourth, in consequence of all this, the scheme of values of capitalist society, though causally related to its economic success, is losing its hold not only upon the public mind but also upon the "capitalist" stratum itself. Little time, though more than I have, would be needed to show how modern drives for security, equality, and regulation (economic engineering) may be explained on these lines.

The best method of satisfying ourselves as to how far this process of disintegration of capitalist society has gone is to observe the extent to which its implications are being taken for granted both by the business class itself and by the large number of economists who feel themselves to be opposed to (one hundred per cent) socialism and are in the habit of denying the existence of any tendency toward it. To speak of the latter only, they accept not only unquestioningly but also approvingly: (1) the various stabilization policies which are to prevent recessions or at least depressions, that is, a large amount of public management of business situations even if not the principle of full employment; (2) the "desirability of greater equality of incomes," rarely defining how far short of absolute equality they are prepared to go, and in connection with this the principle of redistributive taxation; (3) a rich assortment of regulative measures, frequently rationalized by antitrust slogans, as regards prices; (4) public control, though within a wide range of variation, over the labor and the money market; (5) indefinite extension of the sphere of wants that are, now or eventually, to be satisfied by public enterprise, either gratis or on some post-office principle; and (6) of course all types of security legislation. I believe that there is a mountain in Switzerland on which congresses of economists have been held which express disapproval of all or most of these things. But these anathemata have not even provoked attack.

It would spell complete misunderstanding of my argument if you thought that I "disapprove" or wish to criticize any of these policies. Nor am I one of those who label all or some of them "socialist." Some were espoused, even in the eighteenth century, by conservative or even autocratic rulers; others have been on the programs of conservative parties and have been carried by them long before New Deal days. All I wish to emphasize is the fact that we have traveled far indeed from the principles of laissez-faire capitalism and the further fact that it is possible so to develop and regulate capitalist institutions as to condition the working of private enterprise in a manner that differs but little from genuinely socialist planning. The economists I have in mind no doubt emphasize the differences they think likely to persist. They are not all agreed as to the precise location of their movable halfway house. But they all realize what Marx failed to realize: on the one hand, the vast productive possibilities of the capitalist engine that promise indefinitely higher mass standards of life, supplemented by gratis services *without* complete "expropriation of the expropriators"; on the other hand, the extent to which capitalist interests can in fact be expropriated without bringing the economic engine to a standstill and the extent to which this engine may be made to run in the labor interest. Having discovered this possibility of a *laborist capitalism* they go on to conclude that *this* capitalism may survive indefinitely, at least under certain favorable conditions. This may be so, but it does not amount to a denial of my thesis. Capitalism does not merely mean that the housewife may influence production by her choice between peas and beans; or that the youngster may choose whether he wants to work in a factory or on a farm; or that plant managers have some voice in deciding what and how to produce: it means a scheme of values, an attitude toward life, a civilization—the civilization of inequality and of the family fortune. This civilization is rapidly passing away, however. Let us rejoice or else lament the fact as much as everyone of us likes; but do not let us shut our eyes to it.

One genuine problem remains. The diagnoses that support implications which are favorable to the survival of laborism all lean heavily on extrapolations of the present spectacular development of society's productive powers. But there is an element of question-begging in this. Past achievement was the achievement of a more or less unfettered capitalism. It cannot be assumed without further consideration that laborism will continue to perform like this. We need not accept the stagnationist thesis as it stands in order to be disturbed by the possibility that this thesis may come true after all if the private-enterprise system is *permanently* burdened and "regulated" beyond its powers of endurance. In this case, an outright socialist solution may impose itself even on the enemies of socialism as the lesser evil.

II

The transformation of social orders into one another is an incessant process but, in itself, a very slow one. To an observer who studies a moderate span of "quiet" time, it may well seem as if the social framework he beholds did not change at all. Moreover, the process often suffers setbacks which, considered by themselves, may suggest to him the presence of an opposite tendency. But at times we also observe accelerations and one of the most obvious causes of these are major wars. In the past, successful wars may have added to the prestige of the ruling stratum, and to the strength of the institutional framework with which

this stratum was associated. This is no longer so under modern conditions. The First World War of our own epoch affected the social situation in the United States but little because the war effort was neither
exhausting enough nor prolonged enough to leave a permanent mark.
But in Europe it was different. In the vanquished countries where the
social framework caught fire, the latent tendency toward socialist reconstruction proved its existence by emerging to the surface and, for a
brief period, carrying everything before it. Still more significant is the
fact that something similar also happened, though of course on a much
reduced scale, in the victorious countries. In France the bourgeois
republic ceased to function as it had functioned before 1914. In England, a labor party that was not yet socialist but was influenced by a
socialist wing, rose not indeed to power but at least to office. And in
both countries, the attitude of the political sector to the private-
enterprise system quietly underwent a fundamental change.

Given a pre-existing tendency toward the socialist goal, this is easy
to understand. Although voices that called for a continuation of the
policies established during the years of the war economy did not elicit
much response and although, for a time, public resentment of war
regulations blocked further advance on the same lines, no return to
prewar policies proved possible even where it was attempted. This has
been strikingly verified by England's gold policy and its ultimate failure: in a world that was no longer the world of free enterprise, the
gold standard—the naughty child that keeps on telling unpleasant
truths—refused to work.

The world crisis and the Second World War were additional "ac-
celerators" and, this time, they asserted themselves also in the United
States. They created situations that were felt, rightly or wrongly, to be
beyond the remedies that would have recommended themselves to the
men of the free-enterprise age. The business class itself, afraid of the
"adjustments" that application of those remedies would have required,
accepted—though of course grumbling all the time—gadgets of regulation that might prevent the recurrence of the experiences of 1929–
1933, and later on others that might prevent a postwar crisis such as
that of 1921. It has learned much and unlearned still more during the
last quarter of a century. Also, it has accepted new fiscal burdens, a
mere fraction of which it would have felt to be unbearable fifty years
ago—as would, by the way, all the leading economists of that time.
And it does not matter whether the business class accepts this new
situation or not. The power of labor is almost strong enough in itself
—and amply so in alliance with the other groups that have in fact, if
not in words, renounced allegiance to the scheme of values of the
private-profit economy—to prevent any reversal which goes beyond an
occasional scaling off of rough edges.

Let me repeat: I do not hold for a moment that any mere "events,"
even events of the importance of "total wars," or the political situa-

tions created thereby, or any attitudes or feelings entertained by individuals or groups on the subject of these situations, dominate tne long-run contours of social history—these are a matter of much deeper forces. But I do hold that such events and the situations created thereby may remove obstacles from the path of the more fundamental tendencies, obstacles that would otherwise slow up the pace of social evolution. Observe that this does not necessarily constitute a reason for a serious socialist to welcome such events. Evolution toward socialism would be slower in their absence but also steadier. Setbacks and the emergence of unmanageable situations would be less likely. Co-ordination of developments in the various sectors of national life would be more perfect. For, just as the existence of an efficient opposition is a requirement for the orderly functioning of democratic government, so the existence of economic forces that resist institutional change may be necessary in order to keep the speed of this change within the limits of safety.

Now, one of the most powerful factors that make for acceleration of social change is inflation. With so many authorities telling us that nothing undermines the framework of a society as does inflation, it is hardly necessary to dwell upon this proposition. If we accept it, then it follows from what I have just said that from all imaginable standpoints, the standpoint of irresponsible revolutionaries alone excepted, it is of prime importance after a war so to adjust a country's economic process as to stop it from producing further inflation. But it is clear at the same time that this is an extremely difficult thing to do in a world where everybody is afraid of the short-run consequences of such a policy and where some of the adjustments required—especially a rise in many previously controlled prices without a rise in money wage rates—is not "politically possible" at all.[3] The course that was the obvious one to take under the circumstances and that was actually followed after 1945—among mutual recriminations but still with a good deal of common consent—was to mitigate transitional difficulties by a dose of controlled peacetime inflation that was made more effective by the continuance of a high level of expenditure on the armed services and by the policy of European aid. Substantially, all this served its purpose and, as it became evident to most people, though not to all economists, that a period of vigorous economic development, entailing vast investment requirements was at hand, the hope that major disturbances would be avoided and that the economy of the United States would expand on a slowly rising price level was, for a time, not altogether unreasonable—whatever, short of another world war, might happen abroad.

Considerations of this type fail however to take into account an

[3] The alternative course, scaling down other prices and money wages, is not only still less "politically possible" but also much more difficult to do without causing a serious depression.

ominous fact. At a high level of employment (we seem, at long last, to be abandoning full-employment slogans) whether "natural" or enforced by high-employment policies, wage demands or other demands that increase the money cost of employing labor become both inevitable and inflationary. They become inevitable because high-level employment removes the only reason why they should not be raised. And they become inflationary because, with high utilization of resources, borrowing from banks and upward revision of prices provides a perfectly easy method of satisfying them. Though bargaining is still with individual trade unions, the movement is really a general one so that we are drifting into the Keynesian situation in which the money wage rate no longer affects output and employment but only the value of the monetary unit. The situations of trade union leadership and of government being what they are, there is nothing to stop this mechanism which—barring exceptions that are due to the particular situations of certain firms—spells perennial inflationary pressure. Rising demands upon the Treasury and our hyperprogressive methods of taxation aggravate this condition, of course, but they have not created it.

There should be no need to state that breaks in prices such as have occurred and will occur again prove nothing against the presence of inflationary pressure. Even apart from the postwar movements of agricultural prices and other self-explanatory cases, such breaks occur characteristically in the course of every inflation—as could be illustrated nicely from the German inflation that followed upon the First World War. People who are "caught" then cry out about deflation, and so do those fellow economists of ours who have deflationary prognoses to live down and who, in any case, seem incapable of foreseeing anything but deflation. But it is a compliment, the more sincere because unintentional, to the productive powers of American industry that doubts are at all possible as to whether our society is menaced by inflation or deflation.

III

A state of perennial inflationary pressure will have, qualitatively, all the effects of weakening the social framework of society and of strengthening subversive tendencies (however carefully wrapped up in "liberal" phrases) that every competent economist is in the habit of attributing to more spectacular inflations. But this is not all. In addition some of the standard remedies for such situations will not mitigate, and may even aggravate, the present one. It seems to me that this is not being fully understood. Let us therefore, in desperate brevity, discuss three types of such remedies.

1. The most orthodox of all measures for the control of inflation is action upon the volume of borrowing through interest rates or credit rationing and the like. I fully understand of course that money rates

must be freed from the grip of cheap-money policies *if normalcy in the sense of a free-enterprise economy is to be attained* and that for everyone who desires return to such normalcy, the liberation—or reconstruction—of a free money market must be a point of prime importance. But this does not alter the fact that a restrictive credit policy would at present produce consequences quite different from those that the old theory of credit policy would lead us to expect. Accepting the latter without any qualification—for argument's sake—we cannot help observing that it was to apply to a world in which everything was entirely flexible, and which was not afraid of what I may term, remedial recessions. In such a world, an increase in interest rates was supposed to reduce the volume of operations, money wages, and *employment*. Surely these effects would not materialize at present and, if they did, they would immediately provoke government action to neutralize them. In other words, credit restrictions would at present achieve little beyond increasing the difficulties of business. Even restrictions of consumers' credit would have this effect to some extent, though something could no doubt be done in this field.

2. Similar difficulties stand in the way of controlling inflation by means of increasing taxation—a no less orthodox remedy but one which enjoys a popularity with modern economists that is denied to credit restriction. It is quite true that something might be accomplished by increasing taxes on consumption. In an inflationary situation this would even be good Keynesianism. But if it is the corporation tax and the higher-bracket income tax which are to be increased, the effect upon inflationary pressure would be small at best and might even be negative. For if the present rate of industrial progress is to continue and therefore the present rate of obsolescence of equipment is to continue also, increasing resort would have to be taken to inflationary bank credit in order to make up for the decrease in the available noninflationary means of finance. Alternatively, a decrease in those rates of progress and of obsolescence, would indeed decrease inflationary pressure for the moment but increase it in the long run.[4]

3. The third household remedy consists in direct controls—price-fixing, priorities and the like (including subsidies). Why they are so popular with certain sectors of public opinion is a question that need

---

[4] I have no difficulty in understanding why this argument does not impress our radical friends. But I confess that I find it difficult to understand the position of some excellent economists who are quite above any suspicion that they would welcome the failure of our industrial engine to work on successfully and who nevertheless list reduction in industrial investment among the acceptable means for counteracting inflation, both in this country and in England. Incidentally, it should be noticed that the opinion of some conservative stalwarts that high and highly progressive taxation might promote, and that reductions in taxation (at the right spots) might decrease, inflationary dangers does not necessarily merit all the sneers it usually gets.

not detain us. For the bureaucracy, in particular, their reintroduction would spell reconquest of ground that has been lost; for the trade unions it would spell a decisive advantage in the campaign for the conquest of the profit item; for business it would mean the loss of the line of retreat that is open to it so long as most, if not all, attacks upon it can be, partly if not wholly, parried by price adjustments. Or, at least, it would make this retreat dependent upon government permission which there is no reason to believe would be granted for purposes of securing means for improving the productive engine. In other words, price control may result in a surrender of private enterprise to public authority, that is, in a big stride toward the perfectly planned economy.

[At this point Joseph Schumpeter stopped in the writing up of his notes. Those who heard the address will remember that at the end there was little time, and he summed up very briefly, going back to his opening remarks on the relevance, for the economic future of this country, of the present state of inflationary pressure, under existing political conditions. Some of the points touched upon with "desperate brevity" may be found developed at greater length in the second American edition or in the third English edition of *Capitalism, Socialism and Democracy* and in an article, "There is Still Time to Stop Inflation," which appeared in the *Nation's Business* for June, 1948.

The following paragraphs are reconstructed from memory and from the notes used for the address.]

I do not pretend to prophesy; I merely recognize the facts and point out the tendencies which those facts indicate.

Perennial inflationary pressure can play an important part in the eventual conquest of the private-enterprise system by the bureaucracy —the resultant frictions and deadlocks being attributed to private enterprise and used as arguments for further restrictions and regulations. I do not say that any group follows this line with conscious purpose, but purposes are never wholly conscious. A situation may well emerge in which most people will consider complete planning as the smallest of possible evils. They will certainly not call it Socialism or Communism, and presumably they will make some exceptions for the farmer, the retailer and the small producer; under these circumstances, capitalism (the free-enterprise system) as a scheme of values, a way of life, and a civilization may not be worth bothering about.

Whether the American genius for mass production, on whose past performance all optimism for this way of life rests, is up to this test, I dare not affirm; nor do I dare to affirm that the policies responsible for this situation might be reversed.

Marx was wrong in his diagnosis of the manner in which capitalist society would break down; he was not wrong in the prediction that it would break down eventually. The Stagnationists are wrong in their diagnosis of the reasons why the capitalist process should stagnate; they may still turn out to be right in their prognosis that it will stagnate—with sufficient help from the public sector.[5]

December 30, 1949

[5] This paper is here reprinted with the permission of the American Economic Association for whose *Papers and Proceedings* (December, 1949) it was written.

INDEX

A

Accumulation, primitive, 17; theory of, 30, 32
Adler, F., 240
Adler, M., 49, 202n
Adler, V., 202n, 348
Allocation of resources, 174
American Federation of Labor, 332
Anarchism, 307
Ancien régime, social structure of, 135
Anti-intellectualism, Bergsonian, 340
Anti-Semitism, 241
Aristotle, 23n
Austrian socialist party, 348-349
Authority, 210

B

Babeuf, G., 309
Bailey, S., 26n
Bakunin, M., 307, 339
Bank of England, nationalization of, 377
Barone, E., 173
Bauer, O., 15n, 49
Bebel, A., 344, 347, 350
Bentham, J., 214, 260n
Berlepsch, v., 341
Bernstein, E., 12, 346, 353n
Big business and the standard of life, 81
Bismarck, Prince, 343
Blanc, L., 309
Blanquist party, 337
Bolsheviks, 329
Bortkiewicz, L. v., 29n
Breakdown of capitalism, 57
Bureaucracy, problem of, 205-207, 293-294
Burke, E., 283, 292, 295
Burns, A. F., 63n
Business strategy, 88

C

Cabinet, 270, 278
Cabinet ministers, 270
Capital, organic structure of, 26; Marx's definition of, 45
Capital-saving innovations, 119

Capitalism, performance of, 63-71; evolutionary nature of, 82; and government action, 107; and gold, 108; and increase in population, 108; and new countries, 109; and technological progress, 110; classical theory of, 74-76
Catastrophe of capitalism; See *Zusammenbruchstheorie*
Central board, 168
Centralist Socialism, 168
Central (Catholic) party, 344-345, 371
Chamberlain, E. H., 79n
Chartist movement, 309
Chigi, A., 125
Childlessness, 157
Christian Socialism, 309
Clark, C., 115
Clark, J. B., 77n
Class war, 14
Classical economists, 75n
Cobden, R., 282
Commercial society, 167
Committee on socialization, German, 300
Common good, 250, 265
Communism, 168, 358-363, 376, 380
Communist Manifesto, 7, 14, 15, 39, 50, 55, 110, 205n, 236, 308, 317, 372
Competition, perfect, 77-78, 103-105; imperfect, 78; monopolistic, 79; predatory or cutthroat, 80; *modus operandi* of, 84-85
Competitive leadership, 269, 271
Comte, A., 121n
Concentration of economic power, 33, 140
Confédération générale du travail, 340, 355
Constitutional monarchy, 270
Continental congresses, 248
Cost accounting in socialism, 176-177
Cournot, A., 78
Crises, Marx's theory of, 38-42
Croce, B., 319n
Crowds, psychology of, 257

D

Debs, E. V., 335
Defeatism, charge of, xi